PAUL
IN HIS JEWISH *AND* GRAECO-ROMAN CONTEXT

Paul in His Jewish and Graeco-Roman Context:
Theological, Ecclesial, Social, and Political Perspectives
Edited by Constantine R. Campbell and James R. Harrison

© AUCD Press and Contributors 2025

AUCD Press
PO Box 6110
Norwest NSW 2153
Australia
aucdpress@aucd.edu.au

ISBN-13: 978-1-925730-59-3 (Paperback)
ISBN-13: 978-1-925730-60-9 (E-book)

Cover design and typesetting by Lankshear Design.
Cover image: *The Apostle Paul*, portrait by Rembrandt (c. 1657)
Public Domain via National Gallery of Art, Washington D.C.

PAUL
IN HIS JEWISH AND GRAECO-ROMAN CONTEXT

Theological, Ecclesial, Social, and Political Perspectives

Constantine R. Campbell and James R. Harrison
Editors

AUCD Press
2025

INTRODUCTION

Constantine R. Campbell
James R. Harrison

As a Pharisee who had risen to prominence among his Jewish contemporaries, Paul emerged from the cradle of Second Temple Judaism to become, by God's calling, Christ's apostle to the Gentiles. That the apostle was intimately familiar with both worlds, Jewish and Graeco-Roman, has often been overlooked by New Testament scholars, who have tended to gravitate either to one background or the other in explaining the legacy of the apostle in the Western intellectual tradition or in writing commentaries on his epistles. Happily, recent scholarship has begun to shift toward an acceptance that Paul was a Jew of the Second Temple period *and* a diaspora intellectual who negotiated the various challenges of Graeco-Roman cities and cultures. This results in historically thicker exegesis with biblical theology, social history, and classical studies being drawn on to recognise the rich tapestry of influences that gave shape to Paul's person and legacy.

The essays in this volume were presented at the conference *Paul in His Jewish and Graeco-Roman Context*, hosted by the Australian University College of Divinity (formerly Sydney College of Divinity) in Sydney on 26–27 October, 2023. The conference aimed to investigate the legacy of Paul's thought from both Jewish and Graeco-Roman perspectives, allowing that there is a calculated polyvalence in the apostle's reasoning. Whether it is the 'state-of-play' of' the New Perspective debate (Sanders, Dunn, Barclay), situating Paul's Christ-communities within the context of ancient associations (Kloppenborg, Ascough, Harland), locating

Paul among other Hellenistic-Roman 'founder' figures (Hanges), comparisons of Paul with Stoicism and broader Graeco-Roman ethics (Engberg-Pedersen, Thorsteinsson), Paul's views about social issues such as gender and slavery (Westfall, Glancy), or evaluating an apocalyptic re-reading of Paul's gospel (Martyn, Campbell), the debate on both sides is as strong as ever.

Conference papers were invited to discuss the legacy of Paul's thought from either a Jewish or Graeco-Roman perspective (or, indeed, both), either in his socio-historical and rhetorical context or arising from the development of the Western intellectual tradition. Approaches discussing the apostle's theological, ecclesial, social, or political perspectives were welcomed. Four invited plenary papers were delivered by Lynn Cohick (Houston Christian University) and David Starling (Morling College), and a diverse range of other papers filled out the conference. While not all presenters were able to contribute their papers to this volume of collected essays, the majority have done so. The resulting volume you are now reading covers a wide variety of topics of great interest directly related to the Jewish and Graeco-Roman elements within Paul's thought. While the first two essays address general broad themes, the remainder target issues related to Romans, the Corinthian correspondence, and Galatians.

In her first essay, Lynn Cohick explores the social status of freedwomen in Pauline communities. While technically enjoying the same status as free born women, freedwomen bore the stigma of their enslaved past, but this could be mitigated by their inclusion into their ex-owner's *familia* as quasi-family members. Cohick suggests that this historical fact can shed light on Paul's kinship language as he imagines all believers—slave, free, or freed—as members of God's family. Cohick's second essay asks the fascinating questions of whether circumcised males will remain circumcised in their resurrected bodies, or if that physical feature serves no eschatological purpose in Christ—to both of which she tentatively answers positively.

James Harrison draws contrasts between Paul and Aesop in his essay on popular morality and the apostolic gospel. Many of Paul's converts would have been familiar with Aesop through schooling or oral culture and would have felt the conflict between two moral worldviews in relation to the divine world, the role of prayer, and social relations, as well as moral prohibitions and exhortations.

In her essay addressing Jews robbing temples in Romans 2:22, Lyn Kidson argues that Paul uses the trope to refer to Jews blaspheming Gentile gods, thus breaking the commandment against blasphemy. Together with other rhetorical questions issued in the immediate context, Kidson argues that Paul's purpose is to stymie potential objections that his Jewish interlocutor is a sinner like the Gentiles.

Liam Carlton-Jones explores the influence of the Christ-event and Jewish tradition on Paul's thinking about governing authorities in his essay on Romans 13:1–7. He argues that Paul draws on the salvation-historical role of governing authorities in the new creation, which has been inaugurated with the Christ-event. Such salvation-historical purposes are grounded in Jewish soteriological and eschatological expectations, which have been recontextualised in Christ.

DongWoo Oh's essay on Paul as Temple Builder focuses especially on Romans 15:20 to explore the relationship between messianic expectation, the building of God's temple, and Paul's commission as apostle to the Gentiles.

David Starling's first essay explores unity and the Graeco-Roman political tradition within 1 Corinthians 1–4, with critical examination of Margaret Mitchell's conclusions about the text. He argues that Paul's appeal to the Corinthians to think with the mind of Christ is as confronting as it is conciliatory and as disruptive as unifying. It is shaped not only by Graeco-Roman political values but also by Israel's prophetic tradition through the lens of Paul's apocalyptic gospel. Starling's second essay follows from the first by exploring the hermeneutics and epistemology that undergird Paul's appeal to adopt the mind of Christ. He asks what it looks like for a community to possess the mind of Christ and how it shapes believers' lives and conduct.

On the contentious reference to believers and unbelievers vis-à-vis tongues and prophecy in 1 Corinthians 14:22–25, Scott Goode proposes a way forward through recognising two distinct uses of ἄπιστος in 14:22 and 14:23–25. In support of this proposal, Goode draws on the rhetorical strategy of 1 Corinthians 14, the backdrop of Isaiah 28:11–12, and the socio-religious identities of the groups Paul addresses.

Paul Barnett addresses Paul's defence in 2 Corinthians against 'theological piracy' conducted by a counter-mission dedicated to reforming Paul's churches. Paul had to mend his connection to the Corinthian church after sending them a harsh letter and other perceived offences in order to reaffirm his teaching against the theological pirates who sought to sway the Corinthians.

Peter Bolt's extended essay on 2 Corinthians 2:13 explores its grammar and syntax to offer a new assessment of Titus and his role in Paul's mission. Titus emerges as a Corinthian local who served in the final stages of the Pauline mission in Crete and Dalmatia, fueled with apocalyptic vision.

The essays on 2 Corinthians conclude with Emmanuel Nathan's offering on 7:5–16. He explores the possible double meaning of a Hebrew verb in MT Jeremiah 31:15, and argues it ought not be dismissed in accounting for Paul's language and conception in 2 Corinthians 7:10.

In Galatians, Grant Buchanan explores the connection between Paul's language of crucifixion, the Spirit, and Christian identity. He argues that Paul intentionally correlates the crucifixion of Christ and the Spirit throughout the letter, which together establishes the foundation for Christian identity.

Sunny Chen addresses the connection between 'the flesh' and circumcision in Galatians 5:13–26 and draws on Philo to argue that the concept of sexual pleasure serves as the connection between them. He suggests that Paul undermines the importance of physical circumcision by negatively associating it with the realm of the flesh, in opposition to the Spirit.

Brent Niedergall addresses whether Paul's disagreement with Peter over Jew-Gentile table fellowship occurred before or after Paul's visit to Jerusalem, as recorded in Galatians 2:1–14. Niedergall assesses Gerd Lüdermann's claim that the conjunctive phrase ὅτε δὲ interrupts, rather than continues, the chronological narrative presented by Paul by reviewing 282 occurrences of ὅτε δὲ across Greek literature.

And last but not least, Lionel Windsor discusses missionary hospitality, table fellowship, and the occasion of the letter with reference to Galatians 6:16. He pays special attention to the concrete social activities of the agitators in Galatia, which is more closely aligned with Paul's conflict with Peter in Antioch than is commonly supposed, and argues that Paul draws a rule of association in table fellowship derived from the eschatological implications of his gospel.

The essays in this volume track closely with current trajectories within Pauline scholarship on the themes of social history and kinship (Cohick, Windsor, Barnett), Judaism and the eschatology of identity markers (Cohick, Kidson, Chen), Graeco-Roman moral and/or political culture (Harrison, Starling), empire and salvation history (Carlton-Jones), temple and messianism (Oh), prophecy, rhetoric, and community boundaries (Goode, Buchanan), and chronology and historical reconstruction (Bolt, Niedergall). Together these essays offer creative approaches, fresh insights, and novel possibilities. As such, we trust this book will find its place among the burgeoning literature exploring the apostle Paul, his mind, his message, and his legacy.

TABLE OF CONTENTS

1. *Slave Women and Freedwomen in Pauline Communities: Manumission and Freedom in Christ.* Lynn H. Cohick 1

2. *'The Body' in Paul: Christ's Body, the Church as Christ's Body, and Bodily Resurrection.* Lynn H. Cohick 21

3. *Paul and Aesop: Popular Morality and the Apostolic Gospel in the Ancient Mediterranean.* James R. Harrison 41

4. *Do Jews Rob Temples? Paul and his Hypocritical Interlocutor of Romans 2:22.* Lyn M. Kidson 79

5. *How Revolutionary is Romans 13:1–7? The Influence of the Christ-Event and the Jewish Theological Tradition in Paul's Conception of Governing Authorities.* Liam Carlton-Jones 103

6. *Paul: Temple Builder.* DongWoo Oh 123

7. *'In The Same Mind and the Same Purpose': 1 Corinthians, Unity, and the Graeco-Roman Political Tradition.* David I. Starling 139

8. *'But We Have the Mind of Christ': 1 Corinthians, Wisdom, and the Interpretation of Israel's Scriptures.* David I. Starling 153

9. *An Intra-Ecclesial Reading of* οἱ πιστεύοντες *and* οἱ ἄπιστοι *in 1 Corinthians 14:22.* Scott Goode 167

10. *'Letters of Recommendation [...] From You'*
    (2 Corinthians 3:1). A Case of Theological Piracy?
    Paul W. Barnett 183

11. *Locating Titus in the Pauline Mission:*
    Re-reading 2 Corinthians 2:13 with Apocalyptic Vision.
    Peter G. Bolt.. 195

12. *Of Grief that Turns to Comfort: MT Echoes Resounding*
    in the Background of 2 Corinthians 7:5–16?
    Emmanuel Nathan 251

13. *Crucifixion, the Spirit, and Christian Identity*
    in Galatians. Grant Buchanan 265

14. *The Connection of* Σάρξ *and Circumcision in*
    Galatians 5:13–26 in Light of Philo's Writings.
    Sunny Chen 281

15. *'An Antiquated Exegetical Convention'?* Ὅτε δὲ *and*
    Paul's Chronology of the Incident at Antioch in Galatians.
    Brent Niedergall 305

16. *'As Many as will Conform to this Rule' (Galatians 6:16):*
    Missionary Hospitality, Table Fellowship, and the Occasion
    of Galatians. Lionel J. Windsor 323

LIST OF CONTRIBUTORS

Peter G. Bolt
Professor of New Testament and Director of Academic Strategy at Australian University College of Divinity

Grant Buchanan
Senior Lecturer at Alphacrucis University College

Constantine R. Campbell
Professor of New Testament and Research Director at Australian University College of Divinity

Liam Carlton-Jones
PhD candidate at Australian Catholic University

Sunny Chen
Honorary Researcher at University of Divinity

Lynn H. Cohick
Distinguished Professor of New Testament at Houston Christian University

Scott Goode
PhD candidate at Charles Sturt University

James H. Harrison
Distinguished Professor at Australian University College of Divinity

Lyn M. Kidson
New Testament scholar at Australian University of Theology

Emmanuel Nathan
Senior Lecturer in Biblical Studies and Comparative Theology at the Faculty of Theology and Philosophy at Australian Catholic University, and Director of the Research Centre for Studies of the Second Vatican Council

Brent Niedergall
PhD candidate at Australian University College of Divinity

DongWoo Oh
Pastor of Coolum Beach Uniting Church

David I. Starling
Vice-Principal (Academic) and Lecturer in New Testament at Morling College

Lionel J. Windsor
Lecturer in New Testament at Moore Theological College

CHAPTER 1

Slave Women and Freedwomen in Pauline Communities: Manumission and Freedom in Christ

Lynn H. Cohick

Introduction

Epicharis should be famous. Epicharis was a freedwoman who played a key role in the Pisonian conspiracy against Nero and comes out a heroine in Tacitus's telling (*Ann.* 15.51–57). In 65 CE, as hatred grew against Nero, and the senator Piso grew more popular, a conspiracy to murder Nero gained strength. However, the co-conspirators, all men, dithered, so Epicharis took matters into her own hands. She encouraged the sulking Proculus, a navy captain who played a key role in killing Nero's mother, Agrippina. He nursed a grudge that Nero did not reward him sufficiently for his loyalty, and Epicharis stoked his anger. She told him, privately with no witnesses, that a conspiracy was afoot and he could take his vengeance. He promptly went to Nero with this information, but because he had no proof, his claims were dismissed, sort of. Nero arrested several men, and they all gave up names quickly, including one man, Lucan, who turned in his own mother. But despite gruesome tortures on the rack and broken bones, Epicharis revealed no names. She survived a day of torture, then hung herself by her girdle. Tacitus heaps contempt on the men, elite citizens all, and elevates Epicharis, the freewoman, as a noble example of fidelity. Yet Tacitus also hints at her dishonour by introducing her as someone who did not concern herself with honourable matters (*res honestae*), (*Ann.* 15.51).[1]

We will not find many other stories of valiant freedwomen. Part of the reason is the stain of slavery can remain on their persons. Orlando Patterson has said that slavery is social death.[2] Scholars have since nuanced his argument, and I will do so also, but his insight is crucial to understanding slavery as an institution of domination by the owner over his or her slave. Romans added an in-between category, the freed person. As we reflect on this social category, noted only once in Paul's letters, we must ask how their lives changed (1 Cor. 7:22). To use Patterson's language, how socially dead is a freedman? A freedwoman?

Upon manumission, the freedwoman of a Roman citizen is legally equal to a free born female citizen. Yet the freedwoman's sexuality is dubious due to her enslaved past. The tension created by the contrasting identities might be partially resolved by enfolding a freedwoman into her ex-owner's household as the wife of her ex-owner, now patron and husband. Similarly, a freedman was viewed as a quasi-son by his ex-owner, who now functioned as his patron. The manumitted person's *familia* structured his or her social reality, as it was embedded in a fictive kinship framework. This historical context can inform our understanding of Paul's kinship language as he imagines the church, co-heirs with Christ and siblings under their heavenly Father. Paul's fictive kinship language creates realities for manumitted believers, as they participate in the complexity of the ancient household, and the household of God.

I will sketch the practices for manumission in both the Roman and the Greek systems. My focus is Ephesus, which was established as a Greek city. Yet because it was tied closely to Rome through the imperial cult, we should also expect numerous Roman citizens and imperial slaves and freedmen. Second, I will look closely at what a typical urban slave-owning household might look like, focusing on the female slaves and the matron and daughters. We need to see this reality to better understand both the community which received Paul's missive and Paul's own pastoral vision.[3] Third and finally, I will explore the possi-

---

1   Perry, *Gender*, 141.
2   Patterson, *Slavery*, 13–27.
3   For a discussion of Pauline authorship of Ephesians, see Cohick, *Ephesians*, 3–25.

ble ramifications of fictive kinship in Paul's communities, specifically in relation to owners and ex-owners' sexual claims on their female slaves, freed women, and wives. I will underline the key role that marriage played in establishing the freedwoman as a chaste Roman matron.

Part 1: Manumission Practices as Pertains to Women

In the Roman world, conversations about female manumission generally involved either the status of their offspring, or their sexual honour. Considering first the topic of children, the children of a woman in a non-Roman (or non-licit) marriage took her social status. If she was free, then her children were free. If she was a slave, her children were her owner's slaves. But in an unusual case, if a free woman had sexual relations with a slave in a family other than her own, then her own status shifted to freed, from free. Any children born to this union of free woman and slave were the property of the male slave's owner. This legal shift ensured that a male slave could not produce free-born children. Roman law was altered to create a freedwoman who had never been a slave.[4]

Turning to the topic of sexual honour, the freedwoman's sexual autonomy distinguished her new identity as separate from her enslaved status. Her ex-owner, now patron, was to treat her with dignity, but if she married, especially if she married a fellow freedman from the same patron, the latter could not bring a charge of sexual misconduct against his patron if the latter had sex with the freedwoman. Patron rights trumped husband's rights, for the most part. Yet both men were to uphold her dignity as integral to her new status as a manumitted slave.

A. Roman Manumission

Roman law had a few avenues open to manumit slaves. The formal processes included the owner and slave appearing before a Roman magistrate, and with a payment of a five percent tax, the magistrate declared the slave to be free (*manumissio vindicta*). Alternatively, the owner could free the slave by will or codicil, effective at the owner's death

---

4   Mouritzen, *The Freedman*, 22.

(*manumissio ex testament*).⁵ A third option was to include the slave's name in the census (*manumissio censu*). If the owner was a Roman citizen, the slave received citizenship under formal process. This process assumed that the slave had shown himself to be trustworthy and loyal. Once a freedman, he would be part of the family business and network system. For the female slave, as Matthew Perry observes, 'both literary and legal sources indicate that a sexual relationship was the principal means for a female slave to gain favor with her male owner'.⁶ A slave woman (Latin: *ancilla*) could be freed to then be married to her owner. In this two-step process, the owner married a freedwoman, and the event was known as *ancilla matrimonia causa*.⁷ Inscriptional evidence suggests that this form of manumission for women was rather common. A rather well-known example of such practice is the tombstone of Regina, a native Britain, freedwoman and wife of Barates, a man from Palmyra who lived in Britain. Her patron/husband added the line 'Regina, freedwoman of Barate, alas' in his native Palmyrene.⁸

The slave might also self-purchase with money saved, what is known as the *peculium*. This money technically belonged to the owner, who could seize it at any time for any reason. Female slaves had fewer opportunities to gain income; the most common sources were tips for favours done or for access to the matron or others in the household. Perry writes in his careful study of Roman manumission and freedwomen, 'I have yet to find a clear example of a female slave who purchased her freedom solely with her own *peculium*'.⁹ Romans also had informal mechanisms for manumission, but space limitations prevent me from exploring them here.¹⁰

---

5   *Lex Fufia Caninia*, 2 BCE, regulated the number of slaves that could be freed by a will, so that those with more than several slaves could not manumit them all at the owner's death. See Gaius, *Institutes*, 1.
6   Perry, *Gender*, 51.
7   We may have an example of this in Philippi, *I.Phil*2 345; see Pilhofer, *Philippi*, 411–12. Vivia Hilara, a freedwoman of Titus Vibius, is married to Marcus Aurelius Tertius. The Vibii family was an elite family from nearby Thessaloniki, and perhaps Hilara was freed by a freedman of that family.
8   *RIB* 1065. See Millett et al., *Handbook*, 238–39.
9   Perry, *Gender*, 57.
10 Nasrallah, *Archaeology*, 58, remarks that Roman citizenship was granted if the Junian Latin married a Roman or Latin woman, and they had a child who survived one year. Informal processes included manumission by letter, wherein the owner sent to a friend a letter indicating that his/her slave was manumitted (*manumissio per epistulam*). Similarly, the owner could invite friends to observe the manumission (*manumissio inter amicos*). In these informal situations, even if the owner was a Roman citizen, the slave would not be given Roman citizenship, but receive Junian Latin citizenship.

Not only did Roman owners grant citizenship to their slaves, but the relationship shifted to one analogous to patron/client. The Romans saw manumission as a benefit granted by the owner, which strengthened the cords of the wider family unit. The freed slave benefited in that he or she had access to their patron's network and support. The freedman would work alongside free men in the patron's business, or set up shop with the patron's help, and share the profits of the business.[11] In this sense, we see the cultural value of reciprocity in action, as both persons benefited. Nevertheless, this reciprocity was not of equals, for the Roman hierarchical system remained. And this description pertains to the skilled slaves, not the unskilled labour. The latter might save their *peculium* and buy their freedom, which separated them from their owner's family.[12] We can conclude with Perry, 'Roman manumission was not just about freeing a slave; it was also about incorporating a former slave into the citizen community'.[13]

B. Greek Manumission

Greek manumission's key difference from that of Roman manumission is the lack of citizenship granted to the freed slave, or their descendants.[14] While there is no question that Greeks manumitted slaves, the how and the why remain frustratingly vague due to our lack of evidence.[15] Rachel Zelnick-Abramovitz surveys the landscape from classical Athens to the early Roman imperial period and concludes that manumission took

---

11 Perry, *Gender*, 83–88, discusses the substantial and far-reaching legal rights of patrons to their freedwoman's wealth.
12 Flexsenhar, 'No Longer a Slave', 26, concludes that there was little incentive for *peregrini* (non-Roman provincials) to free slaves since that put the slave on basically the same status as the peregrinus. Yet the owner who freed a skilled slave would reinforce loyalty to the family, and the freedman or woman's skills would continue to benefit the family. From the slave's perspective, if they could save a *peculium* and purchase their freedom, they joined the ranks of freedmen and freedwomen who could never be enslaved again.
13 Perry, *Gender*, 155.
14 Zelnick-Abramovitz, *Not Wholly Free*, 52. Greeks spoke of manumitted slaves as *apeleutheros/a*, *exeleutheros/a*, or *aphetheis/eisa*. In the first two terms, one sees the term 'freedom' with a prefix attached. Zelnick-Abramovitz offers definitions of 'freed from someone' and 'thoroughly free', and explains the third term's meaning, 'set away from', which tells us nothing about the slave's social status.
15 *IGUR* 826 = *IG* 14, 856; see Hemelrijk, 92–93.

many forms.¹⁶ Manumission could include an acquiescence clause that meant other family members beside the owner needed to approve the freedom. The female slave master had her own *kurios*, a male who represented her in any legal transaction. Typically, the *kurios* oversaw the manumission, but we have evidence that at times, women owners manumitted their slaves without oversight from the *kurios*. Greek manumission was a commercial transaction process that typically included payments or promises of work as payment. Manumission might include an obligation which places conditions on the slave's freedom that defers its consummation. The agreement stipulates the length of time a slave will work off the remainder of his or her obligations to the ex-owner.¹⁷ A first-century CE example of this is found at Delphi's Temple of Apollo (*Fouilles de Delphes* 3, 6.36). The female slave owner, Sophrona, who has the consent of her son, freed the house-born slave, Onasiphoron, for three silver *minae* and the now freed slave is to remain with Sophrona for the rest of the ex-owner's life, following her orders without complaint. And one more thing: Onasiphoron must give Sophrona's son a child.¹⁸

C. Results of Female Manumission

Several factors related to women's manumission and their sexuality should be highlighted. First, freedwomen were not seen as victims of *stuprum* by their ex-owners, now patrons. That is, it was not illegal for the male patron to have sex with her. Nevertheless, it was bad form, if you will, because her status shifted from slave, wherein she had no agency, to a freedwoman. As such, she had agency and the responsibility to maintain her *pudicitia* or chasteness.

Second, slave women had incentives to build good relationships with their owners if they desired their manumission. Perry concludes, 'Roman lawmakers in the early Principate promoted a vision of citizen

---

16 Zelnick-Abramovitz, *Not Wholly Free*, 127, writes, 'Beside the simple declaration of freedom (whether by the family hearth, at the owner's deathbed, or by a symbolic ritual of pouring wine), manumission could be declared in public by a herald, at the altar, in the theatre, in a sanctuary, or before a magistrate.'
17 Zelnick-Abramovitz, *Not Wholly Free*, 223, cautions that 'all or most manumission agreements included the slaves' obligation to supply further services. Manumission was a social transaction; freedom had to be paid for.'
18 Flexsenhar, 'No Longer a Slave', 145–46 with translation.

manumission conducive to the lifestyles of female slaves because of its emphasis on person relationships'.[19] The owner became her *tutor* and patron at her manumission, and as such had tremendous authority over her subsequent life decisions. The one exception is that the owner could not stipulate that his slave remain unmarried upon her manumission. We see in this stipulation the value that Romans placed on the matron as the ideal Roman female citizen. A citizen freedwoman could guard her *pudicitia*.[20]

Third, freedmen and women's relationships could last a long time. Sarah Pomeroy observes that 'sepulchral inscriptions show that many slave marriages survived over long periods of time, regardless of changes in habitation or changes in status from slave to freed of one or both of the partners'.[21] Pomeroy continues that if a wife died young, her age was often noted on the tombstone, and that of wives of freedmen and imperial slaves, more than fifty percent died before age thirty, with 'the highest proportion dying between twenty and twenty-five'.[22] Emily Hemelrijk provides numerous inscriptions about women from Italy and Latin-speaking provinces from the late Republic through the third century CE. Her study supports Pomeroy's work, including inscriptions celebrating marriage between freed persons of over two decades (*CIL* 6.33087 = *ILS* 8401) and sixty years (*CIL* 6.9499 = *ILS* 7472).[23]

D. Freedmen and Freedwomen in First Century Ephesus

Ephesus had a slave market, although archaeologists have not discovered its location.[24] Katherine Shaner argues from the inscriptional and archaeological evidence in Ephesus that the social landscape included slaves and freed men and women actively engaged 'with larger civic and

---

19 Perry, *Gender*, 67.
20 Perry, *Gender*, 95, writes, 'Behavior that blurred the line between freedwoman and slave—such as sexual obligations, servile punishments, and oaths not to marry—was strictly prohibited.'
21 Pomeroy, *Goddesses*, 193.
22 Pomeroy, *Goddesses*, 194.
23 Hemelrijk, *Women*, 23–25.
24 Two inscriptions speak of a *statarion*. The proconsul of Asia in 42–43 CE, C. Sallustius Crispus Passienus (*IEphesos* 7.2.3025) and a Titus Claudius Secundus (*IEphesos* 3.646, see also *IEphesos* 3.857) are both honoured by those doing commerce in the slave market. Secundus is a common slave name, so we can safely assume he is a freedman.

religious institutions in the city'.²⁵ Some slaves (and by extension, freedmen and women) were priests, cultic specialists, and leaders of various religious groups. For example, we find an inscription in a marble seat in the theater with the names of Timonax and certain slave managers who were public priests of the Artemis temple. To have seats of honour suggests that these slaves 'oversaw the temple's wealth'.²⁶

One of the best-known landmarks in Ephesus today is the arches put up by Mithridates and Mazaeus, freedmen of Livia and Augustus. In 3 BCE, the freedmen erected three large gates near the Celsus library (erected later), through which one passes into the agora. These freedmen benefactors greatly enhanced the city. James Harrison has done extensive work on the epigraphic material in Ephesus. He mentions Stertinia Quieta, freedwoman or *liberta* of Gaius Stertinius Orpex, a freedman of G. Stertinius Maximus (*IEphesos* 3.720, 86). This freedwoman's name is listed with three children, a son who lived eight years, another son who died at age three, and a daughter who lived eight years. A surviving daughter, Marina, was a benefactor to the city, as was her father, who contributed to the stadium. Harrison considers whether Orpex was a public slave in Rome and became 'an upwardly mobile freedman and agent at Ephesus'.²⁷ In another example, Hellenia Meroē was a freedwoman who set up a monument in which she first mentions her patron, Sextus Hellenius, and then honors her husband, Publius Castricius Velanetius, and then clients or dependents (*IvE* VI.2266). Michael Flexsenhar wonders if Meroē was analogous to Chloe, who seems to have owned slaves and kept her own household (1 Cor. 1:11). Meroē may also be comparable to Phoebe whom Paul describes as patroness.²⁸

---

25 Shaner, *Enslaved Leadership*, 13. Inscriptions from Philippi, see Pilhofer, *Katalog*; Inscriptions from the Italy and Latin-speaking provinces, Hemelrijk, *Women*.
26 Shaner, *Enslaved Leadership*, 38.
27 Harrison, 'An Epigraphic Portrait', 31.
28 Flexsenhar, 'No Longer a Slave', 102.

Part 2: The Typical Household: Anthia's and Augustine's Households

We have traced the manumission process of the slave to her freed status. We saw that freedmen and women contributed to the civic and religious life in Ephesus, even as they also supported their patrons and new familial ties. We find freedmen and freedwomen praising their patrons/husbands and benefiting from their new status as members of the *familia*. Yet it is without question that slaves were treated brutally. The physical scars spoke to the accompanying mental and emotional anguish. How did the violence and the praise exist in the same social space?

I would like to make two points that illuminate this contradictory reality. First, slavery itself was not viewed as the same by all. It could be re-examined by those who saw nobility in slaves, and cruelty in owners, at least in some cases. William Owens examines several Graeco-Roman romance novels, including *Ephesiaca*, by Xenophon. In this tale, the protagonists, newly married Habrocomes and Anthia, are captured by pirates, and are separated and enslaved and face all manner of horrible circumstances. Owens argues that the *Ephesiaca* and the novel *Callirhoe* by Chariton of Aphrodisias, both from the first century CE, 'subvert the way the elite thought about slaves'.[29] Owens points to the positive portrait of the real or literal slaves that accompany Anthia and Habrocomes, and to the acceptance or rationalisation of the slave-like behaviour of the elite protagonists in their enslaved circumstances.[30]

Second, we find that violence in the home was not reserved for slaves. Wives could show bruises or scars from their husbands. We will look at a fourth-century document, Augustine's *Confessions*, for his picture of his childhood home, paying close attention to his descriptions of his mother's upbringing and marriage to her non-Christian father. What we find is that violence is a constant in these stories, affecting women at all social levels.

---

29 Owens, *Representation*, 2.
30 Owens, *Representation*, 3, wonders about the 'contradictory subversion and affirmation, that is, this ambivalence toward normative elite thinking, [which] suggests to me the possibility that Xenophon and Chariton could have been ex-slaves writing, in part, for ex-slave readers'.

a. Anthea's Household and Slavery in Xenophon's Ephesiaca

Xenophon's work has been recently dated to the first century, offering us one perspective on slaves and their owners through the lens of fiction. *Ephesiaca* is a five-volume work that spins a rather amazing tale of young married lovers who find themselves separated and facing terrible struggles.[31] Anthia, a daughter of an elite family, falls deeply in love with Habrocomes, the son of another Ephesian leading family. After they wed, they travel down to Egypt with their two personal slaves, Leucon and Rhode. These two slaves are identified as σύντροφοι, which likely means the slaves were raised in the household with our two protagonists (2.3.3). The journey takes a horrible turn, and the four are captured by pirates and sold into slavery. So far, this Graeco-Roman novel follows the basic script that the lovers are separated and face slavery.

In our focus on the slave women and freed women of the story, we find that Anthia, who demonstrates σωφροσύνη, sexual chasteness, is threatened with rape at every encounter with a slave owner. In the early part of the novel, her slave, Rhode, helps her navigate the terrors of slavery. Later the two are separated, and Anthia faces her owners on her own. In all six encounters, Anthia avoids rape. Twice she is ready to die rather than face her assailant, a motif that perhaps takes its power from the Roman origin story of the Rape of Lucretia. In this foundational story, the good wife Lucretia is raped, and then commits suicide. She does so to prove her innocence so that no woman after her might hide an illicit affair under the guise that she was a victim like Lucretia.

The death in our romance novel is Anthia's owner, at her own hand. If Anthia had been accosted on the streets of Ephesus, she would be completely within her rights as an elite woman to kill a man who sought to rape her. But in the novel, she is a slave, one who has no right or even expectation that she might refuse her owner. Xenophon is at pains to explain that she did not premeditate the murder, but merely grabbed what was at hand to fight off her owner. In the novel, the male owners are greedy and cruel (and the female owners fare no better), but most of the slave characters are good, gentle, helpful. One fellow slave, Lampon, rescues Anthia twice from their owners. Throughout her ordeals,

---

31 The novel's current form of five volumes. However, the tenth century Byzantine encyclopedia *Suda* lists the novel at ten volumes, which leads some to see our current work as an epitome.

Anthia retains her σωφροσύνη and thus challenges the 'stereotype of the sexually available and promiscuous female slave'.³²

The adventures resolve themselves as the four lead characters reunite on the island of Rhodes. The two slaves are now freed and wealthy, for their previous owner had made them heirs (5.6.3). Leucon and Rhode recognise Habrocomes, and then he finds Anthia and they reunite in the temple of Isis. She assures her husband that she is as chaste as when they were first together. They return to Ephesus, to find both sets of parents deceased. Habrocomes and Anthia do not resume their past lives; instead, they live in what Owens calls a 'replacement family with Leucon and Rhode'.³³ A new family is a promise given to freed slaves, who can establish a future and inheritance, kinship, and connection. In this sense, the novel mirrors the society, for we find that inscriptions by freedmen often mention individuals beyond parents and children.

Might we have parallels in the house-churches in Ephesus, as all members experience new life in Christ, and face various threats from blood relatives or business associates? Would these new believers have resonated with the character Anthia as one who used tricks and deception to remain true to her love, Habrocomes, and her own modesty? Would they be sympathetic to the survival ploys, including lies and misdirection, that Anthia uses to remain whole? Would they affirm that the slave owners were indeed horrid and cruel, and felt sympathy for slaves and freedwomen in their midst? Most of all, would the young church see themselves in the final chapter, as a fictive family made up of those who felt great love for each other and experienced life-changing events that marked them forever? I will explore the language of fictive kinship in a moment, but before we get there, a further word about family, specifically slave and wife, in a context of familial violence.

b. Augustine's Household as Told in his Confessions

Patricia Clark explores familial details in Augustine's *Confessions*, looking at Monica, her mother-in-law, her husband (Augustine's father),

---

32 Owens, *Representation*, 215.
33 Owens, *Representation*, 48. On page 216, he observes that the novel 'align[s] with commemorative practices of freedmen that similarly asserted the ex-slave's dignity, stressed the importance of family relationships, and indicated continuity with the servile past'.

and the slaves of the household. What emerges is an alarming depiction of Augustine's family life. We see the complicated interactions between slave women and matrons, all within the cultural and family *milieu* of violence. Clark highlights several significant experiences of violence in Monica's life from childhood to adulthood that intertwine with slave women.

As a girl, Monica was supervised by an older slave woman who had the confidence of Monica's parents and is described with words 'analogous to that of a man in the public sphere'.[34] The prevailing view on child-rearing would be labelled criminal neglect or abuse today, but the strict, harsh treatment was commonplace in the ancient world. Augustine speaks about this elder slave woman restricting Monica's access to water, to the point of her extreme thirst, to teach self-discipline. Augustine explains, 'except at the times when they ate their frugal meals at their parents' table, she would not allow them to drink even water, however great their thirst, for fear that they might develop bad habits' (*Confessions,* trans. Pine-Coffin, 9.8.17). Clark's point is that this trusted slave woman taught her to be subordinate to greater authority, even as Monica, as an adult, will be a matron over slaves.

Let us pause for a moment to think about the slaves in Paul's congregations, some of whom could be raising up owners' daughters (and sons), and who had great power over those children. Many families had wetnurses and παιδαγωγός who did much of the childcare, and many of these figures were slaves.

Returning to Monica's story, as she grew up (thirsty!), she was given the task of filling the daily wine jug from the barrel stored in the basement. She was accompanied by a slave girl, probably close to her age. Over time, Monica started drinking the wine as well as filling the jug. At some point the slave girl accused her of being a drunkard, which Monica acknowledged was true, and she sought to change. Augustine explains that the slave girl apparently spoke with a temper during a quarrel. In other words, the slave girl was not thinking of helping Monica, but of getting the better of her (9.8.18).

This is not the only place where we see tensions between free and slave. After marriage to Patricius, Monica seeks to woo her mother-in-law. The

---

34 Clark, 'Women', 111.

latter's slave women are poisoning the well, but Monica persists in pleasantness, and wins the woman's heart. One ramification of this course change is that the mother asks her son to beat those slave women who spread nasty tales, which he does. The mother announces that if she hears anything negative about Monica, those speaking will suffer the same consequences (9.9.20). Recall that Paul said to the slave owners that they are not permitted to threaten their slaves (Eph. 6:9). One sees in Augustine's short vignette how powerful Paul's command could be if it were obeyed. Notice also that the patriarch, Patricius, sought harmony in the household by listening to his mother, as would a good son. The punishment suggested seemed reasonable, given the views about slaves' culpability. Finally, observe that Monica is praised for her kind, quiet demeanour that eventually won out. We are not told at what cost. It's time to do the math.

One last look at Monica as we turn to her marriage. Monica married a pagan; Augustine describes his mother's view on her marriage as serving her lord (*servivit veluti domino*). Clark observes that such is the language of slavery.[35] Augustine relays the advice Monica gave matrons in the community 'whose husbands were far more gentle than her own' and who bore disfiguring marks on their bodies (9.9.19). Monica urges these women not to gossip about their husbands, but to serve their husbands, as they had contracted to do when they were married.

Monica's marriage played out in a few ways, as Augustine describes it. First, Monica accepted expressions of her husband's temper. It is not clear if she was beaten, but it is possible. Yet her husband would not need to connect the punch, only raise his fist, for the desired effect on his wife. In the background is always the threat of violence. What if Patricius asked his slave to beat Monica? We know Tiberius ordered a centurion to beat his daughter-in-law, Agrippina, and she lost sight in one eye (Suet. *Tiberius*, 53). Herodes Attticus got irritated with his wife, Regilla, and told his freedman to beat her. She was eight months pregnant, and both she and the baby she was carrying died; Herodes denied that he instructed his freedman to punish her so severely (Philostratus, *Lives of the Sophists*, 555). A better-known story features Nero, who, though wildly in love with Poppaea, kicked her in the stomach, killing

---

35 Clark, 'Women', 113.

her and her baby. The ancient historians did not praise this rage, but they can rationalise a husband's jealousy or anger. Nero did not mean to kick so hard (Tacitus, *Annals* 16.6; Suetonius, *Nero* 35).

Second, although we find language of slavery in the story, nevertheless, Monica as a wife could wait out her husband's fit of anger. When he was calm, she could speak with him about whatever it was that precipitated the event. As Clark explains,

> One of the most significant markers distinguishing the dominated free woman from the female slave is Augustine's assertion that Monnica (sic) could wait, and later explain or justify her actions, and reason with her husband; this option…is not one that is stressed in a slave's relationship with a violent master or mistress.[36]

Not every woman was as compliant as Monica. A fourth-century Christian woman from Roman Egypt pursued a complaint against her violent husband. This man locked up his and her slaves, plus her foster daughters and his son for seven days in a cellar. He attacked his slaves and her slave, named Zoe, half-killing them. He applied fire to her foster daughters after stripping them naked, neither of which is permitted by law. He refused to honour his wife with having the keys to the house. Yet when he was before bishops and his filial brothers, he said he would change. That did not happen, and in fact, he then declared to his wife that he was getting a mistress.[37] I wish we knew if the law or the church restrained him.

Part 3: Ephesians, Fictive Kinship Expectations, and the Freedwoman

We have looked at the ubiquitous violence that permeated the ancient family and highlighted the ways in which families sought to mitigate it. In a novel, elite owners who were enslaved, and their slaves who were freed and made wealthy, created in the end a family unit based

---

36 Clark, 'Women', 119.
37 Oxy Pap 903, cited in Clark, 126.

on goodwill and mutual love. Freed slaves could become benefactors of their city and, especially important for women, could enter legitimate marriages with their children having the status of Roman citizen in many cases. The evidence shows a complex reality where social honour was fluid and everyone—free, freed, and enslaved—negotiated their space in their social networks.[38]

a. Complicating the Household Codes

How does this complicated reality inform our understanding of Paul's house churches? I think it can in three ways. First, the category of freedwoman helps us understand Roman family loyalty and networking. While I confess that marrying one's ex-owner seems unappealing, even horrible, the social convention reveals that men could view a female slave as worthy of marriage. Second, it helps us see that the categories of wife, enslaved female, and freedwoman had many overlapping realities. They were all judged in terms of the Roman model of *pudicitia*. They did similar jobs in the home and served their husbands/male owners. They faced violence from the adult men (and at times women) in the home. Wives were sexually available for their husbands, and I know of no examples where wives could say 'no' to basic sex, although participating in orgies or activities that harmed their *pudicitia* could be contested.

Therefore, when we exegete the household codes in the New Testament, we should not separate the marriage texts from the slavery texts as we imagine women's lives.[39] Some of the wives would previously have been slaves of their current patron/husband and would have endured his physical abuse. Thus, when Ephesians 5:29 commands a husband to treat his wife's body as his own, we should imagine that a husband, formerly an owner, would likely have to re-frame his sense of entitled self, now through the lens of Christ's self-sacrificial love.

---

38 Kloppenborg, *Christ's Associations*, 345, fruitfully explores early Christian communities through a comparison with ancient associations. His observations reinforce the importance of fictive kinship, in that both types of groups foster '*connectivity* among members, sometimes between members and the elite of society, and often lateral connections between one association and another'. He continues that the shared meals, funeral attendance, and other acts 'were ways of materializing connectivity and displaying the group to itself. These activities were not epiphenomenal but constitutive'.

39 We should not impose the employer/employee grid on the owner/slave reality, especially as this pertains to women.

Perhaps by reckoning with household violence in the first century, we will be more attuned to the home violence faced by women (and children) in our communities today.

b. Kinship Language and Congregational Life

When we turn to Ephesians 6:9, which commands that owners treat slaves *in the same way*, we should consider whether the scope of Paul's command includes refraining from sexual relations with female slaves. Paul Thompson argues that Paul's qualifier τὰ αὐτὰ is best understood as advocating for numerical equality and not proportional equality.[40] He looks back to earlier verses in chapter five, concluding, 'Paul's deliberate inclusivity and rejection of any cover-up in 5:3–12 [...] render Pauline complicity with the specific practice [of male owners having sex with female slaves] implausible'.[41]

Thompson's conclusions can be further strengthened by examining the language of kinship, specifically brother/sister language, that permeates his letters. Siblings, or more specifically brothers, were to be the glue that held the family together, for they continued the family's lineage and reputation after their father died. The fraternal relationship focused on harmony, with brothers encouraged to forgive and mend conflicts. The brothers were not seen as equals, for Romans recognised birth order and natural giftedness. But these differences were expected to work for the betterment of the other. Plutarch's treatise on brotherly affection (*De Fraterno Amore*) makes several points pertinent to our study. First, he observes that brothers' love for each other is rooted in their shared parentage (*Frat. Amor.* 2/478E). Second, demonstrating love for one's brothers effectively shows love of one's parents (*Frat. Amor.* 4/480A; 6/480F). Third, natural and social differences between brothers should be used to advantage the lesser brother or younger brother. There should be no envy, nor dictatorial attitudes between the brothers (*Frat. Amor.* 12/484D; 16/487B). The danger of strife was ever present, as inheritance disputes could tear apart families.

---

40   Thompson, *Pauline Slave Welfare*, 260, writes, 'the pronoun refers to the *same* treatment between persons that is premised upon their *numerical* equality rather than some vague and undefined *mutatis mutandis* proportionate treatment'.
41   Thompson, *Pauline Slave Welfare*, 262.

Paul takes the culture's ideal of brotherly harmony and transposes this into a gospel key.[42] He shifts the focus onto believers' heavenly Father, and their shared inheritance with their 'brother' Jesus Christ, and their shared experience of being sealed with the Holy Spirit. Paul keeps his society's emphasis on brotherly harmony but lifts the hierarchical grid that imposed levels of social worth and status variously onto persons within a family or clan unit. Trevor J. Burke sees this play out in 1 Thessalonians 4:3–8. He argues that the fictive kinship language of brotherly love reveals Paul's concern not only for morality, but for community cohesion and even its very survival. Burke points to the phrase τὸν ἀδελφὸν αὐτοῦ (1 Thess. 4:6; accusative singular, used only here in Pauline epistles in relation to believers) as Paul's attempt to emphasise the group's proper identity as brothers. Burke declares that the 'apostle is more anxious about the fact that such morality could threaten the very existence and survival of the *community* itself'.[43] Burke's observations remind us of the familial context in which Paul's words are read. Fictive kinship language that emphasises brotherly affection plays an important role in Paul's vision for the oneness of the church. The same language provides scaffolding for freedmen and freedwomen's participation in their patron's family as quasi-sons or wives/concubines.

Conclusion

In conclusion, we have seen the messiness of family in the ancient world, or more positively, we have a better sense of the texture and depth of the household in Paul's day. It is a place where love can be expressed, but violence—the physical sort that is illegal in our contexts—is a normal part of life. No one is quite safe from the hand of another, even sons from their fathers. But violence against slaves and wives is of a sanctioned sort that adult free sons did not face. In this context we explored the life of freedwomen. Their very presence challenges the ideology of

---

42 Punt, 'Pauline Brotherhood', argues that the Apostle Paul does not imagine women in his use of the plural *adelphoi*. He cites the few places where Paul uses the feminine 'sisters' to say that Paul intentionally restricted the masculine plural to men. However, Punt fails to give adequate weight to the fact that the places where Paul uses the feminine refer to a 'believing wife' (1 Cor. 9:5) and to a specific woman like Phoebe (Rom. 16:1–2), which would require the feminine form.

43 Burke, *Family Matters*, 180.

slavery's permanent marks of dishonour and reinforces cultural claims that a woman's sexual modesty is her most valuable possession or commodity. The freedwoman is re-made, especially if she marries, and especially if she marries or is the concubine of her ex-owner, now patron and husband (in that social order). She is now family, or at least quasi-family, which gives her a social network and a space to show her virtues of piety and loyalty. This hierarchy promotes reciprocity and grows the family network.

The kinship language that infuses and supports the category of freedmen and freedwomen created a new social reality within a family. Paul might have drawn on this ready model of kinship language and structure as he imagined the household of God, co-heirs together in Christ. The family dynamics embedded in the Roman manumission system offered analogies for believers to visualise social movement towards a closer familial experience. The believer joined a family of adopted siblings, all with equal status in Christ.

Bibliography

Burke, T. J.	*Family Matters: A Socio-Historical Study of Kinship Metaphors in 1 Thessalonians* (Library of New Testament Studies; London: T&T Clark, 2003).
Clark, P.	'Women, Slaves, and the Hierarchies of Domestic Violence: The Family of St. Augustine', in S. R. Joshel and S. Murnaghan (eds.), *Women and Slaves in Greco-Roman Culture: Differential Equations* (London: Routledge, 1998), 109–129.
Cohick, L. H.	*Ephesians* (The New International Commentary on the New Testament; Grand Rapids: Eerdmans, 2020).
Flexsenhar, M.	'No Longer a Slave: Manumission in the Social World of Paul' (MA Thesis, UT Austin, 2013).
Harrison, J. R.	'An Epigraphic Portrait of Ephesus and Its Villages', in J. R. Harrison and L. L. Welborn (eds.), *The First Urban Churches 3: Ephesus* (Atlanta: SBL, 2018), 1–68.
Hemelrijk, E. A.	*Women and Society in the Roman World: A Sourcebook of Inscriptions from the Roman World* (Cambridge: Cambridge University Press, 2021).
Kloppenborg, J. S.	*Christ's Associations: Connecting and Belonging in the Ancient City* (New Haven: Yale University Press, 2019).
Millett, M., Revell, L., and Moore, A. (eds.)	*The Oxford Handbook of Roman Britain* (Oxford: Oxford University Press, 2016).
Mouritzen, H.	*The Freedman in the Roman World* (Cambridge: Cambridge University Press, 2011).
Nasrallah, L. S.	*Archaeology and the Letters of Paul* (Oxford: Oxford University Press, 2019).
Owens, W. M.	*The Representation of Slavery in the Greek Novel: Resistance and Appropriation* (New York: Routledge, 2020).
Patterson, O.	*Slavery and Social Death: A Comparative Study* (Cambridge, MA: Harvard University Press, 1982).
Perry, M. J.	*Gender, Manumission, and the Roman Freedwoman* (Cambridge: Cambridge University Press, 2013).
Pilhofer, P.	*Philippi: Band II, Katalog der Inschriften von Philippi* (2nd edn; WUNT 119; Tübingen: Mohr Siebeck, 2009).
Pomeroy, Sarah B.	*Goddesses, Whores, Wives, and Slaves: Women in Classical Antiquity* (New York, NY: Schocken Press, 1975, 1995).

Punt, J. 'Pauline Brotherhood, Gender and Slaves', *Neotestamentica* 47.1 (2013), 149–169.

Shaner, K. *Enslaved Leadership in Early Christianity* (Oxford: Oxford University Press, 2018).

Thompson, W. H. P. *Pauline Slave Welfare in Historical Context: An Equality Analysis* (Tübingen: Mohr Siebeck, 2023).

Zelnick-Abramovitz, R. *Not Wholly Free: The Concept of Manumission and the Status of Manumitted Slaves in the Ancient Greek World* (Leiden: Brill, 2005).

CHAPTER 2

'The Body' in Paul: Christ's Body, the Church as Christ's Body, and Bodily Resurrection

Lynn H. Cohick

Introduction

My family lived in rural Kenya for three years in the late 1990s. During that time, I got to know Paul Ngoroge, a Kikuyu in his early twenties. He worked in our house, cooking, cleaning, washing, and being a big brother to our young children. At one point he asked if we would be interested in helping his family with a celebration honouring his younger brother who at age fifteen was undergoing circumcision. Paul had been circumcised at his rural home, and I asked him what circumcision meant to him. He said it was a doorway to adulthood, to manhood. I wondered aloud, 'Who would know whether you are circumcised anyway?' And his simple answer was quite profound; he said, 'I would know.'

'I would know.' If we transpose this answer into the key of Philippians, we might catch the note Paul strikes here. 'We are the circumcision,' Paul says to the Philippian Gentiles, the new believers among whose men no one is marked in this way (Phil. 3:3). Both 'Pauls' emphasise the radical, life changing effect of being a circumcised one. And both Pauls are part of a culture, an ethnicity, that values male circumcision.

For Ngoroge, the private knowledge that he underwent the rite to adulthood or manhood made all the difference in his public demeanour. He was a man now; he had standing in the community. And in the apostle Paul's time, it was important for most Jews to circumcise their infant sons. Jesus was circumcised (Luke 2:21). Timothy, Paul's co-worker whose mother was Jewish, was circumcised when he joined Paul's group (Acts 16:3). To the Philippians, the apostle insists that Gentile believers have a new identity based on a real, spiritual change such that one now worships in the spirit of God.

'For it is we who are the circumcision, we who serve God by his Spirit, who boast in Christ Jesus, and who put no confidence in the flesh' (Phil. 3:3, NIV 2011). Paul intends the comment to be understood as a spiritual marker on all believers. This is quite clear in the well-known passage from Galatians 3:28, wherein Paul declares that there, in Christ, there is neither Jew nor Greek. The verse includes two other pairs: slave and free, and male and female. Scholars consider the ramifications of this statement for Paul, and what it should mean for churches today.

The Galatians verse points to difference within the unity of Christ. The differences noted in the second and third pairs are, from Aristotle's point of view, ontological and hierarchical. By Paul's day, Stoics had backed away from a strict sense that there were some population groups that were born to be enslaved. However, in Paul's day, the Gentile would think himself better than the Jew, and the Jew would count himself blessed to be an elect member of the family of the one true God. Paul declares that baptism into Christ, being clothed with Christ, made such hierarchies moot within the fellowship of believers. Scholars today would say that, at the very least, the hierarchy of slave and free is man-made and the institution of slavery, including human trafficking, is a plague that should be exterminated. It is the other two pairs, Jew/Gentile and male/female, that scholars debate as to their eternal status. The Jew/Gentile pair displays both an ethnic distinction, and a religious one, and we must add that the category 'Gentile' includes numerous people groups. From this angle, then, we can re-introduce the slave/free category as it pertains to those situations where the enslaved people's ethnic (racial) identity is a key factor in the slavery ideology, as happened in the United States.

I address two questions in this essay. First, will there be circumcised and uncircumcised male raised bodies in the new heavens and the new earth? I am prompted in this inquiry by the rather common claim that Galatians 3:28 signals that all will be equal in the eschaton. I would agree if what is meant is that the institutions of marriage and slavery would not be relevant or appropriate and are thus absent. But I confess the statement also makes me as a woman nervous. Will male and female remain in the eschatological fellowship of resurrected believers, in the new heavens and new earth? Will the identity markers of being a Jew remain? Will the ethnic identities that shape our self today remain? I am interested in those arguments which suggest that individual bodies, from creation, possess eternally significant differences that are continuous through the resurrection. This has been most acute in the conversations about male/female distinctives, but I think an intriguing parallel can be found in the Jew/Gentile distinctives. I want to explore the questions of whether and how the particularities of our earthly body shape the promised resurrected bodies. The questions are important because we should value more highly that which we think will have continuity into the eschaton.[1]

Second, I want to probe Paul's expectations about particularity and the universal work of God in Christ. If we talk about particularity continuing with the raised body, what then is meant by expression of being 'in Christ'? This takes special urgency when we imagine being a member of Christ's body.[2] By 'particularity' I refer to substantive differences found among humans, including sex (male and female) and cultural/religious identity (Jew and Gentile). The term 'universal' tries to capture that which is common to humanity and to its status as *imago Dei*. The hope is to explore these themes through the lens of Paul within Judaism model, with special attention to one of its leading scholars, Paula Fredriksen.

---

1   Disability Studies is another area which asks similar questions about the body in the eschaton. Speaking about the resurrection body, Yong, *The Bible*, 121, writes that 'a disability perspective would insist that some impairments are so identity-constitutive that their removal would involve the obliteration of the person as well.' The upshot of such: 'Eschatological images without people with disabilities effectively translate into church—harbingers of the coming reign of God—without such people, either.' See Draper et al., *Disabling Leadership*. Due to space constraints, this essay will not engage with this important field of study.
2   Thiessen and Fredriksen, 'Paul and Israel', 371, describe a universal reading of Paul that understands 'Israel' to be 'ethnically non-specific Christians'.

Part 1: Review of Pauline Studies

To set the stage for my argument, a brief word about the recent movements within Pauline scholarship. Most Pauline scholars accept these three tenets. First, Paul was Jewish, born a Jew in a world that emphasised ethnic identity (specific language, gods, dress and diet). Second, Paul followed Jesus as the crucified and resurrected messiah. Third, Paul preached what he called 'good news'. Often the debate about Paul and Judaism centers on whether Paul kept his Judaism (whatever that might look like) or converted to Christianity (again, whatever that looked like in the apostolic era). In this construction, Judaism is primarily defined as a religion, not a cultural/ethnic designation. Within the last sixty years or so, Pauline studies have been upended based on a re-evaluation of Second Temple Judaism. This has been a helpful shift, as it places Paul's letters within their cultural and theological context and highlights the dangers of universalising Paul's message wholesale. Yet for much of the discussion, we still use the lens of sin and salvation in evaluating Law and Jesus Christ. In so doing, we fail to fully appreciate that the Jewish torah focuses extensively on purity/impurity, and that Christ creates a new family, his Body, with his cross, resurrection, and ascension. I hope to develop both these topics as we pursue the question of raised bodies in Christ.

New Perspective on Paul

In the post-WWII world, and with the discovery of the Dead Sea Scrolls, New Testament scholars took a hard look at their discipline's assumptions about Paul and the Judaism of the Second Temple period. Krister Stendahl argued that Paul was called, not converted, that he did not have a crisis of conscience like Luther's, but instead had a robust conscience.[3] Stendahl's work opened the door to the question of Paul and Judaism, and specifically to thinking of Paul remaining within Judaism as he preached his gospel of the risen Christ. One trajectory became known as the New Perspective on Paul (NPP). This position emphasises that Jews at this time assumed their election as the people of God and followed torah to demonstrate their obedience to their God. E. P. Sanders called this 'covenantal nomism.'[4] For Sanders, Paul judged

---

3   Stendahl, 'The Apostle Paul', 199–215.
4   Sanders, *Paul*, 33–59, 183–98, 222–28.

the law irrelevant for salvation in favour of Christ. Since Sanders, others such as Jimmy Dunn and N. T. Wright have argued that Paul decried works of the law, those rites which create ethnic boundaries between Jew and Gentile. The adherents to the NPP decried the antisemitism that infused New Testament studies and left the church without theological courage to fight Nazism. Not everyone is convinced that antisemitism has been removed, but all should agree that we must be vigilant in the pursuit of this goal.[5]

Paul within Judaism

Another trajectory, with a broad range of views fitted under its banner, is known by the name Paul within Judaism (PWJ), or the radical new perspective.[6] I mention first those views that receive near unanimity and emphasis by the PWJ scholars. They argue that the categories of Jew and Gentile are critical for understanding Paul, and Paul's preaching about Christ was intended for Gentile ears, not Jewish ones.[7] I think most scholars agree that Paul wrote to congregations made up primarily of Gentiles. Also, most scholars hold that it is important to use categories of Jew and Gentile, and not simply or only believer/unbeliever. Stephen Westerholm remarks that part of the PWJ view can be summarised thus: Paul thought in Jewish categories, including about the God of Israel, the people of God and the messiah, through the lens of the Old Testament. He concludes, 'If all this is what is meant by saying that Paul remained "within Judaism," then we need have no qualms about adopting the slogan.'[8] But of course, this is not all that is meant.

Additional views held by some who claim the PWJ label include that Paul believed in two paths for salvation: torah for Jews, Christ for Gentiles. In one of the earlier expressions of this position, John Gager, in his book *Reinventing Paul*, explains the 'two paths' position.[9] For Gager, Paul never doubted Israel's salvation, 'what he taught

---

5   Fredriksen, 'What Does It Mean', 361, critiques the NPP, 'this antiritual, postethnic Paul is the Paul-within-Protestantism'.
6   Foster, 'An Apostle', 1–11, reviews Fredriksen, *Paul*.
7   Fredriksen, *Paul*, 86, writes, 'And while his letters are addressed often (I think, only) to Christ-following gentiles, we have no statement from Paul to Jews about their no longer preserving Jewish tradition.'
8   Westerholm, *Romans*, 69.
9   Gager, *Reinventing Paul*.

and preached was instead a special path, a *Sonderweg*, for Gentiles'.[10] Fredriksen, by contrast, argues that Paul preached Jesus to both Jew and Gentile.[11] Rafael Rodriguez is clear in his book, *If You Call Yourself a Jew*, that the two-covenant position is not consistent with Paul's gospel, for 'it excludes Christians from their God-given identity as Israel and it deprives Israel of its own Messiah'.[12] Mark Nanos would agree that the PWJ perspective does not promote two paths to salvation, while Gabriel Boccaccini promotes three paths to salvation: the Mosaic law for righteous Jews, the natural law for righteous Gentiles (these both based on works), and Christ for sinners, in which group Paul would place himself. Mark Nanos suggests that the language of salvation is unhelpful. For example, he suggests that the verb σωζω in Romans 11:26 is best translated as 'keep safe' and that Paul intends that God will keep Jews safe, as 'many are suffering estrangement for not having faithfully carried out the entrusted task'.[13]

Perhaps most basic to the PWJ position is the conviction that Paul thought and acted within the structures and presuppositions of Second Temple Judaism. This includes that he observed Jewish law, including ritual law, and encouraged other Jews to do so. As Rodriguez states, the 'problem is not Torah. The problem is that God never intended Torah for Gentiles'.[14] The Paul of PWJ offered no critique of Judaism *per se*; instead, this Paul limited his comments to areas that were part of the general Jewish conversation. For example, we know that Jews discussed the relative importance of physical circumcision, in light of the biblical texts that stressed spiritual circumcision. So too, Paul talks about circumcision of the identity, not only of the physical member. As Fredriksen asks, 'If Israel is to remain Israel—rejoicing with the Gentiles (Rom. 15:10)—then why would Israel cease enacting their covenant with the god of their redemption?'[15] It is precisely the assumption underpinning this question—if Israel is to remain Israel—that I will explore.

---

10 Gager, *Reinventing Paul*, 146.
11 Fredriksen, *Paul*, 113–114; Fredriksen, 'What Does It Mean', 378.
12 Rodriguez, *If You Call Yourself*, 190.
13 Nanos, 'All Israel', 254.
14 Rodriguez, *If You Call Yourself*, 117.
15 Fredriksen, *Paul*, 113.

Part 2: Circumcision and Jewish Identity

Reflections on Jesus' Circumcision

Andrew Jacobs' book, *Christ Circumcised: A Study in Early Christian History and Difference*, offers helpful information. He discusses imperial Rome's political and cultural control over Jews, including the insistence that circumcision is the signature demarcation of Jewishness. Jacobs wonders whether Paul's interlocutors desired Gentile circumcision as a means of incorporating them into 'that same Roman economy of cultural signs'.[16] Paul sought an invisibility afforded by retaining the foreskin and offered a theological circumcision for all believers in Christ, as seen in Colossians 2:9–13, which speaks of a circumcision not made by hands, a circumcision done by Christ in baptism.[17]

Looking at Christian texts, Jacobs' research shows a few places in the late ancient and medieval Christian writings where circumcision and Jesus' resurrected body are linked. Generally speaking, Patristic writers did not think Jesus' raised body was circumcised and believed that God 'recovered' the circumcised foreskin at his Son's resurrection. For example, for Philoxenus (bishop of Mabbug/Hierapolis, d. 523), the concern is Christ's incorruptibility. Philoxenus battles with those who question Christ's full humanity and encourages the faithful to 'have faith that even the cutting of Christ's circumcision was united to his person in resurrection, and corruption did not have dominion over it, as the living and life-giving body of God. And do not seek impiously where that part is until the time of the resurrection.'[18]

However, in the twelfth century, there was increasing talk about having bits of the foreskin, a part of Christ's divine body, as relics. This relic is

---

16 Jacobs, *Christ*, 24.
17 Cohen, *Why Aren't Jewish Women*, 71, 'Circumcision marks the Jew not the gentile; the slave owned by a Jew, not the free gentile; the male, not the female.' Cohen explores the question from the gender angle, asking why women are not circumcised. He points to the Christian contrast made between baptism, done to both women and men, and circumcision. He highlights Galatians 3:28, declaring that circumcision discriminates. It is not until the 13th century CE with the *Zohar*, the Jewish mystical text written by Moses de Leon, that we have Jews explaining circumcision as making the male infant a Jew, able to study Torah. No longer simply a sign or a commandment, circumcision was now seen as making the man/male infant a Jew. Cohen concludes, 45, that the rite becomes the 'sine qua non of Jewishness'.
18 Jacobs, *Christ*, 138, as cited from Philoxenus, *Commentary on Matthew and Luke* fr. 42 (CSCO 392:39 [Syr.], 393:34 [Eng.]).

known as *sanctus virtus* (holy virtue). Jacobus, a monk who wrote about the legend and how such relics came to be in France, expressed doubt about its veracity. He believed that when Jesus rose, his flesh of foreskin also was raised and put back where it belonged. However, Catherine of Siena said she saw the wedding ring for the church made from Jesus' foreskin.[19] Some said the foreskin was in the Santa Sanctorum in the Lateran Basilica; Pope Innocent III spoke of this belief but did not endorse it. It was under his leadership that transubstantiation became official church doctrine, and the physical body of Christ became a focused topic of discussion.

Reflections on Resurrection, Circumcision, and the Male or Female Body

Perhaps a way forward is to look at the third pair of Galatians 3:28, 'neither male and female' (ἄρσεν καὶ θῆλυ). Will this pair disappear at the eschaton? Origen likely taught this, for he stressed the discontinuity of our current body with the resurrected body. Methodius objected to Origen's views on resurrection bodies, taunting that Origen believed those resurrected would have a geometric shape, such as a sphere, even as Origen taught the sun, moon and stars were spherical and rational beings. Gregory of Nyssa argued for a non-sexed human, without genitalia. Maximus the Confessor picked up Origen and Gregory of Nyssa's views.[20] These men wrestled with the conundrum of the decaying body somehow being brought back to life, and with tentative answers about what perfection looked like. Such concepts are philosophically interesting but are not done in a vacuum. Ideals of perfection were available, understood as rational, non-material, and were mapped onto the male/female pair, with female being non-rational or irrational and material. Augustine identifies the sexism and counters it. He declares women will be raised as female, for 'the sex of a woman is not a vice, but nature' (*City of God*, 22.17.1144–1145).

---

19 Jacobs, *Christ*, preface ix and x.
20 Mitchell, *Origen's Revenge*, xviii, suggests two ways of viewing male and female, based on an understanding of the nature and purpose of the differentiation. The 'Greek' position says that male and female are not essential to the creation of humans as bearing the image of God, and the purpose for male and female is procreation in marriage. The 'Hebrew' position emphasises the differences between male and female, and sees the image of God expressed as a matter of relationships.

The enigmatic phrase 'like the angels' used in Jesus's teaching about the resurrection deserves another look in this context (Matt. 22:30). Timothy Bradford looks at the evidence about the physicality of angels in the Old Testament and Second Temple literature and acknowledges its breadth and even conflicting pictures.[21] He observes that both those who claim resurrection of sexed bodies, and those who argued for a spiritual body, used Jesus' comparison to angels as support for their claims. Bradford, however, argues that Jesus was not speaking about resurrection in his comparison. Instead, Jesus denies the Sadducees' assumption that resurrected life continues similarly to the present existence. The added statement, that the resurrected will live like angels, refers to resurrected life in the presence of God, for angels live in the heavens. Jesus likely points to the resurrected human's exalted status as similar to angels, similar to the descriptions of Moses and David as having angelic appearance because of their exalted circumstances (Exod. 30:29 LXX; Sir. 45.2; 1 Sam. 29:9; 2 Sam. 14:17, 19:27; Zech. 12:8; Dan. 12:3). Bradford concludes, 'While sexual relationships will be transcended at the resurrection, there is nothing explicit to indicate that the sexed bodies of men and women will be transcended or transformed at the resurrection.'[22] Jesus' reference to angels in Matthew 22:30 is better understood as describing 'tangibly the hope of human nature raised from the dead and glorified in the presence of God'.[23]

Candida Moss comes at the question of resurrected body from a different angle. In her book *Divine Bodies: Resurrecting Perfection in the New Testament and Early Christianity*, she includes a scene from Sant'Apollinare Nuovo, Ravenna, specifically the mosaic of the twenty-two female martyrs in procession to the altar. She remarks on the similar dress and hairstyles, that 'in death, they are memorialized as heavenly Stepford wives'.[24] While recognising that iconography is at play in the women's presentation, she continues that we could 'optimistically interpret the scene theologically—these women are all the same because in Christ all other individuating markers are, in the style of

---

21 Bradford, 'Like the Angels'?, 152–53.
22 Bradford, 'Like the Angels'?, 155.
23 Bradford, 'Like the Angels'?, 161.
24 Moss, *Divine Bodies*, 89.

Gal. 3:28, stripped away.'[25] When one looks closely at the depiction of Felicitas and Perpetua, a slave woman and a free, wealthy woman, Moss is correct. Both martyrs are dressed and bejewelled with similar style, only the colours of the jewels and garments differ. One might say, then, that the second pair of the Galatians 3:28 series is believed to be overcome in the eschaton. But they are still women in the eschaton, which is the burden of my argument.

Beth Felker Jones, in her excellent work *Marks of His Wounds: Gender Politics and Bodily Resurrection*, talks about male and female and the resurrected body.[26] She argues persuasively that male and female are raised as such, and her conclusion is based on looking at both creation and the eschatological body. Felker Jones argues that Christ's mission has a representational element as the image of God, the image which was created male and female. She argues further that Jesus' incarnation as a human in space and time affirms each human's particularity. Thus, each member of Christ's body has their own (and good) particularity.

Felker Jones observes that Jesus' particularity in his incarnation expresses itself in maleness and Jewishness.[27] While most of her book focuses on male and female, I want to concentrate here on the 'Jewish' part of Jesus' particularity, as it relates to the question of Jesus' raised and glorified body. Is his raised body a circumcised body? Her work invites us to think about creation and new creation as both important to understand our embodiment now in light of our raised bodies in Christ. Just as the sexism against the female body tarnishes discussions about the raised female body, so too the anti-Judaism permeating the arguments about Jesus' raised, fore-skinned body sharply diminishes the validity of their conclusions. The 'male and female' created in God's image to do life together and steward the earth as described in Genesis, and echoed in Galatians, is a particularity that carries into the eschaton.

Fredriksen makes a similar observation in her interpretation of Paul's argument to Peter in Galatians 2:15. Here Paul speaks of himself and Peter as Jews by nature or by birth (φύσις), suggesting a shared kinship or ethnicity group that, as with all other kinships groups at that time,

---

25   Moss, *Divine Bodies*, 90.
26   Felker Jones, *Marks*.
27   Felker Jones, *Marks*, 111.

regulated and informed piety.[28] Fredriksen states that Paul was an 'ethnic essentialist'.[29] Focusing on 1 Corinthians 15, she continues, '*How does star-body manifest ethnicity?*' Fredriksen concludes that Paul gives no answer, and thus she too will give it a pass.[30]

I would point out, however, Paul's insistence that believers are 'in Christ', the one raised from the dead. Paul claims that believers, those in Christ, have a foot in this present evil age, and one in the age to come. He maintains that 'in Christ' believers are united as one family, siblings adopted into God's family. Here we turn to our second question, the ramifications for particularity when we are also all 'in Christ'.

Part 3: Resurrection and 'in Christ' Identity

Fredriksen rightly emphasises the apocalyptic in Paul's thought; however, there is less on the matter of becoming members of Christ's body, of being 'in Christ'. Instead, she sees 'the inclusion of Gentiles as "ex-pagan pagans"'.[31] She states that 'eschatological pagans *join with* Israel; but they do not 'join' Israel'.[32] She further clarifies that godfearers were '*active*' pagans and that,

> *Like* god-fearers, these eschatological pagans would retain their native ethnicities; *unlike* god-fearers, these pagans would no longer worship their native gods. *Like* proselytes, these pagans would worship exclusively the god of Israel; *unlike* proselytes, these pagans would preserve their own ethnicities and—another way of saying the same thing—they would not assume the bulk of Jewish ancestral custom (such as, for males, circumcision).[33]

Fredriksen speaks about Gentiles turning from lesser gods and turning to the God of Israel but resists the translation 'convert' for the verb ἐπιστέφω (1 Thess. 1:9; Acts 15:3). There is no eschatological conversion, only 'eschatological inclusion'. Margaret Mitchell questions the

---

28 Fredriksen, *The Pagans' Apostle*, 65. See also 'What Does It Mean', 359.
29 Fredriksen, 'Paul the "Convert"?', 43.
30 Fredriksen, 'What Does It Mean', 376. She translates *pneumatikos* as 'star-body.'
31 Fredriksen, *The Pagans' Apostle*, 30.
32 Fredriksen, *The Pagans' Apostle*, 75.
33 Fredriksen, *The Pagans' Apostle*, 74.

translational decision to reject 'convert'. She asks, 'Can they not only be ex pagan pagans but 'ex pagans called in Christ' to that καινὴ κτίσις Paul likes to talk about, as a third category (Gal. 6:15; 2 Cor. 5:17; cf. 1 Cor. 1:22–24)?'[34] Fredriksen argues there would not be anything to convert to, for Paul does not want them to become Jews, and Christianity has yet to be established.[35] She lands on τὰ ἔθνη as Paul's preferred choice to describe Gentile followers of Jesus, although she points to Paul's use of 'the saints/holy ones'.

Fredriksen concludes that Gentiles are adopted children, while Jews 'are God's sons *physei*'.[36] Both Jews and Gentiles who follow Jesus the messiah would be included in God's kingdom, but the two do not become one new humanity.[37] Repeating Fredriksen's question asked at the beginning of the paper, 'If Israel is to remain Israel—rejoicing with the Gentiles (Rom. 15:10)—then why would Israel cease enacting their covenant with the god of their redemption?'[38]

Fredriksen asks about the status of the covenant, about Israel enacting their covenant, as part of what would be included in life in the eschaton. To address her important question, I will, first, suggest a better way to think of the terms 'Israel' and 'Jew'. Here I follow Jason Staples. Second, I will suggest that the messianic age requires a different sort of piety, based on the righteousness the messiah brings, or the new torah establishes, and in the case of Paul, the resurrection life is inaugurated. Third, and relatedly, Paul's refrain of life in Christ, the risen saviour, involves transformation of believers' raised bodies.

Meaning of 'Jew' and 'Israel'

First, a brief word about the terms 'Jew' and 'Israel'. They are often used as synonyms, but Jason Staples, in his work *The Idea of Israel in Second Temple Judaism*, argues the evidence suggests otherwise. After reviewing

---

34 Mitchell, 'Paul and Judaism', 76.
35 Fredriksen, *The Pagans' Apostle*, 117.
36 Fredriksen, *The Pagans' Apostle*, 378.
37 Thiessen and Fredriksen, 'Paul and Israel', 384. Thiessen and Fredriksen suggest that the reference to the full number of Gentiles refers to the descendants from Noah, found in the Table of Nations in Genesis 10. 'Both all Gentile nations and all Israel will, somehow, receive Christ's *pneuma* (Rom. 1:16–17; 10:11–13).' They conclude that Jew and Gentile in Christ, 'though now in one 'family', are not 'one'.
38 Fredriksen, *The Pagans' Apostle*, 113.

most of the Second Temple literature, Staples finds that Jewish authors spoke of 'Israel' when referring to the 'twelve-tribe covenantal people of YHWH' or the Northern Kingdom.[39] The noun 'Israelite' signalled a person claiming ancestry back to Jacob. Interestingly, when we read pre-Christian, Graeco-Roman sources, including inscriptions, we find only Samaritans used this self-identification.[40] For example, from Delos, we have a second-century BCE inscription that reads, 'The Israelites in Delos, who send the temple tax to holy Ar-garizein', which we call Mt. Gerizim.[41] This inscription highlights a diaspora Samaritan community who self-identified with the ancient Israelite faith, and saw its holy place as Mt. Gerizim.[42] We find the term 'Hebrew' almost always refers to the person's language, Aramaic and/or biblical Hebrew. It might also mean a person in the pre-monarchy period of Israel's history.

What about 'Jew' or *Ioudaios*? This term refers to those of Judah, from the Southern Kingdom. As such, they are part of Israel, but not coterminous with Israel. As Staples explains, there exists a '*partitive* relationship between Israel and Judah established in biblical literature [that] persisted within the tradition'.[43] Staples disputes the theory that 'Jew' is a term designating outsider status or carrying negative connotations. This theory was developed by the German scholar Karl G. Kuhn who had strong antisemitic leanings.[44]

How did Jews connect these various terms in their self-understanding? Staples argues that Second Temple Jews relied on restoration eschatology to explain their current circumstances and their future. That is, Jews believed they were experiencing an exile—even those who returned to Judah, such as Ezra and Nehemiah. They awaited the full consummation of God's promise to restore the Twelve Tribes. Until this happened, and the scattered ones were brought home, there was not such a thing as Israel. Therefore, the term 'Israel' is always theological, always expectant, for God is the God of Israel, not simply the God of the Jews. And Jesus would not be merely King of the Jews, for that

---

39 Staples, *The Idea of Israel*, 339.
40 Staples, *The Idea of Israel*, 340.
41 Kartveit, *Origin*, 216, inscriptions from Delos. See also Pummer, *The Samaritans*.
42 Josephus, *Ant* 14.10, indicates a Samaritan synagogue at Delos.
43 Staples, *The Idea of Israel*, 340; see also Staples, *Paul and the Resurrection of Israel*.
44 Carl Georg Kuhn, ' Ἰσραήλ, Ἰουδαῖος, Ἑβραῖος in Jewish Literature after the OT,' *TDNT* 3:359–69.

would limit his reign. As the Samaritans declare in John's Gospel, Jesus is the saviour of the world (John 4:42). As Nathaniel said upon meeting Jesus, 'You are the king of Israel' (John 1:49). If Staples is right, then one answer to Fredriksen's question is that Israel becomes a new entity or family, which includes Jews rejoicing with Gentiles, in Christ.

Torah Expectations in the Messianic Age, Found in Second Temple Judaism

Second, along with our precision about the meaning of the term 'Israel' and the restorative eschatology that underpins the theological impact, we might ask whether Jewish groups in STJ imagined obedience to torah or the function of torah as being different in the coming messianic age. Kevin Grasso explores the ancient sources and finds that a few speculate on what torah observance would look like in the messianic age. Grasso suggests,

> 'While a torah specific to the messianic era is not well-attested in our literature, idealized versions of the Mosaic torah were commonplace, and given that messianism was often associated with an ideal state of righteousness, it is easy to see how the messianic era might be thought to have its own torah that would detail the righteous rules of the new age.'[45]

Grasso points to Sibylline Oracle 3 (ca 163–145 BCE) with its picture of the messianic age as a time of great peace, drawing on Isaiah 11:5–7. People are drawn to the Jerusalem temple from all places, and they will worship the true God. They will cease from adultery, murder, lewdness, and especially idolatry. The king from the East (messiah?) brings peace, obeys God's decrees, and people will prosper with food to eat and righteous wealth (3.973). Grasso contrasts this with the vision presented in the DSS, specifically the Damascus Document (CD) and the Rule of the Congregation (1QSa), which look for two messiahs. The torah takes on a new role, as it is studied more closely and obeyed more strictly, especially the priestly code, as the Qumran community viewed themselves as the priests, sons of Zadok. Grasso points to Nickelsburg's

---

45 Grasso, 'Righteousness', 40.

evaluation of 1 Enoch, which includes the assessment that wisdom is central for Enochic Judaism, and torah is not emphasized.

Grasso's findings invite us to re-examine our ideas about what torah obedience could look like in the messianic age. Or said another way, it complicates the picture by asking whether the messiah might change the way torah is obeyed, or whether torah content is altered. For example, from the Vayikra Rabbah 9:7 (5–7th CE) we read, 'in the world to come, all the sacrifices are annulled, but the thanksgiving sacrifice is not annulled; all the prayers are annulled, but the (prayer of) thanksgiving is not annulled'. Later this text speaks of a 'new torah' and points to Isaiah 51:4. This new torah changes kashrut laws, for the new torah will allow the righteous to eat foods that are now on the list of unclean food. Interestingly, we don't find the word 'new' in the Isaiah text, but Justin Martyr assumes the word in his Dialogue with Trypho the Jew. Justin declares that Isaiah 51:4 proclaims that a new law will come from the messiah, and this is a final law. However, when Justin quotes the text, he writes a 'law shall go forth from me'. Grasso rightly suggests that Justin is aware of a tradition that connects messiah with giving a new law.[46]

Grasso highlights the few texts within STJ where the messianic age is imagined, especially attending to ideas of messiah and torah. Paul Sloan takes a different tack, writing from the Paul within Judaism camp. He rightly emphasises that the torah not only regulates sin and the festival calendar, but also includes much about purity and impurity. Following Milgrom's work on Leviticus,[47] Sloan points out that the purity law regulates mortality. The laws about semen and menstruation and blood in childbirth highlight mortal life, and by extension, death. They underline humanity's mortality, which limits relationship with the Divine. Sloan applies this argument to Jesus' words about marriage, and specifically that angels do not marry and nor will believers in the eschaton. Sloan concludes that the present (evil) age requires marriage, procreation, and laws regulating purity because of mortality. But Christ

---

46 Grasso, 'Righteousness', 64, n.66. He continues, 67, 'it was not necessarily the idea of certain commandments being annulled in the messianic era that troubled Jews during the second temple period (though some certainly may have disagreed with this point), but the contentious issue may have been, at least for some, that the messianic era had been inaugurated in Jesus'.

47 Milgrom, *Leviticus*.

brings immortality, for he opens the door to the life to come. In this new life, purity laws are irrelevant.⁴⁸

I would add that the wedding feast of the Lamb would have perfect food for immortal bodies, neither kosher nor non-kosher. The lack of a temple in the New Jerusalem would mean that festivals and worship would be directly in the presence of God and his Son, the eternal High Priest. That sabbath rest is the constant state of existence, the eternal rest promised in Christ. I wonder if things will seem totally 'Jewish' and not Jewish at all, at the same time, because the promises are perfected and fulfilled.

We have looked at Staples' claims about restorative eschatology for Israel, and explored texts that offer hints of what STJ imagined about the messianic age, specifically concerning the torah and the messiah. We turn lastly to look at transformation into Christ's likeness as a result of being 'in Christ'. Not only does Christ create through his cross one new humanity, but also Christ's body has many members, all of equal value and importance. Willie Jennings speaks to this, declaring that 'just as Torah formed Israel's identity, establishing human life in the presence of God, so Jesus intends the formation of new humanity in his presence, listening to his speaking through the Spirit', adding that this is 'biracial humanity'.⁴⁹

Resurrection and Transformation

In Philippians, we discover another way Paul speaks about the one new humanity. Here Paul speaks about transformation and emphasises the connection between Christ's raised body and his followers' raised bodies at his second coming. The followers are part of Christ's πολίτευμα, they are citizens of heaven, a commonwealth devoted to Christ (Phil. 1:27; 3:20–21). Additionally, Paul identifies Christ here as Saviour, linking his coming with salvation and resurrection. Christ delivers from sin by transforming believers' lowly bodies to be like his glorious one. Paul had earlier in Philippians described Christ in the form of a human (Phil. 2:8, NIV 2011; 2:7, NA28), now he describes his followers as

---

48 Sloan, unpublished, 10. 'Once humans obtain this immortal condition, or exist in Christ for whom such a condition has obtained, some decrees become redundant', citing 1 Cor. 15:1–22.
49 Jennings, *Christian Imagination*, 272.

transformed. This is part of a larger transformation, when all enemies, including death, are finally and forever defeated.

The transformation includes a change in the person's 'glory status', if I could say it that way. The splendour of the raised body includes its imperishability, its glory, its power (1 Cor. 15:42–44). Transformation with particularity preserved; one new humanity with each person's name written in the book of life. Moss asks about the raised body. 'Is there any distinction between accidental attributes and essential markers of identity?'[50] She continues, 'If being 'me' is important, then what essential elements of myself need to be preserved or reformed in order for the resurrected 'me' to be the same 'me' that exists now?'[51] But these are not Paul's questions. Paul's enquiries relate to transformation of the self into Christ's likeness, into one new humanity, a new creation, a transformed body that shares its immortal life because he or she is 'in Christ'.

Conclusion

'We are the circumcision.' Does physical circumcision, a covenant act performed on Jewish male babies, endure with the man into the eschaton? Or does the physical act done now serve no eschatological purpose in the immortal state, in Christ? I tentatively conclude yes to both questions. If we ask whether the Apostle Paul and Paul Ngoroge will be raised circumcised, and we conclude that these are both critical identity markers of ethnicity, then I could imagine both men with raised, circumcised bodies. Jesus' particularity as a Jew is eternally consequential in the salvation history of God's people, as is his title as the King of Israel (John 1:49). The Paul within Judaism school invites us to focus closely on the ethnic particularity of Jesus, and by extension, ourselves. Yet the mention of 'Israel' could signal the Body of Christ, made one new humanity through His cross (Eph. 2:14–15). The element of fulfillment, of something new coming from the 'now', resonates with some Second Temple Jewish expectations.

---

50 Moss, *Divine Bodies*, 2.
51 Moss, *Divine Bodies*, 2.

Paul Ngoroge's brother's circumcision ceremony was a big success, and the boy joined the community of adults. At the time, I wondered whether Paul's sons (should be become a father) would one day undergo this rite. This year, we received word that Paul's son is preparing for his circumcision, and we were delighted to be part of this important rite of passage. Yet this circumcision of Paul's son, made by human hands on the flesh, will never replace, for Paul Ngorge or other Kenyan believers, the figural circumcision marks made by God's hands on each of his children. I've tried to imagine what our raised, glorified bodies will look like, in large part because what is eternal should be valued today.

As we reflect on Galatians 3:28, it seems clear to almost everyone today that social hierarchies expressed by the institution of slavery are temporal, and do not reveal eternal values. Conversely, God's image-bearers, male and female, shine forth like the spectacular mosaics in the procession of the martyrs in Sant'Apollinare Nuovo. As Christ-followers celebrate the one new humanity made up of Jew and Gentile, we remember to value each ethnic group's particularity as we await the full transformation of our mortal bodies to share in Christ's eternal life as the one, unified Body of Christ.

Bibliography

Bradford, T. P. — '"Like the Angels"? Embodiment and Eschatology in Matthew's Gospel', in P. G. Bolt (ed.), *Jesus: Beginning, Middle, and End of Time? Eschatology in Gospels & Acts Research* (CSAR 4; Norwest NSW: SCD Press, 2023), 149–164.

Cohen, S. J. D. — *Why Aren't Jewish Women Circumcised? Gender and Covenant in Judaism* (Oakland, CA: University of California Press, 2005).

Felker Jones, B. — *Marks of His Wounds: Gender Politics and Bodily Resurrection* (Oxford: Oxford University Press, 2007).

Foster, P. — 'An Apostle Too Radical for the Radical Perspective on Paul: Review of *Paul, the Pagans' Apostle* by Paula Fredriksen', *Expository Times* 133.1 (2021).

Fredriksen, P. — 'Paul the "Convert"?', in M. V. Novenson and R. Barry Matlock (eds.), *The Oxford Handbook of Pauline Studies* (Oxford: Oxford University Press, 2022), 31–53.

Fredriksen, P. — *Paul: the Pagans' Apostle* (New Haven: Yale University Press, 2018).

Fredriksen, P. — 'What Does It Mean to See Paul "Within Judaism"?' *Journal of Biblical Literature* 141.2 (2022), 361.

Gager, J. G. — *Reinventing Paul* (Oxford: Oxford University Press, 2000).

Grasso, K. — 'Righteousness in the Christ-era: A Study in the Purpose and Function of Torah in the Messianic Age in Paul within the Context of Second Temple Judaism' (MA Thesis, The Hebrew University of Jerusalem, 2022).

Jacobs, A. — *Christ Circumcised: A Study in Early Christian History and Difference* (Philadelphia: University of Pennsylvania Press, 2012).

Kartveit, M. — *The Origin of the Samaritans* (Leiden: Brill, 2009).

Kuhn, C. G. — ' Ἰσραήλ, Ἰουδαῖος, Ἑβραῖος in Jewish Literature after the OT', in G. Kittel and G. Friedrich, *Theological Dictionary of the New Testament* [vol. 3, tr. G. W. Bromiley; Grand Rapids, MI: Eerdmans, 1964–1976), 359–69.

Milgrom, J. — *Leviticus* (The Anchor Yale Bible Commentaries; New Haven: Yale University Press, 1998–2001).

Mitchell, B. P.   *Origen's Revenge: The Greek and Hebrew Roots of Christian Thinking on Male and Female* (Eugene, OR: Pickwick, 2021).

Mitchell, M. M.   'Paul and Judaism now, Quo vadimus?' *Journal of the Jesus Movement in its Jewish Setting* 5 (2018), 55–78.

Moss, C. R.   *Divine Bodies: Resurrecting Perfection in the New Testament and Early Christianity* (New Haven: Yale University Press, 2019).

Nanos, M.   'All Israel will be "*Saved*" or "*Kept Safe*"? (Rom. 11:26): Israel's Conversion or Irrevocable Calling to Gospel the Nations?', In F. Ábel (ed.), *Israel and Nations: Paul's Gospel in the Context of Jewish Expectation* (Lanham, MD: Lexington Books/Fortress Academic, 2021).

Rodriguez, R.   *If You Call Yourself a Jew: Reappraising Paul's Letter to the Romans* (Eugene, OR: Cascade, 2014).

Thiessen, M. and Fredriksen, P.   'Paul and Israel', in M. V. Novenson and R. Barry Matlock (eds.), *The Oxford Handbook of Pauline Studies* (Oxford: Oxford University Press, 2022),

Sanders, E. P.   *Paul and Palestinian Judaism: A Comparison of Patterns of Religion* (40th Anniversary Edition; Minneapolis: Fortress, 2017 [Philadelphia: Fortress, 1977]).

Sloan, P.   'Once humans obtain this immortal condition, or exist in Christ for whom such a condition has obtained, some decrees become redundant.' Paper presented at the Annual Meeting of the Institute of Biblical Research, 2022.

Staples, J. A.   *The Idea of Israel in Second Temple Judaism: A New Theory of People, Exile, and Israelite Identity* (Cambridge: Cambridge University Press, 2021).

Staples, J. A.   *Paul and the Resurrection of Israel: Jews, Former Gentiles, Israelites* (Cambridge: Cambridge University Press, 2024).

Stendahl, K.   'The Apostle Paul and the Introspective Conscience of the West', *Harvard Theological Review* 56 (1963), 199–215.

Westerholm, S.   *Romans: Text, Readers, and the History of Interpretation* (Grand Rapids: Eerdmans, 2022).

CHAPTER 3

Paul and Aesop: Popular Morality and the Apostolic Gospel in the Ancient Mediterranean

James R. Harrison

1. Prolegomenon

The ground-breaking study of Teresa Morgan on popular morality in the imperial world has failed to grab the attention of New Testament scholars in their discussions of the apostle Paul's ethics.[1] In scholarly consideration of Paul's moral thought against its Graeco-Roman backdrop, ethics have been traditionally approached either through the lens of the established philosophical schools or the public orations of the peripatetic philosophers (e.g. Dio Chrysostom). One of the many significant contributions of Morgan's book was to introduce New Testament scholars to a range of non-traditional ethical sources that stood outside of the predictable boundaries of the philosophical schools and the popular philosophers: namely, writers such as Publilius Syrus, Zenobius and Diogianus, Babrius and Phaedrus, among others, each representing different types of proverbial wisdom. However, New

---

1   See Morgan, *Popular Morality*, 57–83. Additionally, Morgan, 'Divine-Human Relations'; 'Living with the Gods'.

Testament scholars have failed to take up the opportunity offered by Morgan's seminal study to investigate how this popular 'underside' of ethical thought interacted with Paul's gospel, although James Harrison has begun charting a course through some of the material.[2]

This chapter will discuss the ethics articulated in Aesop's fables, as distilled by the late first-century AD Flavian compiler Babrius, who furnishes 143 fables in Greek iambic verse.[3] The earlier first-century AD collection of Phaedrus, a Greek freedman living at the time of Sejanus in Tiberian Rome and beyond, will be bypassed. Phaedrus discusses only 31 Aesopian fables, adds several of his own, and imposes his *Romanitas* on the Aesopic collection by subjecting it to Latin metre, satirising Julio-Claudian Rome, and adopting a civil law viewpoint throughout.[4] There are other fables which have no counterparts in Phaedrus and Babrius, cited in the Greek in Latin and Greek literature and in other collections ascribed to Aesop, which will not form part of our study.[5] While this represents important evidence for negative reactions to Julio-Claudian rule, it does not contribute to our focus on popular morality.

At the outset, we need to establish briefly what scholarly research has been conducted on the intersection of the New Testament documents with the fables of Aesop. First, in terms of the Gospels, Steve Reece has argued that Luke had drawn upon the tradition of Aesopic fables and proverbs widely available throughout Mediterranean

---

2   On Paul and the elite ethics of Delphic canon, see Harrison, *Paul and the Ancient Celebrity Circuit*, 173–216. On Paul and Publilius Syrus, see Harrison, 'Publilius Syrus'. On Aesop hobnobbing at the courts of kings and tyrants with the Seven Sages, whose sayings formed the Delphic canon, see Kurke, *Aesopic Conversations*, 125–42.
3   For the comments of Babrius on his collection, see Babrius, *Fab.* 107 [Beginning of Part II]. On Babrius himself, see Pertsinidis, 'Like a Warhorse'; Mann, *The Fabulist*, 179–246; Morgan ('Living with the Gods', 380) sums up what we possibly know about Babrius with these words: 'Babrius was probably either a hellenised Italian or a Greek who took the name of an Italian patron; features of his verse indicate that he knew Latin and he is speculatively located in the same literary circles as Martial. His fables are dedicated to Alexander, client king of Rough Cilicia c. 72–103 CE, a Judaeo-Armenian with close connections at Rome'. See also Strong, *The Fables of Jesus*, 93–98.
4   See Champlin, 'Phaedrus the Fabulous'; cf. Currie, 'Phaedrus the Fabulist'; Lefkowitz, 'Innovation and Artistry'; Strong, *The Fables of Jesus*, 107–17. On the imperial dimension of the fables of Phaedrus, see Hardie, 'Juvenal'; Henderson, *Telling Tales*; Libby, 'The Intersection'; Edwards, 'Caesar Telling Tales'.
5   See Perry, *Babrius and Phaedrus Fables*, 422–610, §§1–725. All parable numbers and translations cited herein are from the Loeb Classical Library edition.

antiquity in his use of the phrase ὦ ἀνόητοι καὶ βραδεῖς τῇ καρδίᾳ in Luke 24:45.[6] In an innovative contribution to parable studies, Justin Strong has argued innovatively that the parables of Jesus belonged to the ancient fable tradition, proposing that the Lukan parables were identical in genre to first-century fables.[7] Second, in terms of Paul, the 'body' fables of Babrius (*Fab.* 134) have also been brought into dialogue with 1 Corinthians 12.[8] James Harrison has also briefly touched upon Aesop's fables in relation to Paul's understanding of χάρις, highlighting Aesopian reciprocity motifs (e.g. humility before God's beneficence, gratitude towards benefactors) and, conversely, retribution for ingratitude towards benefactors.[9]

This recent interest in the fables of Aesop and their relevance for New Testament scholarship is long overdue. Fables had long been a familiar feature in the evolution of Greek oral, intellectual, and literary culture by New Testament times. The earliest Greek example of the genre is Hesiod's fable of the 'Hawk and Nightingale' (*Op.* 202–212) in the seventh century BC.[10] From the Classical period onwards, fables were employed 'in rhetorical arguments, speeches in Greek tragedies, historical accounts, comic plays,[11] lyric and iambic poetry, philosophical discourses and scientific treatises'.[12] Many of these fables were attributed to Aesop, the most famous Greek exponent of the genre, a slave from sixth-century BC Samos who died in Delphi in 564/563 BC. Aesop may be regarded as a quasi-historical figure if no sources later than the Alexandrian period are adduced, excluding thereby the first-century AD romance, the *Life of Aesop*,[13] an aretalogical novelistic biography.[14] By contrast, M. L. West argues that the earliest evidence regarding Aesop

---

6 Reece, '"Aesop", "Q" and "Luke"'.
7 Strong, *The Fables of Jesus*. See also Elliott, '"Witless"'; Watson, 'The "Life of Aesop"'.
8 Zimmermann, 'The Body Fables'.
9 Harrison, *Paul's Language of Grace*, 177, 180, 186, 201, 204–5.
10 See Hubbard, 'Hesiod's Fable'; Nelson, 'The Justice'.
11 See Rothwell, 'Aristophanes' "Wasps"'.
12 Pertsinidis, '*Like a Warhorse*', 3. Note, too, the presence of fables in Graeco-Roman novels: van Dijk, 'The Function of Fables'. On fables in the rabbinic literature, see Strong, *The Fables of Jesus*, 173–99.
13 Luzzatto, 'Aesop'.
14 Watson, 'The "Life of Aesop"', 669; Strong, *The Fables of Jesus*, 75–77, 123–29, 249–51. Notably, however, Keith Hopkins ('Novel Evidence', 10) highlights the text's value in being the only major 'biography of a slave to survive from the ancient world'.

demonstrably belongs to the realm of legend.[15] He concludes that 'the Greek instinct to attach anonymous compositions or achievements to any appropriate individual ensured that Aesop would attract fables'.[16]

Whatever the truth of Aesopian authorship might be, the first collection of Aesopic fables was compiled by Demetrius of Phalerum (350–280 BC). The work is no longer extant, but it is mentioned by Diogenes Laertius in his biography of Demetrius (*Lives* 5.80: Αἰσωπείων α').[17] This collection was followed by the first-century AD collections of Phaedrus and Babrius, noted above.[18] But importantly for our purposes, the Aesopic fables were still part of a living oral tradition by the first century,[19] referred to in the writings of the Roman and Greek elites and in the exercises of schoolchildren.[20] Several pertinent examples will establish the point.

The rhetorician Quintilian (AD 35–c.100) states that Aesop's fables had to be paraphrased by pupils in simple and restrained language which would be reflected in a simplicity of written form (*Inst. Or.* 1.9.2). Quintilian also mentions that the moral principles of the fables were taught by dry nurses to children from an early age (1.9.2). Furthermore, when Horace (65–8 BC) was brought to Rome c. 50 BC for his grammatical and rhetorical education, he refers to the fables of 'the town mouse and country mouse' (*Sat.* 2.6.79–117) and 'the fox and the sick lion' (*Epist.* 1.1.73–75) as part of his rhetorical curriculum. Regarding citation of fables, Plutarch (AD 46–post 119) routinely relates the Aesopic fable first (e.g. *An seni* [*Mor.* 785e]; *Quaest. conv.* [*Mor.* 614e]) before elaborating on its application, sometimes even using the same Aesopic fable to illustrate different points (e.g. *An. Corp.* [*Mor.* 500d] versus *Sept. sap. conv.* [*Mor.* 155b]). The travelling Greek philosopher

---

15 West, 'The Ascription of Fables', 117.
16 West, 'The Ascription of Fables', 128. By contrast, Kurke, *Aesopic Conversations*, 13, adopts an agnostic position regarding the historicity of Aesop; cf. Strong, *The Fables of Jesus*, 74–77, 123–29.
17 Perry, 'Demetrius'.
18 We omit the later Augustana collection of Aesop's fables. It contains 231 prose fables found in alphabetical order in the thirteenth-century AD Augustanus Monacensis 564 manuscript, kept in the Bayerische Staats-bibliothek, Munich. For discussion of the Aesopian ethics revealed therein, see Zafiropoulos, *Ethics*.
19 Kovacs, *The Aesopic Fable*, 13–46.
20 For discussion and references to the primary and secondary literature, see Kovacs, *The Aesopic Fable*; Fisher, *A History*, 6–64; Laes, 'Children and Fables'; Strong, *The Fables of Jesus*, 131–71.

and miracle worker, Apollonius of Tyana (AD 15–98), whose *Life* was written over a century afterwards by Philostratus (AD 170–247), delineates the moralistic purpose of Aesop's fables thus: 'Aesop [...] uses humble subjects to teach great lessons, and after setting out his tale rounds it off with a "Do this" or a "Don't do that"' (*Vit. Apoll.* 5.14).[21] Finally, in the prologue to a speech, the Latin prose writer and Platonist philosopher, Apuleius (AD 124–post-170), expands Aesop's fable of the crow and the fox (*De deo Socr.*) by means of more elaborate descriptions and longer speeches.

The Greek textbooks of preliminary rhetorical exercises, spanning the late Hellenistic age to Roman times, had also been accepted by Latin rhetoricians by the first century BC, much to the disquiet of more conservative Romans,[22] and had become part of the school curriculum. The authors of these treatises commented on the appropriate rhetorical use of fables, including those of Aesop: i.e. the *progymnasmata* of Aelius Theon §72, Hermogenes §1–4, Antiphonius §21, Nicolaus §§6–11, 22 and John of Sardis §7–8.[23] In sum, the familiarity of the poets, rhetoricians, moral philosophers, and novelists with Aesop indicates the ubiquity of the oral traditions of the Aesopian fables and the creative appropriation of their popular morality in differing social contexts from the first century AD onwards, supplemented by new fables composed by the compilers of the collections such as Phaedrus.[24]

Regarding the availability of papyrological collections of fables, the

---

21 It is beyond the scope of this chapter to discuss the moral introductions prefacing fables (promythium) and the moral conclusions appearing after fables (epimythium). Cf. Strong, *The Fables of Jesus in the Gospel of Luke*, 384–91. It is difficult to determine with certainty whether any of these originated with the quasi-historical Aesop, rhetoricians or schoolmasters, or the collectors of fables (Demetrius, Phraedrus, Babrius). And was their intent clarificatory, exegetical, hortatory, or an index-heading in a handbook of reference? For discussion, see Perry, 'The Origin', passim. In this chapter, the moral applications (epimythia) attached to Aesopian fables will be accepted as one interpretative response of posterity to the message of fables in the Babrian collection, irrespective of its provenance. There are no promythia in the Babrian collection (Strong, *The Fables of Jesus*, 91–92).

22 Fisher, *A History*, 24, 28. Suetonius (*Gramm.* 439; *Rhet.* I *ad. int.*) and Gellius (*NA* 15.11.2) preserve the edict of 92 BC against rhetoricians in which Gnaeus Domitius Ahenobarbus and Lucius Licinius Crassus vent their annoyance over the new Latin rhetoricians who had introduced in their teaching the preliminary exercises in rhetoric known as *progymnasmata*. See Johnson, Coleman-Norton, and Bourne, *Ancient Roman Statutes*, 62–63 §59.

23 For the translations, see Kennedy, *Progymnasmata*.

24 For full discussion, see Kovacs, *The Aesopic Fable*, 68–80; Fisher, *A History*, 24–30; Laes, 'Children and Fables', 898–902.

Rylands papyrus (P.Ryl. 3.493), dated by its editor C. H. Roberts to the first century AD,[25] contains the fragments of fourteen prose fables, among which are five identifiable Aesopian tales, possibly copied from a much earlier collection of fables some two to three hundred years before.[26] Notably, in one of the tales there is a moral saying (epimythium) stylistically placed in the lips of the last speaker, though whether this is a genuine epimythium is disputed.[27] Bonnie Fisher also highlights the continuing availability of Aesop's fables for schoolchildren from the second century AD onwards in various media: '... Babrian fragments on papyri, tablets, and ostraka from the second through to the fifth centuries indicate a widespread, continuous place in the elementary school curriculum: often the handwriting is that of a young child'.[28]

By the first century AD, therefore, Paul's audiences in the eastern Mediterranean basin were not only exposed to the ethical systems of the philosophical schools, heard through the peripatetic philosophers declaiming at the agora or in the private salons of their sponsors, but also through the popular morality absorbed from their elementary school curriculum. The latter moral traditions were initially acquired by students copying out Aesopian fables, paraphrasing a fable in class, or learning their appropriate use in rhetorical exercises designed for hypothetical situations, to cite several pedagogic examples. Paul's gospel would have engaged such first-century auditors who were unconsciously attuned from their elementary education onwards to a host of axiomatic moral assumptions about how the divine and human worlds worked and intersected in everyday life. How would such auditors have responded to the public and private teaching of the apostle? In our investigation of the Aesopian fables, the motifs of the divine world,

---

25 Roberts, *Catalogue (Vol. 3)*, no. 493; for discussion, see Strong, *The Fables of Jesus*, 83–87.
26 Perry, 'The Origin', 400.
27 Perry ('The Origin', 397; cf. 410) comments that the moral saying is 'here put into the mouth of last speaker of the fable, (and) hence (is) not really an epimythium', which routinely comes *after* the fable's conclusion (cf. n.20 above).
28 Fisher, *A History*, 27. Perry (tr., *Babrius and Phaedrus Fables*, lxviii-lxx) cites several examples of papyri and a tablet containing Aesopian fables. (1) Papyrus Bouriant (P.Bour.), no. 1 (3–4 lines of Babrius in a student's reading notebook [IV cent. AD]): see Bouriant, *Les papyrus Bouriant*. (2) Papyrus Amherst (P.Amh.) no. 26 (fables 11, 16, and 17 [III–IV cent AD]). (3) Papyrus Oxyrhynchus (P.Oxy.) 10 (1914) no. 1249 (fables 42, 110, 118, 25 [mid II cent. AD]). (4) *Tabulae ceratae Assendeftianeae* (waxen tablets written on by a schoolboy, containing 13 Babrian fables [III. cent. AD]): see Hesseling, 'On Waxen Tablets'.

social relations, and character analysis will be compared with Paul's ethical and theological teaching. Paul's cruciform gospel offered a holistic moral transformation in Christ that healed the horizontal and vertical dimensions of human relationships in all their brokenness in antiquity.

In such a comparison, however, the fables of Aesop are at a methodological 'disadvantage'. We know little if anything about their redactional history other than the collection they appear in and the epimythium, even if present, does not necessarily reflect the original intent of the fable, whoever its composer might be. The presence of comparative terminology may or may not be present. Ambiguity and uncertainty remain continuing interpretative challenges in the Aesopian tradition. The Pauline epistles, while occasional productions, have a largely recoverable ecclesial context, a wider spread of the comparative terminology and its cognates, and a recoverable literary, archaeological, and epigraphic context for the city to whom the epistles are addressed. The comparison will necessarily be in large brush strokes.

2. Popular Morality in Babrius' Aesop

2.1 *The Divine World of Aesop*

• The Gods, Fates, and Demi-gods

One of the composers of the epimythia concluding the Aesopian fables states that Aesop had a moral intention in including fables about the gods: ['Aesop brings even the gods into his fables in the course of cautioning us one against another'] (Babrius, *Fab.* §112). In the Babrian collection of fables, the divine world is almost exclusively populated by well-known Olympian deities: Zeus (Babrius, *Fab.* §§58, 59, 68, 72, 127, 142); Hermes (§§48 ['the athlete's god'], 57, 68, 117, 127); Athena (§59); Aphrodite (§10 [i.e. Cypris, §32]); Apollo, Ares, and Phoebus (§68); Pan (§§3, 53); Poseidon (§59); Cybele (§141; cf. §97: ['Mother of the Gods']); Rhea (§141); Pallas (§59); Paean (§120); Demeter (§129); Hades (§75); and Iris, the messenger of the Olympians (§72). In the case of these deities, they sometimes appear personally alongside human beings (§20) or grant dream revelations (§§49, 136); however, oneiric revelations could also prove to be 'false dreams' (§136). The only hint we get regarding relations between some of these deities is their rivalry in archery skills, with the chief deity Zeus winning by a clever stratagem which allowed him to win the contest without even shooting an arrow (§68). The Queen of the underworld, Persephone, is mentioned too, as is Pluto, the ruler of the underworld (§75). In a wry twist of humour, dire actions were threatened against all physicians by the underworld deities because, owing to the success of their medical treatments, the physicians were not allowing the sick to die and proceed to Hades and drink Lethe's peaceful waters (§75).

In addition to various demi-gods (*infra*, n.38), there are personified divine beings identified as Fortune (§12: ἡ κακὴ Μοῖρα; Tyche: §49) and Fate (§136 [πέπρωται ταῦτα]). There is no escape from what is fated (§136): one must bear bravely (γενναίως) what is allotted and not attempt to dodge one's destiny by clever devices (μὴ σοφίζου). Elsewhere the fickleness of luck is emphasised, overriding the clever stratagem of a donkey in alleviating its load (§111). The dramatic social humbling (ταπεινός) brought about by ill fortune totally outweighs any other strategy employed to overcome its inevitable outcome (§12). Another personification—in this instance a spirit (daimon)—is the fault-finder Momus (§59), who was expelled by Zeus from heaven for ridiculing the gods. In this fable, however, Momus is presented as still living with the gods in heaven. He criticises the beautiful creations made by Zeus (humankind), Pallas (a house), and Poseidon (a bull), highlighting in each case their design deficiencies. Momus is animated by Envy in his fault-finding, rejecting anything 'entirely pleasing' in his harsh criticism of the creations of others (§59).

A puzzling differentiation is also drawn between the 'simpleton' rural gods and the 'unerring' urban gods (§2). However, this alleged distinction in wisdom, knowledge, and prescience between the rural and urban deities is shown to be spurious when the urban gods are not able to find property stolen from their temple, pathetically offering a thousand drachmas for its return. There are no literary or fable references elsewhere which throw light on this distinction between country and urban gods.[29] Morgan argues that behind the fable lies the prejudice and superiority of sophisticated city-dwellers towards their unsophisticated rural counterparts, the fable unexpectedly adopting 'the country-man's

---

29 Morgan, 'Living with the Gods', 393.

perspective'.[30] The 'religious' location of deities, whether in the splendid temples of the poleis or in the small shrines of rural villages, is an irrelevance for genuine worshippers: what really matters is the power and prescience of the deity involved. Nor is any reference made to the priestly personnel of the gods in either context other than a fleeting mention of the 'begging priests of Cybele' who 'go around to all the villages and gather contributions in the form of provisions' (§141).[31]

The justice of the gods surfaces as an important concern of the fables. The divine drowning of all people on a boat due to the presence of one impious man among all the other virtuous passengers raises acutely the issue of the unjustness of the gods' decrees (§117). The hypocrisy of human evaluations regarding the unjustness of gods here is exposed here by means of the accompanying 'ant' fable. Concerns are also aired over the late implementation of Zeus' will in exacting the penalty for human misdeeds and unjust acts (§127): this is explained by the slow and somewhat inefficient processes of Hermes in recording such misdemeanours on shards for the inspection of Zeus prior to final judgement.[32] Furthermore, the fact that the god relies on human beings to find out who stole property from an urban temple (§2), discussed above, 'points to the conclusion that the gods and human beings collaborate in the administration of justice'.[33] The problem of theodicy, it seems, is resolved by an appeal to the sovereignty of Zeus, the ponderous outworking of the wheels of justice, and the propensity of human beings either to blame Fortune for their own errors (§49) or to blame others for their own failings (§66; cf. §142), as opposed to any consideration of the divine character and the soteriological intentions of the gods.[34]

Finally, two fables call in question the character and sovereignty of the gods. First, Hermes fills his wagon with lies, distributing to every human tribe his deceitful wares, but upon the breakdown of the wagon,

---

30 Morgan, 'Living with the Gods', 393.
31 In terms of additional religious personnel, see the reference to a sacrificing seer in Babrius, *Fab.* §54.
32 An entertaining fable about Zeus' judgement of a beauty contest for birds (Babrius, *Fab.* §72) drives home the moral lesson of not deceitfully parading in the borrowed finery of others. Cf. also Babrius, *Fab.* §56.
33 Morgan, 'Living with the Gods', 395.
34 An example of an Aesopian focus upon the divine character in judgement is found in Babrius, *Fab.* §50: 'The Divinity is wise and cannot be deceived. No one, though he many think his perjury will go unheeded, escapes the penalty for it'.

the Arabs plundered its remaining goods. The epimythium affords the parable interpreter to indulge in some pernicious racial stereotyping: 'That's why the Arabs, as I have learned from personal experience, are liars and imposters; not a word of truth is on their tongues' (§57). As Morgan concludes, 'a third party mediates between Zeus and his creatures, but ... Hermes is carrying out Zeus's orders, so there is no doubt here that Zeus is responsible for something which human beings find morally problematic'.[35]

Second, all good things were brought together by Zeus in a jar, which was then lidded and placed among mankind. Inevitably, mankind opened the jar—possibly the Babrian version of the primeval fall in the Aesopian fables—with the result that the blessings of Zeus fled to the dwellings of the gods, leaving only the (futile?) hope of the return of blessing (§58; cf. §126).[36] The fable poses more questions than it answers. While the fault for the disappearance of blessing is rightly lodged with humanity, there is no secure promise regarding the future return of Zeus's blessing. Hope abides but it may never be realised. Furthermore, why was the jar left exposed to tempt vulnerable human beings, with no warning beforehand about the disastrous consequences if the jar was opened? Zeus ultimately remains inscrutable in his operations.

• **Prayer**

Prayer in the Babrian fables can either reject, refine, re-define, or endorse traditional approaches of humans towards the gods and demi-gods. Four examples will suffice. The personal appearance of the demi-god Heracles beside an ox-driver, whose wagon had plunged into a ravine, seemed to be initially a propitious response to his prayer to the one god 'whom he really worshipped and held in honour' above all other gods (Babrius, *Fab.* §20). Instead, the ox-driver was told to seize the wheels and whip the oxen. Idleness in the face of tragedy or danger did not precipitate the gods to action or even elicit sympathy: 'Pray to the gods only when you are doing something to help yourself. Otherwise, your prayers will be useless' (§20). Synergism, it seems, underlies all divine-human relations, with prayer precipitating human action at the outset as opposed

---

35 Morgan, 'Divine-Human Relations', 13.
36 Despite the deceptiveness of our confident expectations, Babrius, *Fab.* 43 advises its readers not to give up or lose hope.

to divine intervention on behalf of the suppliant. A Stoic resolution in the face of vicissitude should result in self-determination as opposed to a pious passivity before the gods.

In the house of a worshipper of a private hero-cult, the altars were regularly wreathed and drowned in wine libations and the hero prayerfully summoned: 'Hail, O dearest of heroes, and make your fellow-lodger rich in all good things' (§63). In a striking reply the hero says that such beneficence only the gods can bestow, whereas the demi-gods, the heroes, are only the givers of ills. Morgan correctly notes that this is a case where minor divinities 'are not merely incompetent, but malevolent'.[37] The traditional deities are preferred to the demi-gods whose reputation is blackened. This disrespect is unexpected given that there is (a) the regular appearance of demi-gods such as Heracles, Prometheus, and Theseus in the fables;[38] (b) a widespread founding of hero-cults by private individuals or associations for outstanding community members in the third to second century BC; (c) the heroisation of the deceased generally from the first century BC onwards, seen in the later heroisation of Hadrian's prominent paramour, Antinous, and in ἥρως ('hero') becoming a common funerary accolade on epitaphs for close relatives.[39]

A cattle-driver, in search of his lost horned bull, made a vow to the mountain-roaming nymphs, that he would offer a sacrifice in return for the thief's discovery. Upon finding that the bull had been eaten by a lion, the moral (epimythium) of the fable is framed thus: 'From this we may well learn not to pray to the gods for something ill-conceived, moved by a grief brought on us temporarily' (§23). The fable undermines the simplistic *do ut des* mentality of ancient religion ('I give so that you might give'). In reciprocity rituals, therefore, prayer is the art of what

---

37 Morgan, 'Living with the Gods', 386.
38 In a quarrel over the pre-eminence of two cities (Babrius §15), there is a rhetorical debate over the respective 'slave' or 'divine' status of the heroes of Thebes (Heracles) and Athens (Theseus). For the demi-gods in the fables: (a) *Heracles* (Babrius, *Fab*. §15 ['Alemena's son']; Perry, *Babrius and Fabrius*, Appendix, 'Fables of the Augustana Collection', §231). (b) *Theseus* (Babrius §15). (c) *Prometheus* (Babrius, *Fab*. §66; Perry, *Babrius and Fabrius*, Appendix, 'Fables of the Augustana Collection', §240; Perry, *Babrius and Fabrius*, Appendix, 'Odd Fables in Various Manuscripts of Aesop', §259; Perry, *Babrius and Fabrius*, Appendix, 'Fables in the *Life of Aesop*', §383; Perry, *Babrius and Fabrius*, Appendix, 'Fables Excerpted from Various Greek Authors', §§ 430, 458, 467).
39 See Jones, *New Heroes*; Harrison, 'Greater than the Greek and Trojan Heroes'.

is rationally conceivable as opposed to the imprudently inconceivable.[40]

The open-air robbery by a crow of each god's altar of food offerings results in divinely appointed (?) disease and suffering being inflicted upon the bird. Consequently, his prayers for soteriological deliverance by the gods went unheeded (§78). For prayers to be divinely answered, the fable reveals, there needs to be appropriate reverence exercised in cultic rituals.

A series of contrary positions emerge in these Babrian fables regarding the effectiveness of prayer to the gods. The *do ut des* dynamic of traditional religion is rejected while reverential attention to the cult is endorsed; the demigods are designated malevolent, but the traditional gods are considered beneficent; passive dependence on the gods is discouraged, but a prayerful consideration of what is conceivable is sponsored.[41] No resolution to these discordant notes is ever orchestrated in the Babrian fables: all are equally viable options for those seeking moral pathways and deliverance before the gods.

2.2 Paul and the Divine World of Aesop

In discussing the intersection of Paul's thought with Aesop (§§2.2, 3.2, 4.3), we will concentrate upon the collision between their moral worldviews, not opting for detailed exegetical analyses of the Pauline epistolary evidence. Even though Paul does not explicitly quote Aesop— or any other Graeco-Roman author for that matter (*pace*, Menander, *Thais*, Fragment 218 [1 Cor. 15:33]; Epimenides, *Cretica* 1 [Titus 1:12– 13])[42]—his literate converts would have had been familiar with aspects of the Aesopian fable tradition, either through their elementary school curriculum or, in the case of the illiterate, though their recounting in Graeco-Roman oral culture more generally. Therefore, the collision of moral worldviews is worth pursuing.

---

40 Morgan ('Divine-Human Relations', 19) writes: 'The gods and other divinities, it seems, want not only the attention of human beings, but their right understanding as well'.
41 See Morgan's discussion of Babrius §10 ('Living with the Gods', 391–92), according to which, it is argued, 'in the principate ... the gods want to be understood by those who worship them' (392).
42 Furnish (*Theology and Ethics*, 45) comments that Menander 'is probably known to Paul not directly from any literary source, but as an everyday proverb in common use'. On the distinctive ethic of the Christians, see Campbell, *Pauline Dogmatics*, 475–96.

First-century believers would have experienced an internal 'tug-of-war' between the inherited popular morality of their culture and the new Pauline ethic unleashed powerfully in missionary and ecclesial contexts through the indwelling and transformative work of the Spirit in the Body of Christ.[43] The ethical pluralism of Graeco-Roman culture and its multiplicity of gods, comprehensively reflected in Aesop, is excluded by the apostle because of (a) his christologically-modified monotheism;[44] (b) the eschatological reign of divine grace operative in the lives of believers, who experience a soteriological 'dying and rising with Christ' in the past, present, and future;[45] (c) his 'eschatologically transcendent ethic';[46] and (d) the Father, Son, and apostolic paradigms provided for the ethical imitation of believers.[47]

Nor does any confusion exist regarding the heroisation of deceased human beings as demi-gods. Paul only mentions God's transformation of believers into the image of the Lord of glory through the Spirit (2 Cor. 3:18, μεταμορφούμεθα), God having predestined them by grace to be conformed (συμμόρφους) to the image of his Son, as opposed to acquiring post-mortem ἥρως status. This occurs in the present (ἀνακαινοῦνται, ἀνακαινούμενον: 2 Cor. 4:16; Col. 3:10)—given the advent of the new creation (cf. 2 Cor. 5:17)—and at the eschaton (Rom. 8:28–30; Phil. 3:20–21).

The interpersonal rivalry between the Aesopian gods is humorously depicted in the archery competition. But for Paul the interrelationship between the Father and the Son is expressed in mutual honouring and glorification, as opposed to self-promotion (Father: Phil. 2:9–11a; Son: 2:8,11b). This is also expressed by the overarching unity of their soteriological purpose, the Son and Spirit having been sent by the Father to redeem and adopt enslaved humanity (Gal. 4:4–7), uniting in the Spirit diverse ethnicities and classes into one body (1 Cor. 12:12–13).

---

43 Confining ourselves to the indisputably authentic Pauline epistles, see Rom. 1:5; 7:6b; 8:9–17; 14:17; 15:18–19; 1 Cor. 1:22; 2:4–5; 12:4–11; 2 Cor. 3:4–6b, 18; 13:13; Gal. 3:2b–5; 5:16–18,22–26; Phil. 2:3; 3:3; 1 Thess. 1:6; 4:8; 5:19. Cf. Fee, *God's Empowering Presence*.

44 Rom. 9:5b; 1 Cor. 8:5–6; Col. 1:15–20. Cf. Harris, *Jesus as God*.

45 Rom. 5:18b, 19b; 6:14; cf. Rom. 6:1–23; 7:1–6; 8:17; Gal. 2:19–20; 5:24–25; 6:14–15; 2 Cor. 1:3–9; 4:7–14; 5:14–17; 7:3; 12:9; 13:4; Phil. 3:2–11; 1 Thess. 1:3–8; 2:13–16; 4:14; 5:10. Cf. Tannehill, *Dying and Rising*.

46 Campbell, *Pauline Dogmatics*, 494: 1 Cor. 12:13; 3:26–28; 6:15; Col. 3:9–11.

47 μίμησις and its cognates: 1 Thess. 1:6; 2:14; 2 Thess. 3:7,9; 1 Cor. 4:16; 11:1; Eph. 5:1; Phil. 3:17. Cf. Harrison, *Paul and the Ancient Celebrity Circuit*, 217–56.

In the present age, Christ reigns as the risen, ascended, and reigning Lord over the Kingdom of God (1 Cor. 15:25). However, at the eschaton Christ willingly subjects himself in obedience (1 Cor. 15:24) and is divinely subjected to the Father after his triumphant parousia (15:28a),[48] so that 'God may be all in all' (15:28b). Mutual honouring, mutual glorification, pneumatic unity in soteriological purpose,[49] and the God-glorifying submission of the Son to the Father at the eschaton characterises the relationships of the Godhead.

In view of Paul's fulsome paean of praise elicited by Christ's soteriological victory over Sin, Death, and the Powers (Rom. 8:31–39), the vagaries of Fate, the fickleness of Fortune, the inscrutable delay of the justice of Zeus (cf. Plutarch, 'On the Delays of Divine Vengeance', *Mor.* 548B–568), and the impenetrability of theodicy are rendered null and void in the 'Aesopian universe'. In contrast to the impersonal nature of the Aesopian construct, Paul explains the delay in divine judgment as originating in the riches of God's kindness, forbearance, and patience, with a view to his leading humans to repentance (Rom. 2:4). Furthermore, the impersonal forces ranged against believers are demobilised by 'the love of God in Christ Jesus' (Rom. 8:38–39). Believers need not fear judgement before God because they have been reckoned righteous because of Christ's atoning death and vindicatory resurrection (e.g. δίκαιόω: Rom. 3:24,26,28,30; 4:5; 5:1,9; 8:30,33; 1 Cor. 6:11; Gal. 2:16; 3:8,11,24). The compassionate character of God and his liberating soteriological acts are thrust into the foreground.

In terms of the impact of religion upon social and ethnic relations, Paul does not distinguish between the gods of the unsophisticated rural worshippers over against the gods of the sophisticated city-dwellers. Instead, Paul eschews all such cultural comparisons as contrary to his apostolic calling, being indebted equally to barbarian and Greek.[50] While Paul opposes any ethnic stereotyping in his programmatic statements about unity in Christ in his authentic epistles (e.g. Rom. 10:12; 15:7–9a; 1 Cor. 12:13; Gal. 3:28; 6:15), the characterisation of the Jews in 1 Thessalonians 2:14b–16 remains a difficult text in Pauline

---

48 For discussion, see Jamieson, '1 Corinthians 15:28 and the Grammar of Paul's Christology'.
49 For an insightful discussion of the Spirit in the Godhead, see Fee, *God's Empowering Presence*, 831–42.
50 See Harrison, 'Paul's "Indebtedness" to the Barbarian (Rom. 1:14) in Latin West Perspective'.

interpretation.⁵¹ Further, the citation of the sixth-century BC Cretan poet Epimenides (*Cretica* 1), who denigrates his fellow citizens over their claim to host a tomb of Zeus, represents a puzzling departure from practice elsewhere in the (putatively) pseudepigraphic letter of Titus (1:12–13), though the text itself was well known in antiquity.⁵² It is beyond the scope of this chapter to address these two texts contextually, but, at first blush, we find here discordant notes in the Pauline corpus reminiscent of those found in the Aesopian tradition.

Finally, the Aesopian distinction between what is rationally conceivable as opposed to the imprudently inconceivable in prayer is undercut by Paul's homage to the petitionary possibilities, well beyond the scope of human ability, provided by God in Ephesians 3:20 (cf. Rom. 11:33–35): 'Now to him who by the power at work in us is able to accomplish abundantly than all we can ask or imagine'. The overflowing divine grace implied in Paul's rapturous language rules out the *do ut des* contractual arrangement of Aesopian prayers. Further, the synergistic self-reliance recommended in the Aesopian prayer tradition is also inverted by Paul who highlights the weakness (τῇ ἀσθενείᾳ ἡμῶν) of the inadequately informed prayers of believers (Rom. 8:26): their stumbling and imperfect attempts require the intercessory guidance and empowerment of the indwelling and sanctifying Spirit on the earth (8:26b–27) and the mediation of the exalted Christ in heaven (8:34).⁵³

3. Social Relations

3.1 Relationships from the Apex to the Base of the Social Pyramid

Several important aspects of social relations in antiquity are mentioned in the Babrian collection of Aesopian fables, reflecting divergent approaches to social attitudes, groups, and conventions. We will confine our discussion to six Aesopian motifs.⁵⁴

---

51 Recently, see Standhartinger, 'Paul, the Jews, and the Thessalonians'.
52 For a comprehensive discussion of Titus 1:12 in its ancient context, see Spicq, *Saint Paul*, 242–44.
53 See Vollmer, '*The Spirit*'0.
54 In Morgan's discussion of *exempla* (*Popular Morality*, 122–59), she provides examples of courage, friendship, mercy, and self-control etc., to demonstrate how the Romans understood social relations embracing the family, justice and law enforcement, and the divine–human encounter.

- **Attitudes towards the Elites**

The Babrian fables of Aesop reveal sharply diverging attitudes towards the elites, pointing to the multiple authorship of the entire corpus. A later interpreter of Aesop's fables understands the message of Aesop's fable of 'The Humpbacked Camel' in this way: ['A state in which the worst citizens are in power, instead of the best, might tell this story of Aesop's'] (§40). In the fable of 'The Wild Ass and the Lion' (§67; cf. §§36, 41), a strong distrust of the powerful elites emerges: 'Measure yourself: don't get involved in any business or partnership with a man who is more powerful than yourself'. In the fable of 'The Bull and the Mouse' (§112), the following moral is drawn: 'It's not always the big fellow (ὁ μέγας) who has the power: there are times when being small (τὸ μικρόν) and humble (ταπεινόν) has more force'. In each of the fables above the superior power of those attached to the civic authorities and the wealthy elites is spotlighted, but with strong warnings not to overstep oneself, choosing instead to act with judicious caution.

However, a clearly aristocratic viewpoint is endorsed in the fable of 'The Fir Tree and the Bramble' (§64): 'Every distinguished man not only has greater fame (μᾶλλον δόξαν) than lesser men but he also undergoes greater dangers (κινδύνους)'. The aristocrat's quest for glory is not only acknowledged, but also his willingness to undergo greater dangers on behalf of his dependents, either as an 'endangered' benefactor or in military operations on behalf of his city.[55]

- **The Honour System and Boasting Culture**

Graeco-Roman 'boasting' culture was associated with the elite maintenance of ancestral honour and the quest for personal glory on the part of each new generation, with a view to either excelling or adding to the prestige of their forebears.[56] In two Babrian 'boasting' fables, we see departures from the expected honorific protocols. The premature boasting of a cock about his victory over his shamed rival in a fight was brought to nothing when an eagle seized him and flew way. The epimythium explains the significance of the fable thus: ['You, too, man, never be

---

55 On the 'endangered' benefactor, see Danker, *Benefactor*, 417–35; Harrison, *Paul's Language of Grace*, 335–40; Wyman, *Paul's Endangered Benefactor*.
56 See Harrison, 'From Rome'.

boastful when fortune elevates you above another. Many have been saved by the very fact of not succeeding'] (§5). The capriciousness of Fortune pinpricks the inflated expectations associated with the maintenance of ancestral honour and its surpassing by each new generation. A similar observation emerges from the boastful interaction of a ram with a wolf: 'no one should boast whose strength depends on circumstance alone' (§96). Additionally, the inflated boasting of a lamp, with its superior light to all the heavenly stars, is brought to a decisive end when the wind snuffs it out. The light of the stars, by contrast, is never extinguished, so the lamp must learn to remain silent during the time of its shining (§114). Fortune, according to Aesop, is the great social leveller (cf. §4).

In a fable dealing with the ancient honour system, we encounter an unexpected Babrian perspective that diverges from the status quo. In the fable of 'The Crane and the Peacock', the epimythium asserts that it would be socially better, like the crane, to be 'admired in a threadbare coat than to live without honour in (the) rich attire' of the derisive peacock (§65). What is surprising here is the disqualification of the rich, with their 'gilded feathers', from the world of honorific protocols, which were de rigueur in antiquity if the generosity of benefactors was to be maintained in a city. The rationale for this social up-ending is not articulated other than the preference of the crane: is this an example of an Aesopian 'slave' perspective?

Similarly, in the fable of 'The Mice and Their Generals' (§31), the moral conclusion is pointed: 'If to live without danger is one's goal, it is better to be obscure than distinguished (τῆς λαμπρότητος)'. The 'distinguished' generals were, according to the fable, 'those who were foremost in birth, bodily strength and intelligence, and bold in combat'. The traditional aristocratic ethos of noble birth, manliness, military achievement, and public distinction is bypassed here for obscurity to ensure personal survival, the antithesis of how the ancient city-states and their elites operated and survived in antiquity. Utilitarian survival is enjoined at the expense of personal obscurity: but with what social consequences, the elites and their entourage would probably wonder. The elites would be much happier with the advice of Babrius §82: '[Don't allow yourself to be despised by inferiors]'. The boldness of social reconstruction and calculated self-preservation is singular in its ancient context.

Last, the imitation of 'great men' by their social inferiors is not recommended because it results in pointless risks, actual injury, and, potentially, death (§§31, 40, 64, 73, 137). Whether it was (a) the ancestral glory of republican nobles and the iconic examples of virtue in the *forum Augustum* in the Latin West, or (b) the civic achievements of benefactors lauded epigraphically in the cities of the Greek East, or (c) the literary memorialisation of the 'great man' for the imitation of posterity (e.g. *De Viris Illustribus*; Plutarch's ΣΥΓΚΡΙΣΙΣ; Valerius Maximus' *Facta et Dicta Memorabilia*),[57] public virtue was conspicuously an elite phenomenon in antiquity and its imitation was confined to the next generation of aspirants from that select social base.

• Friendship

Four Babrian fables on friendship (φιλία) concentrate on the ways of maintaining cohesive and stable relationships among friends (φίλοι): i.e. discernment regarding who are true friends and who are enemies (§35); holding fast to one's friends lest others divide and conquer (§44); the danger of having a super-abundance of friends (§46); and, last, the provision of vital necessities (§83) and suitable gifts for friends (§130). In each case, the status quo of φιλία relationships is affirmed.

• The Socially Marginalised and Impoverished

Suicidal hares, the feeblest of creatures, were diverted from self-destruction when they realised that they could intimidate frogs, one hare concluding that suicide was no longer necessary: 'I can see others who are weaker (ἀσθενεστέρους) than we' (§25). The classification of groups in antiquity into the 'weak' and 'strong' not only appeared in the Epicurean psychagogy of Philodemus, but it also characterised the social ideology of the military elites and their great men.[58] The desire of a eunuch to have children is also mocked by a seer after viewing the entrails of the sacrificial victim: 'When I look at this it tells me that you'll be a father;

---

57 Harrison, *Paul and the Ancient Celebrity Circuit*, 227–47.
58 On 'weakness'/'strength' terminology in Philodemus, see Glad, *Paul and Philodemus*, 329–32. On 'weakness' in Paul, see Black, *Paul, Apostle of Weakness*. Forbes ('*Strength' and 'Weakness'*, Chapter 2) has argued from the evidence of Homer (fl. IX or VIII cent. BC), Diodorus Siculus (fl. I cent. BC), and Dionysius of Harlicarnassus (60 BC–post 7 AD), that 'strength' and 'weakness' terminology not only designated influence and status—or lack thereof—but also the 'strong' and the 'weak' referred explicitly to the powerful (i.e. in political and military fields) and the powerless (i.e. the helpless) in society.

but when I look into your face you seem not to be even a man' (§54). Seemingly the eunuch's gender assignment at birth is an insuperable barrier in antiquity, assigning them to an ambiguous categorisation ('not even a man') which was not reconcilable with established social roles (i.e. the *paterfamilias*).[59]

The vulnerability of the marginalised at the hands of their superiors is highlighted by later interpreters of a fable about the indigestion of a child: '[One might apply this fable to a guardian who has squandered an orphan's inheritance and wails when he is obliged to pay it back]' (§34). Conversely, 'men of good will', in the fable of 'The Lion and the Mouse', are enjoined to preserve the poor because of the concern of the marginalised displayed for others: '[Spare the poor (σώζειν πένητας), and don't hesitate to rely on them, considering that a mouse freed a lion caught in a trap' (§107).

• **Misogyny**

A wolf, disappointed by the idle threat of a nurse to throw her infant to the wolves, reflects upon the reliability of women generally when he says: 'What can you expect, when I put my trust in a woman'? (§16). Two female mistresses of a middle-aged lover, one young and the other old, variously adjusted his hair colouring by extracting all his undesirable hairs until he was bald. The aim of the fable, our later interpreter opines, was '[to show how pitiable a man is who falls into the hands of women. Women are like the sea; which smiles and lures men on to its sparkling surface, then snuffs them out]' (§23). The untruthfulness of women and their destructive attitudes towards males,[60] disguised by their alluring appearance, is emphasised. There is little doubt that in the hierarchical masculine culture of antiquity such views would have been common.

• **The Political Landscape of Antiquity: Concordia, War, and Utopian Hopes**

In a potential battle between dogs and wolves, the diversity of colouring of the dogs and their different breeds precluded, in the opinion of their

---

59 See Tougher, *Eunuchs*.
60 There is also recognition that bad men lie (Babrius §81). On truth and falsehood in the present age more generally, see §126.

leader, any chance of victory. The political moral of the fable is drawn with salutary clarity: 'Concord (Συμφωνία) is the greatest good for men; dissension involves weakness (ἀσθενές) and servitude (δοῦλον)' (§85).[61]

In a bold vision of the utopian future, where weak creatures were feared by the strong, all animals were at peace because each was called to reciprocal personal account for their deeds in a dramatic social reversal: 'the wolf by the lamb, the leopard by the wild goat, the tiger by the deer' (§102). Accountability to the weak by the strong stands in stark contrast to how ancient states and their elites operated in their protocols of power politics. Here we see an Aesopian slave's perspective on how the world should operate, in which the powerful ruling elites are held responsible for their actions by their powerless subjects.

Finally, a divine perspective on the outbreak of war between nations and city states is provided in the choice of the god War's mate, Insolence, the only goddess left as an option as a bride for marriage (§70). In their marriage relationship, Insolence always preceded War, with War perpetually following. The moral is as follows: 'Let not Insolence (Ὕβρις) ever come among the nations or cities of men, finding favour with the crowd (τοῖς δήμοις); for after her straightway War (Πόλεμος) will be at hand'. The aristocratic disdain for the people, who are portrayed as easily seduced by hybris and therefore susceptible to an ensuing call to arms, is clearly seen in this fable.

3.2 Paul, Social Relations, and the Great Reversal in Christ

A nuanced approach towards the elites, imperial and civic, characterises the thought of Paul in a manner reminiscent of Aesop. Like Aesop, the apostle Paul values the humble person (ταπεινός), presenting humility as a defining characteristic of the believer (ταπεινοφροσύνη: Eph. 4:2; Phil. 2:3; 3:12), and employing 'humility' terminology as an apt description of the fallen earthly body (σῶμα τῆς ταπεινώσεως: Phil. 3:21).[62] Humble believers not only experience God's consolation (παρακαλῶν τοὺς ταπεινούς: 2 Cor. 7:6) but are also subject to the discipline of God's humbling hand (ταπεινώσῃ με: 2 Cor. 12:21). For

---

61 On *concordia* and the absence of its Greek equivalent (ὁμόνοια) in Paul, see Harrison, 'Honouring the Concord'.
62 On humility, see Wengst, *Humility*.

believers, Christ is the exemplum par excellence of cruciform humility (ταπεινός: 2 Cor. 10:1; ἐταπείνωσεν: Phil. 2:8). However, the divine humbling of believers was not only attitudinal: it also involved stepping down socially from a position of privilege and power. Paul's self-funded apostolic work, labouring as a despised artisan on behalf of his converts, represents precisely such a process (ἐμαυτὸν ταπεινῶν: 2 Cor. 11:7).[63] Consequently believers are exhorted to associate with the lowly (Rom. 12:16: τοῖς ταπεινοῖς συναπαγόμενοι).

This perspective of social humiliation is highlighted more profoundly in God's choice of the membership of the Body of Christ at Corinth: not many are wise (σοφοί), powerful (δυνατοί), or of noble birth (εὐγενεῖς) in the social constituency of the Corinthian house churches (1 Cor. 1:26), even if by implication some were.[64] Rather the divinely elect are identified as the foolish (τὰ μωρά) and the weak (τὰ ἀσθενή), chosen by God to shame the wise and the strong (1 Cor. 1:27). Socially, they are the lowborn (τὰ ἀγενῆ) and despised (τὰ ἐξουθενημένα) of the world, the things that are not (τὰ μὴ ὄντα), chosen by God to shame the things that are (1 Cor. 1:28). The rhetoric of disdain and derision employed by Paul here culminates in the startling summation of their significance:[65] those called by God are the 'nothings' of this world, τὰ μὴ ὄντα, reduced in the estimation of the Corinthian cultured elites to being things that 'simply do not exist at all'.[66] One might infer here from Paul's presentation echoes of an Aesopian slave-perspective towards the elites. Paul, however, is articulating a profound and paradoxical social reversal in Christ, orchestrated by God through the foolishness and weakness of the cross (1 Cor. 1:18–25; 2 Cor. 13:4), with a view to dethroning the privileged and powerful, and elevating instead the humble and powerless. As Gerd Theissen observes, 'Paul radicalizes in 1 Cor. 1.26–29 the biblical motif of the God who exalts the low and who chooses those who are nothing. It is not in keeping with this biblical thought pattern to mention people of elevated social rank'.[67]

Another example of this social up-ending can be seen in the reversal

---

63 See Hock, *The Social Context*; Welborn, *Paul, the Fool of Christ*.
64 See Clark, *Secular and Christian Leadership*, 41–45.
65 Welborn, *Paul, the Fool*, 148.
66 Welborn, *Paul, the Fool*, 148.
67 Theissen, 'Social Conflicts', 375.

of status between freedman and slave in Christ (1 Cor. 7:22), which is worked out experientially in a new relationship of brotherhood between each group in the Body of Christ (Phlm. 16). Also, the public eulogies of members of the elite classes as 'endangered benefactors', alluded to by Aesop, are inverted socially by Paul and re-applied to servants of Christ—including the apostle himself (2 Cor. 11:26: κινδύνοις [8x])—who undergo great dangers in serving Christ (e.g. Ephaproditus: Phil. 2:25–30).

Nevertheless, Paul, like Aesop, is acutely aware of the power and potential danger of the elites, as his warning to believers regarding the Roman ruler's sword and the necessity of submission to his rule amply demonstrates (Rom. 13:4). Paul also struggles pastorally with socially prestigious members in the Corinthian house churches who, because of their elite status, resist ecclesial discipline (the incestuous man: 1 Cor. 5:1–5),[68] conduct lawsuits against each other (6:1–11),[69] and publicly oppose the founding apostle of the Corinthian house churches (the 'wrongdoer': 2 Cor. 2:5–11; 7:12).[70]

The eulogistic rituals associated with the recognition of the civic elites are also reconfigured. Divine grace in Christ becomes the great social leveller (e.g. Rom. 3:22b–24,29–30), not the Aesopian precariousness of Fortune, excluding thereby all boasting in self-centred human achievement and its honorific recompense.[71] Instead, in a searing spoof of Graeco-Roman boasting culture,[72] Paul confesses his foolishness in boasting (2 Cor. 11:17), but then proceeds to boast in his weakness in Christ (11:15–18,21,30; 12:1,5,6,9; cf. 13:4). This highly unconventional rhetorical tactic is directed against 'apostolic' interlopers who vaunted their credentials and achievements comparatively with the apostle and competed within their own circles, engaging in stylised rhetorical boasting (2 Cor. 10:12–13; 11:12–13). Where Paul does legitimately boast, he boasts either in his refusal to impose his apostolic financial rights upon his churches (1 Cor. 9:15) or in his ministry of

---

68 See Chow, *Patron*, 130–41; Clark, *Secular and Christian Leadership*, 73–88.
69 See Chow, *Patron*, 123–30; Clark, *Secular and Christian Leadership*, 59–71.
70 See Welborn, *An End*.
71 E.g. Rom. 2:17,23; 3:27; 4:2–3; 5:2,3,11; 15:17; 1 Cor. 1:29,31; 3:21; 4:7; 5:6; Gal. 6:13–14; Phil. 3:4b–11; Eph. 2:8–10. See Gathercole, *Where is Boasting?*; Harrison, 'From Rome'.
72 See Harrison, 'In Quest', 46–55.

building up his converts (2 Cor. 1:12; 10:8,13–16). But, tellingly, in the process, he refuses to boast in his divinely imposed call as a preacher of the gospel (9:16). That is the result of electing grace (Gal. 1:15–16). Instead, Paul boasts in Christ (1 Cor. 1:30; 2 Cor. 10:16b–17; 11:10) and in his churches (1 Cor. 15:31; 2 Cor. 7:4,14; 9:2), deflecting any hint of personal glory.

In this inversion of contemporary boasting rituals, Paul reconfigures the protocols of honorific culture. Honour should be given to those to whom it is due (Rom. 13:7: τῷ τὴν τιμὴν τὴν τιμήν), including the imperial elites (13:1–6), but within the Body of Christ others should be honoured ahead of oneself (Rom. 12:10b), including, as an absolute priority, the weaker and dishonourable members of the community (1 Cor. 12:22–25). Also, behind Paul's re-evaluation of the self-centredness of honorific culture and its status acquisition is the dynamic of love: 'let love be genuine' (Rom. 12:9a; cf. 13:8–10). As a result, in contrast to the Aesopian tradition, the apostle avoids the ubiquitous φιλ-compounds associated with contemporary 'friendship' language (φιλία, φίλος; pace, φιλαδελφία: Rom. 12:10; 1 Thess. 4:9) and its reciprocity culture.[73] Furthermore, Paul ensures that the marginalised are at the centre of God's care amongst believers. The material needs of the saints must be addressed holistically (Rom. 12:13a). Significantly, hospitality should be extended by believers to strangers as much as fellow believers (Rom. 12:13b: τὴν φιλοξενίαν διώκοντες; cf. Gal. 6:10), even going so far as providing beneficence to their persecutors and enemies (Rom. 12:14–21), in obedience to the teaching of Jesus (Matt. 5:44; Luke 6:35).

The humiliation and despising of the poor at Corinth—those having nothing (1 Cor. 11:22: τοὺς μὴ ἔχοντας; cf. 11:21: ὅς μὲν πεινᾷ)—by the wealthy hosts and well-off believers at the Lord's supper, socially expressed in their exclusivist, impatient, and gluttonous behaviour (11:20–21,33–34), was roundly condemned by the apostle. It violated the corporate experience of the Lord's supper and overlooked the costly self-sacrifice of the Lord in securing membership of the new covenant for all believers (11:23–32), the poor included.[74]

---

73 See Harrison, 'Friendship'. Contrast the Gospel of John: φιλέω: 5:20; 11:3,36; 12:25; 15:19; 16:27; 20:2; 21:15,17 [2x]; φίλοι: 15:13,14,15; cf. 3:29; 11:1; 19:12.
74 See Welborn, 'Inequality in Roman Corinth'.

The modern accusation of misogyny against Paul, however, is harder to shake off, notwithstanding the apostle's 'magna carta of humanity' enunciated in Galatians 3:28. In the estimate of some scholars, there remains in Paul a 'stubborn' ecclesial and familial hierarchicalism in male/female relationships (e.g. 1 Cor. 7:3-4; 11:3,7b-12; 14:34-35; cf. Col. 3:18; Eph. 5:22-24; 1 Tim. 2:11-15)—reflecting first-century female subordination and the gendered social roles of antiquity[75]—that diminishes the status of women in Western culture. It is beyond the scope of this chapter to address such a complex issue and the variegated approaches undertaken in grappling with the Pauline evidence. Nevertheless, two brief observations are apposite. First, negatively, Paul does not speak of women in the demeaning manner of our Aesopian parable above. Second, positively, the wide range of women in Paul's ministry circle,[76] supported by the evidence of the narrative of Acts,[77] places a question mark over misogynist portraits of Paul that do not sufficiently consider the epistolary, ecclesial, social, and historical context of the apostle.

4. The Moral Life

In the graphic portrait of human character and social behaviour that emerges in the Aesopian fables, there is a strong emphasis on what must be avoided for effective moral living. Less attention overall is paid in the Babrian corpus to what should be cultivated positively, but it nevertheless carries moral force. In similar manner to the 'virtue and vice' lists of antiquity, Paul also polarises the lifestyles of the 'flesh' with the Spirit (Gal. 5:16-26),[78] the slavery to Sin and Death over against the slavery to God and his righteousness (Rom. 6:15-23), and the old creation in contrast to the new creation (Eph. 4:22-5:1; Col. 3:5-17). A

---

75 On Eph. 5:25-33 and the subordination of women in the Delphic canon, see Harrison, *Paul and the Ancient Celebrity Circuit*, 166-70.
76 Chris Marshall ('Was Paul a Sexist?') mentions Phoebe (Rom. 16:1-2), Prisca (Acts 18:2-3,18-19,26; Rom. 16:3-5; 1 Cor. 16:19; 2 Tim. 4:19), Mary (Rom. 16:6), Junia (Rom. 16:7), Tryphaena and Tryphosa (Rom. 16:12a), Persis (Rom. 16:12b), Eudoia and Syntyche (Phil. 4:2-3), Apphia (Phlm. 2), Nympha (Col. 4:15) and Chloe (1 Cor 1:11).
77 Acts 9:36-43; 12:12; 16:13-16,40; 17:34; 21:9-10 (cf. 1 Cor. 11:5).
78 See Rabins, *The Holy Spirit*; Keener, 'A Comparison'.

comparison of the fables with Paul's letters regarding this ethical intersection will allow us to contextualise better how Paul engages the popular morality of his day.

4.1 The Babrian Fables: What to Avoid

A series of negative injunctions frame the rather bleak portrait of society and human nature that is revealed in Aesop's fables, notwithstanding the ironic twists occurring in their plots and humorous observations delivered by the animal actors in the fables. Human beings are liberated from moral turpitude by living a disciplined lifestyle and the Aesopian prohibitions chart a pathway ahead for auditors. The following character traits and social behaviours are to be avoided: unbounded anger and avenging oneself (Babrius, *Fab.* §§11, 116); the provision of beneficence to scoundrels (§94); flattery leading to personal conceit (§77); greed (§§6, 79); guile (§§81, 87); consorting with evil men (§13); honouring wrong-headed men (§119); pity (§143);[79] premature rejoicing (§24); and self-vaunting (§§29, 66, 84), among other behavioural traits and passions.

No moral agenda from a particular philosophical school is consistently espoused in the self-discipline promoted in the Babrian corpus. The fables are too varied, their epimythia having been created or adapted over a long period of time. Instead, a 'popular' morality is espoused, reflecting a syncretism of viewpoints opportunistically chosen, as opposed to a particular ethical strain rigidly applied.[80] Consequently, a 'multiplicity of possible readings of the fables' exits: 'two listeners or readers will never see or hear them in quite the same way … and no one analysis is definitive'.[81]

4.2 The Babrian Fables: What to Cultivate

We have already touched upon several positive dimensions of moral cultivation in social relations: e.g. concord (§85), preservation of the

---

79 On the positive estimate of *clementia* ('clemency') and negative evaluation of *misericordia* ('pity') in Roman thought, see Harrison, 'The "Clemency" of Nero'.
80 Morgan (*Popular Morality*, 340) writes: '… the central concepts of high philosophy are either absent in popular wisdom, or differently understood, while the relationships between virtues, vices, passions and the mind or soul which suffers and practices them, are quite differently expressed in the two spheres'.
81 Morgan, *Popular Morality*, 63.

poor (§107), and holding fast to one's friends (§44). Further examples are easily supplied. In the fable of 'The North Wind and the Sun' (§18), the epimythium applies the fable to the cultivation of helpful relationships: 'Cultivate gentleness (πρᾳότητα), my son: you will get results oftener by persuasion (πειθοῖ) than by the use of force' (§18). Here an astute use of rhetoric, as an expression of gentleness, is the dynamic for changing deep-seated and recalcitrant attitudes that are routinely countered by harsher disciplinarian approaches.

In another fable about the importance of the combined strength of the worthies of old as opposed to rugged individualism (§47), the moral significance is highlighted with an unexpected social twist at the end: ['Brotherly love (φιλαδελφία) is the greatest good for men; even the humble (ταπεινούς) are exalted by it']. The desire to overcome a significant social gulf here—whether based on ancestry, wealth, civic and military status—by *philadelphia* has interesting resonances with Early Christianity. As noted above, believers are exhorted by God's grace and Christ's cruciform love to address class, economic and social divisions within the house churches and to maintain ethnic unity in Christ.

We have also seen from a fable above (§58) that only hope remains with mankind (ἐλπὶς ἀνθρώποις μόνη σύνεστι) when all the blessings of the gods had disappeared. Again, a comparison of this construction of hope could be profitably made with the Pauline understanding of hope, frequently mentioned in the canonical Paul's writings (ἐλπίζω: 19x; ἐλπίς: 31x). Suffice it to say, in a stance diametrically opposite to Aesop, for Paul eschatological hope exists because of (a) the blessing of divine epiphany—revealed historically in Christ and continued in the Spirit as the down payment of future inheritance (Eph. 1:14)—and (b) the surety of the divine promises in the LXX and the apostolic gospel.[82]

A final injunction opens another positive pathway for auditors to cultivate in their lives. In the fable of 'The Fisherman with the Flute', solid work on everyday necessities and duties must be undertaken first before one can indulge in banter and idle play with any propriety (§9).

---

82 See Moser, 'Grounded Hope'; Campbell, *Paul and the Hope of Glory*.

4.3 The Ethics of Paul and the Popular Morality of the Fables

Some of the ethics to be cultivated (ταπεινός and cognates; φιλαδελφία) and their relevance in Pauline discourse have already been addressed above. We will conclude with two brief case studies pertinent to Paul's epistles: the Aesopian avoidance of 'pity' and the Aesopian cultivation of 'gentleness'. How do they intersect with Paul's thought?

First, why did Aesop recommend the avoidance of 'pity' (§143)? In the fable, a viper bit the hand of the farmer, who had picked up the reptile, almost dead from the cold, to warm it. Before dying the farmer said, 'I suffer what I deserve for showing pity to the wicked (τὸν πονηρὸν οἰκτείρος)'. It is not revealed why the snake is evil, a reputational categorisation that existed prior to the reptile's strike, but it explains the foolishness of the farmer's decision to extend help to the reptile in the first place. Auditors, it is assumed, know why pity should not be exercised to the undeserving.

In the first-century Roman context, there is a clear distinction between the allocation of *clementia* ('clemency' [Greek: ἡ ἐπιείκεια]) and *misericordia* ('pity' [Greek: ὁ ἔλεος, ἡ ἐλεημοσύνη]). From a Stoic viewpoint, *misericordia* is an unstable emotion that is to be avoided. The philosopher Seneca advises his young charge, Nero, to exercise *clementia* only to those who are worthy and who are likely to reform their behaviour, but under no circumstance was the future ruler to be influenced by *misericordia*. *Clementia* was exercised by Caesar and Augustus towards their opponents.[83] *Clementia* was one of the four Augustan virtues that the Senate inscribed on the *clipeus virtutis* ('shield of bravery': *Res Gestae* 34.2; cf. CIL 6.876; RIC 1 §47a, p. 44) in the Roman Senate house, a copy of which has been found at Arles.[84]

By contrast, the Old Testament and Second Temple Judaism present the covenantal God of Israel as inherently merciful to the underserving and it is from this tradition that Paul draws. The Hebrew 'mercy' and 'compassion' credal traditions in Exodus (Exod. 34:6–7 [cf. 33:19]; cf. 2 Chr. 30:9; Neh. 9:17; Pss. 86:15, 103:8, 114:4, 145:8; Joel 2:13; Jon. 4:2) and their appropriation by the New Testament writers are

---

83 For source references and full discussion, see Harrison, 'The "Clemency" of Nero'.
84 Seston, 'Le Clipeus'.

distinctive in the Graeco-Roman context.[85] Paul's οἰκτιρμός/οἰκτίρω terminology emphasises the LXX credal tradition of the 'compassion' of God and the Father (Rom. 9:15b [LXX Exod. 33:19]; 12:1; 2 Cor. 1:3), from which flows the necessity of the believer being clothed with tenderness and compassion (Col. 3:12; Phil. 2:1).

Paul's use of verb ἐλεάω and the noun ἔλεος also draws upon the LXX credal tradition of the 'mercy' of God (Rom. 9:15b [LXX Exod. 33:19]), from which the apostle concludes that God has 'mercy' upon whom he wills (Rom. 9:16,18), whether it be the disobedient Gentiles (11:30; 31a: τῷ ὑμετέρῳ ἐλέει; 15:9: ὑπὲρ ἐλέους) or the disobedient Israelites (11:31). Remarkably, all humanity had been divinely imprisoned in disobedience so that God might have mercy upon all (Rom. 11:32; cf. Gal. 6:16), a glorious plan prepared in advance for the 'vessels of his mercy' (9:23: ἐπὶ σκεύη ἐλέους).[86] Having established the universal soteriological plan of the merciful God in history (Eph. 2:4: ὁ δὲ θεὸς πλούσιος ὢν ἐν ἐλέει), Paul focuses on God's personal mercy granted to him in his apostolate (1 Cor. 7:25; 2 Cor. 4:21; 1 Tim. 1:13,16) and in the ministry of others to him (Phil. 2:27; 2 Tim. 1:16,18). The same merciful God also spares the seriously ill Philippian delegate, Ephaphroditus, from death (Phil. 2:27) and bestows the charism of showing 'mercy' upon the Body of Christ (Rom. 12:8). One wonders whether the greetings of the Pastoral epistles ('grace, mercy, and peace') represent the soteriological fulfilment of the Exod.us credal traditions, accomplished by the Father and the Son (1 Tim. 1:2; 2 Tim. 1:2). In conclusion, we are witnessing a collision between the mercy tradition of the Aesopian fables and those of the LXX and the New Testament.

Second, in the case of πραΰς ('moderate', 'mild', 'lenient') and πραότης / πραΰτης ('mildness', 'meekness', 'gentleness'), the use of the adjective and noun in ancient literature is varied.[87] In the classical period, πραΰτης and cognates are contrasted with rage and savagery; in the hands of the orators, πραΰτης denotes leniency and indulgence; the philosophers view πραΰτης as a quality of the virtuous person; in the *Lives* of Plutarch, πραότης denotes 'a self-restraint which avoids excess

---

85 On the Old Testament 'mercy/compassion' credal traditions, see Bocha, *A Severe Mercy*, passim. On 'mercy' in Second Temple Judaism, see Barclay, '"I will have mercy"'.
86 See Ryliskyte, 'God's Mercy'; Dixon, 'Judgement'.
87 The following observations are indebted to Spicq, 'πραυπάθεια, πραΰς, πραΰτης'.

of every kind, whether physical or emotional'.[88] However, Aesop's fable (§18) links πραότης with rhetorical persuasion, a strategy not aligning with any of the modes of rhetorical persuasion articulated in Aristotle, Cicero, and Quintilian.[89]

In the case of Paul, the apostle expressed his preference to approach the recalcitrant Corinthians with love in a spirit of gentleness (πραΰτητος; cf. Gal. 6:1) as opposed to wielding the stick of discipline (1 Cor. 4:21), reflecting in the process the gentleness of Christ (2 Cor. 10:1 [διὰ τῆς πραΰτητος]; Matt. 11:29 [πραΰς]; cf. 5:5 [οἱ πραεῖς]). Gentleness, therefore, is a characteristic of those called in Christ (Eph. 4:2: πραΰτητος; Col. 3:12: πραΰτητα; Titus 3:2: πραΰτητα), being one of the fruits of the Spirit (Gal. 5:23: πραΰτης). Finally, a rhetorical context loosely approximating Aesop does appear in Paul's description of the Lord's servant as one who should correct his opponents with gentleness (2 Tim. 2:25: ἐν πραΰτητι), including the use of gentleness in discipline, noted above. In sum, the Christocentric and pneumatological focus of πραΰτης and its wider application to the Christian life differentiated Paul's construct from Aesop's highly focused application.

Conclusion

This chapter has explored the popular morality in the Babrian fables, the most extensive collection of the Aesopian tradition roughly contemporary with the apostle Paul. Despite the redactional issues associated with the Aesopian fables, the quasi-historical or legendary status of their creator, and the interpretative legitimacy of the epimythia, their moral world view was familiar in antiquity because of their literary citation, use in elementary school curricula and rhetorical exercises, and recounting in oral culture.

Whether it was the divine world or the role of prayer, variegated social relations, and the prohibitions and exhortations of the morality espoused therein, Aesopian moral assumptions would have invisibly shaped the ethical behaviour of Paul's audiences, as much as the teaching

---

88   See Martin, 'The Concept of Prāotês', 73.
89   See Zhuang, 'Rethinking Ethos'.

of philosophical schools and the peripatetic philosophers—notwithstanding the discordant Aesopian viewpoints evidenced on some issues.

There were, to be sure, some areas of similarity in ethical and social perspective between Paul and the Aesopic tradition. But the Christologically modified monotheism of the apostle, his indebtedness to the LXX, the dramatic social reversal effected by God in the Gospel of Christ crucified, the pneumatic empowerment of believers, and the reconfiguration of Aesopian ethical commonplaces with new theological content, challenged the fundamental structures of the moral life in antiquity. The versatility and theological incisiveness of Pauline ethics are even better appreciated when the Aesopian traditions, long ignored by New Testament scholars, are factored into the competing moral backgrounds of antiquity.

Bibliography

Barclay, J. M. G. — '"I will have mercy on whom I have mercy": The Golden Calf and Divine Mercy in Romans 9–11 and Second Temple Judaism', *Early Christianity* 1.1 (2010), 82–106.

Black, D. A. — *Paul, Apostle of Weakness:* Astheneia *and Its Cognates in the Pauline Literature* (New York: Peter Lang, 1984).

Bocha, M. J. — *A Severe Mercy: Sin and Its Remedy in the Old Testament* (SIPHRUT 1; Winona Lake: Eisenbrauns, 2009).

Bouriant, U. — *Les papyrus Bouriant*, (ed. P. Collart; Paris: Honoré Champion, 1926).

Campbell, C. R. — *Paul and the Hope of Glory: An Exegetical and Theological Study* (Grand Rapids: Zondervan, 2020).

Campbell, D. A. — *Pauline Dogmatics: The Triumph of God's Love* (Grand Rapids: Eerdmans, 2020).

Champlin, E. — 'Phaedrus the Fabulous', *The Journal of Roman Studies*, 95 (2005), 97–123.

Chow, J. K. — *Patron and Power: A Study of Social Networks in Corinth* (JSNTS 75; Sheffield: JSOT Press, 1992).

Clark, A. D. — *Secular and Christian Leadership in Corinth: A Socio-Historical and Exegetical Study of 1 Corinthians* (Leiden: E. J. Brill, 1993).

Currie, H. M. — 'Phaedrus the Fabulist', *Aufstieg und Niedergang der römischen Welt* 2.32.1 (1984), 497–513.

Danker, F. W. — *Benefactor: Epigraphic Study of a Graeco-Roman and New Testament Semantic Field* (Clayton Publishing House: St Louis, 1982).

Dixon, T. P. — 'Judgement for Israel: The Marriage of Wrath and Mercy in Romans 9–11', *New Testament Studies* 66 (2020), 565–81.

Edwards, R. M. — 'Caesar Telling Tales: Phaedrus and Tiberius,' *Rheinisches Museum für Philologie* 2.158 (2015), 167–84.

Elliott, S. S. — '"Witless in Your Own Cause": Divine Plots and Fractured Characters in the Life of Aesop and the Gospel of Mark', *Religion and Theology* 12.2–3 (2005), 397–418.

Fee, G. D. — *God's Empowering Presence: The Holy Spirit in the Letters in Paul* (Peabody: Hendrickson, 2001).

Fisher, B. F.	*A History of the Use of Aesop's Fables as a School Text from the Classical Era through the Nineteenth Century* (PhD Diss., 1987, Indiana University).
Forbes, C. B.	*'Strength' and 'Weakness' as Terminology of Status in St Paul: The Historical and Literary Roots of a Metaphor with Specific Reference to 1 and 2 Corinthians* (BAHons Thesis, Macquarie University, 1978).
Furnish, V. P.	*Theology and Ethics in Paul* (Nashville and New York: Abingdon Press, 1968).
Gathercole, S.	*Where Is Boasting? Early Jewish Soteriology and Paul's Response in Romans 1–5* (Grand Rapids: Eerdmans, 2002).
Glad, C. E.	*Paul and Philodemus: Adaptability in Epicurean and Early Christian Psychagogy* (NovTSup 81; Leiden: E.J. Brill, 1993).
Hardie, A.	'Juvenal, the Phaedrus, and the Truth about Rome', *The Classical Quarterly* 48.1 (1998), 234–51.
Harris, M. J.	*Jesus as God: The New Testament Use of* Theos *in Relation to Jesus* (Grand Rapids: Baker, 1992).
Harrison, J. R.	'The "Clemency" of Nero and Paul's Language of "Mercy" in Romans: Paul's Reconfiguration of Imperial Values in Mid-Fifties Rome', in P. G. Bolt and J. R. Harrison (eds.), *Justice, Mercy, and Well-Being: Interdisciplinary Perspectives*, (Eugene; Pickwick [Wipf & Stock imprint], 2020), 193–220.
Harrison, J. R.	*Paul and the Ancient Celebrity Circuit: The Cross and Moral Transformation* (WUNT 430; Tübingen: Mohr Siebeck, 2019).
Harrison, J. R.	'From Rome to the Colony of Philippi: Roman Boasting in Philippians 3:4–6 in Its Latin West and Philippian Epigraphic Context', in J. R. Harrison and L. L. Welborn (eds.), *The First Urban Churches. Volume 4: Roman Philippi* (Atlanta: SBL Press, 2018), 307–70.
Harrison, J. R.	'Paul's "Indebtedness" to the Barbarian (Rom. 1:14) in Latin West Perspective', *Novum Testamentum* 55.4 (2013), 311–48.
Harrison, J. R.	'In Quest of the Third Heaven: Paul and His Apocalyptic Imitators', *Vigiliae Christianae* 58.1 (2004), 24–55.

Harrison, J. R.	*Paul's Language of Grace in Its Graeco-Roman Context* (WUNT 2.172; Mohr Siebeck, 2003).
Harrison, J. R.	'Friendship and the Local Associations: Philippians in Its Epigraphic Context', in J. R. Harrison and E. R. Richards (eds.), *Ancient Literature for New Testament Study. Volume 10: Inscriptions, Papyri and Other Artifacts* (ALNTS 10; Grand Rapids: Zondervan, 2024), 345–66.
Harrison, J. R.	'Greater than the Greek and Trojan Heroes: The Funerary Epigram of Epigonos and Colossians 3:10', in J. R. Harrison, A. H. Cadwallader, R. Canavan, and M. Trainor (eds.), *New Documents Illustrating the History of Early Christianity 12A: Texts on Colossae, Hierapolis, and Laodicea* (Atlanta: SBL Press, forthcoming).
Harrison, J. R.	'Honouring the Concord of the Ephesian Demos', in J. R. Harrison and B. J. Bitner (eds.), *New Documents Illustrating the History of Early Christianity 11A: Texts from Ephesus* (Atlanta: SBL Press, 2024), 211–30.
Harrison, J. R.	'Publilius Syrus, Popular Morality, and Paul's Epistle to the Romans', in S. E. Porter (ed.), *Pauline Ethics: PAST Volume 11* (Leiden: Brill, forthcoming).
Henderson, J.	*Telling Tales on Caesar: Roman Stories from Phaedrus* (Oxford: Oxford University Press, 2001).
Hesseling, D. C.	'On Waxen Tablets with Fables of Babrius (*Tabulae Ceratae Assendeftianeae*)', *The Journal of Hellenic Studies* 13 (1893), 293–314.
Hock, R.	*The Social Context of Paul's Ministry: Tentmaking and Apostleship* (Philadelphia: Fortress Press, 1980).
Hopkins, K.	'Novel Evidence for Roman Slavery', *Past & Present* 138 (1993), 3–27.
Hubbard, T. K.	'Hesiod's Fable of the Hawk and the Nightingale Reconsidered', *Greek, Roman and Byzantine Studies* 36 (1995), 161–71.
Hubert, M.	'The Concept of Prāotês in Plutarch's *Lives*,' *Greek, Roman, and Byzantine Studies* 2/3.3 (1960), 65–73.
Jamieson, R. B.	'1 Corinthians 15:28 and the Grammar of Paul's Christology', *New Testament Studies* 66 (2020), 187–207.

Johnson, A. C., Coleman-Norton, P. R., and Bourne, F. C. *Ancient Roman Statutes: A Translation with Introduction, Commentary, Glossary and Index* (Austin: University of Texas, 1961).

Jones, C. P. *New Heroes in Antiquity. From Achilles to Antinoos* (Revealing Antiquity; Cambridge, Mass.: Harvard University Press, 2010).

Keener, C. S. 'A Comparison of the Fruit of the Spirit in Galatians 5:22–23 with Ancient Thought on Ethics and Emotion', in L. F. Dow, C. A. Evans, and A. W. Pitts (eds.), *The Language and Literature of the New Testament: Essays in Honour of Stanley E. Porter's 60th Birthday* (BIS 150; Leiden: Brill, 2017), 574–98.

Kennedy, G. A. *Progymnasmata: Greek Textbooks of Prose Composition and Rhetoric* (Atlanta: SBL Press, 2003).

Kovacs, R. F. *The Aesopic Fable in Ancient Rhetorical Theory and Practice* (PhD Diss., University of Illinois, 1950).

Kurke, L. *Aesopic Conversations: Popular Tradition, Cultural Dialogue, and the Invention of Greek Prose* (Princeton: Princeton University Press, 2010).

Laes, C. 'Children and Fables, Children in Fables in Hellenistic and Roman Antiquity', *Latomus* 65.4 (2006), 898–914.

Lefkowitz, J. B. 'Innovation and Artistry in Phaedrus' Morals', *Mnemosyne* 70.3 (2017), 417–35.

Libby, B. B. 'The Intersection of Poetic and Imperial Authority in Phaedrus' Fables', *The Classical Quarterly*, 60.2 (2010), 545–58.

Luzzatto, M. J. (F). 'Aesop', in *Brill's New Pauly* (Antiquity volumes ed. H. Cancik and H. Schneider; English Edition by C. F. Salazar; Classical Tradition volumes ed. M. Landfester; English Edition by F. G. Gentry <https://referenceworks.brill.com/display/db/npoe> [accessed 15 March 2024].

Mann, K. L. *The Fabulist in the Fable Book* (PhD Diss., University of California, 2015).

Marshall, C. 'Was Paul a Sexist? On Reading Paul in Context', *Reality* 4.24 (1997–1998), 19–25.

Morgan, T. 'Living with the Gods in Fables of the Early Roman Empire', *Religion in the Roman Empire* 1.3 (2015), 378–402.

Morgan, T.	'Divine-Human Relations in the Aesopic Corpus', *Journal of Ancient History* 1 (2013), 3–26.
Morgan, T.	*Popular Morality in the Early Roman Empire* (Cambridge: Cambridge University Press, 2007).
Moser, P. K.	'Grounded Hope in God: Epiphany and Promise', *Theology Today* 79.2 (2022), 1–11.
Nelson, S.	'The Justice of Zeus in Hesiod's Fable of the Hawk and the Nightingale', *The Classical Journal* 92 (1997), 235–47.
Perry, B. E., tr.	*Babrius and Phaedrus Fables* (LCL 436; Cambridge, Mass.: Harvard University Press, 1965).
Perry, B. E.	'Demetrius of Phalerum and the Aesopic Fables', *Transactions and Proceedings of the American Philological Association* 93 (1962), 287–346.
Perry, B. E.	'The Origin of the Epimythium', *Transactions and Proceedings of the American Philological Association* 71 (1940), 391–419.
Pertsinidis, S.	*'Like a Warhorse Bridled in Gold': A Study of the Aesopic Fables of Babrius* (PhD, The Australian National University, 2010).
Rabins, V.	*The Holy Spirit and Ethics in Paul: Transformation and Empowering for Religious-Ethical Life* (WUNT 2.283; Tübingen: Mohr Siebeck, 2010).
Reece, S.	'"Aesop", "Q" and "Luke"', *New Testament Studies* 62.3 (2016), 357–77.
Roberts, C.H.	*Catalogue of the Greek and Latin Papyri in the John Rylands Library Manchester, Volume 3: Theological and Literary Texts* (Manchester: Manchester University Press, 1938).
Rothwell, K. S., Jr.	'Aristophanes' "Wasps" and the Sociopolitics of Aesop's Fables', *The Classical Journal*, 90.3 (1995), 233–54.
Ryliskyte, L.	'God's Mercy: The Key Thematic Undercurrent of Paul's Letter to the Romans,' *The Catholic Biblical Quarterly* 81 (2019), 85–105.
Seston, W.	'Le Clipeus virtutis d'Arles et la composition des Res Gestae Divi Augusti', *Comptes rendus des séances de l'Académie des Inscriptions et Belles-Lettres*, 98.3 (1954), 286–29.

Spicq, C. — 'πραυπάθεια, πραΰς, πραΰτης', in J. D. Ernest (tr., ed.), *Theological Lexicon of the New Testament. Volume 3: παι–ψευ* (Hendrickson: Peabody, 1994), 160–71.

Spicq, C. — *Saint Paul: Les épitres pastorales* (Paris: Librairie Lecoffre, 1947).

Standhartinger, A. — 'Paul, the Jews, and the Thessalonians: New Observations on 1 Thessalonians 2:14–16', in J. R. Harrison and L. L. Welborn (eds.), *The First Urban Churches 7: Thessalonica* (Atlanta: SBL Press, 2022), 249–67.

Strong, J. D. — *The Fables of Jesus in the Gospel of Luke: A New Foundation for the Study of Parables* (Leiden: Brill, 2021).

Tannehill, R. C. — *Dying and Rising with Christ: A Study in Pauline Theology* (Berlin: Walter de Gruyter GmbH, 1967).

Theissen, G. — 'Social Conflicts in the Corinthian Community: Further Remarks on J. J. Meggitt, Paul, Poverty and Survival', *Journal for the Study of the New Testament* 25.3 (2003), 371–91.

Tougher, S. — *Eunuchs in Antiquity* and *Beyond* (London: The Classical Press of Wales and Ducksworth, 2002).

van Dijk, J. G. M. — 'The Function of Fables in Graeco-Roman Romance', *Mnemosyne*, 49.5 (1996), 513–41.

Vollmer, T. A. — *'The Spirit Helps our Weakness': Rom. 8.26A in Light of Paul's Missiological Purpose for Writing the Letter to the Romans* (BTS 36; Leuven: Peeters, 2018).

Watson, D. — 'The 'Life of Aesop' and the Gospel of Mark: Two Ancient Approaches to Elite Values', *Journal of Biblical Literature* 129.4 (2010), 699–716.

Welborn, L. L. — 'Inequality in Roman Corinth: Evidence from Diverse Sources Evaluated by a Neo-Ricardian Model', in J. R. Harrison and L. L. Welborn (eds.), *The First Urban Churches 2: Roman Corinth* (Atlanta: SBL Press, 2016), 47–84.

Welborn, L. L. — *An End to Enmity: Paul and the 'Wrongdoer' of Second Corinthians* (Berlin/Boston: De Gruyter, 2011).

Welborn, L. L. — *Paul, the Fool of Christ: A Study of 1 Corinthians 1–4 in the Comic-Philosophic Tradition* (London and New York: T&T Clark/Continuum, 2005).

Wengst, K. — *Humility: Solidarity of the Humiliated. The Transformation of an Attitude* (London: SCM Press, 1968).

West, M. L.	'The Ascription of Fables to Aesop in Archaic and Classical Greece', *Entretiens sur l'Antiquité Classique* 30 (1984), 105–36.
Wyman, D.	*Paul's Endangered Benefactor: Galatians in Its Benefaction Context* (PhD Diss., Southern Baptist Theological Seminary, 2022: forthcoming WUNT 2, Tübingen, Mohr Siebeck).
Zafiropoulos, C. A.	*Ethics in Aesop's Fables: The* Augustana *Collection* (Leiden/Boston/Köln: Brill, 2001).
Zhuang, G.	'Rethinking Ethos: A Comparative Analysis of Persuasive Character Building in Classical Antiquity through the Lenses of Aristotle, Cicero, and Quintilian', *SHS Web of Conferences 178, 02016* (2023), *ICPRSS* 2023 <https://doi.org/10.1051/shsconf/202317802016> [accessed 18 April 2024].
Zimmermann, R.	The Body Fables in Babrius, *Fab*. 134 and 1 Corinthians 12: Hierarchic or Democratic Leadership in Crisis Management?', *HTS Teologiese Studies/Theological Studies* 77.4 (2021), a6524. <htpps.//doi.org/10.4102/hts.v.77iv.6524> [accessed 13 March 2024].

CHAPTER 4

Do Jews Rob Temples? Paul and his Hypocritical Interlocutor of Romans 2:22

Lyn M. Kidson

I have long been intrigued by Paul's question in Romans to his Jewish interlocutor: 'You who abhor idols, do you rob temples?' (Rom. 2:22). My immediate thought is: 'Why would Jews be robbing temples?' Colin Kruse calls this phrase 'problematic'. He says that there are two options to interpret this verse, either metaphorically or literally, but it appears that he finds neither convincing.[1] One instance of the metaphorical interpretation is provided by D. B. Garlington, who argues 'most forcefully that for Paul the new idol is the Torah! The 'sacrilege' in question is Israel's idolatrous attachment to the law itself'.[2] Kruse sees a problem with this view but does not really articulate what it might be, except to offer an example of 'temple robbing' by a Jew reported by Josephus (A.J. 18.81–84). He then suggests that there are similar problems with the literal view. He finds it puzzling that 'Paul's indictment of Jews for this offense when the practice of idolatry was absent in Israel at the time

---

1   Kruse, *Paul's Letter*, 150 (metaphorical); Fitzmyer, *Romans*, 318 (literal); Krentz, 'The Name of God'.
2   Garlington, '"Ierosylein"', 150); Origen, *Commentary*, 138, goes a step even further and suggests that anyone who 'steals from the law and the prophets the word that predicts Christ and conceals it, lest people should hear and believe, is committing temple robbery and is truly violating the temple of God'.

he wrote'.³ He lists a number of explanations, the strongest of which is by Duncan Derrett, who argues that temple robbing involves profiting from the misappropriation of endowments of temples and the dispersal of goods and lands of temples fallen into disuse and neglect.⁴ In the end Kruse concedes that although 'it is difficult to be certain about the precise meaning of Paul's reference to robbing temples, the overall purpose of 2:21–22 is clear enough. It highlights the hypocrisy of his dialogue partner and those whom he represents, that is Jews who teach others but do not teach themselves'.⁵ He thus does not come to any conclusion as to what Paul is referring to in the phrase 'You who abhor idols, do you rob temples?' Many simply gloss over this difficult part of Paul's argument.⁶

Recently, Lionel Windsor has made the argument that 'robbing temples' is a reference to an actual incident in Rome involving a Jewish teacher who defrauded a Roman convert of funds which were intended for the Jerusalem temple (A.J. 18.81–84).⁷ Windsor is to be commended on pursuing an option which locates Paul's discourse within the social context of Rome. Much of what he says about Paul's argument in Romans 2:17–29 is very helpful and I will be drawing on his work throughout this chapter. It is certainly plausible that such a notorious incident may be in the background to Paul's reference to 'robbing temples' and illustrates Paul's point that God's name could be blasphemed among the Gentiles because of Jewish wrongdoing.⁸ However, the lack of adulterous activity in the story weakens the argument that the cascade of rhetorical questions refers to an actual incident.⁹ The series of rhetorical questions in 2:21–24 builds until Paul accuses his interlocutor of bring shame upon God:

> 'You, then, that teach others, will you not teach yourself? While you preach against stealing, do you steal? You that forbid adultery, do you commit adultery? You that abhor idols,

---

3 Kruse, *Paul's Letter*, 150.
4 Derrett, '"You Abominate False Gods"'.
5 Kruse, *Paul's Letter*, 151.
6 Barth, *The Epistle to the Romans*; Gathercole, *Where Is Boasting?*; for an overview of German literature on this verse see Dochhorn, 'Der Vorwurf', 106–8.
7 Windsor, 'The Named Jew'; similarly noted by Kruse, *Paul's Letter*, 150, as an example of a literal case of 'temple robbing'.
8 A closer parallel is in 2 Maccabees which records that the high priest Menelaus stole articles from the temple in Jerusalem (4:32).
9 As Windsor concedes: 'The Named Jew', 230.

do you rob temples? You that boast in the law, do you dishonour God by breaking the law? For, as it is written, "The name of God is blasphemed among the Gentiles because of you."[10]

The difficulty with Windsor's suggestion is that Paul's use of an interlocutor, the rhetorical questioning, the citation of Scripture, and the actual accusations themselves, all point to Paul employing rhetorical devices that direct away from an allusion to an actual event and instead indicate a persuasive purpose within the discourse itself.[11]

Therefore this chapter is primarily concerned with Paul's use of an interlocutor as a standard rhetorical device in Romans 2.[12] Before beginning, it is perhaps best to describe what an interlocutor is and the purpose for using them. An interlocutor was a fictional character used most often in literary dialogues but which could also feature in discourses or letters, whose primary purpose was to persuade an audience.[13] It is a rhetorical device that is related to parables because they both use 'hypothetical circumstances—figures and events that, although invented by the rhetor, are nevertheless in keeping with lived experience'.[14] The interlocutor normally represents commonly held views that an audience may or may not share, which the orator wants to affirm or refute.[15] Used poorly, the interlocutor can appear to the audience to be a straw man.[16] Used well, and the interlocutor will become recognisable as a character and, if based on a historical person, will conform to known traits and voice ideas that are plausible from the perspective of the audience (this is especially important if the reader/hearer of the dialogue is a character themselves).[17] In sum, the interlocutor, when used in the

---

10   All Scripture used in this chapter is taken from NRSV (CENCCC, 1989).
11   Use of the interlocutor: Cicero, 'On Invention', 53. Use of rhetorical questioning: Quintilian, *The Orator's Education*, 9.2.6–10. Citing of poetry adding authority to a series of rhetorical questions see Quintilian, *Inst.*, 9.2.6–16; Dozier, 'Rhetorical Display', 243. Thorsteinsson, *Paul's Interlocutor*, 216–18, cogently argues for the use of an interlocutor at Rom. 2:22 but is defending a larger thesis that the interlocutor is a Gentile.
12   As a standard rhetorical device: Chrysostom, *Hom. Rom.* 6. (v.21); Holloway, 'The Enthymeme', 338.
13   Interlocutor as a device used in letters: Thorsteinsson, *Paul's Interlocutor*, 34–51.
14   McCormick, 'An Ancient Typology', 151.
15   Wynne, 'Cicero's Tusculan Disputations', 217–20.
16   Cicero, *On Invention*, 53.
17   Cicero, *Letters*, 3, in reply to Atticus's criticism, defends his removal of Scaevola as a character based on their shared knowledge of this man when he was alive; Cicero's friend Atticus is a character in his dialogue *On Brutus* (122–6); Dugan, 'Cicero's Rhetorical Theory', 36.

hands of a skilled orator is a useful investigative tool for exposing what the orator believes is the truth to an audience and winning them over to his point of view.[18]

In the first part of this essay, I will pose two questions. First, what was Paul's reason for writing Romans? Secondly, what is the relationship of the audience to the interlocutor/s in Romans? In the second part, I investigate what was Paul's purpose in using this device and what role does the temple robbing trope play in this purpose? I argue that Paul uses this well-known trope to refer to the act of blaspheming against the Gentile gods, which breaks the command not to blaspheme in the Ten Commandments. My conclusion is that Paul's purpose in using the series of rhetorical questions in Romans 2:21–24 is to stymie any objection by a Law observant Jewish interlocutor that he is a sinner like the Gentile Romans (3:9–19).

Paul's Reason for Coming to Rome: Rhetorical Strategies

Romans is a complex document: it contains a discourse within a letter frame. Paul seems to have a number of purposes in mind for this letter.[19] Normally, a writer states his or her purpose in the opening body of the letter but here in Romans he is somewhat opaque.[20] Runar M. Thorsteinsson makes the case, based on epistolary theory, that Paul begins his letter body at Romans 1:8.[21] At the opening of the letter body, it was usual, if the circumstances warranted, to discuss one's travel plans and make arrangements for visiting the recipient/s and discuss any possible hindrances as Paul does in Romans 1:8–12.[22] He says he longs to see them so 'that we may be mutually encouraged' and he wants to come to them 'in order that I may reap some harvest among you as I have

---

18   Cicero, *Tusc.*, 1.8.
19   Holloway, 'The Rhetoric of Romans'.
20   Jewett, 'Romans', 12. Consider the letter body openings of BGU 1.27; P.Oxy 12.1482; P.Tebt 2.289 in Kidson, *Persuading Shipwrecked Men*, 62. Cf. 1 Cor. 1:10–11; Gal. 1:6–7; Phil. 1:12–14; 1 Tim. 1:3–4; Titus 1:5–6.
21   Thorsteinsson, *Paul's Interlocutor*, 41–44.
22   PCair Zen II 59251 (252 BCE): 2–3; V 59816 (257 BCE): 3–4; PTebt I 33 (112 BCE): 4–18; I 59 (99 BCE): 3–8; SelPap II 417 (88 BCE): 3–14; PBour 10 (BCE 88): 2–10; PTebt II 284 (c.88–51 BCE): 2–7; PFay 123 (110m—111 CE): 3–12; PAmh II 131 (early 2nd cent. CE): 3–8. White, *Light*, e.g. Letter 111.

among the rest of the Gentiles' and he feels 'indebted to Greeks and barbarians' (1:14). This letter comes close to being a letter of self-introduction; indeed, by the end of the letter he introduces Phoebe (16:1–2) with a formula conventionally used in letters of introduction.[23]

Certainly, in this letter body opening one gets the feeling that more is going to be said about Paul's purpose in coming to Rome, which Robert Jewett identifies as a feature of Paul's diplomatic tone.[24] Not only was it conventional to open the letter body with a statement of purpose, it was also usual to reiterate it at the close of the letter.[25] Normally, letter writers wanted their addressee to do something so they press them at the end of the letter to do that thing.[26] Paul's revelation at the end of the letter is that he is coming to Rome because he wants to go on and preach the gospel in Spain (15:24,28).[27] After he introduces his plan to go to Spain, he says 'for I do hope to see you on my journey and to be sent on by you' (15:24), which, according to Michael White, was Paul appealing to an obligation that his hosts might extend their hospitality to supply or pay for the next leg of a journey.[28] And here is the purpose for writing because he would need assistance to get to Spain, both economic and human. Paul needed people who could speak Latin and know of people in Spain, who could host him and his party. For this reason, Paul's hoped-for audience becomes important in understanding his argumentative strategies in the letter.

Paul's Implied Audience

The big question is who is the audience here? Paul is a skilled orator. Those trained in rhetoric, like Paul, who must have had some training, prepared their orations with the audience in mind.[29] Here Paul is playing

---

23 Holloway, 'The Rhetoric of Romans', 114; Keyes, 'The Greek Letter'; example of a letter of introduction: POxy II 292 (25 CE).
24 Jewett, 'Romans', 14.
25 Kidson, '1 Timothy', 107–108.
26 Kidson, *Persuading Shipwrecked Men*, 72.
27 Jewett, 'Romans', 5; Das, 'Paul of Tarshish', 60–73 argues against this thesis, however, Das does not supply any purpose for Paul's wish to travel to Rome.
28 White, 'Social Authority', 217. Cf. 1 Corinthians 16:6.
29 Aristotle, *Art of Rhetoric*, 197. On Paul's classical education, see Judge, *Social Distinctives*; Robertson, *Paul's Letters*, 216–17.

with his audience's imagination by the introduction of an interlocutor; that is, the audience he is imagining listening to his letter in Rome. This means that there is an implied audience fashioned out of the intended audience; the implied audience is the one who Paul thinks will be in the room as the letter is read out.[30] All skilled writers use an implied audience to shape their writing for effective communication.[31] Paul knows some of his implied audience in the flesh (Romans 16:3–15). And these people, suggests Mark Nanos, are a group of Christ-believers drawn from the synagogue.[32] They are both Jews and Gentile proselytes and God-fearers.[33] However, these might not be the only people Paul has in mind while writing this letter. Paul might be anticipating Jewish unbelievers in the room, there to hear his letter because they know him by reputation.[34] Thus, when Paul starts his argument with a common Jewish polemic, it is safe to assume that he believes his audience to be familiar with the Torah and the common tropes of Jewish teaching.[35]

It is important to bear in mind that the audience that hears the letter is not necessarily the same as the letter's implied audience. Further, the interlocutors in Romans are fictional characters that are set up by Paul for persuasive reasons. Their characters, whether Jew or Gentile, do not necessarily equate with Paul's implied audience, nor the audience that hears the letter in actuality. This is a point that seems to be confounded in many discussions on Romans 2. Many seem to think that if they can identify the audience in Romans (is the church made up of Gentiles or Jews?), they will have solved the problem of the identity of interlocutors in Romans 2. However, as we will see the location of the identity of the interlocutors is not located in the audience but in the discourse itself.

---

[30] On the implied audience see Kidson, *Persuading Shipwrecked Men*, 49–54.
[31] Kidson, *Persuading Shipwrecked Men*, 49–50; Alecia M. Magnifico, 'Writing for Whom?'.
[32] Nanos, 'The Jewish Context'.
[33] Bird, *Romans*, 2–3.
[34] Bird, *Romans*, 3. We must also consider if Paul also had in mind his Jewish opponents within the church: Luedemann, *Opposition*.
[35] Bird, *Romans*, 2–3; Thorsteinsson makes a similar conclusion: *Paul's Interlocutor*, 121–22, 167–73.

Paul as an Orator

In the central section of the letter, which resembles a discourse (Rom. 1:16—15:13), Paul is demonstrating his rhetorical skill as one worthy to preach the gospel in Rome. Rome was full of highly skilled orators, who came to Rome to make their careers.[36] Paul would need to compete with them for attention if his goal was to proclaim the gospel to Greeks and barbarians (Rom. 1:14). Therefore, he needed to convince his potential hosts in Rome that he had the skill to proclaim the gospel in a manner that goes beyond what they could do themselves.[37] He would desire to engage their minds and their emotions, which was the objective of all orators.[38] However, what comes into play, especially in Rome, are the fashions in oratory, which I think impacts on Paul's choice of rhetorical devices. Paul had spent a good deal of time in Corinth, a Roman colony with pretensions to become a centre of education and rhetoric.[39] In Corinth, he could easily become aware of particular fashions in Roman oratory. For instance, Suetonius describes Augustus' oratorical style:

> He cultivated a style of speaking that was chaste and elegant, avoiding the vanity of attempts at epigram and an artificial order, and as he himself expresses it, 'the noisomeness of far-fetched words,' making it his chief aim to express his thought as clearly as possible... He looked on innovators and archaizers with equal contempt... and as for Mark Antony, he calls him a madman, for writing rather to be admired than to be understood.[40]

What we can glean from Suetonius' description of Augustus' oratory is that clarity of expression was important. In describing this Roman rhetorical fashion, Tonio Holscher says that Augustus wanted his speech to be elegant and temperate, not like Antony whose rhetorical style he thought was designed to elicit more amazement than insight.[41] In the section Romans 1:16—15:13, Paul demonstrates a style that has clarity

---

36   Bowersock, *Greek Sophists*, 28–29.
37   Holloway, 'The Rhetoric of Romans,' 114.
38   Arena, 'The Orator', 203–4.
39   Harrison, 'Paul and the "Agonothetia"', 303–16.
40   Suetonius, 'Augustus'.
41   Hölscher, *The Language of Images*, 53.

and correctness rather than one of elaborate rhetorical display.[42]

In relation to Paul's decision to use interlocutors, Cicero has a discussion which is very helpful. Cicero wrote a number of philosophical dialogues in which he himself was a character.[43] Cicero was an exponent of the philosophical school Scepticism. I am not proposing that there is a parallel between Cicero's philosophical thought and Paul's Judaism, but that they seem to be deploying similar strategies in the use of the interlocutor.[44] Cicero describes how,

> Socrates used this conversational method a good deal, because he wished to present no arguments himself, but preferred to get a result from the material which the interlocutor had given him—a result which the interlocutor was bound to approve as following necessarily from what he had already granted.[45]

We see here that Cicero is critical of Socrates for manipulating the words of his interlocutor in order to make a point in his argument: 'For one who sees that if he gives the proper answer to the first question that he is asked, he will be compelled to grant also a proposition which is displeasing to him, will generally put a stop to further questioning by not answering or by answering incorrectly.'[46]

Cicero's goal, as a sceptic in his Tusculan Disputations, was that the inquirer into philosophy not be persuaded to a certain viewpoint, but to discover the wisest viewpoint for himself because 'it would be an abuse of authority to teach somebody to assent to some conclusion'.[47] Paul's object is to argue for a certain viewpoint, but what is interesting is that like Cicero he is arguing an interlocutor out of a commonly held view. As Wynne describes the strategy of 'Cicero the speaker [within the dialogue, is that he] argues against the sincere views of his interlocutor, in order to argue him out of those views, and not into any others'.[48] Like Cicero, Paul wants to argue his interlocutor out of his view, which in

---

42 Kennedy, *A New History*, 164, 269
43 Wynne, 'Cicero's Tusculan Disputations', 205–38.
44 Wynne, 'Cicero's Tusculan, Disputations', 208–10, 209 n.7.
45 Cicero, *On Invention*, 31 (53).
46 Cicero, *On Invention*, 32 (54).
47 Wynne, 'Cicero's Tusculan Disputations', 205–38.
48 Wynne, 'Cicero's Tusculan Disputations', 208.

Romans 1 is that Gentiles who practice wickedness deserve to die while the person observing God's Law is beyond God's judgement (18–32).

Introduction of an Interlocutor at Romans 2:1

Paul introduces his interlocutor at Romans 2:1 by using the vocative 'Oh person' (ὦ ἄνθρωπε).[49] The vocative was used frequently to address an interlocutor within a philosophical dialogue.[50] Since he is introducing a character into his discourse, Paul is unlikely to be addressing a representative of the human race, but rather a 'character' he has already forecasted.[51] Now this character agrees with the Jewish polemic 1:18–32 and passes judgement on those who practise such things.[52] In traditional scholarship, this character has been identified as a Jew.[53] However, Paul says that the gospel is 'the power of God for salvation to everyone (παντὶ) who believes' in verse 1:16, and then those potential believers are narrowed down to those who agree with the polemic.[54] Therefore, I propose that the general 'O person, each one of you' is referring to Jews and Gentiles who principally belong to the synagogue.[55]

Narrowing the Scope of the Interlocutor at Romans 2:17

However, when Paul moves to the second interlocutor at 2:17, he is narrowing his attention to a subset of those to whom 'Oh person' could apply at 2:1. So I agree with Windsor:

> Paul explicitly marks a shift in topic with respect to his interlocutor. He is thus signalling either the introduction of a new interlocutor or a changed perspective on the same interlocutor.

---

49 Moo, *The Epistle to the Romans*, 127.
50 Dickey, 'Me Autem Nomine Appellabat', 1, 31 (53).
51 The interlocutor identified as interjector from general humanity: Jewett, *Romans*, 196; Barrett, *A Commentary*, 42–44; Engberg-Pedersen, *Paul and the Stoics*, 201–202.
52 Holloway, 'The Rhetoric of Romans', 115.
53 For an overview of the traditional identification see Thorsteinsson, *Paul's Interlocutor*, 3–4.
54 Remembering that the interlocutor must behave in a congruent fashion, not all Gentiles would disagree with the polemic in Romans 1:18–31: Wasserman, 'Philosophical Cosmology'.
55 Translation: Moo, *The Epistle to the Romans*, 127. On Paul's implied audience as Gentile and Jewish members of the synagogue: Nanos, 'The Jewish Context', 283–89.

> In either case, the readers are being encouraged to envisage the interlocutor of 2:17–29 with respect to a conceptual frame that has shifted in some way.[56]

Since we are proposing that the interlocutor here is a representative of the subset of Jew and Gentile (1:16), and this person calls themselves a 'Jew', then Paul is most likely styling the interlocutor as a Jew or a proselyte, who believes themselves to be a Jew. However, we must remind ourselves that this Jew is a fictional character. How might this character be congruent with the knowledge of real Jews? It could be that the character represents Jewish believers who are opposed to Paul's version of the gospel (Gal. 2:12). But more likely, he is styling a character who represents a portion of the implied audience as they once were or is readily identifiable as having the traits he is about to describe (2:17–20). What he is not doing is describing actual people. We must be mindful that he is proclaiming his version of the gospel in order to serve his larger purpose, which is to demonstrate his ability to win both Jews and Gentiles in Rome, which will in turn give them confidence to support him in his mission plans. It is reasonable to assume Paul's intended audience would be concerned about their fellow synagogue attenders, whether Jews or Gentiles, just as Paul is concerned for his kinsmen in Romans 9:1–5. It is these people who are analogous to the interlocutors of 2:1 and 17.

The Character of Paul's Interlocutor at 2:17

Robert Jewett persuasively argues that the interlocutor at 2:17 is styled as a pretentious Jew, whether that be someone who is ethnically Jewish or a proselyte.[57] I would propose that Philo of Alexandria and Josephus can act as informants for the character of this interlocutor. Josephus is of particular interest. In his *Against Apion*, Josephus seeks to defend the Jewish Law against the intellectual attacks of Gentile writers. In the first book, he deals with accusations that the Jews are not an ancient people and their laws are new inventions. In the second book he turns to those who are directly attacking Moses and the Law: 'maligning [Moses] as a charlatan

---

56 Windsor, 'The Named Jew', 234.
57 Jewett, *Romans*, 221–23. The interlocutor as a proselyte: Rodriguez, *If You Call Yourself*, 48–61.

and impostor, and asserting that from the [Law] we receive lessons in vice and none in virtue'.[58] He says that his object 'is not to compose a panegyric upon our nation; but I consider that, in reply to the numerous false accusations which are brought against us, the fairest defence which we can offer is to be found in the laws which govern our daily life.'[59] He may not be composing a panegyric about the Jewish nation but it becomes evident that there is a sense of pride in having the Law and observing it:

> For us, with our conviction that the original institution of the Law was in accordance with the will of God, it would be rank impiety not to observe it. What could one alter in it? What more beautiful one could have been discovered? What improvement imported from elsewhere? Would you change the entire character of the constitution? Could there be a finer or more equitable polity than one which sets God at the head of the universe... [60]

Here Josephus is eulogising the Law, but one can see how there is a potential slide toward conflating the greatness of the Law with the people who observe the Law. Although Josephus was cautious not to indulge in arrogance, in the end he says:

> I would therefore boldly maintain that we have introduced to the rest of the world a very large number of very beautiful ideas. What greater beauty than inviolable piety? What higher justice than obedience to the laws? [...] If, however, it is seen that no one observes them better than ourselves, and if we have shown that we were the first to discover them, then the Apions and Molons and all who delight in lies and abuse may be left to their own confusion.[61]

While I do not want to accuse Josephus of arrogance (286, 295) since he was so careful to avoid it, one can see how pride in the Law could lead to pride in oneself as a Jew or a Gentile observing the Law. And this was

---

58 Flavius Josephus, *Against Apion*, 2.14 (Whiston, 145).
59 Josephus, *Against Apion*, 147.
60 Josephus, *Against Apion*, 184–85.
61 Josephus, *Against Apion*, 293–95 (emphasis added).

a danger as Josephus conceded: 'Indeed, were we not ourselves aware of the excellence of our laws, assuredly we should have been impelled to pride ourselves upon them by the multitude of their admirers.'[62] As Josephus says, it was the Jewish nation who has introduced the beautiful ideas of Scripture to the rest of the world.

We see a similar flow of ideas in Romans. Paul makes the case that Gentiles are ungodly and wicked and he expects that the interlocutor 'oh person' would agree (2:1). The use of the interlocutor places his implied audience at a distance from this charge; it is in a sense a piece of theatre.[63] They are watching him charge the one who has judged the Gentiles without the Law as guilty of the same sins as them. This was sure to capture an audience's attention![64] It is an extraordinary claim in the light of Josephus' assuredness that Jews possessing the Law observe it. I propose that Paul was attempting to entrap the interlocutor into acknowledging that the polemic in 1:18-32 only applied to Gentiles who do not observe the Law, only to switch the cards and condemn them because they pass judgement on these Gentiles.[65] By using the interlocutor, Paul does not fall into the same trap. Given Paul's larger purpose for Romans, it would seem that he expects his implied audience to consider if this strategy was persuasive.[66] Perhaps Paul anticipates that his entrapment strategy would not be considered convincing, so he introduces 'a Jew' at 2:17, as a subset of those represented by the 'person' (2:1), who still needed convincing they are sinners like the Gentiles without the Law.

Temple Robbing and Sacrilege as a *Topos*

Paul intends to convince this assured Jew through a series of rhetorical questions (2:21-23). Rhetorical questioning or imaginary interrogation, says Quintilian, has a number of uses within a discourse. Primarily

---

62   Josephus, *Against Apion*, 286.
63   On creating distance, Tzounakas, 'Persius', 570. On the delivery of Paul's letters: Johnson, 'Paul's Letters Reheard', 60-76. On the relationship of the audience hearing a letter and a theatre audience: Quintilian, *Inst.*, 11.3.3-9; Kidson, *Persuading Shipwrecked Men*, 275-76.
64   The need to capture the audience's attention and inspire emotions: Arena, 'The Orator', 205.
65   Paul's aim as rhetorical 'entrapment', see Jewett, *Romans*, 198.
66   The audience's participation in the drama of the oration: Quintilian, *Inst.*, 11.3.3-9; Aristotle, *Rhetoric* 1.1356a.5-6; Easterling, 'Actors and Voices'.

it emphasises a point, but also can put pressure on an opponent and stop them from pretending to misunderstand.⁶⁷ In Greek rhetoric, 'temple robbing' and the related term 'sacrilege' (ἱεροσυλέω) was commonplace (a *topos*) 'because it applies to every temple robber'.⁶⁸ Let's consider some examples.

1. Aristotle, *Nicomachean Ethics*

Aristotle, in *Nicomachean Ethics*, argues that temple robbing is stealing on a great scale:

> Those who make improper gains from improper sources on a great scale, for instance princes who sack cities and rob temples (ἱερὰ συλῶντας), are not termed mean, but rather wicked or impious or unjust (ἀλλὰ πονηροὺς μᾶλλον καὶ ἀσεβεῖς καὶ ἀδίκους).⁶⁹

He goes on to say that similar people, 'the dicer and the foot-pad or brigand [...] are to be classed as mean, as showing sordid greed'.⁷⁰ What holds all these people together is their greed.

2. Demosthenes, *Against Timocrates*

Demosthenes, in *Against Timocrates*, calls temple robbing (ἱεροσυλοῦσι) a serious crime worthy of imprisonment along with theft from the State:

> On the other hand, he abolishes imprisonment for men who steal the property of the State and rob the temples (ἱεροσυλοῦσι) of the Goddess.⁷¹

---

67 Quintilian, *Inst.*, 9.2.6–10.
68 A temple robber (ἱερόσυλος) seizes offerings to the gods; temple robbing as a *topos*: Hermogenes (attr.), *Preliminary Exercises*, 12–14, in Kennedy, *Progymnasmata*.
69 Aristotle, *Nicomachean Ethics*, 4.1.42–43.
70 Aristotle, *Nicomachean Ethics*, 4.1.43.
71 Demosthenes, 'Oration 24', in LCL 299, 122. The Greeks even had a word for this type of behaviour: 'ἱεροσύληκα'; Antiphon says that murder, sacrilege and treason are a grave malefaction in the *Murder of Herodes*, 5.1. Antiochus IV is depicted by Polybius, *Histories* 30.25–26, as grossly self-indulgent, celebrating games in his honour in the most lavish style possible, all paid for, he says, 'by the robberies he had committed in Egypt when he treacherously attacked King Philometor [...] partly by contributions from his friends. He had also sacrilegiously despoiled (ἱεροσυλήκει) most of the temples' (cf. Aristotle, *NE*, 4.1.42).

Here Demosthenes uses the precise Greek word for robbing temples as does Plato in his *Republic*.

3. Plato, *Republic*

Plato says that the type who become henchmen of a tyrant, in times of peace practice these kinds of evils: 'they just steal, break into houses, cut purses, strip men of their garments, plunder temples (ἱεροσυλοῦσιν), and kidnap, and if they are fluent speakers they become sycophants and bear false witness and take bribes.'[72]

4. Plutarch, *Precepts of Statecraft*

It is in Plutarch's *Precepts of Statecraft* where you feel the full force of the orator's invective against robbing temples. In his advice to the young aspiring politician, Plutarch says that he should keep the orator's platform as a sanctuary to sacredness and justice. The young man should

> strip off all love of wealth and of money, as you would iron full of rust and a disease of the soul, cast them straightway at the beginning into the market-place of hucksters and money-lenders, and turning your back depart from them, believing that a man who makes money out of public funds is stealing from sanctuaries (ἱερῶν κλέπτειν), from tombs, from his friends, through treason and by false testimony, that he is an untrustworthy adviser, a perjured judge, a venal magistrate, in brief not free from any kind of iniquity.

All these things are 'evils' says Plutarch.[73]

In summary we can see, in Greek parlance, that the charge of temple robbing is not associated with adultery and certainly not with idolatry. It is usually viewed as a crime against the state such as stealing public funds; however, in Plutarch we notice that there is a shift in association to more personal crimes such as stealing from friends and breaking into tombs, which bears some similarity to Plato's henchmen types who 'steal (κλέπτουσι), break into houses, cut purses, strip men of their garments.'[74]

---

72 Plato, *Republic*, 9.575b.
73 Plutarch, *Precepts*, 819 E–F (26).
74 Plato, *Republic*, 9.575b.

Vice Lists in the Septuagint and other Jewish Writings

Yet aside from 'rob temples', Paul's accusations in Romans 2:17–29 bear a great deal of similarity to other Jewish writers. We should note that the order of these sins is not the same as the Ten Commandments even though they are drawn from this list of commands (LXX Exod. 20). Jeremiah in the Septuagint (7:8–10) is by far the closer parallel:

> But whereas ye have trusted in lying words, whereby ye shall not be profited; and ye murder, and commit adultery, and steal, and swear falsely, and burn incense to Baal and are gone after strange gods who ye know not, so that it is evil with you.[75]

Jeremiah's order of sins, murder, adultery, stealing, swearing falsely, still follows the Ten Commandments, but the list of vices is capped off by the accusation that the Israelites are idol worshippers. A closer parallel to Paul's order of sins can be found in Philo:

> For assuredly it is better for those who have resolved to steal (τοῖς κλέπτειν) or commit adultery (ἢ μοιχεύειν) or murder to behold each of these purposes brought to failure and ruin.[76]

In this list stealing and adultery are in the same order as Paul in Romans. Another very close parallel is Philo in *The Confusion of Tongues* (32) where he says:

> [the soul lacking good sense] who is not far gone in mortal error would pray that all the promptings of his mind's purposes should fail him, so that when he attempts to commit theft or adultery (μὴ τῷ κλέπτειν ἢ μοιχεύειν), or murder or sacrilege (ἢ ἀνδροφονεῖν ἢ ἱεροσυλεῖν), or any similar deed, he should not find an easy path.[77]

We can see here that Philo adds 'sacrilege', a word that could refer to temple robbing, to a list of sins that are familiar from Jeremiah, but in the order that Paul uses them in Romans 2.

But it is Josephus who really comes to our aid once again in *Against*

---

75 Tr. Brenton (ed.), *The Septuagint with Apocrypha*.
76 Philo, *The Posterity*, 82
77 Philo, *On the Confusion*, 32.

Apion. At the end of the first book Josephus recounts a retelling of the exodus story by the detractor Lysimachus. In this version of the story, the Jewish people who were afflicted with leprosy, scurvy, and other maladies took refuge in Egyptian temples (305). These people were rounded up and murdered, while the rest of the Jewish nation was sent out into the desert to die. Moses had the idea to 'make a straight track until they reached an inhabited country' and 'to overthrow any temples and altars of the gods which they found'.[78] Lysimachus says that they founded a city called Hierosyla (Ἱερόσυλα) because of their sacrilegious propensities.[79] This word Hierosyla is a play on ἱεροσυλέω—to commit sacrilege or rob temples as we saw in Philo. Later, says Lysmachus, the Jews change the name to Hierosolyma (Ἱεροσόλυμα), which is a homonym for ἱεροσύλημα, a 'sacrilegious plunder' (LSJ) and is similar in sound to Ἰερουσαλήμ (Jerusalem). But as Josephus explains, the Jews do not use the same word as the Greeks to express robbery of temples.[80] Thus it seems that the accusation among some Gentile adversaries was that the temple-destroying ancestors of the Jews plundered those temples making them impious. This, of course, Josephus rejects as lies.[81]

In summary, I think it is safe to assume that Paul is relying on a familiar list of vices, both Gentile and Jewish, when he constructs the vice list in Romans 2. While this informs us as to how 'temple robbing' came to be included in Paul's vice list, it does not explain its purpose in the list of rhetorical questions in Romans 2:21–24.

The Purpose of Paul's Rhetorical Questioning

So while we now have a reason for 'temple robbing' in this series of rhetorical questions, we are still left with the perplexing reason why Paul is asking Law-observant Jews whether they steal, commit adultery or rob temples and generally break the Law (2:21–23). Paul must be relying on a recognisable *topos* here for his implied audience not to reject his questions out of hand. It is an argument by comparison where 'the greater ...

---

78   Josephus, *Against Apion*, 309.
79   Josephus, *Against Apion*, 311.
80   Josephus, *Against Apion*, 319.
81   Josephus, *Against Apion*, 319.

inheres in the less'.[82] Jesus uses similar reasoning in the Sermon on the Mount (Matt. 5:21 –22):

> You have heard that it was said to those of ancient times, 'You shall not murder'; and 'whoever murders shall be liable to judgement'. But I say to you that if you are angry with a brother or sister, you will be liable to judgement.

Jesus says something similar in regard to adultery (Matt. 5:27–28):

> You have heard that it was said, 'You shall not commit adultery.' But I say to you that everyone who looks at a woman with lust has already committed adultery with her in his heart.

Paul will go on in Romans to make a similar claim that the inner workings of the heart can be sinful because covetousness is an interior action that breaks the Law (7:7). So breaking the Law, even if it is interior and cannot be seen, is still breaking the Law. I think Paul's rhetorical questions relate to the list of sins that humanity is prone to in 1:22–31. So envy (1:29) is the perquisite for stealing (1 Kgs 21:4); both come from the heart says Jesus (Mark 7:21 –23). Adultery is a type of sexual sin that can also be committed internally as Jesus says (Mark 7:22). Doing these things is still breaking the Law and dishonouring God (2:23). Temple robbing is a type of sacrilege akin to idol worship. And this is where Josephus comes again to our aid. Before making the case for the superiority of the Law over the law of the Gentiles, Josephus explains:

> For it is our traditional custom to observe our own laws and to refrain from criticism of those of aliens. Our legislator has expressly forbidden us to deride or blaspheme the gods recognized by others, out of respect for the very word 'God.'[83]

Therefore, those who overstep the mark and blaspheme the gods recognised by others are breaking the Law not to blaspheme, or in Paul's terms, commit sacrilege like temple robbing.[84] Thus Paul is reflecting Josephus' stance when he says (2:1),

---

82 Hermogenes, *Preliminary Exercises*, 12–14; Aristotle, *Art of Rhetoric*, 1.14.1; Cicero, *Topics*, 23.
83 Josephus, *Against Apion*, 327; cf., Philo, *De Spec. Leg.* 1.53; *De vita Mosis* 2.2053.
84 Jewett, *Romans*, 229.

> you have no excuse, whoever you are, when you judge others; for in passing judgement on another you condemn yourself, because you, the judge, are doing the very same things.

Paul's series of rhetorical questions, therefore, emphasises the sinful habits of the Jewish interlocutor.[85] In this argument, he is repetitively demonstrating that even Jews sin (2:17–24). We know that this is his aim because he concludes in chapter 3 (3:9–10),

> for we have already charged that all, both Jews and Greeks, are under the power of sin, as it is written: "There is no one who is righteous, not even one…"

Conclusion

The use of the interlocutor saves Paul from directly accusing his audience of law-breaking. Indeed, the use of the first person plural 'we' in chapter 3 implies that he expects his audience to join him as a type of character as he expounds how both the Jew and the Gentile (even those who hold to the Torah) are both under the power of sin. In conclusion, the rhetorical question: 'You that abhor idols, do you rob temples?' refers to the act of blasphemy against the Gentile gods, which breaks the command not to blaspheme in the Ten Commandments. Paul's purpose in using these rhetorical questions is to stymie any objection by the Law-observant Jewish interlocutor that he is a sinner like the Gentile, because later Paul is going to make the charge 'for there is no distinction, since all have sinned and fall short of the glory of God' (Romans 3:22–23). And this is a crucial point in Paul's gospel that he hopes to proclaim to Jews, Gentiles, and barbarians in Rome.

---

85 Aristotle suggests a similar strategy (or 'trick') in the courtroom to amplify the accused's guilt: Aristotle, *Art of Rhetoric*, 14.5.

Bibliography

Arena, V. — 'The Orator and His Audience: The Rhetorical Perspective in the Art of Deliberation', in C. Steel and H. van der Blom, *Community and Communication: Oratory and Politics in Republican Rome* (Oxford: Oxford University Press, 2013), 195–209.

Aristotle — *Nicomachean Ethics* (tr. H. Rackham; Loeb Classical Library 73; Cambridge, MA: Harvard University Press, 1926).

Aristotle — *Art of Rhetoric* (tr. J. H. Freese; revised Gisela Striker. Loeb Classical Library 193. Cambridge, MA: Harvard University Press, 2020).

Barrett, A. A. — *A Commentary on the Epistle to the Romans.* London: Adam & Charles Black, 1962.

Barth, Karl. — *The Epistle to the Romans* (tr. E. C. Hoskyns; 6th ed.; London: Oxford University Press, 1933).

Bird, M. F. — *Romans* (The Story of God Bible Commentary; Grand Rapids: Zondervan Academic, 2016).

Bowersock, G. W. — *Greek Sophists in the Roman Empire* (Oxford: Clarendon Press, 1969).

Brenton, L. C. L., ed. — *The Septuagint with Apocrypha: Greek and English* (Peabody: Hendrickson, 2011).

Cicero, M. T. — *On Invention. The Best Kind of Orator. Topics* (tr. H. M. Hubbell; Loeb Classical Library; Cambridge, MA: Harvard University Press, 1949).

Das, A. A. — 'Paul of Tarshish: Isaiah 66.19 and the Spanish Mission of Romans 15.24, 28', *New Testament Studies* 54.1 (2008), 60–73.

Demosthenes — *Orations, Volume III:* [*Oration 24: Against Timocrates*] (tr. J. H. Vince; Loeb Classical Library 299; Cambridge, MA: Harvard University Press, 1935).

Derrett, J. D. M. — '"You Abominate False Gods; but Do You Rob Shrines?" (Rom. 2.22b)', *New Testament Studies* 40.4 (1994), 558–71.

Dickey, E. — 'Me Autem Nomine Appellabat: Avoidance of Cicero's Name in His Dialogues', *The Classical Quarterly* 47.2 (1997), 584–88.

Dochhorn, J.   'Der Vorwurf Des Tempelraubs in Röm 2,22b Und Seine Politischen Hintergründe', *ZNW* 109 (2018), 101–17.

Dozier, C.   'Rhetorical Display and Productive Dissonance in Quintilian's Quotations of Poetry', *Ramus* 51.2 (2022), 241–67.

Dugan, J.   'Cicero's Rhetorical Theory', in C. Steel (ed.), *The Cambridge Companion to Cicero* (Cambridge Companions to Literature; Cambridge, UK: Cambridge University Press, 2013), 25–40.

Easterling, P.   'Actors and Voices: Reading between the Lines in Aeschines and Demosthenes', in S. Goldhill and R. Osborne (eds.), *Performance-Culture and Athenian Democracy* (Cambridge, UK; New York: Cambridge University Press, 1999), 154–66.

Engberg-Pedersen, T.   *Paul and the Stoics* (Louisville: Westminster John Knox Press, 2000).

Fitzmyer, J. A.   *Romans: A New Translation with Introduction and Commentary* (The Anchor Bible; New York: Doubleday, 2007).

Garlington, D. B.   '"Ierosylein" and the Idolatry of Israel (Romans 2.22)', *New Testament Studies* 36 (1990), 142–51.

Gathercole, S. J.   *Where Is Boasting?: Early Jewish Soteriology and Paul's Response in Romans 1–5* (Grand Rapids: Eerdmans, 2002).

Harrison, J. R.   'Paul and the "Agonothetia" at Corinth: Engaging the Civic Values of Antiquity', in J. R. Harrison and L. L. Welborn (eds.), *The First Urban Churches 2: Roman Corinth* (Williston: SBL Press, 2016), 271–326.

Holloway, P. A.   'The Enthymeme as an Element of Style in Paul—Critical Notes (an Application of Ancient Rhetorical Theory to Pauline Epistolary Literature)', *Journal of Biblical Literature* 120.2 (2001), 329–39.

Holloway, P. A.   'The Rhetoric of Romans.' *Review and Expositor* 100.1 (2003), 113–27.

Hölscher, T.   *The Language of Images in Roman Art: Art as a Semantic System in the Roman World* (ed. A. Künzl-Snodgrass, A. M. Snodgrass, and J. Elsner; Cambridge: University Press, 2004).

Jewett, R.   'Romans as an Ambassadorial Letter', *Interpretation* 36.1 (1982), 5–20.

Jewett, R.	*Romans: A Commentary* (Hermeneia; Minneapolis: Fortress Press, 2007).
Johnson, L. A.	'Paul's Letters Reheard: A Performance-Critical Examination of the Preparation, Transportation, and Delivery of Paul's Correspondence', *The Catholic Biblical Quarterly* 79.1 (2017), 60–76.
Josephus, F.	*The Life. Against Apion* (tr. H. St.J. Thackeray; Loeb Classical Library 186; Cambridge, MA: Harvard University Press, 1926).
Judge, E. A.	*Social Distinctives of the Christians in the First Century: Pivotal Essays* (ed. D. M. Scholer; Peabody: Hendrickson Publishers, 2008).
Kennedy, G. A.	*Progymnasmata: Greek Textbooks of Prose Composition and Rhetoric* (Atlanta: Society of Biblical Literature, 2003).
Kennedy, G. A.	*A New History of Classical Rhetoric* (Princeton: Princeton University Press, 1994).
Keyes, C. W.	'The Greek Letter of Introduction', *American Journal of Philology* 56.1 (1935), 28–44.
Kidson, L.	'1 Timothy: An Administrative Letter', *Early Christianity* 5.1 (2014), 97–116.
Kidson, L. M.	*Persuading Shipwrecked Men: Rhetorical Strategies of 1 Timothy 1* (WUNT 526; Tübingen: Mohr Siebeck, 2020).
Krentz, E.	'The Name of God in Disrepute: Romans 2:17–29 [22–23]', *Currents in Theology and Mission* 17.6 (1990), 429–39.
Kruse, C. G.	*Paul's Letter to the Romans* (Pillar; Grand Rapids: Eerdmans, 2012).
Luedemann, G.	*Opposition to Paul in Jewish Christianity* (tr. M. E. Boring; Minneapolis: Fortress Press, 1989).
Magnifico, A. M.	'Writing for Whom? Cognition, Motivation, and a Writer's Audience', *Educational Psychologist* 45.3 (2010), 167–84.
McCormick, S.	'An Ancient Typology: Argument by Comparison', *Rhetorica: A Journal of the History of Rhetoric* 32.2 (2014), 148–64.
Moo, D. J.	*The Epistle to the Romans* (Grand Rapids: Eerdmans, 1996).
Nanos, M. D.	'The Jewish Context of the Gentile Audience Addressed in Paul's Letter to the Romans', *The Catholic Biblical Quarterly* 61.2 (1999), 283–304.

Origen	*Commentary on the Epistle to the Romans, Books 1–5* (tr. T. P. Scheck; The Fathers of the Church; Washington: CUA Press, 2009) .
Philo	*The Posterity and Exile of Cain* (tr. F. H. Colson and G. H. Whitaker; Loeb Classical Library 227; Cambridge, MA: Harvard University Press, 1929).
Philo	*On the Confusion of Tongues* (tr. F. H. Colson and G. H. Whitaker; Loeb Classical Library 261; Cambridge, MA: Harvard University Press, 1932).
Plato	*Republic* (ed. C. J. Emlyn-Jones and W. Preddy; Loeb Classical Library 237; Cambridge, MA: Harvard University Press, 2013).
Plutarch	*Precepts of Statecraft* (ed. H. North Fowler; Loeb Classical Library 321; Cambridge, MA: Harvard University Press, 1936).
Quintilian	*The Orator's Education* (ed. and tr. D. A. Russell; Loeb Classical Library 127; Cambridge, MA: Harvard University Press, 2002).
Robertson, P.	*Paul's Letters and Contemporary Greco-Roman Literature: Theorizing a New Taxonomy* (vol. 167; Boston: Brill, 2016).
Rodriguez, R.	*If You Call Yourself a Jew: Reappraising Paul's Letter to the Romans* (Eugene, OR: Cascade Books, 2015).
Suetonius	*Lives of the Caesars: Julius. Augustus. Tiberius. Gaius. Caligula* (tr. J. C. Rolfe; Loeb Classical Library 31; Cambridge, MA: Harvard University Press, 1914).
Thorsteinsson, R. M.	*Paul's Interloctuor in Romans 2: Function and Identity in the Context of Ancient Epistolography* (Conictanea Biblica: New Testament Series 40; Stockholm: Almquist & Wiksell International, 2012).
Tzounakas, S.	'Persius on His Predecessors: A Re-Examination', *Classical Quarterly* 55.2 (2005), 559–71.
White, J. L.	*Light from Ancient Letters* (Philadelphia: Fortress Press, 1986).
White, L. M.	'Social Authority in the House Church Setting and Ephesians 4:1–16', *Restoration Quarterly* 29.4 (1987), 216–18.

Windsor, L. J.	'The Named Jew and the Name of God the Argument of Romans 2:17–29 in Light of Roman Attitudes to Jewish Teachers', *Novum Testamentum* 63.2 (2021), 229–48.
Wynne, J. P. F.	'Cicero's Tusculan Disputations: A Sceptical Reading', in V. Caston (ed.), *Oxford Studies in Ancient Philosophy* (vol. 58; Oxford: Oxford University Press, 2020), 205–38.

CHAPTER 5

How Revolutionary is Romans 13:1–7? The Influence of the Christ-Event and the Jewish Theological Tradition in Paul's Conception of Governing Authorities

Liam Carlton-Jones

In June 2018, when the Attorney General of the United States Jeff Sessions was seeking justification for the Trump Administration's proposal to separate illegal migrant families at the US/Mexico border, he provoked controversy by pointing to 'the Apostle Paul and his clear and wise command in Romans 13 to obey the laws of the government because God has ordained them for the purpose of order.'[1] It should not be a surprise to hear Romans 13 cited in such a manner at the highest levels of governmental authority. Since the Reformation, Romans 13:1–7 has been the classic text in formulating a Christian understanding of the State and contains perhaps 'the most important words ever written for the history of political thought.'[2] But many wish that this were not so. Mullen presents the Sessions controversy as the latest instalment in a toxic tradition of rulers citing Romans 13 in support of oppressive

---

1   Mullen, 'The Fight'.
2   Allen, *A History*, 132.

policies, with various commentators arguing that no other passage in the Pauline corpus has been wielded in such a devastating manner.[3]

But this text remains in our New Testaments, demanding our continued intellectual and pastoral attention to discern what exactly Paul was saying therein. But this process since the mid-twentieth century has largely focused on presenting Romans 13:1–7 as the manifestation of Paul's *Sitz im Leben*, in what Cassidy has defined collectively as 'situational approaches to the text.'[4] Most of these have been efforts to provide a plausible apologetic against any accusation that Romans 13:1–7 is a dilution of the revolutionary political message of Jesus and grants to governing authorities (ἐξουσίαις ὑπερεχούσαις, 13:1) the licence to consolidate their oppression in the face of a Christianity that is nothing more than an opium for the endurance of worldly suffering.[5] But these approaches fail to see how Romans 13:1–7 stands as a purposeful and tightly constructed theological statement, which not only contributes to the argument of Romans as a whole, but is an application to the political realm of foundational Pauline soteriological and eschatological themes.

The purpose of this essay is to contribute to the academic appreciation for the theology behind Paul's conception of governing authorities in Romans 13:1–7.[6] My thesis is that Romans 13:1–7 includes Paul's presentation of the prescriptive salvation-historical role of governing authorities within God's new creation, which he believed to have been inaugurated within the present age by the Christ-event. More specifically, I argue that Paul understands this role principally to involve governing authorities being appointed by God as God's servants in the manifestation of righteousness and justice primarily through the

---

3   Mullen, 'The Fight'; Hill, 'Romans', 1104; Furnish, *The Moral Teaching*, 117–118; Käsemann, *Commentary on Romans*, 354.
4   Cassidy, 'The Politicization of Paul'.
5   Elliott, *Liberating Paul*, 106.
6   I acknowledge that Paul is not addressing governing authorities specifically in Rom. 13:1–7, but rather Roman Christians concerning their relationship to governing authorities. Nevertheless, he still outlines a specific role for governing authorities therein, which scholars have attempted to understand the impetus behind as a distinct (but not separate) question from the Church and submission. I reject Käsemann's claim that Rom. 13:1–7 'does not in fact say anything about the state as such or about the Roman empire', see Käsemann, *Commentary on Romans*, 354.

prerogative given to them to punish evildoers.[7] In this, Paul situates the role of governing authorities within God's orchestration of God's salvation-historical purposes, as the role is both consistent with traditional Jewish soteriological and eschatological expectations but has also been recontextualised in light of the Christ-event. Thus I intend to use Romans 13:1–7 to highlight the varying degrees to which the Christ-event, as Paul's principal theological hermeneutic, overturns traditional Jewish assumptions in his thinking, a question that has received a renewed emphasis in biblical scholarship.[8]

I argue for this in three parts. First, I outline why 'inaugurated eschatology' is the best framework for understanding how the Christ-event influences Paul's perspective on governing authorities. Second, I briefly note the main themes on the role of governing authorities that are consistent across key texts from the OT and Second Temple Literature. And third, I highlight how Paul's inaugurated eschatological understanding of the Christ-event has recontextualised these traditional Jewish perspectives on the role of governing authorities in his own conceptualisation.

Inaugurated Eschatology

The primary theological implication of the Christ-event that shaped Paul's understanding of the prescriptive role for governing authorities in Romans 13:1–7 is related to 'inaugurated eschatology'. Wright says that Pauline theology is driven by 'the eschatological belief that the crucified Jesus had been raised, and was Israel's Messiah. Only in the light of that belief [...] can appropriate 'application' begin.'[9] And the key text for understanding the Pauline conception of inaugurated eschatology as the crux to his 'eschatology belief' is 1 Corinthians 15:20–28. In this passage, Paul argues that God ordained the resurrection of Christ to be the precursor, or 'first-fruits' (15:20), which guarantees the accomplishment of the eschatological final resurrection. For Paul,

---

7   I maintain that the commendation of the good is not as central a role for governing authorities as the punishment of evildoers in Paul's understanding as far as Rom. 13:1–7 is concerned.
8   Wright, *Paul and His Recent Interpreters*, 300.
9   Wright, *Paul and His Recent Interpreters*, 23.

the final resurrection had thus actually been inaugurated within the present age when Christ was raised from the dead (cf. Rom. 8:29; Col. 1:18).[10] But then in 1 Corinthians 15:21–28, Paul also argues that it was not only the final resurrection that had been inaugurated within the present age, but also soteriological and eschatological pledges related to the Messianic Kingdom and new creation. There are two key facets to Paul's argumentation that demonstrate this. First, Paul uses Adam-Christ typology in 15:21–22 to present Jesus as the one who, following his resurrection, succeeded in launching the transformation that was to mark the cultivation of the new creation.[11] And second, in 1 Corinthians 15:24–27, Paul uses Psalm 8:6 in tandem with Psalm 110:1 to present the idea that God promised to crown 'humanity' ($ἄνθρωπος$) with dominion and glory over all creation (Psalm 8:5–8), through the reign of the Messiah and the subjection of all things under his feet (Psalm 110:1–2).[12] Paul then argues that the resurrected Jesus, the supreme 'Son of Man' (Psalm 8:4), fulfils this promise through his cultivation of God's new creation Kingdom within the present age.[13] Thus, Paul presents the Christ-event as the centrepiece, and point of fulfilment, to God's salvation-historical plan within the present age.

And it is my contention that the prescriptive role Paul gives to governing authorities in Romans 13:1–7 (most likely written after 1 Corinthians) is reflective of this position as applied to politics. The role of governing authorities presented in Romans 13:1–7 both contributes to the revelation that the Christ-event was the inauguration of God's Kingdom within the present age, and also affirms the abiding validity of governing authorities' power and position within this new salvation-historical dispensation.[14] The practical application of Paul's theology to politics (or even discussing these issues as he does) would be unnecessary if the new creation had not been inaugurated within the present age. Romans 13:1–7 is evidence that Paul did not subscribe to an 'escapist eschatology',[15] because he saw the Christ-event not as the

---

10 Witherington, *Conflict and Community*, 303–304; Keener, *1–2 Corinthians*, 126–127.
11 de Boer, *The Defeat of Death*, 111.
12 Hays, *Echoes of Scripture*, 84, 163.
13 Thiselton, *The First Epistle to the Corinthians*, 1235; Keener, *1–2 Corinthians*, 127.
14 Thiselton, *Discovering Romans*, 228–229; Bryan, *Romans*, 390.
15 See Webb, 'Eschatology and Politics'.

end of God's concern with the created order, but its beginning, as God renews all things, including politics, through the reign of the resurrected Jesus.[16] This is reflective of Paul's usage of the 'new creation' motif, with God's promised redemption impacting the entire created order, including governing authorities.[17]

It would have been foreign to the thinking of a first century Jew to suggest that the Messiah's coming would have no discernible impact upon the existing political structures of the world. Much of the Second Temple Literature argues that God's promised eschatological righteousness and justice had not yet been fulfilled because Israel was still awaiting the overturning of idolatrous political order.[18] And so we should expect that Paul, who did believe that this eschatological promise had been inaugurated within the present age through the Christ-event, would have conceptualised the role of governing authorities within this framework, which he did in Romans 13:1–7. But that Paul believed these eschatological promises to have been 'inaugurated' (i.e., set in motion) rather than 'realised' (i.e., reached maturation) means that Romans 13:1–7 remains prescriptive. Thus, we should not interpret Paul's position in Romans 13:1–7 as 'governing authorities behave this way' (descriptive), but rather, 'Christ is risen! Therefore, governing authorities should now behave this way' (prescriptive).[19]

By taking this position, I am situating my interpretation of Romans 13:1–7 within the 'salvation-historical'[20] methodological approach to Pauline theology. That is, I argue that Paul's primary concern across his teaching is to answer the question of 'how then shall we live?' in light of the Christ-event inaugurating a new stage in God's salvation-historical plan for the entire cosmos (Rom. 8:29–30; Eph. 1:4–6; 2 Tim. 1:9; Titus 1:2). The conviction that the Christ-event moved salvation

---

16 Bryan, *Render to Caesar*, 81; Webb, 'Eschatology and Politics', 502; Furnish, *The Moral Teaching of Paul*, 123–124.
17 See Gignilliat, *Paul and Isaiah's Servants*. For more on the 'new creation' motif within the Pauline corpus, see Jackson, *New Creation*, part II.
18 Wright, *Paul and the Faithfulness of God*, 737–764.
19 This, of course, assumes that Roman Christians were familiar with Paul's inaugurated eschatology motif, which I believe to be so since many of his arguments throughout the epistle rely upon it. See Beale, 'The Inaugurated Eschatological Indicative and Imperative', 24–26.
20 I use 'salvation history' as a heuristic to discuss Paul's understanding of the Christ-event and its consequences in relationship to God's salvific dealings with humanity from Eden to Eschaton, as outlined first in the Tanakh and continued on into the NT.

history from promise to proleptic fulfilment necessitates for Paul that the people of God acknowledge the necessary theological implications of this shift, including for governing authorities. But scholars who accept this position disagree over the extent to which the Christ-event revolutionises Paul's theology in contrast to every other hermeneutical framework that preceded it on the salvation-historical timeline. Barclay developed the notion that, for Paul, the incongruous grace of the 'Christ-gift' overrides the Torahic system of worth in establishing the makeup and identity of new Christian communities.[21] From this perspective, the impact the Christ-event had upon Paul's formulation of theological concepts related to justification, merit, and ecclesiastical unity is one that was revolutionary.[22] But we cannot make similar claims for how the Christ-event impacts the role he prescribes for governing authorities in Romans 13:1–7. Instead, in this context its impact was one that was *recontextual* rather than *revolutionary* in comparison to the position outlined in the Tanakh and Second Temple Literature. Apart from the idea that, as we have already seen, the post-Christ-event stage in salvation history did not require the abolishment of government as an institution within the inaugurated new creation, there are three other areas where the Christ-event recontextualises Paul's conception of the role of governing authorities in Romans 13:1–7: (1) the Christ-event places greater accountability upon governing authorities in the exercise of their role now that they operate in obedience to the resurrected Jesus; (2) the Christ-event also established the necessary conditions within which governing authorities are now able to exercise their prescriptive role; and (3) the inauguration of the new creation within the present age recontextualises the overarching salvation-historical purpose for which governing authorities exercise their role as God's servants in the punishment of evildoers.

This is not a rejection of Barclay's position, but rather a call to recognise the nuanced way in which the Christ-event operated in Paul's theology. This is consistent with contemporary Pauline scholarship's recognition that Paul did not see the Christ-event as a 'solution to a problem', but the introduction of a new lens through which to interpret

---

21 Barclay, *Paul and the Gift*, 444, 498–499.
22 Barclay, *Paul and the Gift*, 412–414.

God's actions within salvation history.[23] I now move to examine the parallels that exist between Romans 13:1–7 and the Jewish theological tradition.

Jewish Background

In this section, I examine how Paul founds his conception of the role of governing authorities in Romans 13:1–7 upon the theological assumptions of the Tanakh and Second Temple Literature.[24] In this, I outline the second pillar upon which I argue Paul conceptualised the prescriptive role he gives to governing authorities in Romans 13:1–7. I undertake this with the necessary caveat that there are many 'traditions' within these texts, many of which make up different genres. But as Crabbe convincingly argued in her book on Luke/Acts, themes and perspectives transcend genre.[25]

First, Paul's assertion that governing authorities have been 'appointed' or 'decreed' (τάσσω and διαταγή) by the sovereign power of God (Rom. 13:1–2) is consistent with what is in the OT and Second Temple Literature, to the point where it appears to be an axiom within traditional Jewish theology (1 Sam. 24:6; Prov. 8:15–16; 24:21; Dan. 2:21,37–38; 4:17,25,32; 5:21; Isa. 45:1–7; Jer. 1:10; 27:5–11; Wis. 6:1–4; Sir. 17:4–7; 1 En. 46:5; Arist. 224; 2 Bar. 82:9). This notion is an outgrowth of God's sovereignty over human affairs, including political authority, and the belief that post-Fall humanity would be incapable of autonomously establishing the conditions in which the power and position of governing authorities could arise.[26] Wallace uses Romans 13:1 as a prime example of where the subject (θεοῦ) of the passive verb (τεταγμέναι) highlights the 'ultimate agent' of the action by the use of the preposition ὑπό.[27] Likewise, Gaventa contrasts how Paul presents the appointment of Pharaoh in Romans 9:16–17 compared to others

---

23 Meeks, *The First Urban Christians*, 180.
24 For an overview of how Rom. 13:1–7 reflects Hellenistic political discourse, see Blumenfeld, *The Political Paul*, 391–395. But I maintain that any alleged parallel to the Graeco-Roman tradition does little to explain Paul's use of particular theological language and motifs in Rom. 13:1–7.
25 See Crabbe, *Luke/Acts*, 21–23.
26 O'Donovan, *The Desire of the Nations*, 46–47.
27 Wallace, *Greek Grammar*, 433.

within the Jewish theological tradition in emphasising this point.[28]

Second, the OT not only testifies to God's concern for the proliferation of righteousness and justice[29] across the created order, but also that governing authorities have a role in its accomplishment (1 Kgs 3:9; 2 Kgs 12; 18; 22; 1 Chr. 22:12–13; 29:19; Ps. 72:1–2; Isa. 32:1; Jer. 21:12; 22:3). The history of Israel's reception of the Mosaic Law, which the nation was to uphold as the standard according to which they were to manifest righteousness and justice, is the main evidence of this.[30] The Mosaic Law operated in this manner by commanding governing authorities to promote impartiality (Exod. 23:2–3; Lev. 19:15; 24:22; Deut. 1:17; 16:19), ensure the just distribution of wages (Deut. 24:12–22), denounce unjust judges and statutes (Isa. 10:1–2; Amos 5:7,15), punish those who practised unrighteousness (Exod. 22:23; Lev. 17:4; Num 35:30; Deut. 13:5; 17:6–7,12; 19:11–13; 22:1; 19:15–19; Judg. 20:13; 2 Sam. 4:11; 1 Kgs 2:31), and to support widows, orphans, refugees, and any other societal outcasts who were unable to protect themselves (Deut. 14:29; 16:11; 24:17; Ps. 72:4; Amos 2:4–6). Morgenstern has even noted that the Tanakh presents the capacity of Israel's governing authorities to embody these principles as a requisite for maintaining their God-granted position, even when judging themselves against allegations (cf. Gen. 38:26).[31]

Third, there is an expectation within the Jewish theological tradition that if governing authorities fail to exercise their divine role God will judge and depose them (Ps. 94:20–23; Isa. 3:14–15; 5:21–32; 10:1–2,7–19; 14:4–6; 16:6–7; 41:2–4; 42:14–15; Jer. 8:8–9; Mic. 3:1–4; 4:11–12; Wis. 12:12; Sir. 30:6; Josephus, *J. W.* 5.377). This motif is reflective of an emphasis upon God's sovereignty, including God's prerogative over both the rise and fall of all governing authorities (Prov. 21:1–4; Jer. 27:5–7; Dan. 2:21; 4:13–17,23–25,32; 5:20–21; Wis.

---

28 Gaventa, 'Reading Romans 13', 15–16.
29 The LXX mainly employs δικαιοσύνη when speaking of both righteousness and justice, which Paul likewise does throughout his epistles, and Romans especially (34 times). It is beyond the scope of this essay to untangle the meaning of δικαιοσύνη and its δικα-cognates within the Pauline corpus. But suffice to say that it includes the notion of 'right moral order.' See Becker, *Paul the Apostle*, 209.
30 Ademiluka, 'Romans 13:1–7', 6–7, outlines these issues.
31 Morgenstern, *Conceiving a Nation*, 35–36.

6:3–5; Sir. 10:14; 2 Bar. 82:4–9; 4 Macc. 12:11; Josephus, J. W. 2.140).[32] Although these passages present God as the ultimate cause in the judgement of governing authorities, there are also calls for God's people to act as instrumental causes through remonstrations of prophetic indictment and behavioural defiance directed against unrighteous and unjust governing authorities (Ps. 82:4; Prov. 31:8–9; Isa. 1:17).[33] Likewise, whilst the overthrow of governing authorities occurs in a variety of historical contexts within the Jewish tradition, there are passages that refer to an eschatological moment when God will depose all pertinaciously rebellious governing authorities through a 'Son of Man' figure who reigns victorious over them (Ps. 2; Dan. 7:13–14,23–27; 1 En. 46:1–5).[34] But what of the more positive side to Paul's political theological coin found in Romans 13:1–7?

Four, I argue we can discern this positive attitude by situating Paul's prescriptive role for governing authorities within the broader Jewish eschatological expectation concerning God's establishment of a new creation marked by perfect righteousness and justice (Pss. 2; 9:8; 45:6–7; 72:3,7–8; 96:10; Dan. 7:13–14,23–27; Isa. 2:3–4; 9:6–7; 42:16; 60:21; 61:1; 64:4–5; 65:17–25; Jer. 23:5; Zech. 9:10; Hos. 2:18; Amos 5:24; Hab. 2:14; cf. 1 En. 46:1–5). It is also evident that Paul believed that this expectation had been fulfilled in the Christ-event (1 Cor. 1:30; 2:8–9; 15:25; 2 Cor. 3:17; 5:17; Eph. 2:14).[35] The question then becomes whether the Jewish tradition understood governing authorities to exercise any positive role within this new creation. Was the purpose of governing authorities as instruments in the manifestation of righteousness and justice only typological in anticipation of this eschatological moment, the accomplishment of which would then render such a role obsolete?

---

32 Dunn, *Romans 9–16*, 762; Horrell, 'The Peaceable, Tolerant Community', 88.
33 Ademiluka, 'Romans 13:1–7,' 7.
34 Thiselton, *Discovering Romans*, 230.
35 Paul refers to Jesus as 'Lord' (κύριος) forty-four times in Romans, often in reference to His relationship with God (θεός). This is significant because it identifies Jesus with YHWH of the Tanakh who has ultimate authority over the nations (Ps. 110:1; Isa. 10:5; 45:1; Dan. 4:17,25,32; 5:21). See Cranfield, *The Epistle to the Romans*, 654.

The Prescriptive Role for Governing Authorites

So now we can examine how the Jewish tradition and the Christ-event come together in Paul's thinking on the role of governing authorities in Romans 13:1–7. Consistent with the Jewish theological tradition, Paul understands God's appointment of governing authorities to be towards their accomplishment of a specific prescriptive role within the created order. In Romans 13:4–6 especially, contra Bertschmann,[36] Paul uses strong language to present God granting governing authorities a role with particular salvation-historical significance. In Romans 13:4, Paul refers to governing authorities as a 'servant of God' (θεοῦ γὰρ διάκονος). This not only subverts Plato and Demosthenes's idea that political power exists to serve the interests of the State at large, but the word διάκονος associates the role of governing authorities with those who serve God in soteriological and ecclesiastical contexts in Pauline usage (Rom. 11:13; 12:7; 15:8 16:1; 1 Cor. 3:5; 2 Cor. 3:6; 6:4; 11:23; Eph. 3:7; 6:21; Phil. 1:1; Col. 1:7,23–25; 4:7; 1 Tim. 3:8; 4:6).[37] Paul also describes governing authorities as λειτουργός ('ministers') in Romans 13:6, which is a term within the LXX and NT that refers to those who serve in God's Temple (Num. 4:37,41; 1 Sam. 2:11,18; 3:1; Ezra 7:24; Neh. 10:40; Isa. 61:6; Rom. 15:16; Phil. 2:25; Heb. 1:7; 8:2; 10:11).[38] The purpose of this language is to present the role of governing authorities as having a similar theological legitimisation and significance within God's salvation-historical plan as the Church's, though with differing responsibilities and prerogatives. This contradicts those Roman Christians who were seeking to incorporate the role of governing authorities within the purview of the Church (Rom. 12:19–21), possibly prompted by a rejection of government as an abiding institution within God's new creation.[39]

But Paul would not sympathise with those states who believe that God had uniquely appointed them to be agents in the manifestation of God's Kingdom across the world, whether through liberal interventionism, imperial paternalism, or outright authoritarian conquest.[40] There

---

36 Bertschmann, *Bowing Before Christ*, 170.
37 Jewett, *Romans*, 794.
38 Moo, *The Letter to the Romans*, 820–821.
39 Hultgren, *Paul's Letter to the Romans*, 471.
40 Webb, 'Eschatology and Politics', 506.

is no room in Pauline political theology for Christian Nationalism.[41] Romans 13:1–7 is relevant to all governing authorities, not any one nation. Likewise, Paul limits the role of governing authorities primarily to the punishment of evildoers, with the evangelistic role of manifesting righteousness and justice given to the Church exclusively (Rom. 1:5; 16:26; Matt. 28:19; Mark 16:15–16; Luke 24:47). This attitude is thus an example whereby governing authorities have historically infringed upon the God-ordained role of the Church, even though Paul's concern in Romans 12:19–13:7 is to avoid the Church contravening the role of governing authorities.

In Romans 13:1–7, Paul also presents governing authorities as God's appointed purveyors of God's wrath within the present age through the prerogative bestowed exclusively upon them in the use of violence to punish evildoers, which is their role within God's purpose to manifest God's righteousness and justice across the created order. The rhetorical logic of this position is simple. In Romans 12:19, Paul cautions believers against taking personal vengeance upon evildoers (μὴ ἑαυτοὺς ἐκδικοῦντες, ἀγαπητοί), urging them instead (ἀλλά) to allow God, to whom judgment ultimately belongs, to bring this vengeance himself (δότε τόπον τῇ ὀργῇ, γέγραπται γάρ· ἐμοὶ ἐκδίκησις, ἐγὼ ἀνταποδώσω, λέγει κύριος). Then in Romans 13:3–4 Paul argues that God has ordained governing authorities as 'God's servants' (θεοῦ γὰρ διάκονος) to function as 'avengers' (ἐστιν ἔκδικος) in meting out this wrath against evildoers (εἰς ὀργὴν τῷ τὸ κακὸν πράσσοντι).[42] This position stands between Bertschmann's 'maximalist'/'minimalist' dichotomy, whereby I reject that Paul is talking about the 'good' (Rom. 13:4) of salvation on the 'maximalist' reading, but that he is also speaking beyond the 'good' of political stability, contra the 'minimalist' interpretation.[43]

Thus, Paul's denunciation of personal vengeance in 12:19–21 is not a rejection of retribution against wrongdoers per se. Instead, Paul focuses upon presenting governing authorities in 13:1–7 as the only institution to whom God gave this prerogative within the present

---

41 It is no surprise that in Wolfe's recent horrifically authoritarian and bigoted defence of Christian Nationalism, he makes 'little effort to exegete the biblical text', see Wolfe, *The Case for Christian Nationalism*, 16.
42 Keck, *Romans*; Jewett, *Romans*, 795–796.
43 Bertschmann, *Bowing Before Christ*, 146–147.

age.⁴⁴ And in line with the Jewish theological tradition, the exercise of this prescriptive role is the mechanism by which governing authorities manifest God's righteousness and justice in fulfilment of God's new creation promises that Paul believed to have been inaugurated within the present age by the Christ-event. That they achieve this primarily through the enactment of violent retributive justice is controversial. But Romans 13:1–7 is unequivocal that the punishment of evildoers is the very purpose for which God ordained governing authorities, with such a role reflecting the character of divine justice by making retribution not some pale approximation or alien dimension to God's character as in much contemporary thinking (Rom. 13:4).⁴⁵ That capital punishment is the means by which Paul recognises governing authorities to apportion God's wrath upon evildoers is evidenced by the reference in Rom. 13:4 to them 'wielding the sword' (τὴν μάχαιραν φορεῖ). The NT and secular Greek literature use this phrase to signify one who has authority over life and death (Rom. 8:35; Acts 12:2; 16:27; Heb. 11:34,37; Philostratus, Ap. 7.16–20; Cassius Dio, Rom. Hist. 42:47).⁴⁶ It may also encompass the entire range of means to punish wrongdoers, even if this is not capital punishment in every instance, with contemporary Greek papyri referring to Roman law officers as 'sword-bearers.'⁴⁷ Given that the entire phrase emphasises that governing authorities do not wield this sword 'in vain' (οὐ γὰρ εἰκῇ τὴν μάχαιραν φορεῖ), it is likely that Paul's purpose is to signal to Roman Christians that the presence of governing authorities as God's servants in punishing evildoers is not an empty threat or promise, but a reality to fear (Rom. 13:4).⁴⁸ Some have argued that Paul's use of μάχαιρα is ironic given the spurious boasts of Roman propaganda that Nero forwent the sword as an example of his magnanimity.⁴⁹ But this is unlikely given that Paul presents this aphoristic phrase as evidence for his argument in Romans 13:4–6. My thesis

---

44 This is not the same as Josephus' claim that God had given the Roman Empire its supremacy so that they could bring God's wrath to bear upon Israel for their covenant unfaithfulness in the destruction of the Temple (Josephus, J. W. 1.10; 4.233; 5.19, 367–368, 378, 408–412, 442–445; 6.109–110, 251). See Pinter, 'Josephus and Romans 13:1–14', 145.
45 Johnson, *Reading Romans*, 200; Vandrunen, 'Power to the People', 8.
46 Bertschmann, *Bowing Before Christ*, 127.
47 Kruse, *Paul's Letter to the Romans*, 496–497; Moo, *The Epistle to the Romans*, 818–819; Jewett, *Romans*, 795.
48 Byrne, *Romans*, 388.
49 Elliott, *The Arrogance*, 154–156; Kruse, *Paul's Letter to the Romans*, 491.

that Romans 13:1–7 is prescriptive concerning the role of governing authorities makes this purported incongruity specious and the recommended solution redundant, given its 'descriptive' assumptions.

Paul thus limits the scope of governing authorities' role to, in Vandrunen's terminology, the enactment of primary (retributive) justice (bringing about the judicial consequences of evildoing), rather than positive justice (encouraging ethical behaviour).[50] That Paul gives governing authorities the more reactive of these roles aimed at establishing God's righteousness and justice is likely because he understands God to have tasked the Church with the more proactive (cf. Rom. 12).[51] This is important to note as I am not suggesting that the manifestation of God's righteousness and justice is inherently or exclusively retributive, only that Romans 13:1–7 presents the role of governing authorities within this manifestation as reflecting that component specifically. Nevertheless, in the words of Tertullian, Romans 13:1–7 presents governing authorities as the 'assistants bestowed upon righteousness, as it were handmaids of the divine court of justice, which even here pronounces sentence beforehand upon the guilty.'[52] And the punishment of evildoers is an appropriate means of establishing righteousness and justice in the world given that Paul understands it to be an extension of God's wrath (Rom. 13:4), with the term ὀργή used in the Tanakh to express God's desire to rid God's creation of anything that perpetuates unrighteousness and injustice (Exod. 4:14; 15:7; 32:1–12; Num. 11:1; Isa. 51:7; Jer. 6:11; 21:3–7; 25:25; Hos. 13:11; Zeph. 1:15).[53] But it is possible that Paul is not intending to present the entire role of governing authorities in Romans 13:1–7, with his immediate context dictating that he only outlines their legitimate role in punishing evildoers to prevent the Church at Rome from taking that prerogative upon themselves.[54] Neither is it necessary to read Romans 13:1–7 as Paul suggesting that governing authorities exercise this role perfectly at all times throughout history. We ought instead to read the passage as a statement

---

50 Vandrunen, 'Power to the People', 4.
51 Cole, 'Towards a Christian Ontology', 310–311.
52 Tertullian, *Antidote* 4.1.
53 Matera, *Romans*, 48; Longenecker, *The Epistle to the Romans*, 201–202; Moo, *The Letter to the Romans*, 111–112; Johnson, *Reading Romans*, 33.
54 Cobb and Lull, *Romans*, 169.

concerning the prescriptive role God appointed governing authorities to exercise, the recognition of which informs the proper relationship between them and the Christian Churches.

This perspective on the prescriptive role of governing authorities is consistent with the Jewish theological tradition, but how it reflects Paul's Christ-event and inaugurated eschatology hermeneutic is more nuanced. I argue that it is best summarised by saying that the Christ-event did not alter the *esse* of governing authorities, but rather has transformed their capacity to exercise their *bene esse* as God's servants in the manifestation of righteousness and justice through the punishment of evildoers.[55] That is, Paul's understanding of God's providential role in politics consists of more than God appointing governing authorities to exercise a particular salvation-historical role (*esse*), but that through God's coronation of Jesus as the Messianic Lord of God's inaugurated new creation (cf. 1 Cor. 15:20–28) God has likewise enabled governing authorities to exercise their power and position in fulfilment of that salvation-historical role (*bene esse*). This is consistent with the Pauline notion that part of Christ's redemptive work was to re-establish humanity's rightful place as overseers in the moral stewardship of creation (1 Cor. 15:20–27; cf. Ps. 8:4–6), of which the proper exercise of political power by governing authorities is part. It is also reflective of the Jewish belief that the only possibility for righteousness and justice to flourish in a nation was the appointment of a supreme Messianic Lord over its governing authorities, which Paul believes took place through the Christ-event.[56] O'Donovan relays this position succinctly when he argues that the Christ-event restores the integrity and efficacy of humanity's original God-ordained role within the created order, which has had its essential teleology vindicated and its corrupted qualities redeemed by the present-age inauguration of the new creation.[57] In the context of Romans 13:1–7, we can say that, for Paul, the Christ-event vindicates the abiding legitimacy of governing authorities within God's salvation-historical purposes, while also enabling them properly to exercise their prescriptive role within this framework. Haddad's argument

---

55   Cole, 'Towards a Christian Ontology,' 322.
56   Morgenstern, *Conceiving a Nation*, 184.0
57   O'Donovan, *Resurrection*, 76, 106, 112.

that Romans 13:1–7 is not concerned with discussing the implications of the resurrected Christ's reign per se is accurate enough given the literary context concerning God's delegation of His authority in the punishment of wrongdoers.[58] But my argument is not that Paul is concerned with the per se implications of Christ's reign, but rather with how the outworking of God's eschatological plan of redemption in the present age, accomplished in and through this resurrected reign, acts as the lens through which Paul partly conceptualises the role of governing authorities in Romans 13:1–7.

This idea is present within the Tanakh and Second Temple Literature but is clearer in light of the Christ-event as the inauguration of God's new creation promises within the present age. I am not suggesting that such a reality guarantees that governing authorities will exercise their *bene esse* properly. For submission to the Lordship of Christ (Ps. 2:12) is a necessary prerequisite for them to live in light of the Christ-event's transformative power and righteous and just example, with failure to do so leading to the annihilation that Paul outlines in 1 Corinthians 15:24–26.[59] Thus, in answering Bertschmann's confusion over how Paul believed it possible for governing authorities to exercise their prescriptive role, I argue that he did not believe that they could, outside of their commitment to the salvation-historical vision of the Lordship of Jesus Christ presented throughout the epistle that recontextualises their role and purpose.[60] None of this is Paul's primary purpose to expound in Romans 13:1–7. But what such exegetically potential extrapolations do is help us to appreciate the theological concepts that underpin the passage's formulation, which is necessary if Romans 13:1–7 is to become part of constructing a coherent Pauline political theology.

---

58   Haddad, *Paul, Politics, and New Creation*, 18.
59   This reflects a tension within the Roman Christian community who may have believed that the Roman Empire had a God-ordained role but also anticipated its destruction. See Oakes, 'Christian Attitudes'.
60   Bertschmann, *Bowing Before Christ*, 161–162.

Bibliography

Ademiluka, S. O. — 'Romans 13:1–7 in Relation to Nigerian Christians' Attitudes Towards Social Activism', *In die Skriflig* 53, no. 1 (2019), 1–11.

Allen, J. W. — *A History of Political Thought in the Sixteenth Century* (London: Methuen, 1960).

Barclay, John M. G. — *Paul and the Gift* (Grand Rapids: Eerdmans, 2015).

Beale, G. K. — 'The Inaugurated Eschatological Indicative and Imperative in Relation to Christian Living and Preaching', *MJT* 10, no. 1 (2011), 12–31.

Becker, J. C. — *Paul the Apostle: The Triumph of God in Life and Thought* (Philadelphia: Fortress Press, 1980).

Bertschmann, D. H. — *Bowing Before Christ – Nodding to the State?: Reading Paul Politically with Oliver O'Donovan and John Howard Yoder* (London: Bloomsbury, 2014).

Blumenfeld, B. — *The Political Paul: Democracy and Kingship in Paul's Thought* (London: T&T Clark, 2004).

Bryan, C. — *Render to Caesar: Jesus, the Early Church, and the Roman Superpower* (Oxford: Oxford University Press, 2005).

Byrne, B. — *Romans* (Collegeville: The Liturgical Press, 1996).

Cassidy, R. — 'The Politicization of Paul: Romans 13:1–7 in Recent Discussion', *ET* 121, no. 8 (2010), 383–389.

Cobb, J. B. and Lull, D. J. — *Romans* (St. Louis: Chalice, 2005).

Cole, J. — 'Towards a Christian Ontology of Political Authority: The Relationship Between Created Order and Providence in Oliver O'Donovan's Theology of Political Authority', *SCE* 32, no. 3 (2019), 307–325.

Cranfield, C. E. B. — *The Epistle to the Romans: Volume Two* (Edinburgh: T&T Clark, 1979).

De Boer, M. C. — *The Defeat of Death: Apocalyptic Eschatology in 1 Corinthians 15 and Romans 5* (Sheffield: Sheffield Academic, 1988).

Dunn, J. D. G. — *Romans 9–16* (Dallas: Word Books, 1988).

Elliott, N. — *Liberating Paul: The Justice of God and the Politics of the Apostle* (Sheffield: Sheffield Academic Press, 1995).

Elliott, N.	*The Arrogance of Nations: Reading Romans in the Shadow of Empire* (Minneapolis: Fortress Press, 2008)
Furnish, V. P.	*The Moral Teaching of Paul: Selected Issues* (Nashville: Abingdon, 1986).
Gaventa, B. R.	'Reading Romans 13 with Simone Weil: Toward a More Generous Hermeneutic', *JBL* 136, no. 1 (2017), 3–22.
Gignilliat, M. S.	*Paul and Isaiah's Servants: Paul's Theological Reading of Isaiah 40–66 in 2 Corinthians 5:14–6:10* (London: T&T Clark, 2007).
Haddad, N. T.	Paul, *Politics, and New Creation: Reconsidering Paul and Empire* (Lanham: Lexington Books, 2021).
Hays, R. B.	*Echoes of Scripture in the Letters of Paul* (London: Yale University Press, 1989).
Hill, C. C.	'Romans', in J. Barton and J. Muddiman (eds.), *The Oxford Bible Commentary* (Oxford: Oxford University Press, 2001), 1083–1108.
Horrell, D. G.	'The Peaceable, Tolerant Community and the Legitimate Role of the State: Ethics and Ethical Dilemmas in Romans 12:1–15:13', *Review and Expositor* 100 (2003), 81–99.
Jackson, T. R.	*New Creation in Paul's Letters: A Study of the Historical and Social Setting of a Pauline Concept* (Tübingen: Mohr Siebeck, 2010).
Jewett, R.	*Romans: A Commentary* (Minneapolis: Fortress, 2007).
Johnson, L. T.	*Reading Romans: A Literary and Theological Commentary* (Macon: Smyth & Helwys Publishing, 2001).
Käsemann, E.	*Commentary on Romans* (tr. G. W. Bromiley; Grand Rapids: Eerdmans, 1980).
Keck, L. E.	*Romans* (Nashville: Abingdon, 2005).
Keener, C. S.	*1–2 Corinthians* (New York: Cambridge University Press, 2005).
Kruse, C. G.	*Paul's Letter to the Romans* (Grand Rapids: Eerdmans, 2012).
Longenecker, R. N.	*The Epistle to the Romans: A Commentary on the Greek Text* (Grand Rapids: Eerdmans, 2016).
Matera, F. J.	*Romans* (Grand Rapids: Baker Academics, 2010).

Meeks, W. A.   *The First Urban Christians: The Social World of the Apostle Paul* (New Haven: Yale University Press, 1983).

Moo, D. J.   *The Letter to the Romans* (2nd ed.; Grand Rapids: Eerdmans, 2018).

Morgenstern, M.   *Conceiving a Nation: The Development of Political Discourse in the Hebrew Bible* (University Park: Pennsylvania State University Press, 2009).

Mullen, L.   'The Fight to Define Romans 13: Jeff Sessions Used It to Justify His Policy of Family Separation, but He's Not the First to Invoke the Biblical Passage', *The Atlantic* 2018. <https://www.theatlantic.com/ideas/archive/2018/06/romans-13/562916/>

Oakes, P.   'Christian Attitudes to Rome at the Time of Paul's Letter', *R&E* 100 (2003), 103–111.

O'Donovan, O.   *Resurrection and Moral Order: An Outline for Evangelical Ethics* (Grand Rapids: Eerdmans, 1986).

O'Donovan, O.   *The Desire of the Nations: Rediscovering the Roots of Political Theology* (Cambridge: Cambridge University Press, 1996).

Pinter, D.   'Josephus and Romans 13:1–14: Providence and Imperial Power,' in B. C. Blackwell, J. K. Goodrich and J. Maston (eds.), *Reading Romans in Context: Paul and Second Temple Judaism* (Grand Rapids: Zondervan, 2015), 143–150.

Tertullian   *Antidote for the Scorpion's Sting* (tr. S. Thelwall, Wheaton College, 1998) <https://ccel.org/ccel/tertullian/scorpiace/anf03.v.x.xiv.html>

Thiselton, A. C.   *The First Epistle to the Corinthians: A Commentary on the Greek Text* (Grand Rapids: Eerdmans, 2000).

Thiselton, A. C.   *Discovering Romans: Content, Interpretation, Reception* (Grand Rapids: Eerdmans, 2016).

Vandrunen, D.   'Power to the People: Revisiting Civil Resistance in Romans 13:1–7 in Light of the Noahic Covenant', *JLR* 31, no. 1 (2016), 4–18.

Wallace, D. B.   *Greek Grammar: Beyond the Basics* (Grand Rapids: Zondervan, 1996).

Webb, S. H.   'Eschatology and Politics', in J. L. Walls (ed.), *The Oxford Handbook of Eschatology* (Oxford: Oxford University Press, 2007), 500–518.

Witherington, B.	*Conflict and Community in Corinth: A Socio-Rhetorical Commentary on 1 and 2 Corinthians* (Grand Rapids: Eerdmans, 1995).
Wolfe, S.	*The Case for Christian Nationalism* (Moscow, ID: Canon Press, 2022).
Wright, N. T.	*Paul and the Faithfulness of God* (London: SPCK, 2013).
Wright, N. T.	*Paul and His Recent Interpreters: Some Contemporary Debates* (London: SPCK, 2015).

CHAPTER 6

Paul: Temple Builder
DongWoo Oh

Introduction

In his epistles, Paul identifies Jesus of Nazareth with several appellations. Among them, the most frequently used is *the Christ, the Messiah*. There have, historically, been two dominant opinions on the manner in which this designation can be interpreted. Firstly, it has been argued that it functions as a surname of Jesus, without having any further significance. Secondly, recent studies have proposed this term as a translation of the Hebrew Messiah (מָשִׁיחַ), the Anointed one, expressing Jesus as the promised Messiah. In this view, the designation is an honorific title with a Davidic royal connotation. This is a better understanding of the Christ. Frequent references to Jesus' messianic identity in Pauline letters show its significance in Paul's thought and theology.

Considering the importance of Paul's Christology, one wonders whether it also accounts for the reason Paul went out to preach the gospel among the Gentiles. Matthew Novenson has proposed that Paul's messianic understanding drove Paul to conduct his apostolic ministry. Novenson emphasises the military aspect of the messianic task which resulted in the obedience of faith from the Gentile believers (cf. Rom. 1:5; 15:18, etc). Paul preached the gospel to elicit this obedience to Jesus the Messiah. While emphasising the military aspect, however, Novenson seems to ignore the cultic facet. In relating his life and ministry, Paul uses cultic metaphors on several occasions. For example, he compares his life to a sacrifice in Phil. 2:17: 'even if I am being poured out as a libation over the sacrifice and the offering of your faith, I am glad'. Paul also likens himself to a priest in describing his apostolic work in Romans 15:16 (cf. 1 Cor. 9:13–14). There is a Jewish messianic hope which can explain Paul's appeal to cultic images to describe his apostolic ministry. According to this understanding, God's temple would be (re)built with the coming of the Messiah, the Christ. Given the distinct cultic language in Paul's writing, this biblical idea of the Messiah has not received sufficient attention, even among those who advocate Paul's messianic Christology. The connection between the Messiah and God's temple is clearly used in his writing and deserves closer scrutiny. Paul expresses his apostolic ambition in Romans 15:20 - 'Thus I make it my ambition to proclaim the good news (φιλοτιμούμενον εὐαγγελίζεσθαι), not where Christ has already been named'. The rationale for Paul's apostolic ministry can also be gained from this verse. The strength of this view is that one can derive the rationale of Paul's apostolic ministry from the place where he expresses his apostolic ambition. Paul understood his apostolic ministry as a temple-building project which was initiated with the coming of Jesus Christ, the Messiah.

The Messiah and the Temple

A tangible Jewish expectation of the Messiah is that his arrival would be accompanied by the (re)building of God's temple. Several aspects of this messianic hope are not unambiguous: how would God build this temple? What role would the Messiah play?[1] Nevertheless, one thing remained certain: God's new temple would appear with the coming of the Messiah. N. T. Wright has highlighted the close relationship between God's Messiah and the temple. In reviewing Matthew Novenson's book, *The Grammar of Messianism: An Ancient Jewish Political Idiom and Its Users*,[2] Wright notes: 'The question "what are you

---

1 Bryan, *Jesus and Israel's Traditions*, 193–99.
2 Novenson, *The Grammar of Messianism*.

saying about the Temple?" is the other side of the coin of "are you the Messiah?"[3] The result of this dialogue between Novenson and Wright is to confirm the importance of the temple in relation to the promised Messiah.[4] Historical incidents demonstrate this point. King Herod's obsession to build the Second Temple can also be explained by this connection between God's Messiah and his temple. Since he could not claim to be a descendant of David, one way of claiming the legitimacy of his monarchy was to build the temple.[5] A similar point can be made concerning Simon Bar Kokhba who led a revolt against the Roman Empire. Bar Kokhba, like King Herod, could not claim David's lineage. Yet, he was regarded as the Messiah because of his military conquest.[6] The inscription of the temple on the coins during the revolt reflects the popular messianic hope that the Messiah would build God's temple.[7]

This messianic hope for God's temple has a strong biblical attestation. In 2 Samuel 7:12–13, the Lord promised King David that his son would build the temple for the name of the Lord: 'I will raise up your offspring after you [...]. He shall build a house for my name.' This verse sets the unambiguous expectation that a Davidic descendant would build God's temple. This is also the way the text is understood in 4Q 174.[8] A similar understanding appears in Zech. 6: 12–13, where the LORD promises Zechariah that the man, identified as 'the Branch' would 'build the temple of the Lord'. In this context, the Branch is presented as a royal figure: 'he shall bear royal honour and shall sit upon his throne and rule' (Zech 6:13). These verses present a royal messianic figure who would build God's temple as the interpretation in *Targum Jonathan* demonstrates: 'Behold the man whose name is Anointed will be revealed, and he shall be raised up, and shall build the temple of the Lord' (*Tg.* Zech. 6:12). In addition to these scriptural witnesses, other literature during Second Temple Judaism attest to the promise of rebuilding the temple with the coming of the Messiah (Sir. 50.1–2,5–6; T. Dan. 5.10–12; 1 En. 53.6; 90.29; Pss. Sol. 17.21–23; Sib. Or. 5.414–27,432–33).[9]

---

3   Wright, 'Messianic Grammar?', 298.
4   Novenson, 'On the Grammar', 303–06.
5   See Horbury, 'Herod's Temple', 115–128. See also Novenson, *The Grammar of Messianism*, 77–82.
6   Novenson, *The Grammar of Messianism*, 91–96.
7   See Johnson, 'The Messianic Temple Builder', 202–203.
8   Juel, *Messiah and Temple*, 172–79; see also Johnson, 'The Messianic Temple Builder,' 208–13.
9   See Perrin, *Jesus the Temple*, 169–71.

The Messiah and the Temple in the NT

It is not surprising then to find this correlation between the Messiah and God's temple in the NT in which Jesus is understood as the Messiah. The recent work of Joshua Jipp on the messianic Christology in the NT is helpful in this regard. In his writing, Jipp argues that Jesus' messianic identity is the central theme of New Testament Theology.[10] Jipp demonstrates how God's temple is projected in relation to Jesus' identity as the Messiah in the Gospels. For example, in responding to Jesus' question about who he is at Caesarea Philippi, Peter reveals Jesus' messianic identity: 'You are the Messiah, the Son of the living God' (Matt. 16:16). As a response, Jesus announces his intention to build his church. This building of the church reflects the messianic expectation to build God's temple.[11] When it comes to the Gospel of Mark, the messianic task of building God's temple stands behind Jesus' trial. In Mark 14:58, Jesus is accused of (after destroying the existing one) building another temple, not made with hands (ἀχειροποίητος). Different opinions exist concerning what this new temple refers to.[12] Yet, it seems certain that building this new temple has ssomething to do with Jesus' identity as the Messiah. It explains why Jesus' claim to build the new temple is followed by the high priest's question about Jesus' messianic identity in Mark 14:61.[13] The messianic expectation to build God's temple can also account for the temple Christology in the Fourth Gospel: 'Destroy this temple, and in three days I will raise it up' (John 2:19).[14]

Jipp provides insightful discussions on how the messianic task of building God's temple is referred to in the Gospels. Yet, there is a lack of such discussion in relation to the Pauline epistles. Its absence is interesting, since, in addition to New Testament Theology, Jipp wrote a separate monograph on the topic to demonstrate that 'Paul used, reworked, and applied ancient conception of the good king—both Greco-Roman and Jewish—to Christ in order to structure reality [...]

---

10 Jipp, *The Messianic Theology*.
11 Jipp, *The Messianic Theology*, 55–56; Barber, 'Jesus as the Davidic Temple Builder'. See also Rucker, *Temple Keys*, 144–57.
12 For Christian community see Juel, *Messiah and Temple*, 56–57, 208; for the heavenly sanctuary see Botner, 'A Sanctuary'.
13 Jipp, *The Messianic Theology*, 75–76.
14 For the temple Christology in the Fourth Gospel, see Coloe, *God Dwells*; Kerr, *The Temple*; Hoskins, *Jesus as the Fulfillment*; Behr, *John the Theologian*, 137–93.

of his congregation.'[15] Even in this elaborated volume, however, messianic temple building does not receive any meaningful attention. It does not mean that Jipp is unaware of this correlation between the temple and the Messiah. Instead, Jipp attributes this lack of discussion to the nature of his book as 'more illustrative than comprehensive'.[16] In addition to the illustrative nature of his book, Jipp's purpose may also explain why the temple has not received a distinct treatment in exploring Paul's messianic Christology. As noted in the above quotation, Jipp intends to explore the concept of kingship in Paul's work, based not only on Jewish Scripture but also Graeco-Roman kingship discourse.[17] Yet, from a Jewish perspective based on the OT, the idea of the messianic temple building is a concept too important to be set aside. This present study attempts to show that the messianic hope to rebuild the temple was an important concept for Paul as he appropriated it to demonstrate the purpose and rationale for his apostolic ministry for the Gentiles.

The Messiah and the Temple in Paul's Epistles

Even though many commentaries do not recognise it, one can see that Paul exhibits the relationship between the Messiah and God's temple in Romans 15:20: 'It has always been my ambition to preach the gospel where Christ was not known, so that I would not be building on someone else's foundation'. Paul describes the future location of his apostolic ministry as the place where Christ is not named (οὐχ ὅπου ὠνομάσθη Χριστός). This unusual phrase deserves careful attention in the context. In Romans 15:14–20, Paul explains his purpose in writing to the Romans and how he understood his apostolic ministry. Paul states that, even though the believers in Rome are 'filled with all knowledge and able to instruct each other' (Rom. 15:14), Paul writes (or dictates) this letter since, because of divine grace, he is 'a minister of Christ Jesus to the Gentiles' (Rom. 15:16). This correlation between divine grace and

---

15 Jipp, *Christ Is King*, 9.
16 Jipp, *Christ Is King*, 275, writes: 'Given that my study has been more illustrative than comprehensive, further studies might examine with profit Paul's use of priestly metaphors (Rom. 12:1–2; 15:14–25) and his depiction of the church as sacred temple (1 Cor. 3:16; 6:19; 2 Cor. 6:14–7:1; Eph. 2:19–22) in light of the notion of the king as priestly figure and temple builder'.
17 See Jipp, *Christ Is King*, 9–10.

Paul's apostleship echoes the beginning of the letter: 'we have received grace and apostleship to bring about the obedience of faith among all the Gentiles for the sake of his name' (Rom. 1:5). And, importantly, Paul expresses the purpose of his ministry as follows in Romans 15:16: 'so that (ἵνα) the offering of the Gentiles may be acceptable, sanctified by the Holy Spirit'.[18] Here the conjunction of ἵνα functions as a 'marker to denote purpose, aim or goal'.[19] Paul relates further that he accomplished such apostolic purpose during his past ministry in the Eastern Mediterranean in Romans 15:19: 'In Christ Jesus, then, I have reason to boast of my work for God. [...] from Jerusalem and as far around as Illyricum I have fully proclaimed the good news of Christ'. But what did it look like when the gospel is fully proclaimed? Paul seems to give an answer by stating the goal of his apostolic ministry again in Romans 15:20. Paul aspired (φιλοτιμούμενον) to preach the gospel where Christ is not named.

What does the phrase *where Christ has not been named* (οὐχ ὅπου ὠνομάσθη Χριστός) mean? One way to interpret the phrase in question is to regard it as an expression of knowing Christ. This view has several significant proponents. The NIV's rendering (both 1984 and 2011) is representative of this view: 'It has always been my ambition to preach the gospel *where Christ was not known*'. When it comes to lexicons, both BAGD and BDAG support this view.[20] A recent advocate among the commentaries is that of Robert Jewett: 'The use of the word "name" in these contexts refers to making someone known for the first time, which is Paul's particular calling as an apostle of Christ'.[21] Many commentators, however, find it insufficient to interpret the word 'name' in terms of knowing Christ. Instead, they propose that the name of Christ in the verse contains cultic connotations. C. E. B. Cranfield writes, 'It is probably better, with Sanday and Headlam, Michel, Leenhardt, Murray, Käsemann, and others, to take the passive of ὀνομάζειν to be used here with some such solemn sense as "be named in worship" or

---

18 Many interpreters understand the genitive structure of 'the offering of the Gentiles' (ἡ προσφορὰ τῶν ἐθνῶν) as an objective (epexegetic) genitive. It means that the Gentile believers are equated with the offering. Reading it as a subjective genitive, David J. Downs proposes that this refers to the collection made by the Gentiles believers for the saints in Jerusalem in Rom. 15:25–32. See Downs, 'The Offering'. For different opinions on the issue see Moo, *The Letter to the Romans*, 906.
19 'ἵνα,' *BDAG*, 475.
20 'ὀνομάζω', *BDAG*, 574, states: 'not where Christ is already known'. 'ὀνομάζω', *BDAG*, 714.
21 Jewett, *Romans*, 915.

"be acknowledged and confessed" or "be proclaimed (as Lord)", than to understand it as signifying merely "be known".[22]

Many commentaries have correctly pointed out that the word 'name' in Romans 15:20 should be understood beyond the scope of epistemology. Yet, none of them specifically points out its temple background. The context supports this reading. For example, in describing his apostolic ministry in Romans 15:16 ('to be a minister of Christ Jesus to the Gentiles in the priestly service of the gospel of God, so that the offering of the Gentiles may be acceptable'), Paul chooses metaphorical expressions which show 'the analogy between Paul's gospel mission and cultic worship'.[23] Further, the building imagery, which follows the name phrase in question ('so that I do not build on someone else's foundation'), makes it more likely that Paul was mindful of the temple. The building metaphor is also used to express the believers' temple identity in 1 Cor. 3:10–17 and in other parts in the NT (Matt. 16:18; Acts 4:10–12; Eph. 2:18–22; 1 Pet. 2:5; Rev. 3:12). Hence, Mark Seifrid writes on Romans 15:20: 'as elsewhere in Paul's letters, the language of building suggests "temple" imagery'.[24] Both what comes before and what follows makes it possible to read Paul's description of the location of his future ministry in Romans 15:20, *where Christ has not been named*, as a reference to the temple in the NT.

Based on its temple background in the context, I propose a reading which has not been raised before. Paul appropriates one important characteristic of the temple when he uses the verb (ὀνομάζω) to describes the place of his apostolic ministry in Romans 15:20. It refers to the temple's connection with the name of the Lord. In the OT, the temple is known as the dwelling place of the name of the Lord. In Deuteronomy, this idea is reflected in the injunction to offer sacrifices to the Lord only in the place that bears the name of the Lord. (Deut. 12:5,11,21,26; 14:23–24; 16:2,6,11). King Solomon, who was responsible for building the temple, was also aware of this correlation between the temple and

---

22 Cranfield, *A Critical and Exegetical Commentary*, 764. In addition to it, see also Fitzmyer, *Romans*, 715, and Dunn, *Romans 9–16*, 865.
23 Hogeterp, *Paul and God's Temple*, 287. Paul's understanding of his apostolic ministry against the cultic background is not limited to 1 Cor. 15:16. See Gal. 1:15; 1 Cor. 9:13–14; Phil. 2:17. For a further discussion, refer Donaldson, *Paul and the Gentiles*, 255.
24 Seifrid, 'Romans', 691.

the name of the Lord as he repeatedly noted in his letter to Hiram, King of Tyre (1 Kgs 5:3–5, etc). Solomon's understanding reflects the Lord's promise to David by the prophet Nathan in 2 Samuel 7:13: 'He [David's descendant] shall build a house for my name.' The same verb, which is used in Romans 15:20, is employed to express the temple's connection with the name of the Lord in 1 Esd. 4:63: 'to go up and build Jerusalem and the temple that is called by his name' (ἀναβῆναι καὶ οἰκοδομῆσαι Ιερουσαλημ καὶ τὸ ἱερόν οὗ ὠνομάσθη τὸ ὄνομα αὐτοῦ ἐπ' αὐτῷ).

It is then possible to understand the verb 'to name' (ὀνομάζω) in connection with the most used expression for the OT temple: *called by the name of the Lord*. [25] In his 'sermon' at the temple, Jeremiah also consistently described the temple as the place called by the name of the Lord (Jer. 7:10,11,14). The same phrase is used by Greek translators to render two Hebrew expressions for the chosen place of worship (לְשַׁכֵּן שְׁמוֹ שָׁם and לָשׂוּם אֶת־שְׁמוֹ שָׁם) in Deuteronomy 12. The Israelites are to worship at the place where the Lord would choose for his name to be called. (ὃν ἂν ἐκλέξηται κύριος ὁ θεὸς ὑμῶν ἐπικληθῆναι τὸ ὄνομα αὐτοῦ ἐκεῖ; Deut. 12:5,11,21,26).[26] All of these examples point to the temple's connection with the name of the Lord in the OT, and this relationship is alluded to, when Paul identifies his future mission field as the place where Christ is not named.

It is possible to postulate why Paul appeals to the temple's connection with the name of the Lord. Several recent studies have shown that the name of the Lord at the temple in the OT is a theological way of expressing the immanent presence of the transcendent Lord. The name of the Lord at the temple 'asserts YHWH's practical presence in the temple to reassure the people, yet equivocate about its nature to avoid divine limitation'.[27] Further, the divine name functions as a means for the Israelites to receive access to this presence of the Lord: 'Invoking God's name at God's shrine was a powerful prelude to a direct existential encounter with God'.[28] This name theology serves as a theological resource to express the active presence of the transcendent Christ in Paul's apostolic ministry

---

25 See Talshir, *1 Esdras*, 243.
26 This Greek expression is a common rendering of two different Hebrew phrases (לְשַׁכֵּן שְׁמוֹ שָׁם and לָשׂוּם אֶת־שְׁמוֹ שָׁם) for the temple in Deuteronomy 12.
27 Hundley, 'To Be or Not to Be', 555.
28 Cook, 'God's Real Absence', 145.

in Romans 15:20. Christ sits at the right hand of God in heaven (cf. Rom. 8:34) which means that Christ is absent from the earthly domain. Nevertheless, Paul claims that Christ was active in his apostolic ministry through the Spirit, as he notes in Romans 15:18–19: 'What Christ has accomplished through me to win obedience from the Gentiles.'[29] By utilising the temple theology in the OT in Romans 15:20, Paul demonstrates that the immanent presence of the transcendent Lord at the temple in the OT is one way of construing the presence of the exalted Christ which is available to the Gentiles through his apostolic ministry.

Christology and Paul's Apostolic Ministry for the Gentiles

There is one more factor to consider when discerning why Paul appropriates the temple's connection with the name of the Lord to describe his apostolic ministry. In Paul's journey to become a preacher of the gospel among the Gentiles, his experience on the road to Damascus was a turning point (cf. Acts 9:1–8; Gal. 1:13–17; Phil. 3:5–6). What came out of this experience is Paul's realisation of the identity of Jesus as the Messiah: 'it must have been an experience in which he [i.e. Paul] became convinced that the crucified Jesus was even so and after all the "Messiah" and "Son of God"'.[30] Jesus' messiahship likely shaped Paul's gospel message: 'the proclamation of Jesus the Messiah of Israel was a fundamental part of his [i.e., Paul's] announcement of the good news'.[31] It is not surprising then to observe a close connection between Paul's Christology and his apostolic ministry. It is especially the case in Romans. At the beginning of the letter, Paul states his messianic Christology in Romans 1:3–4.[32] It is followed by Paul's receiving his apostleship in Romans 1:5: 'we have received grace and apostleship'.[33]

Because of this close correlation, it is possible to derive a rationale

---

29 See Orr, *Christ Absent*, 165–68; Tilling, *Paul's Divine Christology*, 164–65.
30 Donaldson, *Paul and the Gentiles*, 250. See also Kim, *The Origin*, 100: 'The gospel that he received on the Damascus road Paul defines, first of all, Christologically'.
31 Collins and Collins, *King and Messiah as Son of God*, 122.
32 See Whitsett, 'Son of God'.
33 It is better to take 'we' in Rom. 1:5 as epistolary, referring to Paul himself. See Barret, *The Epistle to the Romans*, 22. For a different opinion which takes 'we' as a reference to other apostles, see Jewett, *Romans*, 109.

for Paul's apostolic ministry from his Christology. One such attempt is made by Novenson. According to Novenson, Paul understood his apostolic ministry in line with the OT expectation that the Gentiles render obedience to a Jewish king. Novenson makes his case against a popular scholarly view on the topic. According to this view, the Gentiles were expected to come to Jerusalem to worship the Lord.[34] There are several OT passages which express such an expectation (e.g., Isa. 2:2–3/Mic. 4:1–2, Isa. 56:6–7, Zech. 8:22–23). Nevertheless, as Novenson argues, Paul does not appropriate this OT eschatological expectation in his epistles: 'Paul, apostle to the Gentiles and a virtuosic interpreter of the prophets, cites precisely none of these texts. None at all. Not so much as an allusion or an echo'.[35] Instead, Paul cites Isaiah 11:10 in Romans 15:12, which shows 'the subjection of the pagan nations to the root of Jesse'.[36] Based on its thematic resemblance in the LXX (Ps. 17:44–45 and Isa. 11:13–14), Novenson further argues that this messianic expectation stands behind the obedience of the Gentiles in Romans 1:5: 'The Gentiles are to be neither converted nor destroyed; rather they share in the blessedness of the age to come by virtue of their obedience to the Davidic king of Israel'.[37] This messianic understanding shows how Paul regarded his apostolic ministry among the Gentiles: 'Paul believed that God had enlisted him to recruit pagan subjects for his Jewish king'.[38]

While Novenson proposes a valid reading, there is a better reading which reflects the importance of the temple in relation to the Messiah. When it comes to Romans 1:5, there is one important piece of information that Novenson does not focus on. The Gentiles' obedience is associated with the *name* of Jesus Christ: 'we have received grace and

---

34 See Fredriksen, *Paul: The Pagans' Apostle*, 164–65.
35 Novenson, *Paul, Then and Now*, 146. A similar point can be made concerning a popular reading of Rom. 15:16. According to this reading, Paul makes the reverse of the eschatological hope of Isa. 66:20 in Rom. 15:16 since Paul, a Jew, brings the Gentiles as an acceptable offering while the Gentiles bring the dispersed Jews to Jerusalem in Isa. 66:20. For this view, see, among others, Aus, 'Paul's Travel Plans', 236–37. Many commentaries support this reading. As a recent example see Moo, *The Letter to the Romans*, 906. Yet, it is questionable whether there is an echo of the Isaiah text in Rom. 15:16. More importantly, the Isaiah text is not appropriated in Paul's epistles. Donaldson, *Paul and the Gentiles*, 363n38, writes: 'while understanding the attractiveness of Isa. 66:18–21 for Pauline interpreters [...], the complete absence of any citation or allusion by Paul himself cautions us against any substantial reliance on it'.
36 Novenson, 'The Jewish Messiahs', 369.
37 Novenson, 'The Jewish Messiahs', 373.
38 Novenson, 'The Jewish Messiahs', 372.

apostleship to bring about the obedience of faith among all the Gentiles *for the sake of his name*'. According to Douglas Moo, '[T]he ultimate focus of Paul's apostleship is expressed with the phrase "for the sake of his name"'.[39] The name of Christ in Romans 1:5 likely has a cultic connotation. It is possible that, as it is the case with 'where Christ has not been named' in Romans 15:20, 'the name' in Romans 1:5 can be understood as a reference to the temple's connection with the name of the Lord. As noted above, Paul's receiving apostleship in Romans 1:5 is associated with Jesus' messiahship in Romans 1:3–4. And many scholars read Romans 1:3–4 in connection with 2 Samuel 7:12–14.[40] In 2 Samuel 7:12, the Lord promises to give David a descendant who would succeed him on the throne. According to 2 Samuel 7:13, a task of this Davidic descendant is to build the temple for the name of the Lord. In Romans 1:3–4, Jesus' identity as a Davidic descendant is proclaimed. Based on this, Paul went out to do his mission work for the sake of the name of Christ ὑπὲρ τοῦ ὀνόματος αὐτοῦ. Because of its link with the OT, it is not unlikely to read the usage of the name in Romans 1:5 in line with the divine promise that a Davidic descendant would build a temple for the name of the Lord in 2 Samuel 7:13. The point is that the military aspect of the Messiah, as argued by Novenson, does not provide the best background to interpret the obedience of the Gentiles in Romans 1:5. When it is associated with the *name* of Christ the Gentiles' obedience for the name of Christ has a cultic connotation.[41]

Novenson is correct, however, to emphasise the role of Pauline Christology to understand the rationale behind Paul's apostolic ministry to the Gentiles. The contention of this paper is that the messianic hope of (re)building the temple plays an important role for Paul's apostolic ministry among the Gentiles. Paul understood that he labours in building God's temple with the coming of Jesus Christ. That is the reason why he describes the location of his future apostolic ministry by utilising a phrase for the relationship between the temple and the name of the Lord in Romans 15:20. And the identity of Jesus as *Christ*

---

39 Moo, *The Letter to the Romans*, 51.
40 For a bibliography information see Johnson, 'Jesus as Divine Son', 470n14. See also Whitsett, 'Son of God', 675–76.
41 In this aspect, it is interesting to note that the expected obedience of the Gentile believers is expressed against the cultic background in Rom. 12:1: 'I appeal to you therefore [...] to present your bodies as a living sacrifice, holy and acceptable to God, which is your spiritual worship'.

is the driving force. Hence, instead of *the Lord* as it was the case in the temple in the OT, it is the name of *Christ* which Paul uses to explain his apostolic ministry among the Gentiles: 'Thus I make it my ambition to proclaim the good news, *not where Christ has already been named* (οὐχ ὅπου ὠνομάσθη Χριστός)'. Further, Paul makes it clear that the main builder of this temple building project is Christ: 'For I will not venture to speak of anything except what Christ has accomplished through me to win obedience from the Gentiles' (Rom. 15:18).[42]

Paul expresses his apostolic ministry with building imageries in 1 Corinthians 3:10 as well: 'According to the grace of God given to me, like a skilled master builder I laid a foundation'. Paul understood himself in such a way since the Corinthian congregation is regarded as the temple (1 Cor. 3:16; 6:19 [individual members]; 2 Cor. 6:16). This building metaphor is used in reference to the temple in Jerusalem.[43] And the purpose of this metaphorical usage of the temple is unambiguous in the context. Paul seeks for unity among the congregation. Building God's temple in Corinth should not be understood in a parochial manner. As Paul states in 1 Corinthians 1:2, the Corinthian congregation had spiritual unity 'with all those who in every place call on the name of our Lord Jesus Christ'. The phrase 'in every place' is derived from Malachi 1:11. In Malachi, it is a criticism against the priests in Jerusalem for their abuses of the temple sacrifices (see Mal. 1:6–10). The background of this criticism is the Deuteronomic understanding of the place of sacrifice as the dwelling place of the name of the Lord.[44] In addition to Jerusalem, Malachi predicts that every place would become the dwelling place of the name of the Lord in the future.[45] By echoing

---

42 In understanding the work of Christ in Paul's ministry, the role of the Holy Spirit is also evident as the rest of Rom. 15:19 states.
43 See Basham, 'Paul, the Temple, and Building a Metaphor', 49–50. From a biblical theology perspective, the change of the metaphors from agriculture to building in 1 Cor. 3 can be explained when Solomon's temple is in view. See Beale, *The Temple*, 245–50.
44 See Ciampa and Rosner, *The First Letter to the Corinthians*, 57–58.
45 In describing the new cultic centre in every place, Malachi employs the idea that the temple in Jerusalem is the chosen dwelling place of the name of the Lord. The fact that every place is expected to be the dwelling place of the name of the Lord implies depreciation of the importance of the temple in Jerusalem. It dovetails with Paul's intention of using metaphors in 1 Corinthians. Basham, 'Paul, the Temple, and Building a Metaphor', 63, writes: 'Paul's temple metaphors in light of the ritual realities for uncircumcised Corinthians work in both directions as creating new cultic access for them whilst pronouncing judgement on the cult in Jerusalem for them. In his use of the temple metaphor, Paul has created something new—a new understanding and self-understanding of the Corinthian community as a legitimate dwelling place of God by using the image of the Jerusalem temple'.

this prophecy in Malachi 1:11, 'Paul depicts the Corinthians as part of the end-time temple, one in which God's name will be great among the nations and in every place incense will be offered'.[46]

This promise in Malachi 1:11 is important for Paul. In fact, it can be seen as a rationale for Paul's work among the Gentiles. Paul is the only NT writer who uses this phrase 'in every place' from Malachi (cf. 1 Cor. 1:2; 2 Cor. 2:4; 1 Thess. 1:8; 1 Tim. 2:8). It shows that through his ministry, Paul hoped that, as the Israelites called on the name of the Lord at one chosen dwelling place of the name of the Lord, the Gentile believers would call on the name of Jesus Christ in every place. Paul makes it clear that the driving force of his ministry is the identity of Jesus. It is the name of Christ which is to be called. Romans 15:20 shows that Paul was still working based on God's prophecy in Malachi 1:11 when he was planning for his next mission project. Paul understood himself as participating in building the dwelling place of the name of Christ.

Conclusion

In Romans 15:20, Paul expressed his apostolic ambition not to labour in places where Christ had already been named. With it, Paul reflects the messianic expectation that God's temple would be built with the coming of the Messiah. It is important to recognise that the phrase *Christ has been named* echoes the understanding of the OT temple as the dwelling place of the name of the Lord. The name of Christ replaces the name of the Lord in the verse. This shows the importance of Paul's messianic Christology for his apostolic ministry. The correlation between the Messiah and the temple can further account for the rationale behind Paul's apostolic ministry. As Romans 15:20 shows, Paul aspired to labour in the places where Christ has not been named. Paul's effort should be understood against the background of the prophecy in Malachi 1:11 that, instead of one place in Jerusalem, it is promised that every place would be the place of sacrifice. Paul's apostolic ministry among the Gentiles is a temple building project to make every place the dwelling place of the name of Christ.

---

46 See Ciampa and Rosner, *The First Letter to the Corinthians*, 153.

Bibliography

Aus, R. D.   'Paul's Travel Plans to Spain and the 'Full Number of the Gentiles' of Rom. XI 25.' *Novum Testamentum* 21 (1979), 232–62.

Barber, M. P.   'Jesus as the Davidic Temple Builder and Peter's Priestly Role', *Journal of Biblical Literature* 132 (2013), 935–953.

Basham, D. A.   'Paul, the Temple, and Building a Metaphor' (PhD diss., McGill University, 2022).

Barret, C. K.   *The Epistle to the Romans* (2nd ed.; London: A&C Black, 1991).

Behr, J.   *John the Theologian and his Paschal Gospel: A Prologue to Theology* (Oxford: Oxford University Press, 2019).

Botner, M.   'A Sanctuary in the Heavens and the Ascension of the Son of Man: Reassessing the Logic of Jesus' Trial in Mark 14.53–65', *Journal for the New Testament Studies* 41 (2019), 1–25.

Bryan, S. M.   *Jesus and Israel's Traditions of Judgement and Restoration* (SNTSMS 117; New York, Cambridge University Press, 2002).

Ciampa, R. E. and Rosner, B. S.   *The First Letter to the Corinthians* (Pillar New Testament Commentary; Grand Rapids: Eerdmans, 2010).

Collins, A. Y. and Collins, J. J.   *King and Messiah as Son of God: Divine, Human, and Angelic Messianic Figures in Biblical and Related Literature* (Grand Rapids: Eerdmans, 2008).

Coloe, M.   *God Dwells with Us: Temple Symbolism in the Fourth Gospel* (Collegeville, Minn: Liturgical Press, 2001).

Cook, S. L.   'God's Real Absence and Real Presence in Deuteronomy and Deuteronomism', in N. MacDonald and I. J. de Hulster (eds.), *Divine Presence and Absence in Exilic and Post-Exilic Judaism* (Tübingen: Mohr Siebeck, 2013).

Cranfield, C. E. B.   *A Critical and Exegetical Commentary on the Epistle to the Romans* (International Critical Commentary; Edinburgh: T&T Clark, 1975–1979).

Donaldson, T. L.   *Paul and the Gentiles: Remapping the Apostle's Convictional World* (Minneapolis: Fortress, 2006).

Dunn, J. D. G.	*Romans 9–16* (WBC 38B; Dallas: Word Book, 1998).
Fitzmyer, J. A.	*Romans: A New Translation with Introduction and Commentary* (AB 33; New Haven: Yale University Press, 2008).
Fredriksen, P.	*Paul: The Pagans' Apostle* (New Haven: Yale University Press, 2017).
Hogeterp, A. L. A.	*Paul and God's Temple: A Historical Interpretation of Cultic Imagery in the Corinthian Correspondence* (Biblical Tools and Studies 2; Leuven: Peeters, 2006).
Hoskins, P.	*Jesus as the Fulfillment of the Temple in the Gospel of John* (Milton Keynes: Paternoster, 2006.)
Horbury, W.	*Messianism Among Jews and Christians: Biblical and Historical Studies* (2nd ed.; London: Bloomsbury, 2016).
Hundley, M.	'To Be or Not to Be: A Reexamination of Name Language in Deuteronomy and the Deuteronomistic History', *Vetus Testamentum* 59 (2009), 533–55.
Jewett, R.	*Romans* (Hermeneia; Minneapolis: Fortress, 2007).
Jipp, J. W.	*Christ Is King: Paul's Royal Ideology* (Minneapolis, MN: Fortress, 2015).
Jipp, J. W.	*The Messianic Theology of the New Testament* (Grand Rapids: Eerdmans, 2020).
Johnson, N. C.	'The Messianic Temple Builder in the Dead Sea Scrolls, Midrash Rabbah, and Targum Jonathan', *Judaïsme ancien – Ancient Judaism* 8 (2020), 199–232.
Juel, D.	*Messiah and Temple: The Trial of Jesus in the Gospel of Mark* (SBLDS 31; Missoula, MT: Scholars Press, 1977).
Kerr, A. R.	*The Temple of Jesus' Body: The Temple Theme in the Gospel of John* (JSNTSup 220; Sheffield: Sheffield Academic Press, 2002).
Kim, S.	*The Origin of Paul's Gospel* (Wissenschaftliche Untersuchungen zum Neuen Testament 2, Reihe 4; Tübingen: Mohr Siebeck, 1981).
Moo, D. J.	*The Letter to the Romans* (2nd ed.; New International Commentary on the New Testament; Grand Rapids: Eerdmans, 2018).
Novenson, M. V.	'The Jewish Messiahs, the Pauline Christ, and the Gentile Question', *Journal of Biblical Literature* 120 (2009), 357–373.

Novenson, M. V.	*The Grammar of Messianism: An Ancient Jewish Political Idiom and Its Users* (New York: Oxford University Press, 2017).
Novenson, M. V.	'On the Grammar of Messianism, in Dialogue with N.T. Wright', *The Expository Times* 129 (2018), 303–306.
Novenson, M. V.	*Paul, Then and Now* (Grand Rapids: Eerdmans, 2022).
Orr, P.	*Christ Absent and Present: A Study in Pauline Christology* (Wissenschaftliche Untersuchungen zum Neuen Testament 2, Reihe 354; Tübingen: Mohr Siebeck, 2014).
Perrin, N.	*Jesus the Temple* (London: SPCK, 2010).
Rucker, T. M.	*Temple Keys of Isaiah 22:22, Revelation 3:7, and Matthew 16:19: The Isaianic Temple Background and Its Spatial Significance for the Mission of Early Christ Followers* (Wissenschaftliche Untersuchungen zum Neuen Testament 2, Reihe 559; Tübingen: Mohr Siebeck, 2021).
Seifrid, M. A.	'Romans', in D. A. Carson and G. K. Beale (eds.), *Commentary on the New Testament Use of the Old Testament* (Grand Rapids: Baker, 2007), 607–94.
Talshir, Z.	*1 Esdras: A Text Critical Commentary* (Atlanta: SBL, 2001).
Tilling, C.	*Paul's Divine Christology* (Grand Rapids: Eerdmans, 2012).
Whitsett, C. G.	'Son of God, Seed of David: Paul's Messianic Exegesis in Romans 2[sic]:3–4', *Journal of Biblical Literature* 119 (2000), 661–681.
Wright, N.T.	'Messianic Grammar? A Response to Matthew V. Novenson, *The Grammar of Messianism: An Ancient Jewish Political Idiom and Its Users*', *The Expository Times* 129 (2018), 295–302.

CHAPTER 7

'In The Same Mind and the Same Purpose': 1 Corinthians, Unity, and the Graeco-Roman Political Tradition

David I. Starling

'The history of Pauline interpretation,' Ernst Käsemann famously asserted in 1971, 'is the history of the apostle's ecclesiastical domestication.'[1] If there is any truth in that assertion (and I suspect that it contains at least a grain of truth) then one obvious place where we might expect to find it is in the history of interpretation of Paul's first letter to the Corinthians.

As early as the mid-90s AD (if we assume the correctness of the majority opinion regarding the date of 1 Clement), Paul's first letter to the Corinthians was being appealed to as support for a call to the church in Corinth to put down a rebellion of the congregation against certain of their presbyters, repent of their seditiousness, and return to a more peaceable, orderly and reputable pattern of conduct:

> 1. Take up the epistle of that blessed apostle, Paul. 2. What did he write to you at first, at the beginning of his proclamation of the gospel? 3. To be sure, he sent you a letter in the Spirit

---

1   Käsemann, *Perspectives*, 46–47.

> concerning himself and Cephas and Apollos, since you were even then engaged in partisanship. 4. But that partisanship involved you in a relatively minor sin, for you were partisan towards reputable apostles and a man approved by them. 5. But now consider who has corrupted you and diminished the respect you had because of your esteemed love of others. 6. It is shameful, loved ones, exceedingly shameful and unworthy of your conduct in Christ, that the most secure and ancient church of the Corinthians is reported to have created a faction against its presbyters, at the instigation of one or two persons. 7. And this report has reached not only us but even those who stand opposed to us, so that blasphemies have been uttered against the Lord's name because of your foolishness; and you are exposing yourselves to danger.[2]

The letter that we call 1 Corinthians was, according to Clement,[3] a letter that Paul wrote 'concerning himself and Cephas and Apollos', created as a response to the 'partisanship' (πρόσκλισις) of the Corinthian church. It functioned for Clement as a source of apostolic support for his rebuke of the 'shameful and unworthy' conduct of those who had formed a 'faction against [the] presbyters' and had in so doing given ammunition to 'those who stand opposed to us' and utter 'blasphemies ... against the Lord's name' (presumably because of the way in which the Corinthian factionalism offended against the value that the Graeco-Roman elite placed on harmonious and orderly political conduct).

The authors of the Muratorian Canon (traditionally dated to the late second century), similarly epitomised 1 Corinthians as a letter 'admonishing against schism of heresy' (*schisma haeresis interdicens*), and subsequent patristic interpretation and use of the letter frequently followed the same path: 1 Corinthians was to be read as medicine against factionalism, written by the Apostle to rebuke the divisions that had arisen within the Corinthian church and call the readers back to a path of harmony, concord and good order.

---

2   1 Clement 47:1–7 (trans. Ehrman [LCL]).
3   Strictly speaking, the letter is anonymous, and is introduced in the opening greeting as from 'the church of God that temporarily resides in Rome', but its authorship has traditionally been attributed to Clement.

Interpreters in the modern period have not always been so convinced. Writing in the mid-twentieth century, for example, Walter Bauer commented on the way in which 1 Corinthians was read and used by Clement, marvelling at how 'peculiar and in need of an explanation' it was that 'this extensive and multifaceted epistle [was] supposed to have had only this purpose'.[4] For most of the twentieth century the majority of the letter's scholarly interpreters concurred with this judgment. Some commentators, pointing to the wide diversity of themes discussed within the letter, the abrupt transitions from one theme to the next, and the infrequency with which matters of factionalism are explicitly addressed outside of chapters 1–4, proposed partition theories of various kinds, dividing the canonical letter into as many as four originally separate letters or letter fragments.[5] Others, while remaining convinced of the letter's integrity, stressed the variegated nature of its contents, in keeping with the multiplicity of issues raised within the letter and oral reports to which Paul is responding.[6]

But the Clementine reading of 1 Corinthians was not that easily laid to rest. In the last decade of the twentieth century, it found a powerful champion in Margaret Mitchell, whose groundbreaking work *Paul and the Rhetoric of Reconciliation* made a vigorously argued case for its rehabilitation. Mitchell's reading of the letter was by no means an attempt to reassert the normativity of patristic interpretation over modern, critical readings. While it is true that the introductory chapter of her book included a warm commendation of the earliest Christian interpreters of 1 Corinthians as 'readers far closer to the text, the language and the social situation of Paul than we',[7] the primary frame within which she interpreted the letter was not the patristic interpretive tradition but the wider political culture and rhetorical conventions of the Graeco-Roman world. The language of the letter, she argued, is 'throughout filled with terms and *topoi* which were of general commerce

---

4 Bauer, *Orthodoxy and Heresy*, 220, quoted in Mitchell, *Paul and the Rhetoric of Reconciliation*, 19.
5 E.g. Weiss, *Der erste Korintherbrief*, xl–xliii; Héring, *The First Epistle*, xii–xiv.
6 E.g. Robertson and Plummer, *A Critical and Exegetical Commentary*, xxxiv–xlvi; Barrett, *A Commentary*, 17–22; Conzelmann, *1 Corinthians*, 6–7; Orr and Walther, *1 Corinthians*, 121–22; Fee, *The First Epistle*, 6–8, 11–13.
7 Mitchell, *Paul and the Rhetoric of Reconciliation*, 19; cf. 298.

in the Imperial period for urging divided groups to become reunified.'[8] Its form, she likewise sought to demonstrate, is consistently in keeping with the conventions of Graeco-Roman deliberative rhetoric. Hence, she concluded, 1 Corinthians should be read as 'a single letter of unitary composition which contains a deliberative argument persuading the Christian community at Corinth to become reunified.'[9] From start to finish, according to her reading, the letter hangs together as 'an argument for ecclesial unity, as centered in the πρόθεσις, or thesis statement of the argument, in 1:10'.[10]

Mitchell's work was a monumentally important contribution to the interpretation of 1 Corinthians, and numerous scholars across the subsequent decades have accepted her conclusions as foundational for their interpretation of the letter.[11] Readings of 1 Corinthians that have been influenced by this tradition of interpretation tend to characterise the politics of the letter as conventional, conservative, and conciliatory, appealing to traditional Graeco-Roman political values to urge the readers to reconcile with one another and restore the internal harmony of the congregation.

In this chapter I subject Mitchell's influential thesis to critical examination, posing two main questions: (i) whether Mitchell's claim that 1:10 functions as the as the πρόθεσις for the rest of the letter is borne out by the content and emphases of the chapters that follow; and (ii) whether her reading of 1 Corinthians 1–4 gives sufficient weight to the particularity of the 'mind' and 'purpose' in which Paul hopes to see the Corinthians united and the potentially contentious nature of his appeal. On both scores, I argue that there is a need for significant revisions to Mitchell's thesis, with greater emphasis placed on the content and distinctiveness of the mind Paul urges the Corinthians to adopt.

---

8   Mitchell, *Paul and the Rhetoric of Reconciliation*, 296.
9   Mitchell, *Paul and the Rhetoric of Reconciliation*, 1.
10 Mitchell, *Paul and the Rhetoric of Reconciliation*, 1.
11 Recent examples include Barton, 'Paul on Oneness', Oropeza, *1 Corinthians*, 9, and Brookins, *Reading 1 Corinthians*, 5–8.

1 Corinthians 1:10 and the Unity of 1 Corinthians

Because of the limitations of time and space I will address only very briefly the first of these two issues—that is, the question of whether Paul's appeal for unity in 1:10 should be read as the thesis statement for the entire letter, with all of the various topics that follow functioning within the rhetoric of the letter as arguments in support of that appeal.[12] The brevity with which I intend to deal with this first issue should not be taken as a sign of its relative unimportance but as a reflection of the fact that the main arguments for and against Mitchell's claim are already readily available within the existing scholarly literature.

In partial support for Mitchell's reading, it should be acknowledged at the outset of the discussion that issues of division, disunity, and disorder are undoubtedly a recurring concern within the letter, not only in chapters 1–4 but also in subsequent passages such as 11:17–34 and chapters 12–14. Even in chapter 15, where Paul climactically restates for the Corinthians the gospel traditions that he passed on to them 'as of first importance' (15:3), his reminder includes not only the content of the gospel he preached but also the fact that he preached it in solidarity with Cephas (v.5), the Twelve (v.5), James (v.7) and 'all the apostles' (v.7): 'Whether then it was I or they, so we proclaim and so you have come to believe', he concludes in verse 11.[13] In chapter 16, as the letter draws toward its conclusion, the name of Apollos (which has not appeared since it was last mentioned in 4:6) resurfaces in a brief assurance that Paul offers to the church that he is as eager as they are to see Apollos revisit them, and the commendation of Stephanas, Fortunatus and Achaicus in 16:15–18 includes a mention of the way in which they have 'devoted themselves' (ἔταξαν ἑαυτούς) to the service of the saints and a call for the Corinthians to 'put yourselves at the service (καὶ ὑμεῖς ὑποτάσσησθε) of such people, and of everyone who works and toils with them' (16:16).

Nevertheless, as a number of commentators have pointed out, it would be unreasonable to expect that a letter as long as 1 Corinthians, addressing a situation as complex as the one Paul is faced with in

---

12 E.g. Mitchell, *Paul and the Rhetoric of Reconciliation*, 16; Witherington, *Conflict and Community*, 69, 94. Cf. the criticisms of this approach in Thiselton, *The First Epistle*, 33–34; Ciampa and Rosner, *The First Letter*, 19–21.
13 All scriptural quotations within this chapter are from the NRSV.

Corinth, should be expected to have the kind of tight unity of theme and neatness of structure that one might look for in a textbook piece of deliberative rhetoric.[14] Given the ubiquity with which students of rhetoric within the Graeco-Roman tradition were taught to think of their exercises of persuasive speechwriting as falling into one of the three traditional rhetorical species—i.e., forensic, epideictic and deliberative rhetoric—there is an undoubted heuristic value in appealing to those three categories as options for describing the intended function of a letter, or a portion of a letter, intended for oral delivery within the context of a gathered assembly of believers. But the further the rhetorical situation addressed within a letter diverges from kind of situations laid out as the prototypical contexts addressed, respectively, by a forensic, epideictic or deliberative oration, the less useful those categories become. And the rhetorical situation addressed by 1 Corinthians is quite demonstrably not one in which the gathered assembly of believers will be convening to make a decision about a single, particular course of action that has been proposed by one party and contested by another. Nor are the various issues that Paul does wish the Corinthians to deal with within the letter all reducible to the common denominator of matters on which they are problematically divided and need to come to a common mind for the sake of harmony and good order.

The attempt to read the entire letter through the lens of 1:10 as a rhetorical *propositio* thus requires us to force quite a number of its sections out of shape to make them fit. The call for an urgent exercise of church discipline that Paul issues in chapter 5, for example, certainly includes a depiction of the church as a single 'batch of dough' (5:6), but the function of that image in the context of Paul's appeal is not to speak about the divisive consequences that the man's actions might give rise to but to highlight the contagiousness of unrepentant sin when it is tolerated within the community.[15] The section that follows, in which Paul responds to reports regarding the lawsuits that members of the congregation have initiated, is focused at least as much on the injustice that the lawsuits have perpetrated as on the disunity between fellow believers that they have created. The response in chapters 8–10 to the

---

14 Cf. the comments in Collins, 'Reflections', 39–61.
15 *Contra* Mitchell, *Paul and the Rhetoric of Reconciliation*, 112.

Corinthians' questions about food sacrificed to idols is framed not as an adjudication or mediation between two warring factions but as a warning to the 'knowledgeable' members of the congregation about the dangers of arrogance and complacency (both to themselves and to their weaker brothers and sisters). And even in chapter 12, where the unity and solidarity of the congregation are undeniably evoked by the image of the church as the body of Christ, Paul's use of the metaphor transcends and at several points sharply subverts its conventional function as a reinforcement of the harmonious ordering of a hierarchical political community. Unlike the standard traditional appeals to the notion of a political community as a single, united body, Paul's use of the body metaphor in chapter 12 is framed as a vigorous appeal for the special honour that ought to be given to the body's weakest and most vulnerable members, berating the 'eye' and the 'head' for the condescending and elitist manner in which they have been relating to the lower-status 'hand' and 'feet' (v.21).

All things considered, the range of issues Paul addresses and the various ways in which he frames his responses suggest that his concern is at least as much for the ethical distinctiveness of the Corinthian community and the maintenance of its boundaries with the surrounding culture as it is for the preservation of the community's internal unity and concord.[16] Attempting to tie the entire letter together as a single deliberative argument for unity and concord simply does not do justice to the diversity of its contents and themes.[17]

But acknowledging the inadequacy of approaches that attempt to read everything through the lens of the call to unity in 1:10 does not require us to give up altogether on the idea that there might be some form of underlying coherence that ties the letter together or a pastoral/rhetorical logic that informs the sequence and arrangement of its parts. At the very least, it is worth noting the implied pastoral/rhetorical strategy at work in the structuring decision Paul makes to address (most of) the reports that he has received before he turns to the questions and

---

16 Cf. the comments in Ciampa and Rosner, *The First Letter*, 21–25, and Thielman, *Theology of the New Testament*, 291–99, and the analysis in Schnabel, *Der erste Brief*, 33–34.
17 Even Oropeza, who is broadly in agreement with Mitchell's reading of the letter, acknowledges that the complex set of problems Paul is responding to means that his letter should not be read as 'a one-tracked, perfect piece of rhetoric on bodily solidarity': Oropeza, *1 Corinthians*, 9.

theories that have been conveyed to him within the Corinthians' letter. A further indication of how the various issues addressed within the letter cohere within Paul's mind can be seen in the recurring rhetorical question, 'Do you not know that... ?' (οὐκ οἴδατε ὅτι ...;) that Paul asks ten times across the various sections of the letter (cf. 3:16; 5:6; 6:2,3,9,15,16,19; 9:13,24), frequently followed by a reminder of basic entailments of the gospel and the Corinthians' experience of the outpoured Spirit (3:18; 6:2,3,9,15,19) or of other elementary facts, drawn from Scripture or from common knowledge, that a congregation as 'knowledgeable' as the Corinthians ought to have been well aware of (5:6; 6:16; 9:13,24). In addition to these are the various other rhetorical questions that Paul puts to the Corinthians, frequently expressing his incredulity at their apparent forgetfulness of the gospel and its immediate implications, or of the events surrounding their own conversion (e.g. 1:13,20; 4:7), and the points at which he offers the Corinthians extended and explicit reminders of core gospel tradition (e.g. 11:23–26; 15:1–11).

As a remedy for this apparent forgetfulness, manifested in a wide variety of attitudes and practices that are antithetical to the values implied by the gospel, Paul begins and ends the central core of the letter body with passages that remind his readers of the message he preached to them during the time of his original ministry in Corinth.[18] The former of these two reminders, in 1:18—2:5, focuses on the message of the cross as the judgement of God on all human arrogance and the heart of the wisdom that Paul urges the Corinthians to live by; the latter, in chapter 15, focuses on the apostolic testimony to the resurrection as the foundation for the assurance Paul gives to the Corinthians that all who live by that humble, counter-cultural wisdom will one day be vindicated and glorified with Christ as participants in his victory over the rulers of the present age.[19] Everything between is framed by these two reminders, and applies the wisdom that is revealed in the message of the cross and vindicated in the resurrection to the multiplicity of issues that have been raised by the Corinthians in their letter or made known to Paul in the reports that he has received.[20]

---

18 Properly speaking, the letter body of 1 Corinthians commences at 1:10 and extends to 16:12, but its theological core is contained in 1:18—15:58.
19 See especially Malcolm, *Paul and the Rhetoric of Reversal*, ch. 5.
20 Cf. Starling, "'As to Sensible People'", 113–26.

In *Which* Mind, and Speaking *What*?

Which leads us back to the language of Paul's appeal in 1:10, and the question of what he has in mind when he urges the Corinthians to 'be in agreement' with one another (literally: τὸ αὐτὸ λέγητε, 'that you all speak the same thing'), 'united in the same mind and the same purpose'. If Paul's appeal in 1:10 cannot be stretched to encompass all of the themes and intended functions of the entire letter, can we at least say that it sets us up to read the first major block of the letter body (i.e. 1:10—4:21) as an expression of the conventional Graeco-Roman preference for concord and good order in political communities?[21]

As has been noted by a line of commentators extending at least as far back as Joseph Lightfoot, Paul's language in 1 Corinthians 1:10 is steeped in the idioms of ancient Greek politics. Those who 'say the same thing' are (as Mitchell puts it, summarising this tradition of usage) 'allies, compatriots, even co-partisans'.[22] Something similar can be observed regarding the participle κατηρτισμένοι ('united,' or 'knitted together'),[23] and the two prepositional phrases that follow it in the second half of the verse: 'in the same mind' (ἐν τῷ αὐτῷ νοΐ), which is rarely attested but is cognate with the noun ὁμόνοια, the standard term for political unity or concord, and '[in] the same purpose' (ἐν τῇ αὐτῇ γνώμῃ), which can be found, along with other closely similar expressions, in contexts where it refers (as Mitchell puts it) to 'those in political agreement'.[24] The conclusion Mitchell draws from the evidence is unqualified and emphatic: each of the four phrases that Paul uses to make his appeal in 1:10 is 'a stock phrase in Greek literature for political order and peace: the use of four such phrases gives this πρόθεσις a vehemence and undeniable clarity'.[25]

There is an indisputable element of truth in these observations, but the evidence that Mitchell provides in support of her conclusion is not quite as unanimous or unambiguous as the language in which she frames it.

---

21 Cf. the brief discussion and works cited in Mitchell, *Paul and the Rhetoric of Reconciliation*, 60–64, as well as the more recent, extended exploration of the topic in Stanton, *Unity and Disunity*.
22 Mitchell, *Paul and the Rhetoric of Reconciliation*, 68.
23 Cf. the discussion in Mitchell, *Paul and the Rhetoric of Reconciliation*, 74–75.
24 Mitchell, *Paul and the Rhetoric of Reconciliation*, 79.
25 Mitchell, *Paul and the Rhetoric of Reconciliation*, 68.

To begin with, of course, there is the third of the four expressions, 'in the same mind' (ἐν τῷ αὐτῷ νοΐ), for Mitchell is unable to produce a single example in which it carries the sense she claims, and is compelled to direct our attention away from the phrase itself toward its cognate noun, ὁμόνοια, speculating that Paul's choice not to use the latter was probably in order to avoid being understood as referring to the pagan goddess who personified that virtue.[26] That explanation is certainly possible, but it falls a long way short of establishing that the expression Paul chooses in preference to the noun, ὁμόνοια, would have fallen on the ears of his hearers as a 'stock phrase' for exactly the same meaning. Something similar can be said regarding the verb καταρτίζειν, which can certainly be used to speak of actions taken to reconcile or reunite a divided political community, as the examples cited by Mitchell illustrate, but also carries a wide variety of other literal and metaphorical senses depending on the context of use.[27]

The situation is also somewhat more complex than Mitchell's summation would suggest in relation to the first and last of the four phrases under discussion. It is true that the first expression, τὸ αὐτὸ λέγητε πάντες (literally, 'that you all speak the same thing') can be used, in various grammatical configurations, to refer to parties who are in political agreement with one another (e.g. Attica and Sparta, in Thuc. 4.20.4, or the Jews and the Syrians in Josephus, *AJ* 18.375), or to internally unified political communities (e.g. the Greeks, collectively, in Polybius, *Hist.* 5.104.1), but the expression does not always carry that sense. It can also be used by Josephus, for example, to refer to the words of two prophets who foretell the same event—or, in this instance, to speak about a point of detail concerning the fate of Zedekiah on which the prophets Jeremiah and Ezekiel appear to differ and do not 'say the same thing' (*AJ* 10.105)—without any suggestion at the political inter-relationship between the two prophets is in view.

Similarly, in the case of the verse's final phrase, ἐν τῇ αὐτῇ γνώμῃ ('[in] the same purpose'), the examples that Mitchell cites include some in which, as she claims, the phrase carries the meaning of 'those in political agreement'—either the members of group A in agreement

---

26 Mitchell, *Paul and the rhetoric of reconciliation*, 78.
27 Cf. BDAG, s.v. 'καταρτίζω.'

with the members of group B (e.g. the plebeians and the consuls, in Dio. Hal. *Ant. Rom.* 6.32.2) or the members of a single group, who are all in agreement with one another (e.g. the members of the βουλή in Dion. Hal. *Ant. Rom.* 6.49.3, or the assembled statesmen of the city, in Plutarch's *Precepts of Statecraft* [*Moralia* 813B]). But an equal or greater number of the examples she cites do not carry that meaning at all, referring variously to situations in which the people spoken of are, or ought to be, 'of the same mind' in relation to one matter as they are in relation to another (e.g. in relation to Sparta and Messene, Isocrates *Or.* 6.25; or in relation to their personal glory and the glory of the state, Isocrates *Or.* 6.93), or in one kind of situation as in another (e.g. in fortunate and in unfortunate circumstances, Isocrates *Or.* 6.34; in relation to the previous demands made by the Peloponnesians and their present demands, Thucydides 1.140.1; or in relation to the past invasion of the Peloponnesians and their present invasion, Thucydides 2.55.2).

A meaning almost but not quite the same as the meaning attributed to the phrase by Mitchell is conveyed at yet another point in Isocrates' sixth oration (*Or.* 6.37), where he uses the expression to speak about members of a community who are agreed in relation to one matter ('what is just'; περὶ ... τοῦ δικαίου) but then goes on immediately to speak of how they differ on another ('what is expedient'; περὶ ... τοῦ συμφέροντος). In this instance at least, the expression clearly refers not just to a generic state of harmony and good order but to a position of conscious agreement on a particular matter in question.

In the case of Paul's appeal in 1 Corinthians 1:10, the accumulation of all four phrases and their juxtaposition with the reference that Paul goes on to make in verse 11 to the reports that he has received about the 'quarrels' (ἔριδες) that have been occurring among the Corinthians make it clear that issues of unity and disunity within the Corinthian church are most definitely in view. A strong case can also be made for the broadly 'political' nature of the divisions that Paul is addressing, with factions defined primarily in relation to the figureheads with which they associate themselves and addressed not by critiquing the distinguishing theological ideas of each faction but by exposing the underlying attitudes toward human wisdom and human leadership that the partisans of all the factions have in common.

But it is going beyond the evidence to say that the expressions that

Paul makes use of in addressing the Corinthians' factionalism are simply and one-dimensionally 'stock phrases' giving fourfold expression to the generic Graeco-Roman preference for concord and stability within political communities. In framing his appeal the way he does, Paul goes out of his way to express the fact that the kind of unity he has in mind is a unity that is bound together in a common message, a common mind and a common purpose, leaving himself room to do precisely what he goes on to do in the following chapter, where he makes explicit what is already implicit in the fact that his appeal is made 'by the name of the Lord Jesus Christ' (1:10). (The first two chapters of his letter to the Philippians contain a similar movement of thought, from the appeal in 1:27 for the readers to '[stand] firm in one spirit, striving side by side in one mind' [μιᾷ ψυχῇ] to the exhortation in 2:5 for them to 'let the same mind be in you that was in Christ Jesus' [τοῦτο φρονεῖτε ἐν ὑμῖν ὃ καὶ ἐν Χριστῷ Ἰησοῦ]). What matters to Paul is not just that the Corinthians speak the same thing; it is that they speak the message that has been granted to them by the Spirit through the message of the gospel—'not a wisdom of this age or of the rulers of this age, who are doomed to perish. But we speak God's wisdom, secret and hidden, which God decreed before the ages for our glory' (2:6–7). What matters is not merely that they are united in 'the same mind' but that they understand their world and order their lives in accordance with 'the mind of Christ' (2:16).

That appeal—despite the best attempts of interpreters ancient and modern to accomplish its ecclesiastical domestication—is far from the conventional, conservative and conciliatory message that it is sometimes taken to be. An appeal to think with the mind of Christ is a call that is potentially as confronting as it is conciliatory and as disruptive as it is unifying. And it is grounded not merely in the conventional values of the Graeco-Roman political tradition but in the prophetic message of the Scriptures of Israel and the apocalyptic gospel of the crucified Jesus. In the following chapter I will turn to those themes, exploring the interplay between Scripture, gospel and the work of the Spirit that is involved in thinking with the mind of Christ, and trace the outworkings of that mindset within the politics and ecclesiology of 1 Corinthians.

Bibliography

Barrett, C. K. — *A Commentary on the First Epistle to the Corinthians* (BNTC; 2nd ed.; London: A&C Black, 1971).

Barton, S. C. — 'Paul on Oneness and Unity in 1 Corinthians', in S. C. Barton and A. J. Byers (eds.), *One God, One People: Oneness and Unity in Early Christianity* (Atlanta: SBL Press, 2023), 237–58.

Bauer, W. — *Orthodoxy and Heresy in Earliest Christianity* (tr. Philadelphia Seminar on Christian Origins; Philadelphia: Fortress, 1971).

Brookins, T. A. — *Reading 1 Corinthians: A Literary and Theological Commentary* (Rnt. Macon, GA: Smyth & Helwys, 2020).

Ciampa, R. E. and Rosner, B. S. — *The First Letter to the Corinthians* (PNTC; Grand Rapids: Eerdmans, 2010).

Collins, R. F. — 'Reflections on 1 Corinthians as a Hellenistic Letter', in R. Bieringer (ed.), *The Corinthian Correspondence* (BETL; Leuven: Peeters, 1996), 39–61.

Conzelmann, H. — *1 Corinthians: A Commentary on the First Epistle to the Corinthians* (Hermeneia; Philadelphia: Fortress, 1975).

Fee, G. D. — *The First Epistle to the Corinthians* (NICNT; 2nd ed; Grand Rapids: Eerdmans, 2014).

Héring, J. — *The First Epistle of Saint Paul to the Corinthians* (tr. A. W. Heathcote and P. J. Allcock; London: Epworth, 1962).

Käsemann, E. — *Perspectives on Paul* (Philadelphia: Fortress, 1971).

Malcolm, M. R. — *Paul and the Rhetoric of Reversal in 1 Corinthians: The Impact of Paul's Gospel on His Macro-Rhetoric* (SNTSMS; Cambridge: CUP, 2013).

Mitchell, M. M. — *Paul and the Rhetoric of Reconciliation: An Exegetical Investigation of the Language and Composition of 1 Corinthians* (Louisville: WJK, 1993).

Oropeza, B. J. — *1 Corinthians* (NCCS; Eugene: Cascade Books, 2017).

Orr, W. F. and Walther, J. A. — *1 Corinthians: A New Translation* (AB; Garden City, NY: Doubleday, 1976).

Robertson, A. and Plummer, A. — *A Critical and Exegetical Commentary on the First Epistle of St. Paul to the Corinthians* (ICC; New York: Scribner, 1911).

Schnabel, E. J.	*Der Erste Brief Des Paulus an Die Korinther* (HTA; Wuppertal: Brockhaus, 2006).
Stanton, G.	*Unity and Disunity in Greek and Christian Thought under the Roman Peace* (Tübingen: Mohr Siebeck, 2021).
Starling, D. I.	'"As to Sensible People": Human Reason and Divine Revelation in 1 Corinthians 8–10', in D. I. Starling and C. C. Green (eds.), *Revelation and Reason in Christian Theology* (Bellingham: Lexham, 2018), 113–26.
Thielman, F.	*Theology of the New Testament: A Canonical and Synthetic Approach* (Grand Rapids: Zondervan, 2005).
Thiselton, A. C.	*The First Epistle to the Corinthians: A Commentary on the Greek Text* (NIGTC; Grand Rapids: Eerdmans, 2000).
Weiss, J.	*Der Erste Korintherbrief* (KEK; 9th ed.; Göttingen: Vandenhoeck & Ruprecht, 1910).
Witherington, B.	*Conflict and Community in Corinth: A Socio-Rhetorical Commentary on 1 and 2 Corinthians* (Grand Rapids: Eerdmans, 1995).

CHAPTER 8

'But We Have the Mind of Christ': 1 Corinthians, Wisdom, and the Interpretation of Israel's Scriptures

David I. Starling

In the first of my two chapters within this volume, focusing on Paul's appeal to the believers in Corinth in 1 Corinthians 1:10, I argued for the particularity and distinctiveness of the 'mind' in which Paul wishes the Corinthians to be united—not just 'the *same* mind' but 'the mind *of Christ*'—and the basic, underlying commitment that informs the appeal—not merely, and not ultimately, the conventional Graeco-Roman preference for concord and harmony but the common allegiance of Paul and the Corinthians to the Lord Jesus, in whose name the appeal is issued.

In this second chapter I go on to explore the hermeneutics and implicit epistemology that inform Paul's appeal and shape the politics and ecclesiology of the letter. What does it mean for a community to possess the mind of Christ, and to think and act and speak in a manner that is shaped and determined by it? What is the content of that mind? What are its sources and how are they interrelated? And how does Paul envisage it shaping the life and conduct of those who possess it?

The starting point and primary focus of our investigation is the account that Paul offers in chapter 2 of the form and content of the message he taught in Corinth, including the description that he gives in verses 6–16 of the wisdom which that message made known and which, through the work of the Spirit, has become the possession of the Corinthians.

The chapter begins with a reminder of the message that Paul proclaimed during his original ministry in Corinth and the manner in which he proclaimed it. Paul describes the gospel that he came to Corinth to proclaim as 'the mystery of God',[1] drawing on the use of μυστήριον in Old Testament apocalyptic contexts (e.g. Dan. 2:28,30,47) to describe something inaccessible to human reason and investigation but revealed by God as he chooses. Paul's proclamation of that mystery, he reminds the Corinthians, was 'not ... in lofty words or wisdom' (οὐ καθ' ὑπεροχὴν λόγου ἢ σοφίας), but with a simplicity and unpretentiousness that was the outworking of a deliberate decision 'to know nothing among you except Jesus Christ, and him crucified' (2:2).[2]

Having made that point emphatically in verses 1–5, Paul goes on in verses 6–16 to clarify that in renouncing the kind of human wisdom which consists in 'lofty' and 'plausible' words, he is not rejecting wisdom itself.[3] The real conflict, as Paul sees it, is not between the gospel and wisdom but between 'the wisdom of this age' (v.6) and 'God's [...] wisdom' (v.7), revealed by the Spirit in the message of the gospel. Those to whom this wisdom of God is revealed are described as 'the mature' (v.6) and as 'spiritual' people (v.13), referring not to a privileged subset of the Christian community, but to everyone who has received the Spirit of God (v.12).

Paul's description of the people among whom he and his fellow teachers (and, by extension, his fellow Christians)[4] speak their message

---

1 The evidence of the early manuscripts is divided between those that read 'the mystery [μυστήριον] of God' (cf. CSB; NRSV) and those that read 'the testimony [μαρτύριον] of God' (cf. NIV). Arguments in favour of μυστήριον include the fact that this appears to be the reading in the earliest surviving manuscript ($\mathfrak{P}^{46}$), the further development of the 'mystery' concept in 2:6–16, and the possibility that a later copyist could have corrected the potentially ambiguous μυστήριον (occurring here for the first time in the letter) to μαρτύριον, to harmonize with the language previously used in 1:6. Cf. Gladd, *Revealing the Mysterion*, 123–26.
2 All scriptural quotations within this chapter are from the NRSV.
3 The NRSV's 'Yet ...' correctly captures the adversative sense that is carried by the Greek conjunction δέ as it is used in this context and the close link that it suggests between this paragraph and the preceding ones.
4 If the 'we' in vv.12–13 is referring to the same group as the 'we' in v.6 (i.e., if the scope of the 'we' who communicate the message is the same as the scope of the 'we' who receive and understand it), then the implication of those verses is that Paul's words apply to all who have received the Spirit, not just to his fellow apostles or fellow teachers. Cf. Ciampa and Rosner, '1 Corinthians', 702.

as 'the mature' (οἱ τέλειοι) is possibly borrowed from the self-description of the elitists within the Corinthian congregation, who used the word to mark out their superiority to the rest of the congregation (in social status, knowledge and/or spiritual gifts).[5] If that is the case, Paul takes the word back and redefines it (along with the 'wisdom' that went with it) in terms of the message of the cross.

The wisdom that they speak is 'not a wisdom of this age or of the rulers of this age, who are doomed to perish' (v.6b). 'This age', as in 1:20, is apocalyptic language, contrasting the power structures and belief systems of the present world with those that are established and informed by the coming kingdom of God. Paul's further characterisation of the wisdom that he disavows as 'a wisdom ... of the rulers of this age' reflects the particular role of the powerful and the privileged in shaping that wisdom. Whilst some read this as a reference to demonic or angelic powers,[6] it is more likely that Paul is referring, as he does in Romans 13:3, to earthly authorities and power-brokers (cf. Pss. 2:2, 33:10 [LXX Ps. 32:10]), epitomised (v.8) by the earthly rulers who authorised and consented to the crucifixion of Jesus. Given the context here in 1 Corinthians, Paul probably also includes within the scope of the term a broader reference to the cultural, economic, and political elites, local as well as imperial, that the Corinthians admired and emulated. All these powers are depicted by Paul as 'doomed to perish' (καταργουμένων)—a present participle, picturing them as already under the shadow of their eschatological condemnation (cf. his use of the same verb in 1:28). In place of their wisdom, the message that Paul made known in Corinth proclaimed 'God's wisdom, secret and hidden' (v.7), 'revealed ... through the Spirit' (v.10) and received by 'those who are spiritual' (v.15).

The paragraph concludes with a climactic flourish in verse 16, our particular focus in this chapter. The verse commences with a quotation from Isaiah 40:13: 'For who has known the mind of the Lord so as to instruct him?' The wording of Paul's quotation differs slightly from surviving Greek translations of the original, with the second of the three clauses in the original omitted for brevity's sake, the form of the verb in

---

5   Cf. Brookins, *Reading 1 Corinthians*, 28–29; Fee, *The First Epistle*, 109–10.
6   E.g. Barrett, *A Commentary*, 70; Collins, *First Corinthians*, 129.

the third clause altered slightly, and the conjunction γάρ ('For') inserted into the first clause, presumably by Paul, as a signal that the quotation's function, here in its new textual location, is to provide support for the assertions in the preceding verses.

But the nature of the relationship between the Isaiah quotation and the point Paul wishes to assert is a little more complicated than simply an appeal to Scripture as the source and authority for Paul's claim. Having quoted the rhetorical question of the prophet in verse 16a ('For who has known the mind of the Lord so as to instruct him?') Paul immediately offers a response to it in verse 16b: 'But (δέ) we have the mind of Christ.'

This is not the only point in the letter at which Paul will quote from or allude to Scripture and then say: 'But ... '. In the opening verses of chapter 8, for example, at the start of his lengthy discussion of matters relating to food that has been sacrificed to idols, Paul offers a brief synopsis of the 'knowledge' to which some of the Corinthians are appealing, which he draws together in verse 6 as a kind of credal formulation adapted from the Shema of Deuteronomy 6:4. We have every reason to believe that the knowledge referred to here, as it is summed up by Paul in this formulation, is being represented by him as true, genuine knowledge, an assertion with which he concurs. Immediately, though, in the verse that follows, he offers a qualifying or counter-balancing reminder, introduced by the adversative conjunction ἀλλά ('however'), urging the Corinthians to take account of the fact that 'it is not everyone [...] who has this knowledge' (v.7).⁷

A similar dynamic can be seen in chapter 9, where a string of assertions in verses 4–12a regarding the rights of workers to their wages, reinforced in verses 8–9 by a quotation from Deuteronomy 25:4 to establish that Paul says these things not merely on human authority but with the support of the Law of Moses, is followed in verse 12b with the same strong adversative ἀλλά ('nevertheless') and a reminder that Paul has not made use of these rights.

Perhaps most strikingly of all, in 15:55–57, Paul quotes a verse from Hosea 13 that functioned, in its original context, as a summons to Death

---

7   Cf. the similar reminder in 10:26 (quoting from Ps. 24:1), followed in 10:28 by the 'But if ...' (ἐὰν δέ) that follows it.

and Hades to come and execute judgement, follows it in verse 56 with a statement of the basis on which the legitimacy of that judgement is founded ('The sting of death is sin, and the power of sin is the law'), and then pivots triumphantly in verse 57 to say: 'But (δέ) thanks be to God, who gives us the victory through our Lord Jesus Christ.' The reversal proclaimed in verse 57 is so complete and so spectacular that the scripture quotation itself, back in 55, is modified in anticipation, so that an oracle originally functioning to summon Death and Hades for judgement is transformed into a taunt over death, whose penal role has been made redundant by the work of Christ on behalf of those who are in him.[8]

One obvious factor that contributes to this dynamic, especially and most directly in the first and fourth of these examples, is the apocalyptic nature of Paul's gospel: he represents himself to the Corinthians not merely as an exegete of the Old Testament Scriptures or a sage reflecting wisely on life under the sun, but as a 'steward of God's mysteries' (4:1), and encourages his readers to see themselves as a community 'on whom the ends of the ages have come' (10:11). The wisdom that he makes known is a 'secret and hidden' wisdom (2:7), which 'no eye has seen, nor ear heard' (2:9), but which 'God has revealed to us through the Spirit' (2:10).

Language like this has led some interpreters in recent years to champion the notion of an 'apocalyptic Paul' who depicts God's salvific action in the world as a liberating invasion of the cosmos so entirely unprecedented and unforeseeable as to transform the situation of those who receive it into a kind of epistemological ground zero.[9] For Paul, according to the proponents of this view, the disruptive and world-recreating effect of the gospel is so total as to demolish—at least in principle—all prior knowledge and criteria of judgement, compelling believers to rebuild everything on entirely new foundations.[10]

The last few decades' discussion of apocalyptic themes in Paul's letters has embraced a variety of intersecting concerns (including the apocalyptic dimensions of Paul's eschatology, cosmology, soteriology,

---

8   Cf. Starling, *Hermeneutics*, 143–45.
9   See especially Martyn, 'Apocalyptic Antinomies'; Martyn, *Galatians*; Martyn, 'Epistemology'; Campbell, *The Deliverance*, 36–61; Campbell, 'Apocalyptic Epistemology'; Campbell, 'An Evangelical Paul'.
10 The material in the following chapters is adapted from Starling, '"As to Sensible People"', 116–17.

politics and epistemology) and has been plagued by a notorious lack of clarity in the use of key terms, including the word 'apocalyptic' itself.[11] According to some, it should be understood principally or exclusively as a 'literary' term, designating a particular genre of early Jewish revelatory literature;[12] others, however, make use of the term to refer to a theological viewpoint characteristically but not exclusively expressed in literature of that genre.[13] In this chapter I will be focusing on the claims of those who use the word 'apocalyptic' in that latter, theological, sense, and who place the accent on the epistemological implications of an apocalyptic worldview.

Those who understand Paul as an 'apocalyptic' thinker in this sense of the word frequently go on to make a further, related assertion, that all of the important truth claims and exhortations contained within his letters are presented by Paul to his readers not as reasoned arguments but as proclamations and reproclamations of the singular, eschatological mystery made known by God in the gospel.

In his influential commentary on Galatians, for example, J. Louis Martyn insists that Paul's gospel 'has the effect of placing at issue the nature of argument itself.' Because it is a message that is, at its heart, a matter of divine revelation—'God's own utterance'—'it is not and can never be subject to ratiocinative criteria that have been developed apart from it.'[14] The relevance of Martyn's claim to Paul's initial proclamation of the gospel is obvious: as Martyn puts it, 'what human beings already have in their minds [e.g., their pre-existing "notions of justice, of guilt and innocence, of unrighteousness and righteousness"] cannot serve as the point of departure from which one can book a through train to the gospel'.[15] But Martyn's assertion goes further than that: he considers and explicitly rejects the possibility that Paul might have 'distinguishe[d] an initial and nonrhetorical proclamation of the gospel from a later and

---

11 Cf. the helpful survey of the scholarly terrain in Shaw, '"Then I Proceeded"'.
12 The classic definition is that of Collins, who defined apocalyptic as 'a genre of revelatory literature with a narrative framework, in which a revelation is mediated by an otherworldly being to a human recipient [...] envisag[ing] eschatological salvation and involv[ing] a supernatural world [...] intended to interpret present earthly circumstances in light of the supernatural world and of the future, and to influence both the understanding and the behaviour of the audience by means of divine authority' ('Early Jewish Apocalypticism', 282).
13 Cf. the argument in favour of a theological definition, in Sturm, 'Defining the Word "Apocalyptic"'.
14 Martyn, *Galatians*, 22.
15 Martyn, *Galatians*, 146.

rhetorically sophisticated formulation of a written argument addressed to persons who are already Christians'.[16] Even when Paul is writing to Christians, Martyn insists, his rhetoric is 'more revelatory and performative than hortatory and persuasive'. Paul's letter to the Galatians should thus be read, according to Martyn, not as 'an argument designed to persuade the Galatians that faith is better than observance of the Law', but as 'an announcement designed to wake the Galatians up to the real cosmos, made what it is by the fact that faith has now *arrived* with the advent of Christ'.[17]

Martyn's writings on Galatians (along with, in more recent years, Douglas Campbell's on Romans) are certainly the most widely known and influential articulations of this interpretive approach.[18] But any adequate account of Paul's epistemology must include not only those letters but also, crucially, his letters to the Corinthian church, in which the themes of knowledge and revelation occupy such a prominent place. Amongst the various works that have argued for the presence of an 'apocalyptic epistemology' of this sort in the Corinthian letters, the case is made most explicitly and vigorously by Alexandra Brown in her study of the epistemology and rhetoric of 1 Corinthians, *The Cross and Human Transformation*.[19]

In chapter four of that book, Paul's rewording of the quotation from the prophet Jeremiah in 1 Corinthians 1:31 becomes the occasion for a series of sweeping statements that Brown makes about the differences between the prophetic epistemology of Jeremiah and the apocalyptic epistemology of Paul:

> In Jeremiah, the knowledge of God is available to those who do not 'refuse to know' (Jer. 9:6), that is, to those who 'hear the words of the covenant' and do them (Jer. 11:6–8). Knowledge in Jeremiah has primarily to do with recognition and observance of the sacred tradition that defines true knowledge and wisdom. The definition is not itself foreign to the consciousness of Israel, however far astray the people may have gone.

---

16   Martyn, *Galatians*, 147.
17   Martyn, *Galatians*, 23.
18   E.g. especially Martyn, *Galatians*, 22–23, 146–47; Campbell, *The Deliverance*, 36–61.
19   Brown, *The Cross*. Brown's work builds on the earlier discussion in Martyn, 'Epistemology', 269–87.

Jeremiah can appeal to sacred memory (Jer. 9:7). He calls Israel back to the covenant they once knew and observed, albeit a covenant in need of mending (Jer. 9:10).

Paul, on the other hand, makes no appeal to the Deuteronomic past, nor even, as in the wisdom tradition, to the myth of the creation of the world (cf. Jer. 9:12). For Paul, God's faithfulness (1:9) stands now on wholly new premises. While it is still Yahweh alone who rules, Yahweh is now 'pleased' to save believers through means other than salvation history, or the acquisition of wisdom or reason. As Paul sees it, God 'in God's wisdom' has chosen to save through the apokalypsis of something entirely apart from history, tradition, and reason. That something new, moreover, is expressed in language that points unmistakable toward the dissolution of the world defined by sacred, social, or intellectual traditions, and toward the creation of a new world.[20]

The discontinuities between the old world and the new, according to Brown's reading of Paul, are comprehensive and radical: after the deconstructive work of the gospel is complete, all that is left of the old world is 'rubble' to be cleared aside in order to create space for a new structure, which makes use of the occasional word salvaged from the linguistic remains of the old order but gives to such words a fundamentally new meaning:

> In act 1 [i.e., 1 Cor. 1:1—2:5], the Word of the Cross works to expose and 'de-center' the perceptions of the hearer. This de-centering is the first step in its powerful and transformative play against what Paul calls the 'wisdom of the world.' At the next level of the discourse, the burden of Paul's rhetoric is to clear a path through the rubble of his hearers' now-deconstructed language, building a new framework for perception. Act 2 of the drama [i.e., 2:6–16] brings the completion of the new structure—in our text, Paul's refiguring of the terms wisdom and folly, power and emptiness, psyche and spirit—and

---

20 Brown, *The cross and human transformation*, 92–93.

invokes the power of the Spirit, already at work throughout act 1, to bring the hearer into the transformed mind.[21]

There is an obvious and important element of truth in accounts such these. The mind with which Paul thinks, and wishes believers to think, is a mind that has been illumined by an apocalypse. As he writes in a subsequent letter to the Corinthians: 'The God who said, "Let light shine out of darkness" [...] has shone in our hearts to give the light of the knowledge of the glory of God in the face of Jesus Christ' (2 Cor. 4:6). 'From now on, therefore' (he goes on to write in the following chapter of that letter), 'we regard no one from a human point of view; even though we once knew Christ from a human point of view, we know him no longer in that way. So if anyone is in Christ, there is a new creation: everything old has passed away; see, everything has become new!' (2 Cor. 5:16–17).

It is important not to over-reach in the epistemological conclusions that we draw from statements such as these. Paul's sweeping assertion that 'everything old has passed away,' for example, does not mean for him that the scriptures of Israel have been set aside by the apocalyptic events proclaimed in the gospel. The very words that he uses in 1 Corinthians 2:16 to speak about the inaccessibility of the mind of the Lord to human understanding are, after all, words that he has taken from the prophet Isaiah, and the 'for' (γάρ) that he inserts into the verse makes it clear, as we have already noted, that he is agreeing with the truth that it states and offering it as support for his own assertion in the previous verse. Something similar can be said regarding the lines from Isaiah 64:4 that he quotes several verses earlier (in 2:9), and indeed the whole series of scriptural quotations and allusions that are a recurring feature of Paul's rhetoric in 1:18—4:5, and are the most likely referent of Paul's words in 4:6 urging the readers not to go 'beyond what is written' (ὑπὲρ ἃ γέγραπται). Paul's gospel is a newly revealed message but it is still, he insists, an announcement of things that have taken place 'in accordance with the Scriptures' (15:3,4). Scripture, for Paul, is not set aside by a superseding revelation, even if the way in which it is to be interpreted must now be retrospectively reconfigured in light of the revelation of the messianic identity of the crucified Jesus.[22] The

---

21 Brown, *The Cross*, 29.
22 For a discussion of some of the key dimensions of that retrospective reconfiguration, see Starling, '"Nothing Beyond"'.

disjunction between the state of affairs described in the words of Isaiah and the new state of affairs that Paul asserts in the following verse is not a collision between two mutually incompatible ways of seeing the world; it is a temporal disjunction between two moments in the same narrative, two chapters in the same story.

Paul is not unique in the appeal that he makes to Isaiah 40:13 as prophetic support for an assertion regarding the hiddenness of the divine counsels, in the fact that he claims in the same breath to have been given privileged access to God's mind and purposes through act of special divine revelation, or in the complex interplay between the prospective and retrospective elements of the understanding that this new revelation conveys. Claims of that sort, accompanied by a quotation from or allusion to precisely that verse from Isaiah, are in fact a commonplace among Jewish writers of the Second Temple period and in the aftermath of the second temple's destruction.[23] In 2 Baruch 75, for example, an allusion to Isaiah 40:13 in verses 3–5 ('[W]ho can understand your intelligence? Or who can narrate the thoughts of your spirit? Or who of those born who can hope to arrive at these things[?]') is followed immediately by the proviso, 'apart from those to whom you are merciful and gracious'. The knowledge that is granted to those who are included within that fortunate category includes not only the revelation of 'that which will happen to you after these things' (2 Bar. 76:1) but also the ability to 'know why we have come', 'subject ourselves to him who brought us out of Egypt', 'remember those things which have passed', and 'rejoice with regard to the things which have been' (2 Bar. 75:7–8, trans. Klijn). For the author of 2 Baruch, as for Paul, the apocalypse sheds its light backward as well as forward, imparting understanding of the past as well as knowledge of the future.[24]

But the nature of Paul's claims is not in all respects identical to the kind of claims typically made by the authors of the apocalyptic texts written within the Second Temple period and its aftermath. In Paul's

---

23 For a discussion of the reception of Isa. 40:13 in early Jewish literature, see Williams, *The Wisdom*.

24 Ostensibly, of course, the timeframe 'after these things' concerns events that will take place in *Baruch's* future, after the destruction of the original Jerusalem temple in 587 BC. But the revelation that is given to him is presented as a message that has been given not only for the people of his own time but also for those who live in 'the end of times' (76:2) and its content includes events that are still within the future of the author of 2 Baruch and his intended readers.

case, the revelatory event that has unveiled the previously hidden counsels of God is not a visionary experience in the heavens (though Paul, it seems, does lay claim in 2 Cor. 12 to an experience of this nature) but an historical event on earth—i.e., the crucifixion of the Messiah Jesus— and the subsequent confirmation of his messianic identity, made known through the testimony of those (Paul included) to whom he appeared after his resurrection. Thus, for example, in 2 Corinthians 5, Paul's assertion that 'from now on we regard no one from a worldly point of view' (2 Cor. 5:16) is presented as an inference from the fact that he and his fellow missionaries have become 'convinced that one died for all, and therefore all died', and therefore know that 'those who live should no longer live for themselves but for him who died for them and was raised again' (2 Cor. 5:14–15).

The 'mystery' that Paul makes known through his proclamation can thus be summed up by him as 'the message about the cross' (1 Cor. 1:18)—a message which, for Paul, conveys not only 'righteousness and sanctification and redemption' but also a 'wisdom from God' (1 Cor. 1:30) that reshapes the judgement and the conduct of those who have received it. (More precisely, of course, it is Christ himself who is described in those terms within that verse, but—as he goes on in the immediately following verses to make clear—the message that makes Christ known can also be described, by extension, as 'God's wisdom' [cf. 2:6–7,13].) Those who shape their lives according to this mind (as Paul elsewhere reminds the Philippian believers) put aside 'selfish ambition' (ἐριθεία) and 'conceit' (κενοδοξία), subordinating their own interests to the interests of others (Phil. 2:3–4). They live not to please themselves but to build up their neighbour, in imitation of the example of Christ, who 'did not please himself' (Rom. 15:3). As Paul sums up in a later chapter of this letter, they seek not their own advantage but the advantage of the many, so that they may be saved (1 Cor. 10:31).

There is, of course, a strong connection in Paul's thought between the mindset of humility and mutual service that he commends within these verses and the outcome of concord and harmony that he anticipates it giving rise to. In all three of the passages cited above, an explicit connection is drawn between the two ideas, with the latter envisaged as conducive to the former. But the dominant idea is not concord for concord's sake, or (still less) the kind of civility and good order that merely reinscribes the value systems of the prevailing social order and reinforces the status hierarchies that reflect them.[25] The concord of the new covenant community is a new and distinctive kind of concord, emerging out of a mindset in which the strong seek the advantage of the weak and the parts of the body conventionally regarded as dishonourable are clothed with the greatest honour.[26] If the divisions within the Corinthian church are to be fully and properly healed, then the rhetorical response required will need to be (at some points, at least) confronting before it is conciliatory and disruptive before it is restorative.[27] What matters is not merely that the church gathers together for a common meal, but that it does so in a manner that 'proclaim[s] the Lord's death', faithfully and authentically, 'until he comes' (11:26).

The context in which we are called to follow Christ as twenty-first century Western Christians is—as social commentators frequently remind us—a strident and polarised time, both outside the church and within it. But the dysfunctions of our time, like the dysfunctions of the context addressed by Paul in 1 Corinthians, are not limited to the problems of disorder and disharmony. Coexisting with those dysfunctions, and at times reinforcing or reinforced by them, are the dysfunctions of unequal or oppressive order, which multiply advantages and honours for the powerful and perpetuate disadvantage and dishonour for the weak. Within a context such as this, we are called in the gospel to a way of life that is as difficult as it is beautiful. If we are to fulfil that calling it will require of us not merely a conventional civility or an openness to compromise and cooperation (as valuable as those things can be) but the kind of transformation by which our minds are renewed so as to think with the mind of Christ and our communities are re-ordered by the inbreaking of the coming age.

---

25 Cf. the carefully nuanced discussion in Newson, *The End of Civility*, ch. 4.
26 See especially Dale B. Martin, *The Corinthian body* (New Haven: Yale University Press, 1995), 94–96.
27 Cf. the comments on 1 Cor. 11:17–19 and the suggested paraphrase of v.19 in Richard A. Horsley, *1 Corinthians* (Nashville: Abingdon, 1998), 159. For a slightly reading of the tone of Paul's comments in v.19, but with a similar insistence on the need for 'specific discernments of which rifts genuinely need healing to result in a real rather than a superficial unity,' see Brian Brock and Bernd Wannenwetsch, *The therapy of the Christian body: a theological exposition of Paul's first letter to the Corinthians, Volume 2* (Eugene: Cascade, 2018), 50.

Bibliography

Barrett, C. K.   *A Commentary on the First Epistle to the Corinthians* (BNTC; 2nd ed.; London: A&C Black, 1971).

Brock, B. and Wannenwetsch, B.   *The Therapy of the Christian Body: A Theological Exposition of Paul's First Letter to the Corinthians* (vol. 2; Eugene: Cascade, 2018).

Brookins, T. A.   *Reading 1 Corinthians: A Literary and Theological Commentary* (Rnt. Macon, GA: Smyth & Helwys, 2020).

Brown, A. R.   *The Cross and Human Transformation: Paul's Apocalyptic Word in 1 Corinthians.* (Minneapolis: Fortress, 1995).

Campbell, D. A.   'Apocalyptic Epistemology: The Sine Qua Non of Valid Pauline Interpretation', in B. C. Blackwell, J. K. Goodrich, and J. Maston (eds.), *Paul and the Apocalyptic Imagination* (Minneapolis: Fortress, 2016), 65–86.

Campbell, D. A.   *The Deliverance of God: An Apocalyptic Rereading of Justification in Paul* (Grand Rapids: Eerdmans, 2009).

Campbell, D. A.   'An Evangelical Paul: A Response to Francis Watson's *Paul and the Hermeneutics of Faith*', *JSNT* 28 (2006), 337–51.

Ciampa, R. E. and Rosner, B. S.   *The First Letter to the Corinthians* (PNTC; Grand Rapids: Eerdmans, 2010).

Collins, J. J.   'Early Jewish Apocalypticism', in D. N. Freedman (ed.), *Anchor Bible Dictionary* (New York: Doubleday, 1992), 1.282–88.

Collins, R. F.   *First Corinthians* (Sacra Pagina; Collegeville: Liturgical Press, 1999).

Fee, G. D.   *The First Epistle to the Corinthians* (NICNT; 2nd ed; Grand Rapids: Eerdmans, 2014).

Gladd, B. L.   *Revealing the Mysterion: The Use of Mystery in Daniel and Second Temple Judaism with Its Bearing on First Corinthians* (BZNW; Berlin: De Gruyter, 2009).

Horsley, R. A.   *1 Corinthians* (Nashville: Abingdon, 1998).

Martin, D. B.   *The Corinthian Body* (New Haven: Yale University Press, 1995).

Martyn, J. L.   'Apocalyptic Antinomies in Paul's Letter to the Galatians', *NTS* 31 (1985), 410–24.

Martyn, J. L. — 'Epistemology at the Turn of the Ages: 2 Corinthians 5:16', in W. R. Farmer (ed.), *Christian History and Interpretation; Studies Presented to John Knox* (Cambridge: Cambridge University Press, 1967), 269–87.

Martyn, J. L. — *Galatians: A New Translation with Introduction and Commentary* (AB. New York: Doubleday, 1997).

Newson, R. A. — *The End of Civility: Christ and Prophetic Division* (Waco: Baylor University Press, 2023).

Shaw, D. A. — '"Then I Proceeded to Where Things Were Chaotic" (1 Enoch 21:1): Mapping the Apocalyptic Landscape', in B. C. Blackwell, J. K. Goodrich, and J. Maston (eds.), *Paul and the Apocalyptic Imagination* (Minneapolis: Fortress, 2016), 23–41.

Starling, D. I. — '"As to Sensible People": Human Reason and Divine Revelation in 1 Corinthians 8–10', in D. I. Starling and C. C. Green (eds.), *Revelation and Reason in Christian Theology* (Bellingham: Lexham, 2018), 113–26.

Starling, D. I. — *Hermeneutics as Apprenticeship: How the Bible Shapes Our Interpretive Habits and Practices* (Grand Rapids: Baker, 2016).

Starling, D. I. — '"Nothing Beyond What Is Written"? First Corinthians and the Hermeneutics of Early Christian *Theologia*', *JTI* 8 (2014), 45–62.

Sturm, R. E. — 'Defining the Word "Apocalyptic"', in J. Marcus and M. Soards (eds.), *Apocalyptic and the New Testament: Essays in Honor of J. L. Martyn* (Sheffield: JSOT Press, 1989), 17–48.

Williams, H. H. D. — *The Wisdom of the Wise: The Presence and Function of Scripture within 1 Cor. 1:18—3:23* (Agju; Leiden: Brill, 2001).

CHAPTER 9

An Intra-Ecclesial Reading of οἱ πιστεύοντες and οἱ ἄπιστοι in 1 Corinthians 14:22[1]

Scott Goode

Introduction

After reviewing the literature associated with 1 Corinthians 14:22, Anthony Thiselton concludes, 'This is acknowledged to be one of the most difficult verses in our epistle.'[2] Having asserted that tongues εἰς σημεῖόν εἰσιν οὐ τοῖς πιστεύουσιν ἀλλὰ τοῖς ἀπίστοις, and that prophecy οὐ τοῖς ἀπίστοις ἀλλὰ τοῖς πιστεύουσιν (v.22), Paul apparently contradicts himself by describing two groups (ἰδιῶται and ἄπιστοι, vv.23–25) entering the assembly and being repelled by tongues but converted through prophecy. Despite the vast amount of literature associated with 1 Corinthians, no scholarly consensus regarding the

---

1 The proposal in this essay is an adaption, and extension, of part of the argument of Chapter 4: Salvific Intentionality in the Gathering, in my monograph *Salvific Intentionality in 1 Corinthians: How Paul Cultivates the Missional Imagination of the Corinthian Community* (Eugene, OR: Wipf & Stock, 2023). Used by permission of Wipf and Stock Publishers, www.wipfandstock.com.

2 Thiselton, *The First Epistle*, 1122.

coherence of Paul's argument has emerged.³ It is my contention that this long-standing conundrum is resolved by recognising two distinct usages of ἄπιστος. In verse 22, Paul draws from the Old Testament covenant categories of faithless/faithful to state a summarising principle that tongues are indicative of faithless Judah/Corinth (οἱ ἄπιστοι), while prophecy is the sign of the authentic believing community (οἱ πιστεύοντες). This intra-ecclesial usage is distinct from that employed in verses 23–25 where the ἄπιστοι are one of two 'outsider' groups (the other being the ἰδιῶται) whose reactions serve as a reinforcing argument of the tongues/prophecy contrast which Paul has just stated (v.22), and which he has developed throughout the wider literary unit (vv.1–19). The following exegetical considerations will be offered to support this reading: (1) the developing tongues/prophecy rhetoric throughout 1 Corinthians 14 and its implications for the structure and coherence of the argument in verses 20–25; (2) the significance of Isaiah 28:11–12 in its initial context and then in Paul's argument; and (3) the socio-religious identities of the various groups within the pericope.

Tongues/prophecy throughout 1 Corinthians 14

Beginning in 1 Corinthians 14:1, the benefit of προφητεία (hereafter prophecy) is contrasted with the shortcomings associated with γλῶσσαι (hereafter tongues). Prophecy corresponds with an ethic of love (v.1) and serves as an intelligible speech-mode (vv.9,19) directed towards the edification, encouragement, and comfort of others (v.3).⁴ Tongues, on the other hand, refer to a mysterious speech-mode (v.2), corresponding to one's own spirit (v.14) that, given their orientation towards God (v.2), provides benefit only to oneself (v.4), and alienates

---

3   The main proposals are that (1) Paul is, in v.22, stating a rhetorical question from the mouths of Paul's Corinthian opponents which he subsequently rebuts (vv.23–25), on which see Johanson, 'Tongues'. More recently Lucy Peppiatt has offered an adaption of Johanson's general thesis. She argues that v.21 is the Corinthians' own manipulated version of Isaiah which they have previously cited to Paul, on which see Peppiatt, *Women and Worship*; (2) the effects of tongues/prophecy upon unbelievers in vv.23–25 fulfills the Isaiah passage quoted in v.21 and serves as the illustration of Paul's assertion in v.22, on which see Fee, *First Epistle*, 677, 681; (3) prophecy completes the salvific work which tongues can only commence, on which see Bailey, Paul, 402–3; or (4) Paul's rhetoric led him to overstate the matter, on which see Nash, *1 Corinthians*, 378.
4   This description of prophecy is sufficient for this essay. For a comprehensive review of the literature and possibilities, see Thiselton, *The First Epistle*, 956–65, 1087–94.

others (v.11).⁵ Even the logic of Paul's 'exception clauses' holds true to this fundamental tongues/prophecy contrast. Yes, tongues are acceptable when translated (vv.5,13,27,40), but this very act of translation transforms this mysterious speech into that which can be understood, and thus they become analogous to prophecy. While the phenomenon of Corinthian tongues remains a matter of some opaqueness to the modern interpreter, it is likely they are functioning as a status-indicator within the church.⁶ It seems from what Paul writes that he sees no place for tongues in the assembly, at least not in the way the Corinthians are practising them untranslated.

The language of ἀδελφοί (v.20), signalling a subtle development in Paul's argument towards a summarising statement, introduces a child/mature contrast which corresponds to this preceding tongues/prophecy rhetoric. Rather than being mature, the Corinthians are behaving as children, a criticism which has been previously levelled at them (3:1; see 13:11). Moreover, this reference to children may well echo the wider context of Isaiah 28:11–12 which will come into focus in the very next verse (1 Cor. 14:21). The complaint of the religious leaders of Isaiah's day was that his message was too simple—it was for children: 'Who is it he is trying to teach? To whom is he explaining his message? To children weaned from their milk, to those just taken from the breast?' (Isa. 28:9, NIV). Paul draws a comparison between the way those leaders demonstrated their own puerile attitude by taunting the prophet and that of

---

5   This description of tongues is sufficient for this essay. For a comprehensive review of the literature and possibilities, see Thiselton, *The First Epistle*, 970–89, 1098–1100. It is unclear if Paul is simply critical of the misuse of tongues, or whether he completely disapproves of their use in the assembly. The purpose of any potential translation (1 Cor. 14:27–28) is to transform this speech-mode into that which is analogous to prophecy. Whether such translation is even possible is opaque to the modern interpreter—perhaps Paul is conceding that translating a tongue would make the practice acceptable while anticipating that such a possibility is unlikely to take place. I lean towards this latter possibility. Indeed, the meaning of Paul's 'wish' (θέλω) that they all spoke in tongues (v.5) is contested and may be, according to Chadick, a rhetorical strategy designed to prevent 'a fatal barrier between himself and the Corinthians enthusiasts', on which see 'All Things', 268. See also discussion in Thiselton, *The First Epistle*, 1096–8. Furthermore, v.18 is the only other possible place in which Paul offers a favourable opinion of tongues and yet he is clearly drawing a contrast between a private practice and prophesy which should occur in a public setting (ἀλλὰ ἐν ἐκκλησίᾳ, v.19). This private practice may also be in view in 1 Cor. 12:28 (where it is listed last) and 14:39.
6   This view, that tongues were functioning as a status-indicator over the ἰδιῶται will be developed later in this essay. For scholarly support see Moberly, *Prophecy and Discernment*, 179; and Perkins, *First Corinthians*, 156.

the Corinthians' childish resistance to his apostolic words.[7] Similarly, while the Corinthians were critical of Paul's teaching, it was, in fact, *they* who needed to become mature. In the context of 1 Corinthians 14 such maturity would be demonstrated by the cessation of untranslated tongues and the prioritisation of prophecy. Hence, this appeal for maturity in verse 20 commences a summary of the preceding section (vv.1–19) which, I argue, reaches its conclusion in verse 22. Paul's paraphrase of Isaiah 28:11–12 (in 1 Cor. 14:21) builds towards this summarising statement about the place of tongues and prophecy in the church, after which two scenarios (vv.23–25) serve as the reinforcing proof of Paul's prior conclusion. The internal logic of Paul's argument may be outlined as follows:

Appeal (v.20)	Exhortation to maturity.
Premise (v.21)	Despite Assyrian tongues, Judah remained faithless (Isa. 28:11–12).
Conclusion A (v.22a)	Tongues are a sign of unbelieving Judah/Corinth.
Conclusion B (v.22b)	Prophecy is a sign of believing Judah/Corinth.
Further proof A (v.23)	The negative salvific effect of Corinthian tongues upon two 'outsider' groups.
Further proof B (vv.24–25)	The positive salvific effect of Corinthian prophecy upon two 'outsider' groups.

---

7   It is likely that Isa. 28:10 ('For it is: Do this, do that, a rule for this, a rule for that, a little here, a little there', NIV) represents the taunting of the prophet by drawing on the use of mimicking sounds used for teaching a child the Hebrew alphabet, on which see Ciampa and Rosner, *The First Letter*, 697. Webb explains, 'The drunken leaders mock the word of God through the prophet as infantile nonsense, childish prattle.' See *The Message*, 120.

The significance of Isaiah 28:11–12 in Paul's argument

Paul's paraphrase of Isaiah 28:11–12 is fundamental to the coherence of his argument.[8] Despite a tendency for interpreters to understand the effect of tongues/prophecy upon unbelievers in verses 23–25 as the fulfillment of the Isaiah text,[9] the inferential ὥστε, which commences verse 22, indicates that the more immediate statements about tongues and prophecy (v.22) are Paul's primary application of Isaiah 28:11–12. These may be paraphrased as two principles related to their gatherings:

> Tongues are the speech-mode of faithless Judah/Corinth.
> Prophecy is the speech-mode of faithful Judah/Corinth.

The text Paul paraphrases is found at the centre of Isaiah's judgement oracle against Ephraim, Judah, and their leadership (Isa. 28–29). The divine complaint points out the intoxicated state of the priests and prophets who are muddled in their visions and stumble in their judgements (Isa. 28:1,7). In mocking the prophetic word they fail to hear the clear voice of the Lord which contains wisdom (Isa. 28:9–10,14,22–29). Paul's loose quotation of Isaiah 28:11–12 references this first context of divine judgement and its association with Assyrian (foreign) 'prattle' which will accompany the covenant curse of exile (Isa. 28:2–3,22; 29:1–8; see Deut. 28:45–50; Jer. 5:13–15).[10] Paul's application then is relatively straightforward, but confronting: tongues are not an indication of divine spiritual endorsement as the Corinthians thought, but of God's judgement:

> ὥστε αἱ γλῶσσαι εἰς σημεῖόν εἰσιν οὐ τοῖς πιστεύουσιν ἀλλὰ τοῖς ἀπίστοις,
> Therefore, tongues are a sign, not of the faithful, but of the faithless;[11]

---

8 Paul seems to draw from the MT rather than his usual source of the LXX (although the MT is also preferred in 1 Cor. 3:19–20). The correlation of meaning between the MT and Paul's paraphrase is sufficiently aligned to render Peppiatt's proposal (see note 3) unlikely. Moreover, if v.21 is a misquoted version of Isaiah by the Corinthians (as she argues), one would expect a conjunction between v.22 and v.23 which indicates Paul's rebuttal.
9 For example, see Fee, *First Corinthians*, 677, 681.
10 Heil, *The Rhetorical Role*, 202.
11 My translation of 1 Cor. 14:22a.

The term σημεῖον simply means *indication* and the preposition εἰς connects tongues with reference to the ἄπιστοι.[12] Paul is thus drawing an analogy between the presence of Assyrian tongues in Isaiah's time, and the practice of tongues in Corinth: that they too are associated with judgement. Importantly, he has already anticipated this connection when previously explaining the exilic-like effect of Corinthian tongues upon others: 'If then I do not grasp the meaning of what someone is saying, I am a foreigner (βάρβαρος) to the speaker, and the speaker is a foreigner to me' (1 Cor. 14:11, NIV).

This suggests a possibility that the descriptors which immediately follow the Isaiah reference, οἱ πιστεύοντες and οἱ ἄπιστοι (v.22), apply as internal covenant categories pertaining to the people of God. As Paul paraphrases Isaiah, he is applying an intra-ecclesial distinction between *believing* and *unbelieving* Judah/Corinth, the *faithful* and the *faithless*. This is a well-recognised Old Testament tradition which seeks to provoke a faithful response from within: 'The Lord said to me, "Faithless Israel is more righteous than unfaithful Judah. Go, proclaim this message toward the north: Return, faithless Israel," declares the Lord' (Jer. 3:11–12, NIV; see Jer. 3:6–22;[13] Deut. 29–30; Isa. 29:13; Hos. 1; 14:1–3; Rom. 9–11). Indeed, Isaiah's opening homily is framed in just this way: 'Wash and make yourselves clean. Take your evil deeds out of my sight; stop doing wrong [...]. See how the faithful city has become a prostitute!' (Isa. 1:16, 21a, NIV). As Isaiah addressed those within the covenant people as faithless, Paul is also addressing the Corinthian community in these same terms.

---

12 BDAG, s.v. 'σημεῖον'. This is the normal sense in which the term is used throughout Isaiah where it is often an eschatological indication of God's salvific action, on which see Isa. 7:17; 11:12; 13:2; 18:3; 19:20; 38:7; 55:13; 66:19. In support of this reading of σημεῖον as a divine attitude see Carson, *Showing the Spirit*, 115; Collins, *First Corinthians*, 508. For an alternative view that the proposition εἰς with the accusative is for the advantage of, or conveys an effect upon, hearers see Bender, *1 Corinthians*; Dickson, *Mission-Commitment*, 297–98; Fee, *First Corinthians*, 677, 680; Garland, *1 Corinthians*, 650–51; Witherington III, *Conflict and Community*, 284–85. Uniquely, Lang argues that 'the sign function of tongues is disciplinary; it is reserved not for generic outsiders but for unfaithful insiders ... [who] ... in the presence of the worshipping community, are similarly resistant to God's demands and so stand under judgement.' See 'Trouble with Insiders', 994. By insiders, Lang means unbelievers who were socially connected to the church. This is a different line of argument from the one I am advancing by drawing on covenant insider categories.

13 ἀφίστημι in LXX Jer. 3:14 refers to faithless Israel and is a term closely associated with an unbelieving (ἀπιστία) heart in Heb. 3:12. See Luke 8:13.

Such prophetic warnings—in this case referencing the historic threat of pending Assyrian invasion (foreign tongues)—were intended to elicit a believing response from within the people of God. Isaiah is engaging in speech which R. W. L. Moberly describes as 'response-seeking':

> Prophetic speech is response-seeking speech—in the first instance the purpose of pronouncing impending disaster is that the sinful respond by turning to God, but there is also the further prospect that God may then respond by withholding the disaster.[14]

The implication of Paul's paraphrase of Isaiah 28:11–12 in 1 Corinthians 14:21 is that the Corinthians ought not to be like deaf and disobedient Judah/Israel. Tongues, both in Isaiah's time and as practised by the Corinthians, were an indication of the church's unbelief and associated with a response-seeking warning of divine judgement. This is why Paul has commenced his summary with a sharp rebuke: 'Stop thinking like children [...] be adults' (v.20, NIV).

The critical question arising from this intra-ecclesial reading is whether the term ἄπιστος can bear the weight of such a translation. And the answer is most certainly yes. Paul uses the cognate terms ἀπιστέω and ἀπιστία in Romans 3:3 in just such a way when he refers to some among the Jews: 'What if some were unfaithful [ἠπίστησάν]? Will their unfaithfulness [ἀπιστία] nullify God's faithfulness?' (NIV). Consider also Jesus' rebuke of his disciples for their unbelief (ἀπιστία, Mark 16:14) and the warning in Hebrews against an unbelieving (ἀπιστία) heart (Heb. 3:12).[15] In fact, two recent studies have demonstrated that Graeco-Roman and Jewish texts can certainly support the use of the term ἄπιστος as an insider-type reference.[16]

That there are faithless insiders within the Christian community at Corinth is evident throughout the letter. The most infamous example is that of the immoral man whom Paul seeks to expel for his own salvific

---

14 Moberly, *Prophecy and Discernment*, 52–53, see also 95–99. The scope of Moberly's study focuses on Jeremiah but his observations are intended as principles exemplified elsewhere in the Old Testament.
15 Consider also the following examples: 2 Macc. 8:13; Matt. 13:58; 17:17; Mark 6:6; 9:24; 16:11; Luke 24:11, 41; John 20:27; Rom. 4:20; 11:20,23; 1 Tim. 1:13; 2 Tim. 2:13; Heb. 3:19.
16 BDAG, s.v. 'ἄπιστος'. See Trebilco, 'Creativity'; Lang, 'Trouble with Insiders'.

welfare (1 Cor. 5:1–8). This and other cases of immorality (6:12–20), along with idolatry (8:10; 10:14–22) and serious mistreatment of others (11:17–34; 12:12–31) are all factors in T. J. Lang's proposal that 'the fundamental issue animating Paul's correspondence with the Corinthian assembly is the definition of authentic Christian identity [...] to distinguish between types of insiders, assorted degrees of deviancy, and fitting responses to untidy social circumstances'.[17] Thus, in 1 Corinthians 14, Paul, echoing an Old Testament response-seeking prophetic tradition, is exhorting the people of God to be faithful to their covenant identity. Indeed, an analogous relationship between Israel and the people of God in Corinth is explicitly laid out in 1 Corinthians 10:1–14 in which Israel's example serves as a warning to the community at Corinth: 'These things happened to them as examples and were written down as warnings for us, on whom the culmination of the ages has come' (10:11, NIV; see 10:6). This typological connection further reinforces the application of the Isaiah citation in the way I have described. Paul is inviting his readers to be characterised not by tongues but by the maturity which values the presence of God's message: prophecy. Thus, the parallel assertion concerning prophecy in v.22b:

ἡ δὲ προφητεία οὐ τοῖς ἀπίστοις ἀλλὰ τοῖς πιστεύουσιν.
prophecy, however, is [a sign] not of the faithless but of the faithful.[18]

Corinthian prophecy corresponds to the Isaiah ideal of the voice of the Lord (Isa. 28:23–29). This prophetic word received by the redeemed community will extend to 'children', and 'those who are wayward in spirit will gain understanding' (Isa. 29:22–24, NIV). Prophecy, then, is an indication that faithless Judah/Israel has repented and that the Lord has reversed the exile and gathered his people from the places to which they were scattered (Deut. 30:3–4). The presence of prophetic ministry among the Corinthians will likewise indicate that they have come into an adult understanding and thus represent the authentic believing (οἱ πιστεύοντες) community of God's people.

So, to summarise, 1 Corinthians 14:22 functions as a conclusion

---

17 Lang, 'Trouble with Insiders', 981–82. See also Barclay, 'Deviance and Apostasy', 136–38.
18 My translation of 1 Cor. 14:22b.

of Paul's argument thus far in relation to untranslated tongues in the assembly: they fail to edify in verses 1–6, they alienate in verses 6–12, and in verses 12–19 ten thousand of them are no match for five intelligible alternatives. For such reasons, tongues are an indication not of faithfulness, but faithlessness—they are associated with the judgement which unfaithful Judah faced in Isaiah's day.

The socio-religious profile of Corinthian groups

It is in 1 Corinthians 14:23–25 that the salvific effect of the two speech-modes becomes clear. Whereas the οὖν commencing verse 23 is widely translated as an inferential (e.g. 'therefore'), its place within a conditional clause, Ἐὰν οὖν ..., is better understood as conveying a transitional function (e.g. 'now, then'; see 1 Cor. 6:4; 14:11). This observation, along with the abrupt return to internal matters from verse 26, further weakens the view that verses 23–25 is the climactic summary to which Paul is moving. It is my contention that the logical coherence of Paul's argument, along with his rhetorical emphasis, is best explained when verses 23–25 are understood not as the illustration of Paul's assertion in verse 22 but as a reinforcing argument to an already stated conclusion. Thus, the identities of the two 'outsider' groups, ἰδιῶται and ἄπιστοι, become a critical interpretive concern when analysing verses 23–25.[19]

Although ἰδιώτης can refer to an 'amateur' or one who is 'unskilled', in this context it identifies 'one not knowledgeable about a particular group's experience.'[20] For this reason, I adopt the term *ungifted*, recognising Paul's rhetorical use of this term as describing the attitude of the 'spiritual' tongue-speakers towards those who do not speak in tongues.[21] This reading may be compared to Irenaeus' *Against Heresies* (1.6.4, *ANF*) in which he describes the Gnostics as those who 'run us

---

19 Although there are some who argue that the two descriptors are in fact synonymous, on which see Garland, *1 Corinthians*, 651; Hays, *First Corinthians*, 238; Fee, *First Corinthians*, 685. Uniquely, Dickson argues that in v.23, due to the effect of tongues, the uninformed person is revealed as an unbeliever, while in vv.24–25 the order is reversed and the apparent unbeliever turns out to be only uninformed, showing themselves to be among those who would believe. See *Mission-Commitment*, 298–99.
20 BDAG, s.v. 'ἰδιώτης'.
21 The range of possibilities are discussed by Thiselton, *The First Epistle*, 1114–15.

down [...] as utterly contemptible [ὡς ἰδωτῶν] and ignorant persons [καὶ μηδὲν ἐπισταμένων], while they highly exalt themselves, and claim to be perfect, and the elect seed'.²² Similarly, the elites of Corinth have wrongly treated some as less honourable members of the body (1 Cor. 12:22–23), preferring to alienate rather than edify the 'ungifted' (14:11,16–17). It is for this reason that the ἰδιῶται appear first (v.23), as a means of emphasising a continuity in Paul's argument. Although present in the community they are treated as 'outsiders' by the 'spiritual'. Their experience of alienation in verse 23 further reinforces the preceding conclusion of verse 22 that untranslated tongues in the Corinthian assembly are a speech-mode unfitting for God's people.

In the second scenario in which the whole church is prophesying (vv.24–25), the 'ungifted' appear second because Paul wants to emphasise the effect of prophecy upon the ἄπιστοι for whom the experience of conversion is most pertinent.²³ The most coherent reading of Paul's argument throughout verses 20–25 is that ἄπιστος is employed differently in verses 23–25 than in verse 22. In verses 23–25, the translation *unbeliever* corresponds to an outsider group whose response to tongues/prophecy reinforces Paul's prior conclusion about the priority of prophecy (v.22). While, as previously noted, the semantic range of the ἄπιστος word group can certainly reflect a faithless insider-type designation (as I argue it does in v.22),²⁴ the typical Pauline usage is to an unbeliever-type reference.²⁵ Such unbelievers are the unrighteous before whom the Corinthians appear for court cases (6:6), they are those to whom believers may be married (7:12–16), and they are dining hosts

---

22 See discussion by Clarke who proposes that the ἰδιώτης 'has a recognised place but does not fully comprehend the Corinthian cultic practices'. See 'Church Membership', 207–9. My argument extends this proposal further, identifying it as a term of contempt which the elite use to describe the 'ungifted' in the community.
23 For persuasive purposes Paul includes the ἰδιῶται as those who still need 'converting', at least in the minds of the 'spiritual' ones.
24 See notes 15 and 16.
25 Consider Luke 12:46; 1 Cor. 6:6; 7:12–16; 10:27; 2 Cor. 4:4; 6:14–15; 1 Tim. 5:8; Rev. 21:8. See also Josephus, *Ant*. 14.13.6; Mart. *Pol*. 16.1; Ign. *Magn*. 5.1; Justin, *Dial*. 91.3. The verb ἀπιστέω in Wis. 18:13 LXX is a reference to the Egyptians during the Passover: 'For though they had disbelieved [ἀπιστοῦντες] everything because of their magic arts, yet, when their firstborn were destroyed, they acknowledged your people to be God's child' (NRSV). The cognate noun ἀπιστία occurs in Wis. 14:25 LXX to describe the vices associate with generic idolatry: 'All is a raging riot of blood and murder, theft and deceit, corruption, faithlessness [ἀπιστία], tumult, perjury' (NRSV). See Trebilco, 'Creativity', 187–91.

into whose homes the Christians are invited (10:27). While 'outsiders' in terms of Christ-loyalty, they are, according to Lang, '"insiders" in the most socially serious way'.[26] Indeed, the Corinthian community was a relatively small association whose members would have necessarily been embedded in diverse social networks—friends, neighbours, families, coworkers, business associates, patrons, and clients.[27] This explains why Paul can assume that the Corinthians will recognise his point, in verses 23–25, that such unbelievers may be present in the Christian gathering.

While the effect of tongues upon the two groups reinforces the inappropriateness of their use in the assembly, the presence of prophecy results in what John Dickson calls an 'idealized portrait of conversion, styled on the great "conversions" described in the Jewish scriptures'.[28] The new convert assumes a posture of humility and worship (1 Cor. 14:25) which contrasts sharply with the inflated egos of the Corinthians (4:6,18–19; 5:2; 8:1; see 13:4). The recognition by such unbelievers that 'God is truly among you!' (v.25, NIV) echoes both Zechariah 8:23 and Isaiah 45:15 (see Isa. 49:23; 20:20–36) in which the outside Gentile nations are witnessing the post-exilic restoration of God's people and their temple (see Isa. 41:8–10; 42:6; 43:10,12; 44:8; 61:1–3; 66:19; Exod. 19:4–6).[29] That is, the faithful (οἱ πιστεύοντες) ministry of the prophesying Corinthian church is analogous to the restoration of Israel and her temple. The priestly and prophetic role of Israel is realised in Corinth not by the exilic effect of tongues, but when, through prophecy, the ἰδιῶται are edified and the ἄπιστοι are converted.

Conclusion

Despite the semantic range of the ἄπιστος word group, only recently has the possibility of an 'insider' reading of 1 Corinthians 14:22 been explored. By emphasising the logical connection between Paul's

---

26 Lang interacts with Trebilco's study, 'Creativity'. Lang argues that ἄπιστοι retains its (insider) semantic norm by referencing 'deviant insiders' who are socially connected with the community and welcome in worship, and yet 'they are not counted as siblings in the ecclesial family'. See 'Trouble with Insiders', 983, 985–1001.
27 Munoz, 'How Not to Go Out', 115.
28 Dickson, *Mission-Commitment*, 300.
29 Ciampa and Rosner, *First Corinthians*, 706–7; Hays, *First Corinthians*, 239.

paraphrase of Isaiah 28:11–12 (1 Cor. 14:21) and, what I argue is, his subsequent summarising statement of the entire section, I have proposed an intra-ecclesial covenantal reading of 1 Corinthians 14:22. That Paul might address the Corinthians as faithless is no surprise given the range of problems that he addresses: factional pride (1:10–17; 3:1–4; 4:4–21; 5:1–8; 11:19), immorality (5:1; 6:12–20; 7:2; 10:8), inappropriate legal disputes (6:1–11), disregard for the 'weak' (8:1–13), idolatrous engagement (8:1-13; 10:10–22), social disparity and elitism (11:17–34; 12:12–26; 14:1–40), drunkenness (11:21), and deficient views about the resurrection (15:1–58). In chapter 14, Paul extends his criticism to include their practice of untranslated tongues. Whereas the Corinthians thought that their tongues were indicative of an elite spiritual status, Paul compares their practices with the Assyrian tongues of Isaiah's day which were associated with God's judgement. Using insider covenant categories in verse 22, Paul depicts the tongues-speaking church (without translation) as faithless while simultaneously exhorting them to faithful maturity evidenced by prophecy. This is further reinforced in a final scene (vv.23–25) where the reaction of two 'outsider' groups completes Paul's appeal for maturity by showing that it is indeed prophecy, and not tongues, which elicits the exclamation that 'God is truly among you!' (v.25, NIV).

Bibliography

Bailey, K. E. — *Paul through Mediterranean Eyes: Cultural Studies in 1 Corinthians* (Dowers Grove: IVP Academic, 2011).

Barclay, J. M. G. — 'Deviance and Apostasy: Some Applications of Deviance Theory to First-Century Judaism and Christianity', in *Pauline Churches and Diaspora Jews* (WUNT 275; Tübingen: Mohr Siebeck, 2011), 123–140.

Bender, K. J. — *1 Corinthians* (Brazos Theological Commentary on the Bible; Grand Rapids, Brazos, 2022).

Carson, D. A. — *Showing the Spirit: A Theological Exposition of 1 Corinthians 12–14* (Moore Theological College Lecture Series; Homebush West, NSW: Lancer, 1988).

Chadwick, H. — 'All Things to all Men', *New Testament Studies* 1/4 (1955): 261–275.

Ciampa, R. E. and Rosner, B. S. — *The First Letter to the Corinthians* (The Pillar New Testament Commentary; Grand Rapids: Eerdmans, 2010).

Clarke, A. D. — 'Church Membership and the ἰδιώτης in the Early Corinthian Community', in J. C. Laansma et al. (eds.), *New Testament Theology in Light of the Church's Mission: Essays in Honor of I. Howard Marshall* (Eugene, OR: Cascade, 2011), 197–211.

Collins, R. F. — *First Corinthians* (Sacra Pagina; Collegeville, MN: Liturgical, 1999).

Danker, F. W., Bauer, W., Arndt, W. F. and Gingrich, F. W. — *Greek-English Lexicon of the New Testament and Other Early Christian Literature* (3rd ed; Chicago: University of Chicago Press, 2000).

Dickson, J. P. — *Mission-Commitment in Ancient Judaism and in the Pauline Communities: The Shape, Extent and Background of Early Christian Mission* (WUNT 2.159; Tübingen: Mohr Siebeck, 2003).

Fee, Gordon D. — *First Epistle to the Corinthians* (NICNT. Grand Rapids: Eerdmans, 1987).

Garland, D. E. — *1 Corinthians* (Baker Exegetical Commentary on the New Testament; Grand Rapids: Baker Academic, 2003).

Goode, S.	*Salvific Intentionality in 1 Corinthians: How Paul Cultivates the Missional Imagination of the Corinthian Community* (Eugene, OR: Wipf and Stock, 2023).
Hays, R. B.	*First Corinthians* (Interpretation; Louisville, KY: John Knox, 1997).
Heil, J. P.	*The Rhetorical Role of Scripture in 1 Corinthians* (SBL 15; Atlanta: Society of Biblical Literature, 2005).
Johanson, B. C.	'Tongues, a Sign for Unbelievers? A Structural and Exegetical Study of 1 Corinthians 14:20–25', *New Testament Studies* 25 (1978–79): 180–203.
Josephus.	*Jewish Antiquities* (tr. W. Whiston, 1 vol; Peabody, MA: Hendrickson, 1987).
Lake, K. (tr.)	*The Apostolic Fathers* (vols. 24 and 25, LCL; Bellingham, WA: Logos Bible Software, 2005).
Lang, T. J.	'Trouble with Insiders: The Social Profile of the ἄπιστοι in Paul's Corinthian Correspondence', *Journal of Biblical Literature* 137/4 (2018): 981–1001.
Moberly, R. W. L.	*Prophecy and Discernment* (Cambridge Studies in Christian Doctrine; Cambridge: Cambridge University Press, 2006).
Munoz, K. A.	'How Not to Go Out of the World: First Corinthians 14:13–25 and the Social Foundations of Early Christian Expansion' (Ph.D. dissertation, Graduate School of Emory University, 2008).
Nash, R. S.	*1 Corinthians* (Smyth & Helwys Bible Commentary; Macon, GA: Smyth & Helwys, 2009).
Peppiatt, L.	*Women and Worship at Corinth: Paul's Rhetorical Arguments in 1 Corinthians* (Eugene, OR: Cascade, 2015).
Perkins, P.	*First Corinthians* (ΠΑΙΔΕΙΑ Paideia: Commentaries on the New Testament; Grand Rapids: Baker Academic, 2012).
Roberts, A. and Donaldson, J. (eds.)	*The Ante-Nicene Fathers* (1885–1887, 10 vols., repr.; Buffalo: The Christian Literature Company, 1885).
Thiselton, A. C.	*The First Epistle to the Corinthians: A Commentary on the Greek Text* (NIGTC; Grand Rapids: Eerdmans, 2000).

Trebilco, P.	'Creativity and the Boundary: Features of the Linguistic and Conceptual Construction of Outsiders in the Pauline Corpus', *New Testament Studies* 60/2 (2014): 185–201.
Webb, B.	*The Message of Isaiah: On Eagle's Wings* (The Bible Speaks Today; Leicester: IVP, 1996).
Witherington, B. III.	*Conflict and Community in Corinth: A Socio-Rhetorical Commentary on 1 and 2 Corinthians* (Grand Rapids: Eerdmans, 1995.)

CHAPTER 10

'Letters of Recommendation [...] From You' (2 Corinthians 3:1).[1] A Case of Theological Piracy?

Paul W. Barnett

Paul's questions at the beginning of his third chapter in 2 Corinthians are easy to dismiss as pious justification for the strength and credibility of his ministry:

> Are we beginning again to commend ourselves?
> Or, do we need, as some do,
> letters of recommendation to (*pros*) you or from (*ex*) you?

His answer is that the church in Corinth *is* his letter which is both in his heart and able to be known and read by everyone. At the same time, it is

---

1 I am assuming the unity of the epistle; that it was written circa 56 AD, and from Macedonia (probably Berea); and that Paul wrote it to prepare the way for his own coming to Corinth soon afterwards. For extended surveys of the literary integrity of Second Corinthians see Harris, *The Second Epistle*, 8–51. In defence of its unity also see Vegge, *2 Corinthians*, 12–34 and for the contra view see Welborn, *An End to Enmity*, xix–xxii for advocacy of a partition theory. Welborn goes so far as to say, 'the composition of 2 Corinthians is so problematic that the unity of 2 Corinthians must be regarded as a hypothesis in need of demonstration' (xix). Welborn thinks that there were five original letters that were later combined as our Second Corinthians. Dunn, *Beginning from Jerusalem*, 835, however, strikes a fatal blow against partition theories: 'My only problem is with envisaging the situation and motivation which caused some anonymous collector or editor to chop off the introductions and conclusions to each letter and simply to stick the torsos together in such an awkward way as to raise the questions which the various amalgamation hypotheses are designed to resolve. Why not retain them as complete letters?'

manifest that they are a letter from Christ, delivered by Paul.

In short, Paul has no need for letters from others accrediting and authorising his ministry.

The force and complexity of the first paragraph of chapter three are such that we tend to pass over the opening question about 'letters of recommendation *to* you or *from* you.'

Easy to miss is the unusual reference to the church in Corinth providing 'letters of recommendation' to be borne to other churches. Who was to bear such letters? Most likely it was to be those who had arrived bearing letters, whose mission in Corinth was to receive a letter of commendation which they were to carry to other churches of the Pauline mission.

Thus understood, the goal of the newly arrived mission was to correct the faulty theology of Paul as taught to the church in Corinth. Thus reformed, the church would endorse a letter of recommendation to those who would travel to another Pauline church, let us say for example in Ephesus. Their primary objective was to modify Paul's theology and replace it with a new teaching, 'a different gospel' (11:4).

These opening questions open a window that reveals a dedicated counter-mission whose objective was to seize and reform churches established by Paul dotted around the Aegean. It was nothing less than theological piracy. Lest we think this is an overstatement, consider Paul's scathing epithets for these opponents—as those who 'peddle God's word' (2:17), as 'pseudo-apostles' (11:13), and ironically as 'super-apostles' (11:5, 12:11).

So we ask: what was the origin of the initial letter to Paul? What was it about Paul's teaching that called for reformation or re-statement under the leadership of the newcomers?

To complicate matters Paul had been struggling for more than a year to sort out an internal problem within this church.[2] It appears related to the failure of the church to resolve the issue of the incestuous man (1 Cor. 5:1) that forced Paul to make an emergency visit to Corinth, but which proved to be 'painful' (2 Cor. 2:1).[3] Paul then failed to make

---

2 C. Kruse, 'The Offender'. Welborn, *An End to Enmity*, 23–59, argues that Paul was 'caused pain' and 'wronged' by a friend who accused him of fraudulent use of money, whom he identifies as Gaius. For a survey of earlier opinion see Harris, *The Second Epistle*, 223–227.
3 Chow, *Patronage and Power*, 130–140.

a promised return visit but instead sent a strong letter ('written in tears' —2 Cor. 2:4), borne by Titus, which he regretted having sent (2 Cor. 7:8). Forced from Ephesus by the Artemis incident he came to Troas to meet Titus and to hear the Corinthians' response to 'that' letter. No Titus (2 Cor. 2:13). So, he crossed the Northern Aegean to Macedonia (i.e. Neapolis) to wait for Titus who eventually arrived.

Titus' news was mixed. There was strong resentment against Paul's 'painful' letter, as reported by Titus ('His letters are weighty and strong, but his bodily presence is weak, and his speech of no account'—2 Cor. 10:10). Regarding the incestuous man, a majority of the members now agreed to some form of discipline—probably exclusion—but a minority disagreed. Paul argued for his reinstatement (2 Cor. 2:6–7).

Thus, Titus's report in Macedonia confronted Paul with two problems. Most serious was the arrival of those he calls 'peddlers, false apostles, super-apostles' whose mission was to win over the Corinthians to a revised form of Paul's teachings, to reshape the theological underpinning of the church.[4] At the same time, however, it was necessary for Paul to win back the loyalty of the church regarding the disciplinary issue of the incestuous man. Success in the former depended on success in the latter.

2 Corinthians is a complex text, as most would agree. Perhaps, though, the following schema will help.

2 Corinthians
1:1—2:13	The internal Corinthian issue
2:14—7:1	The counter-mission
7:2—10:12	The internal Corinthian issue
10:13—12:13	The counter-mission
12:14—13:14	The internal Corinthian issue

The abrupt changes are what complicate the letter and lead some to suggest that 2 Corinthians is a collection of earlier texts that were later bundled together. It is freely admitted that some of these joints are rubbery.

There is some relief, however, if we understand that Paul splices his responses to the counter-mission between his address to 'the internal

---

4 Barrett, 'Paul's Opponents', 251. For a contra view see Watson, *Paul, Judaism and the Gentiles*, which identifies the false apostles with Apollos and his companions, in my opinion, implausibly.

Corinthian issue'. Evidently Paul understood that he must win the Corinthians' hearts and minds if he was to defeat and discredit the teachings of the newly arrived counter-mission. This would explain the apparently fractured nature of the letter.

As noted, the intention of the counter-mission, apparently, was to reshape Paul's theology in Corinth to win support for a 'letter of commendation' to endorse their onward journey and mission which was to capture other churches of the Pauline mission.

Many problems for modern readers are eased once we understand the reasons for the unusual 'anatomy' of the letter. To repeat, Paul is addressing two concurrent issues, the existing internal problem, and the new problem. He must address both, but the priority was the former.

Accordingly, I will address the two blocks of text that defend his theology against the attacks of the counter-mission.

First Tranche (2:14—7:1)

Coming immediately after reference to 'letters to you or from you' is this assertion of the New Covenant: 'God...who has made us sufficient to be ministers of a New Covenant, not of the letter but of the Spirit. For the letter kills, but the Spirit gives life' (v.14).

Paul then contrasts the Old Covenant (v.14) as a 'ministry of the letter' (i.e. the law) which, he says, 'kills' (v.6), is a 'ministry of condemnation' (v.9), that was in principle annulled from the moment of its inception (v.11), and that 'veils' the heart when it is heard when read in the synagogue (v.15).

Why is Paul so negative about 'the ministry of the Old Covenant' and positive about the 'ministry of the New Covenant'? There must be a reason for the contrastive reference between the two ministries. What makes best sense is that Paul is offering defence for his New Covenant ministry and his condemnation of the ministry of the Old Covenant. This, in turn, suggests that the counter-mission sought to reinstate the Old Covenant among the Corinthians, blaming Paul and his teaching for allowing that Covenant to be superseded and thereby annulled.

During much of the remainder of the first tranche of teaching (2:14—6:13), Paul applies 'New Covenant' teaching to the Corinthians which he says is spiritually 'transformative' (3:18). He introduces chapter 4 with the words, 'having this ministry by the mercy of God...'. By 'this ministry' he means the ministry of the New Covenant, as in the previous chapter. His words 'by the mercy of God' remind the Corinthians of the Damascus 'revelation' in obedience to which Paul had preached the Son of God among them. He then reminds them that his ministry has opened their hearts to 'the light of the knowledge of the glory of God in the face of Jesus Christ' (4:6), their treasure in 'jars of clay' (4:6–7). He reassures them of their hope from the New Covenant: '... knowing that he who raised the Lord Jesus will raise us also with Jesus and bring us with you into his presence' (4:14), adding, 'For we know that if the tent that is our earthly home is destroyed, we have a building from God, a house not made with hands, eternal in the heavens' (5:1).

Perhaps, though, these great New Covenant promises make no provision for answerability before the Almighty, Paul's version of 'cheap grace' (as it were). Not so, he declares: 'For we must all appear before the judgement seat of Christ, so that each one may receive what is due for what he has done in the body, whether good or evil' (5:10).

Paul memorably declares that he is motivated by the love of Christ, that is, the Saviour's love of humanity, revealed in his sacrificial death for others, by which he reconciled the alienated to God. Mindful of the sufferings of the crucified Jesus he wrote, 'For our sake [God] made him to be sin who knew no sin, so that in him we might become the righteousness of God' (5:21).

Paul has more to say to the Corinthians before he completes the tranche. Thus far he has reminded the church of his New Covenant-based ministry and the blessings it has proved to be among the members of the church. Nevertheless, he has also written these words for the counter-missionaries to overhear. They have come to seize his church and to weaponise it for (disaffected?) letter-bearing emissaries in Corinth to move to another of Paul's churches, perhaps in Ephesus (from which Paul had recently come). Corinth was a remarkable city, both in its location and composition. The counter-mission had probably calculated that if they seized Corinth, other churches in the Aegean basin would also fall to them.

Second Tranche (10:13—12:13)

The first verses in the second tranche are informative. What does he mean by 'we will not boast beyond limits, but will boast only with regard to the area of influence God has assigned to us' (10:13)? 'Area of influence' translates the single word *kanōn*, which then referred to a defined territory assigned to an administrator (as noted by Edwin Judge[5]). It was later used to identify and define approved ('canonical') writings of the Bible.

To what is Paul referring? Most likely he has in mind the missionary agreement between James, Cephas, John, and himself in Jerusalem whereby it was agreed that Cephas would go to the circumcised and Paul would go to the Gentiles (Gal. 2:7–9).

This suggests that Cephas and/or his associates have trespassed into Paul's *kanōn*. For he goes on, 'we have not overextended ourselves [...] but were the first to come all the way to you with the gospel of Christ'. Paul is asserting that in coming to a (predominantly) Gentile city he has observed the Jerusalem agreement, but that those from the Jewish apostolate have 'overextended' themselves in trespassing into his *kanōn*.

Here, then, is a clue to the identity of this rival apostolate. They are Jewish missionaries who, despite the careful terms of the Jerusalem agreement distinguishing Jews from Gentiles, seek to impose the former covenant on Gentiles, and to reimpose it on Jews. Very pointedly, Paul accuses them of proclaiming 'another Jesus', which issued in the Corinthians receiving a 'different Spirit' and of 'accepting a different gospel' (11:4).

These words are exceptionally important. Their ministry message was not about the crucified and resurrected Son of God but an earthbound Jewish figure, Jesus, who affirmed and lived circumscribed by the then current covenant.

Furthermore, the counter-mission sought to impose this 'Old Covenant' Jesus upon the Corinthians so that it became central to the belief structure of their church. The next step would be for the now 'reformed' Corinthians to commend by letter the missionaries of this message to take it to another church of the Pauline mission, that is, for

---

5 Judge, 'The Regional *Kanōn*', 36–45.

them to leapfrog from Corinth eventually to other churches established by Paul.

So, it was fundamentally important for Paul to thwart these destructive plans. Accordingly, Paul's carefully stated teaching was not just to shore up the Corinthians belief as 'apostolic'. Paul's concern was immediately and urgently to halt these erroneous teachings in their tracks.

By reinforcing the Corinthians in apostolic truth, which he was engaged in doing, he was effectively sucking the oxygen from the opponents' objectives, their reformed version of the gospel, that would be 'fit for purpose' to send on to other Pauline churches.

This second tranche is dominated by what some call 'The Fool's Speech' (11:1; 11:16—12:14), perhaps imitating a then current genre of mockery: Paul's catalogue of his missionary sufferings. Writing with heavy irony, he alludes to the Corinthians' mistreatment of him (11:20–22), and to privations in the course of his ministry—to greater labours, imprisonments, countless beatings, often near death, a five-fold beating of the thirty nine lashes, thrice beaten with rods, thrice shipwrecked (but briefly), a day and a night adrift at sea, once stoned, the experience of danger from rivers, robbers, fellow Jews, Gentiles; danger in the city, the wilderness, at sea, from false brothers. He writes of toil, hardship, many sleepless nights, in hunger and thirst, often without food, in cold and exposure. Then he writes of his anxiety for all the churches.

This is a revelatory catalogue of Paul's sufferings incurred as he proclaimed the message of the crucified Jesus, which was hated by both Jews and Gentiles. But what was Paul seeking to achieve by this self-mockery?

It is a statement of his sufferings that Paul purposely connects with the sufferings of Christ, the One he serves and with whom he identifies. (Paul's references to the 'sufferings of Christ' are a feature of this epistle: 1:5; 4:8–12; 5:21; 13:4.)

Paul implies that the counter-missionaries have not suffered during their mission, but that Paul has, abundantly so. In fact, their easy ride implies that they didn't preach the crucified Christ and moreover were reticent to do so. By contrast, Paul's missionary suffering validate his claimed proclamation of the suffering, crucified Christ.

The Role of Cephas

Was Paul implying that Cephas was to blame for a Jewish mission intruding into Paul's Gentile-dominated *kanōn*?

There is no reference to Cephas in 2 Corinthians. This is in contrast with 1 Corinthians where Paul refers to him four times. Overall, Paul's references to Cephas in 1 Corinthians are positive.

- 1:12 Cephas had a following in Corinth. Most likely they were Jews who met in several distinct house groups. Unlike those who followed Apollos who seemed to have created an anti-Paul faction, Paul makes no implied criticism of Cephas.
- 3:22 Paul refers warmly to Cephas in these stirring words: 'all things are yours, whether Paul, or Apollos, or Cephas [...] all are yours and you are Christ's, and Christ is God's'.
- 9:5 Paul opens a window for us to see that when Cephas came to Corinth he was accompanied by his wife.
- 15:5 Most important of all, in citing the 'received' resurrection 'tradition' Paul names Cephas as the first to whom the risen Lord appeared.

We don't know when Cephas left Corinth or where he and his wife went next. However, Paul's letter to the Romans written c. 57 AD implies that by then Cephas was in Rome as the apostolic foundation layer of the church, upon whose structure Paul will not build (Rom. 15:20).

Paul made his first return visit to Corinth in c. 56 AD which he refers to as 'painful' (2 Cor. 2:1–4). There is no hint that Cephas was still in Corinth when Paul made that visit.

The Identity of the Counter-Missionaries

One hypothesis worth considering is that the counter-mission validated its coming to Corinth in that Cephas had already been there, and arguably for as long as two years. Since Cephas was the leader of the apostolic mission to the circumcised who had come to Corinth, it appeared to have justified the arrival of the counter-mission in Corinth. It was as if Cephas had planted a flag in Corinth for the Old Covenant mission of the Jews in that city.

What more are we able to say about them? He writes dramatically:

Are they Hebrews? So am I.
    Are they Israelites? So am I.
    Are they offspring of Abraham? So am I.
    Are they servants (*diakonoi*) of Christ? I am a better one.

Like Paul they are Jews. Furthermore, he concedes that they are 'ministers (*diakonoi*) of Christ'. They present themselves as 'apostles', but Paul says they are 'pseudo-apostles' (11:13). In fact, says Paul, they are 'deceitful workmen', in reality 'servants (*diakonoi*) of Satan' (11:15).

Paul's intense mode of argument in chapter 3 is rabbinic in character. Verse 7 employs *qal wahomer*—a 'light to heavy' linguistic device employed by the rabbis—as in, e.g., 3:7: 'For *if* there was glory in the ministry of condemnation, the ministry of righteousness *must far* exceed it in glory.' Paul's mode of argument in chapter 3 suggests that those for whom he was writing were Pharisaic in outlook and teaching. This implies that they and the letter of recommendation came from Jerusalem.

It appears that they were Christian, yet at the same time deeply and conservatively Jewish.

Here we run into a problem. These newcomers must have been fluent Greek-speakers to have come confidently to koine-speaking Corinth. Furthermore, Paul implies that in the employment of oratory these pseudo-apostles were superior to him (11:5). We don't associate Jerusalem Pharisees with superior competence in koine Greek and verbal oratory. However, it is now increasingly recognised that Jerusalem was a 'Greek city' (as Martin Hengel observed). Furthermore, Paul himself, a Pharisee was an accomplished writer of Greek and most likely an effective, if not a stellar, verbal communicator.

Their Message

Depending on 'mirror exegesis', it seems that their message against Paul was that the 'covenant' and the 'letter' (i.e., the law) remained in place, un-annulled, and fully applicable to Jews and Gentiles. The epistle is silent about circumcision but that doesn't necessarily mean it wasn't an issue. That they 'preached Jesus' (11:4) may be taken to mean that their focus was the historical, earth-bound Jesus rather than the crucified and resurrected Son of God, Lord (*Kyrios*) and Messiah.

This may explain the great emphasis Paul makes to the propitiatory death of Christ in the latter part of chapter 5 and the sure hope previously stated of those who belong to him.

Paul's self-mockery in the 'Fool's Speech', where he catalogues his sufferings, was designed to expose the newcomers' lack of missionary sacrifice. His sufferings mirroring Christ's sufferings and expose the newcomers' lack of sufferings, which is consistent with their failure to identify with and proclaim the redemptive sufferings of the crucified Christ. In his earlier letter Paul observed that the message of Christ crucified was a 'stumbling block to Jews' (1 Cor. 1:23).

What was the outcome of this powerful message when the Corinthians received it? The most important observation was that the church received Paul's letter, which they would not have done if the false apostles had prevailed. I assume that they returned, defeated, to Jerusalem.

Conclusion

Paul was faced with the critical possibility of losing this church and, through its letter-bearing emissaries, other churches in the Pauline mission. It was a desperate situation. Paul was already criticised for his handling of the disciplinary matter, for failure to return and instead sending a harsh letter. He must repair the damage in Corinth to have any hope of persuading the members to reaffirm his teachings against the challenge of the pseudo-apostles. This he sought to do in the first, third, and fifth parts of the letter. He then concentrates his defensive apologetic in the second and fourth parts. This explains the anatomy of the letter and its various purposes.

His ultimate objective in writing was to reinforce the church against the attempts of the rival mission to reform its message. Paul understood the power of the newcomers' message and their capacity to win other churches of his mission to their re-stated version of the gospel.

Bibliography

Barrett, C. K.	'Paul's Opponents in II Corinthians', *New Testament Studies* 17 (1971), 233–254.
Chow, J. K.	*Patronage and Power: A Study of Social Networks in Corinth* (JSNT 75; Sheffield: Academic Press, 1992).
Dunn, J. D. G.	*Beginning from Jerusalem* (Grand Rapids: Eerdmans, 2009).
Harris, M. J.	*The Second Epistle to the Corinthians* (NIGTC; Grand Rapids: Eerdmans, 2005).
Judge, E. A.	'The regional *kanōn* for requisitioned transport', in G. H. R. Horsley (ed.), *New Documents Illustrating Early Christianity* (Macquarie University, 1981), 36–45.
Kruse, C.	'The Offender and the Offence in 2 Corinthians 2:5 and 7:12', *Evangelical Quarterly* 88 (1988), 129–139.
Vegge, I.	*2 Corinthians – A Letter about Reconciliation: A Psychagogical, Epistolographical and Rhetorical Analysis* (WUNT 239; Tübingen: Mohr Siebeck, 2008).
Watson, F.	*Paul, Judaism and the Gentiles* (SNTS 56; Cambridge University Press: Cambridge, 1988).
Welborn, L. L.	*An End to Enmity: Paul and the Wrongdoer in Second Corinthians* (Berlin: Walter de Gruyter, 2011).

CHAPTER 11

Locating Titus in the Pauline Mission: Re-reading 2 Corinthians 2:13 with Apocalyptic Vision

Peter G. Bolt

1. Introduction: The Key Role of the Enigmatic Titus

a. The Enigmatic Titus

Despite being named in the New Testament twelve times (2 Cor. 2:13; 7:6,13–14; 8:6,16,23; 12:18; Gal. 2:1,3; 2 Tim. 4:10; Titus 1:4) and being addressed by an entire pastoral epistle, Titus is something of a mystery—according to Sir William Ramsay, 'the most enigmatic figure in early Christian history'.[1]

According to the usual broad conceptions of the Pauline literature, with some data in Galatians and the Pastoral Epistles and two-thirds of it in 2 Corinthians, Titus spans the corpus from early to late and (according to the critical theories) from authentic to inauthentic. Similarly in regard to the history of the apostle Paul and the chronology of his mission to the nations, Titus had a role from beginning to end.

From the data, certain things are clearly known about Titus. In the early days of the Gentile mission, when the apostle Paul visited Jerusalem for only the second time since his conversion, he took Titus with him

---

1   Ramsay, *St Paul the Traveller*, 284; cf. Plummer, *2 Corinthians*, on 2:13, 'we know very little of Titus'; Kruse, *2 Corinthians*, 85, '… we know nothing of Titus's background'.

from Antioch (Gal. 2:1–10). Because Titus was a Greek who remained uncircumcised despite Jewish urgings to the contrary, he became something of a 'test case' for Paul's Gentile mission, showing that Gentiles do not need to become Jews in order to be saved. This visit also concluded with an arrangement that, while the Jerusalem church would work amongst the Jews, Paul's team would take the gospel to the Gentiles—while nevertheless remembering the Jerusalem church, 'the saints', who self-identified as 'the eschatological poor' (2:9–10).[2] Consistent with this beginning, Titus later had a special role in assisting the Corinthian congregation with the collection for the saints, from initiation (2 Cor. 8:6a,10; cf. 1 Cor. 16:1–4) through to completion (2 Cor. 8:6b,17; cf. 9:5). Not only did this collection come as the mission to the nations was completed (Rom. 15:17–33), it also acted as a symbol and harbinger of the End.[3]

Amongst the personal remarks found in the Pastoral Epistles,[4] in the letter bearing Titus' name we learn that Titus was in Crete when Paul instructed him to join him in Nicopolis—towards Dalmatia on the coast of Epirus northwest of Corinth—for the coming winter (Titus 1:5; 3:12). In addition, as Paul urged Timothy to come to him by winter (2 Tim. 4:21), we learn that Titus had taken the gospel to Dalmatia (2 Tim. 4:10).

But given that the known facts indicate that he was closely associated with the apostle in significant roles across the course of at least a decade,[5] what is not known becomes all the more remarkable. Why isn't he mentioned in 1 Corinthians?[6] Why, apart from Timothy, is he the only other 'fellow-worker' of Paul to receive a 'pastoral epistle'? Why is the book of Acts apparently silent about the apostle's beloved compan-

---

2   Georgi, *Remembering*, 17–18, noting Holl, 'Kirchenbegriff', 57.
3   For the eschatological role of the collection see Georgi, *Remembering*, 47, 99, etc, who identifies (p.17) Holl, 'Kirchenbegriff', as 'the first to realise that it had been the eschatological expectation that prompted the Jewish believers in Jerusalem to participate actively in promoting the collection plan'; for a further discussion, see, Young, 'Eschatological Significance'.
4   Kee, 'Titus', 656, notes that 'even those scholars who deny the authenticity of the Pastorals as a whole, acknowledge that the personal remarks at the end of II Timothy and Titus may well include fragments of otherwise unknown correspondence from Paul'.
5   Exactly how long depends upon a full reconstruction of his (and Paul's) chronology, but, on the arguments to follow in this letter, Titus was associated with Paul from (a short time?) prior to the Jerusalem Council to the writing of Romans.
6   Ramsay, *St Paul the Traveller*, 284, following Plumptre; and then Plummer, *2 Corinthians*, on 2:13; reason that this is because Titus is the letter's carrier.

ion?⁷ What was his role, exactly, towards the Corinthians? What was his role in the mission further afield?

The mysteries are significant enough to have prompted attempts to identify Paul's 'Titus' with some other person known to the New Testament, but operating under another name. In the light of the Roman practice of having three names, the practice in bilingual contexts of adopting names from each language, and the wide-spread human practice of possessing a formal name but using an informal (shortened forms; nicknames), did Titus have an 'a.k.a.'—whether 'Timothy', or 'Silas', or, within Luke's presentation, 'Tit(i)us Justus' (Acts 18:7)?⁸

b. Titus' Role in 2 Corinthians ... and Beyond

This exploration will begin with Paul's second letter to the Corinthians, since this is where Titus comes into view most sharply. Although the interrelated literary and historical difficulties of 2 Corinthians were first raised in the eighteenth century,⁹ they have continued to trouble interpreters sufficient to dominate the letter's interpretation. Those who argue for a minimalist partition theory would see the canonical letter as a composition of two separate letters; Weiss and Schmithals, with six and nine separate letters respectively, represent maximalist positions; and the middle ground is occupied by numerous scholars suggesting a composition of three or four.¹⁰ Despite this long debate, however, the case continues to be made that modern interpreters have overcomplicated matters and, 'despite its uneven and disordered character,

---

7   His name appears in some manuscripts at 18:7; because of Gal. 2:1–10 he is often assumed to be amongst the companions of Paul in 15:2; some have identified him with Silas at 15:22; and it is common to assume that Paul met Titus in Macedonia at 20:2; see Barrett, 'Titus', 119, who concludes 'we leave Acts, therefore, having learnt nothing whatever about Titus'.
8   **Timothy**: Fellows, 'Was Titus Timothy?'; **Silas**: Schmiedel, 'Silas', whose efforts in relation to Acts 15:22, Barrett, 'Titus', 119, deemed 'a tortuous eccentricity of criticism'; further discussion noted by Knowling, 'Acts', 316, 326 and Kerr, 'Silas'; **Tit(i)us Justus**: see below.
9   The critical discussion dates to J. S. Semler (1776). For an overview of, and interaction with, the arguments, see Thrall, *2 Corinthians*, 3–77.
10 See Thrall, *2 Corinthians*, 47–49.

2 Corinthians possesses an intrinsic unity'.[11]

After surveying some of the literary and historical problems associated with 2 Corinthians, C. K. Barrett claimed that

> In all probability, the questions never will be finally settled; and we are unlikely to make much advance towards their solution by surveying them as a whole and trying to think out a comprehensive hypothesis capable of explaining everything at once. If advance is to be made at all it will be made by the pursuit, and eventual integration, of a number of details. Among such details we may count the career of Titus. 'Career' is indeed a somewhat grand word for one of whom we know so little, but it is precisely from 2 Corinthians that we learn most about this evidently trusted helper of Paul's, and a careful tracing of his probable movements can only serve to clarify the historical background of the epistle. It may also appear that there are some passages where commonly accepted exegesis needs to be revised.[12]

More recently, in raising the question 'Was Titus Timothy?', Richard Fellows argued that a proper understanding of Titus has a significance even beyond the second letter to the Corinthians. For him, properly determining Titus' identity is the key to solving Paul's interactions with Corinth, identifying his opponents, determining his relationship with the Jerusalem Church, and, indeed, 'shed[ding] new light on the origins of the Christian faith'.[13]

In agreement with Barrett and Fellows that understanding the enigmatic Titus provides a key to solving other thorny issues, this essay will follow Barrett's line of inquiry by 'tracing the probable movements' of Titus, 'revis[ing] some commonly accepted exegesis' (especially on 2 Cor. 2:13), and thereby 'clarify[ing] the historical background of the

---

11 Barnett, *2 Corinthians*, 16, calling attention to the similar position taken by his predecessor, Hughes, *2 Corinthians*, and noting that the letter 'is also consistent with Paul's historical situation between the second and third visits'. In 1994, Thrall, *2 Corinthians*, 1.49, provided a list of eighteen scholars arguing for the unity of the letter. This could now be supplemented by the commentaries of Barnett (1997), Garland (1999), Pratt (2000), Harris (2005), and Seifrid (2014). See also Kümmel, *Introduction*, 287.
12 Barrett, 'Titus', 118.
13 Fellows, 'Was Titus Timothy?', 33–34.

epistle' in relation to Titus. Part of the alternative picture that emerges will be a different solution to Titus' identity from that proposed by Fellows, which, in turn, charts the direction for reconfiguring Titus' role in Paul's mission to the nations.

2. A Turning Point in Troas (2 Cor. 2:13)

a. Missing Pieces of a Larger Puzzle

Tracing the movements of Titus from the Pauline correspondence necessarily requires some 'filling in the blanks' to arrive at a probable (but never certain) reconstruction. As noted by Betz:

> As with all other correspondence, the letters must be interpreted consecutively and in their entirety, for every section has its place in the context of the entire correspondence. Earlier statements may explain why later events occurred, just as later statements may throw light on what was said earlier. In literary terms, a correspondence contains components of an ongoing conversation the missing parts of which must be reconstructed to as great a degree as possible. Such reconstruction is a major task for the interpretation of 2 Corinthians.[14]

In the interpretation of 2 Corinthians, the passage 2:12–13 has played a major role by suggesting some 'missing parts' that have then been reconstructed into a fairly consistent usual picture. This essay, however, will argue that interpreters have not fully explored other possibilities latent in the grammar and syntax of Paul's language and when these are followed, a different picture emerges which is capable of greater explanatory power. A key plank in revisiting these pivotal verses speaking of Titus' absence is to read them in the light thrown by the later account of his arrival in Macedonia to be with Paul (7:5–16, especially vv.5–7), thus closing off a great time of suffering for the apostle in which his leaving Troas marked a most significant turning point in his missionary movements.

---

14 Betz, 'Corinthians, Second Epistle', 1148.

b. A Turning Point in 2 Corinthians

Paul's recount of the turning point in his mission also acts as a turning point for the epistle, and his recount of the arrival of Titus is such a fitting completion of the story, that these two passages have played a pivotal role in the partition theories of the letter, since what begins in 2:12–13 aligns with 7:5–7 sufficient to encourage the suggestion that the intervening material interrupts an originally contiguous letter.

Although also effecting a transition into Paul's long apologia for his new covenant ministry (2:14–7:4), 2 Corinthians 2:12–13 continues the highly emotional autobiographical narrative with which the apostle opens the letter (1:1—2:11).[15] In terms of his movements, 2 Corinthians 2:12–13 reports the simple fact that Paul and Titus were not in Troas at the same time, and this was associated with Paul truncating his visit to Troas in order to go to Macedonia.

This event came at a defining moment in the apostle's missionary journeying. He had endured a time of suffering (θλίψις, 1:8a) in Asia of such severity that he even despaired of life itself (1:8b), but had come through it—as if risen from the dead. He is now on the eve of his third visit to the Corinthians (12:13; 13:1; cf. 2:1–10) before he embarks on his final journey to deliver the collection made amongst the Gentiles for the Jerusalem church. But despite originally wishing to visit the Corinthians twice before departing for Judea, first on the way to and then on his return from Macedonia, his plans had changed (1:15–17). This was not because he was fickle, but in order to spare the Corinthians another 'painful visit' (1:1:17,23; 2:1), he had decided to pour out his heart in a letter, which, although written to show his love, had (as he subsequently learned) actually caused them pain (2:1–11; cf. 7:8). After explaining the motivations for his change of plans, he briefly recounted the turning-point in his missionary movements that took place in Troas (2:12–13).

c. 2 Corinthians 2:12–13: The Greek Text

The structure of the Greek text of these verses can be displayed quite simply:

---

15 See Furnish, *2 Corinthians*, 172; Barnett, *2 Corinthians*, 132–134; so also Garland, *2 Corinthians*, 132, 135.

12. Ἐλθὼν δὲ εἰς τὴν Τρῳάδα εἰς τὸ εὐαγγέλιον τοῦ Χριστοῦ
    καὶ θύρας μοι ἀνεῳγμένης ἐν κυρίῳ,
13. οὐκ ἔσχηκα ἄνεσιν τῷ πνεύματί μου
    τῷ μὴ εὑρεῖν με Τίτον τὸν ἀδελφόν μου,
    ἀλλ᾽ ἀποταξάμενος αὐτοῖς ἐξῆλθον εἰς Μακεδονίαν.

In terms of the manuscript record, apart from some manuscripts having a full lacuna at this point ($\mathfrak{P}^{34}$ $\mathfrak{P}^{117}$ $\mathfrak{P}^{124}$) and others with minor orthographical variations, verse 13b has several significant variations that can be placed into two groups.[16]

Instead of τῷ	το	69 218 1319 1646 1720 1874 1877
	του	ℵ(=01)* Ephraim (=04)c
	εν τω	D(=06) 33 2400
	δια το	945
Variations of word order around the infinitive	μη ευρειν με	ℵ(=01) A(=02) B(=03) Ephraim (=04) D(=06)c 010 012 049 1 33 35 69 76 131 209 218 424 489 927 945 999 1243 1244 1245 1249 1315 1319 1448 1563 1573 1628 1646 1720 1739 1768 1874 1876 1877 1881 1900 1962 2374 2400 MT SBL TR
	μη ευρειν	$\mathfrak{P}$46^{vid} 1505 2495
	μη ευρισκιν με	D(=06)*
	με μη ευρειν	Ψ(=044)
	μη με ευρειν	1735

The first group indicates some scribal discontent around the articular infinitive being in the dative case and without a preceding preposition. Since this is the only New Testament instance of this construction, all of these variations can be taken as evidence of scribal correction towards something deemed less difficult, whether by modifying the article to a case more common with the infinitive (τό, τοῦ), or by supplying a

---

16 UBS⁵ (2014) provides no textual variations, for those supplied see CNTTS.

preposition to formally align with the more usual practice in New Testament writers and materially to clarify the meaning the scribes found latent in the raw dative article. This clarification went in two different directions, with the eleventh century 945 creating a causal expression (διὰ τό), but three other manuscripts—the sixth century D(=06); ninth century 33; and thirteenth century 2400;— supplying the preposition ἐν, which would usually indicate a temporal expression, or perhaps one indicating means.[17]

The second group of variants indicate that the scribes apparently found some difficulty with the placement of the accusative personal pronoun με. The 9th/10th century Ψ(=044) and eleventh century 1735 both advance the pronoun so that it precedes the infinitive—even if Ψ(=044) mistakenly goes too far so that it even precedes the negating particle μή. This adjustment probably indicates that, finding ambiguity in the presence of two accusatives, the scribes sought to clarify through word order which item acted as the 'subject' of the infinitive, with their choice indicating Paul, rather than Titus.

d. Paul's (Aborted) Mission in Troas

Paul commences the account of his sudden change of direction by referring to the beginnings of something good in Troas. Verse 12 consists of two adverbial participial clauses that support the main clause to follow in v.13a (οὐκ ἔσχηκα ἄνεσιν ...), both providing antecedent circumstances.

The first (ἐλθών), registering antecedency because aorist, reports Paul's arrival—on his own (singular).[18] A following prepositional phrase indicates the destination; and a second the goal of his visit: 'after coming into Troas for the gospel of the Christ ...'. Interpreters discuss whether

---

17 BDF §401 regards neither το μη nor του μη as correct 'in all probability', but that εν τω μη is 'perhaps correct'; Plummer, *2 Corinthians*, s.v., appears to tentatively agree. The variants are noted without comment by Moulton-Turner, *Grammar-Syntax*, 142.
18 Harris, *2 Corinthians*, 235.

he came to the city or the region ('the Troad').[19] But even if it was the city (with population estimates ranging from 30,000 to 100,000),[20] since 'the gospel of the Christ' is an expression for the gospel mission (cf. 1 Thess. 3:2; Gal. 1:7; 1 Cor. 9:12b; 2 Cor. 9:13; Phil. 1:27; Rom. 15:19–20),[21] on Paul's usual missionary strategy, this would have been because the city held strategic importance for the region (cf. 1 Thess. 1:7–10; cf. Acts 18:11; 19:8–10).[22]

Switching subjects to a metaphorical door by way of a genitive absolute (θύρας),[23] the second adverbial clause registers its antecedency by way of the perfect tense (ἀνεῳγμένης). On older approaches, the perfect tense was taken to indicate that the initial promising gospel work continued until the time of the action of the main verb (yet to come in v.13), which, being negated, would then suggest a concessive translation for this clause: 'and although a door was standing open for me in the Lord ...', which then forges an opposition with Paul's restlessness.[24]

However, if the aspect of the perfect tense-form is granted an

---

19 Thrall, *2 Corinthians*, 183; Harris, *2 Corinthians*, 236. LSJ indicates that Τρῳάς is a frequent contraction of Τρῳϊάς, and that 'the Troad' can be indicated by γῆ Τρῳάς (Soph. *Aj.* 819) or by ἡ Τρῳάς alone (Hdt 5.122). Originally established in 334 BC with the name Sigia, in 301 BC it was renamed Alexandria, and called Alexandria Troas to distinguish it from other Alexandrias, then simply Troas by New Testament times; Strabo 13.1.47; 13.1.26; Yamauchi, 'Troas', 666. Harris explains the presence of the article in line with this history: 'its full name was Ἀλεξάνδρεια (ἡ) Τρῳάς, 'the Trojan Alexandria,' to distinguish it from other cities called Alexandria, so that Τρῳάς is adjectival in function and therefore technically subject to an article'. This makes it unnecessary to give credence to his alternative suggestion that contrary to four anarthrous uses in the NT (Acts 16:8,11; 20:5; 2 Tim. 4:13), like the anaphoric articular occurrence in Acts 20:6, Paul's use may '[refer] back to the mutually assumed knowledge of where Paul and Titus would meet'. This mutual knowledge is not only insufficiently argued by Harris, but in this essay it is denied.
20 For the history and descriptions of Troas, see, e.g. Burdick, 'Troad', 50; Yamauchi, 'Troas', 666; Thrall, *2 Corinthians*, 184–185; Hemer, 'Alexandria Troas'.
21 Thrall, *2 Corinthians*, 183–184, affirms that his primary purpose was evangelism, even if a small congregation may have already been in existence.
22 Harris, *2 Corinthians*, 237: 'Troas was a strategic center for missionary activity', referring to Ramsay, '*Roads*', 389, 400; Leaf, *Strabo*, 234; Murphy-O'Connor, *Paul*, 300 (for a similar strategic significance of Corinth, see pp.108–110, 256–273); Hemer, 'Troas', 103; Burdick, 'Troad', 31–65; Yamauchi, 'Troas', 666–67; Barnett, *2 Corinthians*, 134 and n.8. Furnish, *2 Corinthians*, 171.
23 Harris, *2 Corinthians*, 238.
24 As Thrall, *2 Corinthians*, 185; Furnish, *2 Corinthians*, 169; Plummer, *2 Corinthians*, 53, 64; Barrett, *Second Corinthians*, 83; cf. Burton, *Syntax*, §452. See also Harris, *2 Corinthians*, 237–240: It is difficult, however, to agree with Harris that the perfect indicated that the door stood open 'down to the time of writing', or that this constituted 'the lifting of the previous prohibition to preach in Asia (cf. Acts 16:6)' (p.237), since by this time Paul has had extensive activity in that province, despite its unfortunate conclusion (Acts 19; 1 Cor. 16:8–9; 2 Cor. 1:8–11).

'enhanced imperfective' sense,²⁵ it functions to draw the reader into Paul's viewpoint at the time of the open(ing) door, as he entered Troas. The compound sentence that makes up verses 12–13 is a contrast, pivoting around ἀλλά, and thus bringing the two verbs (with their independent clauses) into opposition: οὐκ ἔσχηκα ἄνεσιν 'I did not have rest' [...] ἐξῆλθον 'I went out'. In the flow of the sentence—and especially noting the lexical overlap ἐλθών / ἐξῆλθον— the 'enhanced imperfective' sense of the perfect has the effect of forming a more dramatic contrast with his departure, given in the contrastive clause of v.13b (ἀλλ' ἀποταξάμενος αὐτοῖς ἐξῆλθον εἰς Μακεδονίαν). 'After coming to Troas for the gospel of Christ, even with a door opening up before me in the Lord, I did not find rest [...] but [...] went out for Macedonia'.²⁶

e. A Dramatic Departure

In the final contrastive clause, the main verb ἐξῆλθον is supported by an adverbial clause, in which the aorist tense-form of the participle indicates that this was action antecedent to the main verb. According to LSJ (ἀποτάσσω IV) the middle form ἀποτάσσομαί τινι, is used for '*bid adieu* to a person, *part from them* (including Luke 9:61; Acts 18:21; Mark 6:46), or even '*have done with, get rid of* a person'.

Commentators tend to explain the referent of the personal pronoun (αὐτοῖς) in terms of the small congregation of believers that had sprung up in Troas either on a previous visit (proven by Acts 16:6–10) or as part of the initial promise of the most recent visit to which Paul is alluding.²⁷ However, as much as it can be assumed that Paul would have been operating in Troas with his usual strategy of working with and through local believers, the syntax of the larger sentence suggests that the pronoun refers to those who represented the 'door' that was opening up before him.²⁸

---

25 Campbell, *Verbal Aspect. Non-Indicative*, 28–29.
26 His stay in Troas was probably very short; as suggested by Thrall, *2 Corinthians*, 185–186.
27 See, e.g., cf. Thrall, *2 Corinthians*, 183–184, 187; Plummer, *2 Corinthians*, s.v.; Barnett, *2 Corinthians*, 137 and n.20; Harris, *2 Corinthians*, 240, suggests the pronoun refers to 'some believers'; and Seifrid, *Second Corinthians*, 81–82, to 'a small church' which sprang into existence on Paul's first visit to Troas (Acts 16:8–10).
28 Thrall, *2 Corinthians*, 183–184, 187, notes the emphasis falls upon Paul's breaking off of the evangelistic mission that was just commencing.

The nuances of the verb itself allude to a proper, formal farewell. His movement towards Macedonia indicates that he has now resumed the travel itinerary he had outlined to the Corinthians the year before, having previously modified it to allow a brief second visit which had not gone well (1 Cor. 16:5–7; 2 Cor. 1:15–16; 2:1–4).[29] With his ultimate goal Jerusalem (1 Cor. 16:3–4; 2 Cor. 1:16), his farewell is consistent with him saying final goodbyes (cf. Acts 18:18,21; and perhaps 20:13–38).[30] No matter what opportunity it presented, Troas was now a mission field that he was leaving behind. Even if it not fully exploited, it was now completed.

Despite the fruitful mission field opening up for him at Troas, Paul had turned on his heels and left it all behind.

3. Paul Without Remission

a. The 'Unremitted' Paul (v.13a)

What circumstances led Paul to discern that the Lord was prompting him to make such a major change in direction and leave, despite the opening door? He briefly explains these circumstances in the main clause at the heart of the sentence (v.13a), which consists of the lexically stative verb ἔχω, in the perfect tense-form and negated, with the noun ἄνεσις as its direct object, followed by a prepositional phrase in the dative.

This noun ἄνεσις is cognate with the verb ἀνίημι—with both being rare in biblical Greek.[31] In its formation, the suffix -σις denotes the action itself, rather than its outcome (-μα),[32] so the activity denoted by the verb is paramount. In its basic meaning ἀνίημι denotes 'the relaxation of tension,'[33] such as when a guitar string is tuned down from

---

29 Cf. Harris, *2 Corinthians*, 240: 'he was now once again following the itinerary of 1 Cor. 16:5 and because if he had proceeded from Troas to Corinth without hearing of the state of affairs in the Corinthian church he would have been risking a second visit ἐν λύπῃ (which he had resolved to avoid, 2 Cor. 2:1)'.

30 Barnett, *2 Corinthians*, 137 n.19.

31 In the LXX, the verb occurs 37 (Swete) or 40 (Rahlfs) times, and ἄνεσις five (Rahlfs) or six (Swete): 2 Chr. 23:15; 1 Esdr. 4:62; Ezra 4:22; [Wis. 13:13]; Sir. 15:20; 26:10.

32 Goodwin, *Greek Grammar*, §§834, 835.

33 Bultmann, 'ἀνίημι, ἄνεσις', 365. This paragraph draws upon Bultmann's brief entry at several points.

being too taut (ἐπίτασις; Plato, *Resp.*, I, 349e), which may include (with BDAG) the loosening of bonds (Acts 16:26; 27:40), the abandoning of persons (Heb. 13:5; cf. Deut. 31:6), or the ceasing of a threatening activity (Eph. 6:9).

According to Bultmann, in the New Testament the noun ἄνεσις is used once in its 'basic meaning', for relaxation of the strictures of imprisonment (Acts 24:23; cf. Josephus, *Ant* 18.235), and four times (2 Thess. 1:7; 2 Cor. 2:13; 7:5; and 8:13) with 'the metaphorical sense of 'refreshment' or 'rest,' which is also common in Greek (e.g., Plat. *Leg.*, IV, 724a: opp. σπουδή; M. Ant., I, 16, 6)'.[34] However, to capture the idea of 'relaxation from tension', perhaps a better translation might be 'relief' or 'remission',[35] in order to cover not only Paul's inner anxieties,[36] whether about the Corinthians or Titus,[37] but also the external realities from which relief is ultimately required. This certainly seems warranted in 2 Corinthians,[38] where Paul uses it in the context of not finding relief from his afflictions (cf. θλῖψις: 1:4,8; 2:4; 4:17; 6:4; 7:4; 8:2,13; and θλίβω: 1:6; 4:8; 7:5), including those he experienced in Macedonia, inside and out (7:5; cf. 2 Thess. 1:6–7, note ἄνεσιν), until he receives the good news brought by Titus that enabled him to rejoice even in the midst of those troubles (7:5–16). Because the state of being that he lacked in Troas (2:13) was delivered to him in Macedonia (7:5–7), the later account allows for its better understanding.

For both the θλῖψις and the ἄνεσις must be understood in relation to the time of eschatological sufferings that were promised in apocalyptic expectation for prior to the End (Dan 12:1) and realised in the sufferings of Christ, before then being experienced in the apostle's ministry and amongst the Gentile churches.[39]

---

34 Bultmann, ἀνίημι, ἄνεσις', 365.
35 So Plummer, *2 Corinthians*, s.v.; Furnish, *2 Corinthians*, 169.
36 Cf. the language of Furnish, *2 Corinthians*, 169; Garland, *2 Corinthians*, 133.
37 **Corinthians:** Kruse, *2 Corinthians*, 85; Lambrecht, *2 Corinthians*, 33; Seifrid, *2 Corinthians*, 79–81 ('he was so taken up with worry over the Corinthians that he was paralyzed, unable to make use of the *God-given* opportunity that lay before him', p.81); **Titus himself:** Barrett, 'Titus'; **Both:** Harris, *2 Corinthians*, 235, 239.
38 The suffering in Macedonia is not simply that the second planned rendezvous with Titus also failed as they missed each other on the road; so Barrett, 'Titus', 124.
39 See the exposition of Schlier, 'θλῖψις', 3.139–148.

b. The 'Resurrected' Apostle

As a popular concept in the Graeco-Roman world, as also in the Biblical conceptuality, θλῖψις 'tribulation', 'pressure', 'affliction', both external and internal, encompasses 'the afflictions of life, of which the last and strongest is death'.[40] Experienced in particular by Israel amongst the nations (Exod. 4:31; cf. 3:9; Deut. 4:29; cf. 28:47ff.), or, at the individual level, by the righteous Israelite,[41] this takes on the sense of 'days of suffering' experienced as visitations of God (4 Kgs 19:3 = Isa. 37:3; Obad. 1,12,14; Isa. 33:2; Nah. 1:7 etc.), foreshadowing the future 'day of suffering' of the end times prior to the day of resurrection (Dan. 12:1; cf. Hab. 3:16; Zeph. 1:15).[42] Paul has already revealed to the Corinthians, that, in his perspective, the suffering being experienced 'because of the present necessity' (cf. διὰ τὴν ἐνεστῶσαν ἀνάγκην, 1 Cor. 7:26), has come upon the world because of the coming of Jesus Christ (1 Cor. 10:11; 7:26,28–29).

This theme continues to be particularly prominent in 2 Corinthians, in fact, for Plummer 'being set free from θλίψις is the main idea in this letter'.[43] This is brought out well in Schlier's discussion:

> The power common to all θλῖψις is that of death at work in it. The apostle sees death in the almost intolerable weight of his sufferings (2 Cor. 1:8–9). In palpable afflictions he experiences the νέκρωσις τοῦ Ἰησοῦ in his own body (2 Cor. 4:10). He regards these sufferings as an abandonment to death (2 Cor. 4:11), as the ἐνεργεῖσθαι of death in us (2 Cor. 4:12). Thus at the end of his list of afflictions in Rom. 8:36 he quotes LXX Ps 43:23 [ET 22]: ἕνεκεν σοῦ θανατούμεθα ὅλην τὴν ἡμέραν, ἐλογίσθημεν ὡς πρόβατα σφαγῆς. The θλίψεις are θάνατοι, in the pregnant expression of 2 Cor. 11:23. And it is clear that in this last time the necessary suffering of Christ in His members is an experience of the concrete effects of the power of death which Christ has already broken in His death and resurrection. κοινωνία παθημάτων αὐτοῦ is by συμμορφιζόμενος

---

40 Schlier 'θλῖψις', 3.139–140.
41 Schlier 'θλῖψις', 3.141–143.
42 Schlier 'θλῖψις', 3.142–144.
43 Plummer, *2 Corinthians*, s.v.

τῷ θανάτῳ αὐτοῦ (Phil. 3:10). The power of death in θλίψεις affects man in his carnal existence (2 Cor. 7:5–6). The apostle fulfils the sufferings of Christ in his own σάρξ (Col. 1:24). He bears the marks of the νέκρωσις τοῦ Ἰησοῦ in his σῶμα (2 Cor. 4:10), in his total psycho-physical constitution (2 Cor. 7:5). In θλίψεις death shatters the earthen vessel (2 Cor. 4:7). It destroys our outward man, the outwardly orientated and outwardly experienced life with its essential contingency and corruptibility (2 Cor. 4:16).[44]

It is important, however, not to domesticate such a view of suffering into a cycle of regular Christian existence, but to set it firmly within the crisis Christ brought to the world's timeframe.

c. Suffering, Remission and the Day of Resurrection

Against the backdrop of a suffering world, the afflictions Paul experienced in Asia appear to have triggered a larger reality for him. The 'sufferings of the Messiah that abound for us' (1:5) were expected for the times of the end.[45] Paul had previously spoken to the Corinthians of an 'end' (1 Cor. 1:8; 13:8,10; 15:24), and told them that because 'the end of the ages has come' (1 Cor. 10:11), the time is short which has brought an urgency to ordinary life (1 Cor. 7:29–31). Prior to the arrival of the Day of Resurrection, apocalyptic expectation looked to a day of affliction such as has never previously been experienced—the 'great tribulation' (Dan. 12:1 ἡ ἡμέρα θλίψεως; cf. Matt. 24:21,29; Mark 13:19,24; Rev. 2:10; 7:14; 1QM 1:11ff; 1.8–9; 2 Bar. 48:31; Test. Mos. 8:1).[46] Once this expectation was generated, particular periods of affliction could provoke a sense that the great distress was commencing (e.g. 1 Macc. 9:27; *Midr.* Ps. 119.31). For the New Testament authors what began with the sufferings of Christ continued in the afflictions

---

44 Schlier 'θλῖψις', 3.147.
45 This connection makes it unlikely that the event in Asia was simply Paul's despair over the Corinthians or even a severe sickness; similarly, see Thrall, *2 Corinthians*, 115–116. It must be something 'within and without' (7:6) and so is likely a severe persecution, perhaps an imprisonment with a death penalty hanging over Paul's head. See also Winter, '"He will Rescue"', 2–3, 6.
46 Although not specifically mentioning 'the great distress', Winter, '"He will Rescue"', also understands Paul's view of suffering in general and this suffering in particular within an apocalyptic setting.

of his followers,⁴⁷ but these 'birth pangs' nevertheless foreshadowed a definite future moment when the End would come (e.g. 1 Cor. 15:24). Although he had experienced sufferings before, the extremity of the Asian afflictions⁴⁸ seems to have led Paul to see them in the light of Daniel's 'great distress' that would fall upon God's people just before the future resurrection day (12:1–3).⁴⁹ This realisation, in turn, had a bearing upon the urgency with which the mission to the nations should be conducted, because the time remaining had become even shorter, such that, 'Now is the time of God's favour; Now is the day of salvation' (2 Cor. 6:2).

According to 2:13, Paul experienced his lack of relaxation from his afflictions τῷ πνεύματί μου, 'in my spirit',⁵⁰ just as Titus later experienced a contrasting rest 'in his spirit' (7:13).⁵¹ Noting in its retrospective parallel in 7:5 he uses ἡ σὰρξ ἡμῶν, 'our flesh', Paul's reference to his spirit should not be pressed to indicate something purely internal. However, neither should the two terms be declared 'synonymous'. Instead, encompassing 'his total psycho-physical constitution',⁵² they each refer to Paul's whole person viewed from a particular perspective', 'the seat of spiritual sensitivity [...] the seat of physical suffering'.⁵³ The experience of such urgent θλῖψις shapes the believer by putting it into eternal perspective (2 Cor. 4:17–18). With the suffering comes the comfort of Christ which then brings the ability to comfort others (1:5–7) and with the mutual comfort, the experience of great joy

---

47   For this paragraph, see Beale, *Revelation*, 433–435, on 'the great tribulation' in Rev 7:14. See also Schlier, 'θλῖψις', 3.145–146.
48   Thrall, *2 Corinthians*, 114–117, lists the alternatives as: 1. Depression and anguish; 2. Severe illness; 3. Severe persecution, perhaps incarceration under the shadow of a death sentence.
49   In an excursus, Harris, *2 Corinthians*, 164–183, explored the impact of the experience upon Paul's eschatological expectations, but very much in relation to his personal eschatology. The position taken here is that Paul saw the Asian troubles as the beginning of the afflictions to fall upon the world, prior to the resurrection day. As opposed to the view that 'Paul's trouble with the Corinthians is the fundamental trouble of the letter' (Seifrid, *Second Corinthians*, 79–80), I would argue that Paul was dominated by his view that the eschatological sufferings had commenced, which included the desertion of the Corinthians (11:3) and others (cf. 2 Tim. 1:15).
50   Identified here as a dative of reference, 'with respect to my spirit'; with Wallace, *Greek Grammar*, 154.
51   The 'refreshment of the inner man' (1 Cor. 16:18; 2 Cor. 7:13; Phlm. 7,20) noted by Bauernfeind, 'ἀναπαύω', 350, should also be taken with the same eschatological loading.
52   Schlier 'θλῖψις', 3.147.
53   Harris, *2 Corinthians*, 238.

and overflowing generosity (7:5–7; 8:2).⁵⁴ Paul's experience therefore becomes a pastoral vehicle to move the Corinthians into this better experience, corresponding to his lack of relaxation in his spirit through to his refreshment of spirit, or, to put it another way, that they might know the comfort of someone brought from death to life (1:9–10).

2. Entering Paul's Experience

To express Paul's lack of 'relaxation from tension', the main clause at the centre of Paul's compound sentence (13a) utilises the perfect tense-form of ἔχω—which is found only five times in the New Testament, four of which are in Paul, and of those, three in 2 Corinthians (Mark 5:15; Rom. 5:2; 2 Cor. 1:9; 2:13; 7:5):

οὐκ ἔσχηκα ἄνεσιν τῷ πνεύματί μου.

As more generally,⁵⁵ the function of the perfect tense-form has not been well understood here, with commentators usually deferring to another, and/or providing only scant discussion.

a. Paul's Distress as a Past Experience

One well-established suggestion is that, although perfect in form, ἔσχηκα should not be read as a true perfect but as an 'aoristic' perfect, for it is 'apparently used exactly like [an] Aorist',⁵⁶ or an 'aorist used in/for historical narration',⁵⁷ or 'a narrative or aoristic perfect, simply indicating something that happened (or did not happen) at some point in the past'.⁵⁸

Lurking in the background here are the older discussions of Burton and Moulton, who both identify some New Testament perfects as early examples of a diachronic shift taking place in the perfect tense-form

---

54 Schlier, 'θλῖψις', 3.147.
55 Even though he deliberately avoids dealing with the New Testament, for the difficulties in understanding the behaviour and semantics of the perfect tense-form as a cause of 'unwarranted exegesis', see Crellin, 'Abstract', 158–159; for further accounts of the discussion see n.82 below.
56 Moule, *Idiom Book*, 14, and for 7:5.
57 BDF §343 (2), although conceding Rom. 5:2; 2 Cor. 1:9; 7:5 could be true perfects; Martin, *2 Corinthians*, 177; Harris, *2 Corinthians*, 238 and n.20, also for 7:5.
58 Despite noting the 'considerable support' for this view, Thrall, *2 Corinthians*, 185 n.401, regards it as 'more likely that it is a true perfect'.

as the Greek language evolved.⁵⁹ Both, however, are fairly circumspect about this usage in the New Testament.

Under the heading 'The Aoristic Perfect', Burton claimed that

> The Perfect Indicative is sometimes used in the New Testament of a simple past fact where it is scarcely possible to suppose that the thought of existing result was in the writer's mind.⁶⁰

Although tracing 'the beginnings of this departure' to the Classical Greek period and noting that it was 'in Greek writers of a time later than the New Testament that this tendency was still further developed, until the sense of difference between the tenses was lost', he claims that 'in the New Testament we see the earlier stages of this process', even if 'the idiom is confined within narrow limits in the New Testament':

> The Perfect is still, with very few exceptions, a true Perfect, but it has begun to be an Aorist. [...] it is impossible to decide with certainty. While there is clear evidence that the Perfect tense was in the New Testament sometimes an Aorist in force, yet it is to be observed that the New Testament writers had perfect command of the distinction between the Aorist and the Perfect. The instances of the Perfect in the sense of the Aorist are confined almost entirely to a few forms, ἔσχηκα, εἴληφα, ἑώρακα, εἴρηκα, and γέγονα, and the use of each of these forms in the sense of an Aorist mainly to one or more writers whose use of it is apparently almost a personal idiosyncrasy.⁶¹

To illustrate the latter category he cites the aoristic use of ἔσχηκα as belonging to Paul.

Regarding the perfect as 'the most important, exegetically, of all the Greek Tenses',⁶² Moulton argued that 'in Greek, as in English, the line between aorist and perfect is not always easy to draw'. Although he noted that, diachronically, 'the perfect was increasingly used, as the language grew older, as a substitute for what would formerly have been

---

59 Although I have not fully digested his contribution, Robert Crellin provides more recent diachronic study; see his several works on the bibliography.
60 Burton, *Syntax*, §80.
61 Burton, *Syntax*, §88.
62 Moulton, *Grammar*, 140.

a narrative aorist' and that the papyri indicate 'how much more the vernacular tends to use this [sense of the] tense', he was also clear that the previous sense of the perfect was certainly not obsolete at an early stage:

> There are extremely few passages in the papyri of the earlier centuries AD in which an aoristic perfect is demanded, or even suggested, by the context. It is simply that a preference grows in popular speech for the expression which links the past act with present consequences.[63]

> [Although] it was not the perfect which survived in the struggle for existence, these processes do not fairly set in for at least two centuries after the NT was complete.[64]

Because 'aoristic perfects' appear before and after its epoch, their identification in the New Testament 'must be settled on its merits, without any appeal to the *a priori*'.[65] After reviewing the small number admitted by predecessors Blass, W.F. Moulton, and Burton, (J. H.) Moulton notes that 'the extremely small proportion of even possible examples will naturally prevent us from accepting any except under very clear necessity'.[66] After clearing out a number of the suggested examples, he turns to 'the residuum of genuinely aoristic perfects, or those which have a fair claim to be thus regarded', into which group he concedes, first, εἴληφεν and εἴρηκα in Revelation (5:7; 8:5; and probably 3:3, 11:17, 2:27), and then, second, ἔσχηκα in 2 Cor. 2:13; 1:9; 7:5; Rom. 5:2a—and, the only instance outside Paul, Mark 5:15.[67]

In this second group, which is of the greatest interest to this present essay, he acknowledges that 'Blass believes the perfect justifiable except

---

63 Moulton, *Grammar*, 141. Arguing that the traditional distinction survives 'very clearly in the papyri for some centuries' (p.143), he proceeds to dismiss the evidence provided by Jannaris, concluding that Matt. 13:46 'is the only NT example cited by Jannaris which makes any impression' (p.142).
64 Moulton, *Grammar*, 141–142, even if 'the LXX and inscriptions show a few examples of a semi-aoristic perfect in the pre-Roman age'.
65 Moulton, *Grammar*, 143.
66 Moulton, *Grammar*, 143.
67 Moulton, *Grammar*, 144–145. Like his diachronic predecessors, Crellin, *Syntax*, 5 n.6, acknowledges that 'so-called "aoristic" uses of the perfect occur, as may be seen especially in the New Testament' (only citing Matt. 13:46 and Rev. 8:5, however), before admitting that he could only come up with one in his corpus of investigation (Josephus, *AJ* 16.254). 'Given the very marginal nature of this usage within literary Koine', he saw no need to account for it.

in 2 Corinthians 2:13', but considers that 'we must, I think, treat all the Pauline passages alike', before arguing that 'it seems clear that an aorist would suit all four passages, and in [2 Cor. 2:13] it seems hopeless to squeeze a natural perfect force into the Greek'.[68]

If even the proponents of the diachronic argument realise it must be at least taken with a grain of salt, the few synchronic, or textual, arguments that have been offered are even less persuasive. Isn't it reasonably clear that even if the perfect simply denoted a past action whose consequences abided to the present, that the 'present' of which Paul was speaking does not have to be his time of writing, when 'he had in fact gained relief' (7:6,13,16),[69] but could equally well apply to the time of his experience in Troas? The influential comments of BDF, furthermore, seem to be particularly weak. How can the argument that the 'aoristic' nature of ἔσχηκα is derived from being surrounded by aorists in the context, therefore appearing 'in historical narration',[70] or its derivative, 'that ἔσχηκα is structurally opposed to the aorist ἐξῆλθον',[71] really be taken seriously? From an aspectual point of view, since the aorist is the background tense of historical narration, a field of aorists then provides exactly the landscape against which the imperfective present and perfect tense-forms can stand tall to bring an even greater prominence for the reader.

So, not everyone is convinced that reading ἔσχηκα as a 'natural perfect' would be 'squeezing' it in, nor that it would be 'hopeless' to try. McKay, for example, differs with the commonly adopted position 'that the perfect was being confused with the aorist and was on its way to being absorbed by it', because

> the fact remains that however willing we are to see decay in the perfect we must acknowledge that the ancient function of the Greek perfect is clearly fulfilled by many perfects, and this continues to be true for several centuries after the New Testament.[72]

---

68 Moulton, *Grammar*, 145, arguing that whereas ἔσχον is used as the ingressive aorist 'got', the perfect was appropriated for the constative aorist sense 'possessed'.
69 See, e.g. Harris, *2 Corinthians*, 238.
70 BDF §343 (2).
71 Bachmann, *Der zweite Brief*, 125; Harris, *2 Corinthians*, 238. Answered by Thrall, 185 n.401, see in text.
72 McKay, 'Syntax', 52–53; noting his study 'Use of the Ancient Greek Perfect'.

Supplying evidence for an alternative view, he notes that, as in Thucydides, 'frequently in the New Testament the perfect is used where we might expect the aorist, in order to draw attention to the identity of the subject'.[73] He differs from Moulton's treatment of ἔσχηκα, including its occurrence in 2 Cor. 2:13 (which has been followed by many):

> Moulton argued in his *Prolegomena* that ἔσχηκα may have come to be regarded as an aorist form. Yet in some of its occurrences there is no difficulty in taking it as really perfect: e.g. in Romans 5:2 an aorist would be possible but the perfect is more expressive of the Christian's position. The example that is, I think, generally regarded as the most difficult to accept as perfect is 2 Corinthians 2:13 οὐκ ἔσχηκα ἄνεσιν. On the face of it an aorist seems natural: 'When I went to Troas, although a door of opportunity was open I got no respite because I didn't find Titus, but I went away ...'. The context stresses Paul's concern for the Corinthians and his eagerness to get news. In view of the extent to which the perfect can be used to highlight the continuing effect of his action on the subject's life, or even on his reputation beyond his lifetime, I think this may be just a means of emphasizing the emotional effect, not only at the time but ever since, of his not getting the expected news. It amounts to 'I got no respite—and I still feel the effect—because ...'.[74]

In speaking of the perfect 'drawing attention to the subject' and 'highlighting the continuing [emotional] effect' upon the subject's life, McKay shows the aspectual stance that he has championed in regard to the verbal system. Others, however, have also noticed the effect that the perfect has upon the reader. Even Moulton notes a text from Plato's *Crito* in which Socrates uses ἑώρακα instead of εἶδον, 'to emphasise the present vividness of the vision'.[75] Robertson insisted that the perfect forms of ἔχω in 2 Corinthians, even that in 2:13, 'were not to be treated as "for" the aorist', but were instances of 'vivid dramatic recital',[76] where

---

73 McKay, 'Syntax', 52–53, illustrating from Acts 7:35; Heb. 1:13, cf. v.5; and Mark 14:44, cf. Matt. 26:48.
74 McKay, 'Syntax', 53–54; referring to his 'Use of the Ancient Greek Perfect', 11.
75 Moulton, *Grammar*, 141.
76 Robertson, *Word Pictures*, 217; cf. 211, 239.

'an action completed in the past is conceived in terms of the present time for the sake of vividness'.⁷⁷ Although finally opting for the 'aoristic use', Plummer admitted that 'we may explain the perfect as vividly recalling the moment when the Apostle had this experience and could say "I have not got relief"'.⁷⁸ More recently still, Thrall notes that rather than ἐξῆλθον domesticating the perfect ἔσχηκα to operate as an aoristic:

> the force of the οὐκ ἔσχηκα ... ἀλλ' ... ἐξῆλθον antithesis is arguably sharpened, since the aorists ἀποταξάμενος and ἐξῆλθον mark the point of sudden decisive action when the continuing anxiety becomes too great to be borne.⁷⁹

These 'felt observations' can be reinforced by a greater sensitivity to the aspect of the verb, which causes the reader to view the action from a certain perspective. So, for example, this sense of the 'vividness' of the perfect appears to be what more recent writers mean when referring to the 'aoristic/dramatic perfect'. Drawing upon Fanning, Wallace includes 2 Corinthians 2:13 in this category, noting that along with other examples in 2 Corinthians, it acts as 'a narrative within an epistle', and that without concern for present consequences, such perfects are used 'in a rhetorical manner to describe an event in a highly vivid way'.⁸⁰

In relation to the perfect tense-form, Paul's language draws his readers into the events of his 'historical narration' by portraying them with what Campbell has called 'heightened proximity'.

b. Paul's Distress in Heightened Proximity

The unique contribution of the perfect tense-form to the communicative transaction between ancient authors writing in Greek and their readers has been the subject of scholarly debate for more than a century, and this has only intensified as interest in Greek verbal aspect has

---

77 Robertson, *Grammar*, 896–898, and 900–901.
78 Plummer, *2 Corinthians*, s.v.
79 Cf. Thrall, *2 Corinthians*, 185 n.401: 'it is more likely that it is a true perfect, serving to emphasise the seriousness of Paul's uneasiness: it was no merely momentary reaction (cf. Windisch, *Der zweite Korintherbrief*, 95)'.
80 Wallace, *Greek Grammar*, 578–579; cf. Fanning, *Verbal Aspect*, 301.

grown.⁸¹ Both Burton and Moulton operated with the traditional view that the perfect 'conveys the thought of existing result',⁸² thus linking 'the past act with present consequences'.⁸³

Responding to the view drawn by the diachronic analysis that the perfect is collapsing into the aorist, Campbell draws attention to how the perfect indicative aligns with the present tense-form, rather than the aorist. Like the present, the perfect encodes 'imperfective aspect at the semantic level', which 'views an action or state from the inside; it is the internal viewpoint'.⁸⁴ Viewed spatially, just like the present encodes proximity, the perfect encodes 'heightened proximity'.⁸⁵ With this as its core semantic value, it has two pragmatic implicatures: intensification and prominence.⁸⁶ This is particularly significant when a writer or speaker wishes to draw the reader into the intensity, vividness, or even the drama, of their emotional experience.⁸⁷ Because it 'creates a proximate-imperfective context as the speech or thought is presented immediately before the reader's eyes, as though unfolding',⁸⁸ the perfect is a characteristic of discourse—its most frequent New Testament context.⁸⁹ Like the viewer of a passing parade who steps forward to take a closer look, 'the parade becomes more dramatic from the viewpoint of the reporter; he is *experiencing* the parade in an intimate way'.⁹⁰

In 2 Corinthians 2:13, because Paul writes a narrative of the past with an oft-noted 'autobiographical style',⁹¹ his words can be regarded as 'authorial discourse', with the recognition that this also attracts the perfect tense.⁹² In addition, he depicts his state of being with the stative verb

---

81   For the debate, see McKay, 'Syntax'; Campbell, *Verbal Aspect: Indicative Mood*, Chapter 6; for updates on the debate within New Testament circles, see Campbell, Fanning and Porter, *The Perfect Storm* (briefly summarised in Campbell, *Advances*, 117–119); and within the linguistics of Ancient Greek more generally, see Crellin, 'Abstract'; *Syntax*; 'Perfect System'.
82   Burton, *Syntax*, §80.
83   Moulton, *Grammar*, 141. Cf. BDF §340
84   Campbell, *Verbal Aspect. Indicative*, 184–185; *Basics*, 103.
85   Campbell, *Verbal Aspect. Indicative*, 205–206; *Basics*, 104.
86   Campbell, *Verbal Aspect. Indicative*, 205–206.
87   Cf. Campbell, *Verbal Aspect. Indicative*, 191, 199, 210, on the Gospel of John. See also *Basics*, 110–111.
88   Campbell, *Basics*, 105; Campbell, *Verbal Aspect. Indicative*, 185–186, 196.
89   Campbell, *Verbal Aspect. Indicative*, 183, argues that the evidence in his sample shows that the perfect indicative is 'primarily a discourse tense-form'; cf. 175–178, 187 'even more exclusively than the present', 192 and 196 'almost exclusively', 210 'very clearly'.
90   Campbell, *Verbal Aspect. Indicative*, 199; for 'heightened proximity', pp. 195–211.
91   Pratt, *I & II Corinthians*, 320.
92   Campbell, *Verbal Aspect. Indicative*, 210.

ἔχω. Stativity is a lexical property that contrasts with that of dynamicity across all languages, and 'combines with aspectual properties across languages, most often and most naturally with imperfective aspect'.[93] This is because 'imperfective aspect does not portray verbal occurrences with either the beginning or end of such occurrences in view [... but] it views verbal occurrences internally as they unfold'.[94] The stative verb adds its lexical force to the 'intensification and prominence'[95] of the perfect's 'heightened proximity' to draw the reader into the highly emotional experience that Paul is describing.

οὐκ ἔσχηκα is not 'aoristic', or a 'virtual aorist',[96] it is a true perfect, and 'the heightened proximity' created by its imperfective aspect therefore enables Paul's Corinthian readers to enter into his state of being stretched to the limit, without remission. This was the state in which he came to Troas and out of which he departed from Troas for Macedonia, leaving fruitful mission opportunities behind. Through his language, the resurrected apostle draws the Corinthians into his experience of 'the great distress', with a view to them also sharing in the comfort of his own 'resurrection' (cf. 1:9).

Since Paul's 'lack of remission' in the midst of his death-like θλῖψις ceased after Titus brought him resurrection-like comfort, to understand the rhetorical impact of the letter, it is important to follow the movements of Titus.

5. The Absence of Titus

a. Paul Missing Titus in Troas

As the sentence in 2 Corinthians 2:12–13 moves towards its finale, an articular infinitive is supplied in further support of the main clause. It is here that the reader first meets Titus in the letter, and so (at last!) we arrive at the heart of this essay:

---

93 Campbell, *Verbal Aspect: Indicative Mood*, 173, referring to Comrie, *Aspect*, 48–51.
94 Campbell, *Verbal Aspect: Indicative Mood*, 188, cf. 189.
95 Campbell, *Verbal Aspect. Indicative*, 201–205.
96 In relation to the diachronic analysis that some verbs, including ἔσχηκα, became 'virtual aorists', Campbell, *Verbal Aspect. Indicative*, 190, notes that 'imperfective aspect comfortably accomodates οἶδα and ἕστηκα, as well as transitive verbs'—and presumably also ἔσχηκα.

> τῷ μὴ εὑρεῖν με Τίτον τὸν ἀδελφόν μου.

Since this is an adverbial clause, Paul clearly gives Titus a role in relation to the restless tension that led to his dramatic *volte-face*, but what, exactly, was that role? On the usual view, the infinitival clause provides the cause of Paul's disturbed state: when he came to Troas he did not find Titus. Exegetically, this view takes the articular infinitive as causal, and its (accusative) subject the pronoun με, which, in the context of the preceding main clause, refers to Paul. In what follows, these twin underpinnings will be questioned and alternatives offered in order to shape a different picture of events.

Much rides on the interpretation of this adverbial clause. Once the usual exegetical decisions have been made, other ramifications are proposed that make the picture increasingly complex.[97] If Paul was disappointed at not finding Titus, he must have expected him to be in Troas. If Paul had expected to find Titus, then they must have made prior arrangements for a rendezvous.[98] If they were previously together, then Paul must have sent him (to the Corinthians) in the first place, with some task to do (whether carrying letters, sorting out problems, gauging their attitude to Paul, or preparing for the collection), and him bringing news to the apostle (7:5–16) indicates that he has returned with the task completed. That he was sent means that when Paul describes him as 'my partner and fellow worker for you' (κοινωνὸς ἐμὸς καὶ εἰς ὑμᾶς συνεργός, 8:23), Titus, like Timothy, must have not only been a (long-term, see Gal. 2:1–10)[99] travelling companion of Paul, but also one who acted in 'a special role as Paul's envoy to the Corinthians'.[100] Always a visitor to the Corinthians, he is usually granted three visits to Corinth (as are both Paul and Timothy), two of them prior to carrying the latest letter

---

97 The details of this paragraph can be readily found in the commentaries, e.g. Plummer, *2 Corinthians*, on 12:18; Harris, *2 Corinthians*, 235, 240; Barnett, *2 Corinthians*, 136 n.13, 589; Thrall, *2 Corinthians*, 186; Seifrid, *2 Corinthians*, 79–80; Martin, *2 Corinthians*, 179; Kruse, *2 Corinthians*, 85; Betz, 'Corinthians', 1151; Barrett, 'Titus', 125.

98 For an example of much of the following scenario, see Kümmel, *Introduction*, 286. It is readily apparent in the commentaries.

99 E.g. Gillman, 'Titus', 581.

100 Barnett, *2 Corinthians*, 136 n.13. Cf. Thrall, *2 Corinthians*, 186: 'by the time the present letter was written he was one of the apostle's chief fellow-workers, since he had been sent to Corinth at a time of particular tension. He was probably the bearer of the Painful Letter. At any rate, he was to bring news of how it had been received (7:6–15). Whether he had visited Corinth prior to this occasion depends on the interpretation of the reference to him in 8:6'.

from the apostle (whether our 2 Corinthians, or an originally separate portion of it),[101] sent on the brink of Paul's third (12:14; 13:1–4).

Other ramifications are drawn for Paul from Titus missing the rendezvous. Was the apostle purely concerned about Titus' safety on the road, especially if carrying the collection money?[102] Was he worried about what Titus' absence meant for the Corinthians' (continuing?) hostilities to himself especially since his brief (second) visit had ended in disaster? Or was it abiding worry about the internal problems of the congregation that had issued in such disaster in the first place? Was it simply personal, with Paul moving towards Macedonia specifically in quest of Titus with an eagerness to reunite with him,[103] perhaps aiming for a second rendezvous pre-arranged in case the first one fell through? Or with all else going on around him, was he concerned about the Gentile mission as a whole? All these speculations (and any others) lie behind the usual rendering: '*because* I did not find Titus my brother'.

As briefly noted already, at the base of this reconstruction and super-struction lie two decisions about what is the New Testament's only instance of a dative articular infinitival clause: 1. It expresses the cause of Paul's distress; 2. By way of the personal pronoun με, Paul is the (accusative) subject of the infinitive, and, by way of being explicitly named, Titus is its (accusative) object. However, as sometimes noted but not fully explored, the Greek contains latent possibilities which allow both decisions to be challenged, resulting in a very different picture emerging for Titus, his movements, and their wider implications.

b. Not Cause but Circumstance

i. Cause?

It is entirely natural for human beings to connect two sequential events —whether those of real life or of a narration—by proposing causation,

---

101 These three visits are a point of commonality across proponents of different views of the letter's composition. See, for example, Betz, 'Corinthians, Second Epistle to the', 1151, operating with a moderate partition theory for the letter (six letter fragments); and Barnett, *2 Corinthians*, 136 n.13, seeing the letter as a unity.
102 Barrett, 'Titus', 125–126, 131 n.33. Thrall, *2 Corinthians*, 186–187, notes that it is unlikely that Titus would cart back to Troas money collected from Corinth, if the collection for Jerusalem was set to leave from there (cf. Acts 40:4).
103 See Martin, *2 Corinthians*, 178; Kruse, *2 Corinthians*, 85; Lambrecht, *Second Corinthians*, 33; Seifrid, *Second Corinthians*, 79–81; Harris, *2 Corinthians*, 235–236, 239.

in order to prevent human life/history being 'just one damn thing after another'.[104]

The usual reconstruction, that Paul's failure to find Titus in Troas becomes the cause for him to say his goodbyes and go into Macedonia, is grounded upon the view that the articular infinitive, τῷ μὴ εὑρεῖν, should be understood as 'causal', that is, in its adverbial relationship to the main verb of the sentence, the articular infinitive provides the grounds for Paul 'not having rest', and so to be translated along the lines suggested by Plummer: 'by reason of my not finding Titus'.

Given the complex picture that arises from this exegetical decision, the arguments in favour of it are often surprisingly thin, and often simply by declaration.[105] With no New Testament analogies for the dative, or for its causal nature, commentators understandably defer to the grammarians.[106] But these also provide very little argument. Votaw declares the infinitive of 2 Corinthians 2:13 to be 'denoting the cause of the state indicated by the governing verb', before citing six LXX (Swete) instances of the construction, 'expressing manner or means', all of which display textual variation.[107] Moule decides it is instrumental,[108] as does Jannaris, who notes that the dative of cause denotes the motive of some action and particularly emotion.[109] Robertson lists 2 Corinthians 2:13 under the dative indicating cause, without further argument;[110] Winer says this is 'according to the inherent import of that case';[111] and Burton similarly appeals to the dative for cause in classical usage, providing 2 Corinthians 2:13 as the NT's sole example,[112] but neither explains why 'cause' should rise above the many other senses of the dative to become

---

104 According to Copilot, although attributed to Henry Ford (amongst others), this cynical and fatalistic phrase of (probably) anonymous proverbial 'wisdom', emerged in 1909 as a quip about life in an article by Elbert Hubbard in the *Philistine*, before being applied to 'facts' by Plowman (1932), and finally to 'history', as noted (of others) by Arnold Toynbee, *A Study of History* (1954).
105 Harris, *2 Corinthians*, 239; Thrall, *2 Corinthians*, 186 n.405.
106 E.g. Thrall, *2 Corinthians*, 186 n.405 and Harris, *2 Corinthians*, 239 n.24, between them: BDR, §401 [=BDF, 401]; Moulton & Turner, *Grammar: Syntax*, 142; Winer, *Grammar*, 328; Burton, *Syntax*, §396; Robertson, *Grammar*, 532; Moule, *Idiom Book*, 44.
107 Votaw, *Use*, 29.
108 Moule, *Idiom Book*, 44. As noted by Wallace, *Grammar*, 158, then 167–168, the causal sense of the dative is one of the subgroups of its instrumental uses, which is 'built on the root idea of *means*'.
109 Jannaris, *Historical Greek Grammar*, 1387, also referring to 1388; 1582; 2128.
110 Robertson, *Grammar*, 532. In *Shorter*, 112, he lists 2 Cor. 2:13 to illustrate predicate datives, but without any mention of cause.
111 Winer, *Grammar*, 328.
112 Burton, *Syntax*, §396, noting that its other only use is after the preposition ἐν.

the significant one here. According to Moulton-Turner, although 'τῷ c. infin. is sometimes instrumental in the Koine but usually causal', the dative of cause in the New Testament is 'extraordinary', with most examples found in Paul (including 2 Cor. 2:13).[113]

ii. Circumstance (Temporal)
In the evolution of the Greek language, by the time of the New Testament the simple dative was being replaced by prepositions (especially ἐν).[114] This means that the sense of a simple dative might be clarified by reference to the evolving prepositional system. Thus for the infinitive at 2 Cor. 2:13, McKay notes that the causal sense is similar to 'an articular infinitive with the preposition διά [taking] the place of a subordinate causal clause'.[115] However, since the simple dative is moving towards being phased out especially by the preposition ἐν, perhaps McKay's lead can be followed in a different direction, with the infinitive at 2 Corinthians 2:13 acting with a sense similar to 'an articular infinitive with the preposition [ἐν] [taking] the place of a subordinate [circumstantial] clause'? Wallace not only hints at this usage, but by saying that Paul's infinitive is 'perhaps causal', he appears to even favour his only alternative, namely, 'contemporaneous time'.[116]

According to Votaw, the articular infinitive construction with ἐν τῷ 'indicates generally a relation of contemporaneous or attendant circumstances between the act or state denoted by its infinitive and that of the verb to which it stands related'.[117] With its subordinate clause granted this sense, it is no longer providing the grounds for Paul's main clause. Instead, Paul is simply explaining that in Troas, without an encounter with Titus, he was also without relaxation from his troubles.

c. *The Infinitive Subject: Not Paul but Titus*

The second decision lying behind the usual account is to read Paul, who is the referent of the personal pronoun με, as the subject of the negated

---

113 Moulton-Turner, *Grammar-Syntax*, 142; 242, 'more commonly a preposition takes the place of the dative at this period'.
114 Moulton-Turner, *Grammar-Syntax*, 242; Wallace, *Grammar*, 138.
115 McKay, *A New Syntax*, 125.
116 Wallace, *Grammar*, 595 n.20, 597 n.24, 610; and 155–157 for his explanation of this category.
117 Votaw, *Use*, 19–20.

infinitive,[118] and Titus, who is explicitly named and then described, as its object: 'I did not find Titus my brother'.[119] However, the ambiguity arising from the fact that both are in the accusative case (and so potentially the infinitival subject)[120] presents another alternative that is well worth exploring: What if Titus was the accusative subject of the infinitive and the pronoun (Paul) the accusative object?

In New Testament instances of this kind of ambiguity, it is generally agreed that 2 Corinthians 2:13 is one of the four most difficult to resolve.[121] Each of the proposals to disambiguate results in an affirmation of the usual opinion.

Although not specifically casting a vote on 2 Corinthians 2:13, the usual rendering would arise from Votaw's proposal (1896) to disambiguate by proximity to the infinitive:

> When the subject of the infinitive is expressed it is always in the accusative case. The position of the subject in the clause regularly is immediately before, or less frequently after, the infinitive. The object of the infinitive follows the infinitive, and follows also the subject if that stands after the infinitive.[122]

However, noting that Votaw's rule is ultimately not really one of proximity but word order,[123] Cripe (1992) criticises him, along with Moeller and Kramer (1963) and Reed (1991), for attempting to disambiguate

---

118 Rather than using the term 'subject', some prefer 'accusative of general reference', e.g. Robertson, *Pictures*, 217 (on 2 Cor. 2:13).
119 This, or a close version, is the rendering for all English Bibles accessible through biblegateway.com.
120 The notorious difficulty of this question may be as ancient as $\mathfrak{P}^{45}$ attempting a solution by dropping με altogether. As he joins the discussion himself, Cripe, 'Analysis', 2–3, suggests that since Votaw, this ambiguity has become 'something of a hot grammatical topic', by the publications of Moeller and Kramer, and Reed.
121 Luke 18:5; 2 Cor. 2:13; 8:6; and Phil. 1:7. See Cripe, 'Analysis', 60, 83–87; Wallace, *Greek Grammar*, 196–197. For Moeller and Kramer, 'Overlooked Pattern', 26, 29, 2 Cor. 2:13 is among the problem examples; and for Reed, 'Infinitive', 1, it is the parade example that demonstrates the ambiguity.
122 Votaw, *Use*, 58. To cover the problem that accusative objects occur before both the infinitive and the subject, Cripe, 'Analysis', 16, 26–27, reports that the Dallas Theological Seminary New Testament Department operates with an improvement on Votaw's rule: 'the accusative word immediately preceding or following the infinitive is usually the subject', noting that this overlooks where the infinitive comes between the substantives.
123 Cripe, 'Analysis', 27.

through word order rules (each with their inevitable exceptions),[124] which basically state that the first accusative is the subject, the second the object.[125] Hence to follow these authors, in 2 Corinthians 2:13, με (Paul) would be the subject and Τίτον (Titus) the predicate term.

Over against disambiguation by way of word order, Cripe tests Wallace's proposal[126] made while investigating the object-complement construction, to draw on the analogy of the subject-predicate nominative construction, which Wallace argued was 'semantically equivalent'.

> I would also suggest that this analogy between the object-complement and subject-predicate nominative constructions is valid in distinguishing the subject of an infinitive from a predicate accusative. [...] there is a better semantic approach than mere word order. Perhaps the principles for distinguishing subject from predicate nominative are even valid for *all* seventy-seven infinitival constructions examined by Moeller and Kramer.[127]

The principles Wallace refers to are those of Goetchius, that rest upon the primary principle that 'if two nouns in the nominative case are connected by an equative verb in Greek, the more definite of the two is the subject', or, as refined by Wallace, the more specific.[128] Distilled further, this would mean that the subject is the noun that: a) is a proper name; b) has the article; c) has a narrower reference; d) is referred to in the immediately preceding context; or e) a pronoun.[129] Although Goetchius has been criticised for not ordering his principles, Wallace's ranking is accepted by Cripe, that the subject is:

---

124 See Cripe, 'Analysis', 35: 'a rule based only on word order may *help* solve a problem but will never be definitive since there is always the possibility that the construction under discussion does not conform to the *normal* word order. Thus word order rules are helpful for demonstrating emphasis in unambiguous constructions but do not really help in solving problems related to ambiguous constructions'; cf. 67 n.45. This was later endorsed by Wallace, *Greek Grammar*, 193–194.
125 See Moeller and Kramer, 'An Overlooked Structure', 27; Reed, 'The Infinitive', 8.
126 Cripe, 'Analysis', 28, 40; who tests the proposal in Chapter 3.
127 Wallace, 'Semantics', 105 n.65, cf. 101.
128 Goetchius, *Language*, 46; cited by Wallace, 'Semantics', 104.
129 Goetchius, *Language*, 46; cited by Wallace, 'Semantics', 104; and Cripe, 'Analysis', 38–39, who indicates Wallace counsels disregarding rule (c) as it is unwarranted and misleading, because it does not allow for the possibility of a convertible proposition.

1. the pronoun (Goetchius, e)
2. the articular noun (b)
3. the proper name (a)
4. the noun mentioned in the previous context (d).[130]

It should be noted, however, that, having already (1992) dispensed with rule (c), Wallace later (1996) also dispensed with rule (d),[131] leaving the subject to be distinguished from the predicate nominative by means of only three rules (1–3 above).[132] Additionally, while explaining the 'pecking order' to be applied if both the subject and the predicate nominative have one of these three grammatical tags he argues that:

1. The pronoun has the greatest priority; and
2. Articular nouns and proper names seem to have equal priority.[133]

After testing these principles in relation to 'copula constructions' (equative verbs), Cripe affirms the Goetchius-Wallace principles as valid and helpful.[134] However, both Wallace and Cripe insist upon treating constructions with the equative verb differently from those with a transitive verb, which they argue does not have semantic equivalence.[135] When it comes to 2 Corinthians 2:13, therefore, the principle of greater specificity is left to one side, and, while both agree that the infinitive subject could go either way, both seek to resolve the ambiguity purportedly on the basis of 'applying common sense (e.g., noticing the context),'[136] or 'the common sense use of the context [which] will almost always reveal the subject and object or predicate in this type of construction, as opposed to word order'.[137] In doing so, however, both reveal that this is not exactly a straightforward exercise and it seems that both fall into the problem for which Cripe criticises Reed, namely, that of having already decided in advance[138]—no doubt under the influence of the long tradition of English Bible translation.

---

130 Cripe, 'Analysis', 40, drawing upon an unpublished class lecture from Wallace.
131 Wallace, *Greek Grammar*, 44 n.23.
132 Wallace, *Greek Grammar*, 43.
133 Wallace, *Greek Grammar*, 44.
134 Cripe, 'Analysis', 87–88.
135 Cripe, 'Analysis', 24, 28 n.73, 87–88; Wallace, *Greek Grammar*, 193–194, differing from his earlier suggestion as quoted above, 'Semantics', 105 n.65.
136 Wallace, *Greek Grammar*, 194, noting Luke 18:5; 2 Cor. 2:13; 8:6; Phil. 1:7.
137 For the expression, see Cripes, 'Analysis', 88; for its application to 2 Cor. 2:13, see 84.
138 Cripe, 'Analysis', 10, 32.

Although admitting that 'this text [could] be read either way', Wallace opts for 'I did not find Titus' as most probable, because of the connection between the ἔσχηκα ἄνεσιν and the infinitive clause: 'if Paul is looking for Titus, he is not resting'.[139] This, however, is more a lexical than semantic argument (and one importing the notion of Paul 'looking for' Titus) and syntactically it appears to assume what needs to be argued. To state that there is a connection between main and subordinate clauses is simply to re-assert an abstract fundamental of syntax. However, for any given text, it is the nature of that connection that must be explained, and this requires identifying the textual clues that resolve any potential ambiguities for the reader.[140]

Similarly, Cripe confidently endorses the usual translation, because 'the context would seem to argue for [it]', noting '*he* had no rest for *his* spirit' in the preceding clause.[141] His three points of corroboration are not strong. 1. It is a temporal infinitive, and other examples in the New Testament (Luke 2:27; 11:28; 24:51), show an Infinitive–Subject–Object word order; 2. An Infinitive–Object–Subject word order is not very common; and 3. The subject of the previous clause is Paul. Here the last appears to simply restate the overall context statement, and the first two are based upon word order statistics, which Cripe admits cannot be determinative,[142] perhaps especially when the size of the comparative samples is so small. Finally he dismisses the alternative suggestion 'that Paul was troubled because he was expecting Titus to find him and when Titus did not do this Paul was upset' as 'very unlikely', to conclude that 'the Infinitive-Subject-Object is almost certain for this construction'. But this half-hearted alternative is parasitic on the usual rendition that the statement tells us something about Paul's expectations. With a better understanding of the circumstantial infinitive (see below), a stronger alternative scenario can be proposed that better resists dismissal by trivialisation.

But before moving on to draw that different picture, although it may be far short of the further analysis of the S-O construction that Wallace

---

139 Wallace, *Greek Grammar*, 196–197.
140 Wallace, *Greek Grammar*, 196 n.77: 'Thus, in an otherwise ambiguous text, an author might be expected to give us some clue on what he means'.
141 Cripe, 'Analysis', 84.
142 Cripe, 'Analysis', 67 n.45: 'Word order rules cannot legitimately be used to clear up ambiguous constructions since they are never 100% accurate but are merely generalizations of word order patterns'.

invites,[143] the question can be raised as to why Cripe and Wallace's analogy can't be pressed beyond the limits that they set for it. Summarising Cripe's results, Wallace notes that for 'subject accusative –predicate accusative (S–P)' constructions, just like their nominative counterparts,

> neither word order nor proximity to the infinitive are helpful guides for determining the subject. What matters is whether one of the accusatives is a pronoun or articular or a proper name (in which case, it is the subject term).[144]

Here Wallace restates the principle of specificity as the proper disambiguator. However, immediately after this, he denies that it relates to the 'subject accusative–direct object (S–O)', 'since there is no semantic correlation between this construction and the S-P construction'.[145] But is this dismissal well-founded?

Whatever Wallace might mean by 'semantic equivalence' or 'semantic correlation', it is not completely clear why the equative (copula) infinitival constructions and the transitive (non-copula) constructions need to be treated differently, or why the type of verb is the determinative feature of the aptness of the proposed Wallace-Cripe analogy. Rather than the relation of the component parts to the verbal form, surely it is the presence of ambiguity arising from two substantives in the same case that is the point of analogy. If so, the process by which a reader resolves ambiguity of substantives in relation to one kind of construction is most likely how they resolve the same ambiguity in relation to another.

Although operating from the author's end of the equation, Wallace is similarly confident that recourse to the text itself should provide the key to its disambiguation.

> [A]lthough *normal* word order in Greek is difficult to determine, almost all studies conclude that the subject term usually precedes the object term. Thus, in an otherwise ambiguous text, an author might be expected to give us some clue on what he means.[146]

---

143 Wallace, *Greek Grammar*, 194.
144 Wallace, *Greek Grammar*, 194.
145 Wallace, *Greek Grammar*, 194.
146 Wallace, *Greek Grammar*, 196 n.77.

When embarking on this quest in relation to two accusatives associated with a transitive verb, however, it might be asked why it is not part of 'contextual common sense' to adopt the Wallace-Cripe analogy and to apply the same linguistic hierarchy of specificity, that operates to disentangle the ambiguity of Subject-Predicate constructions?[147]

At first glance, the application of the Goetchius–Wallace principles may seem to favour the usual translation of the adjectival infinitive clause in 2 Corinthians 2:13, especially on Wallace's ranking. Although there is no articular noun (ranking 2), because με is a pronoun (ranking 1) whose antecedent is the subject of the verb in the main clause (ranking 4), on this analysis, it emerges easily as the subject. On the other hand, the fact that the second accusative is a proper name (ranking 3) should be taken more seriously than perhaps it has been previously, for surely it was proper, even if he is not regarded as supplying a hierarchy, for Goetchius to list this first in his list of 'greater definiteness' (or specificity).

In view of the fact that a proper name is more definite than a pronoun, why was it only third on Wallace's ranking? This can probably be attributed to the fact that, as Wallace explains, in relation to the predicate-nominative, the principles of disambiguation operate on the basic premise that the subject is already known from the context.[148] Apart from the interrogative, pronouns 'are a substitute for something already revealed in the context (a known quantity), [... rather than] anticipatory of a substantive not yet revealed (an unknown quantity)'.[149]

Without troubling to assemble a body of evidence, it is a common-sense observation of communication, however, that a speaker or writer may begin with a focus upon one person and, for the sake of their communicative ends, proceed to switch focus to another. Such a switch of focus is possible mid-story, mid-paragraph, mid-sentence, or even mid-clause. Although in a performance context with a living voice, there may well be oral/aural techniques to make such a switch

---

147 In solving potentially ambiguous examples, Wallace, *Greek Grammar*, 195, determines that: [on Mark 14:64] unless functioning substantivally, an adjective is the predicate term; [on Acts 28:6] if one of the two is a pronoun, it is the subject; [on 1 Tim. 6:5, see other examples in n.72] if one of the two is articular, it is the subject; and [Luke 20:6] if one of the two is a proper name, it is the subject, noting (n.73) Cripe only finding three examples (Luke 20:6; Acts 17:7; Rom. 15:8).
148 Wallace, *Greek Grammar*, 42: 'The general principle for distinguishing Subject from Predicate Nominative is that the Subject is the *known* entity'.
149 Wallace, *Greek Grammar*, 44 n.24.

absolutely clear to a live audience, any necessary disambiguation should also be apparent in a text which, at the least, required reading out to the assembled listeners. This is where we may be assisted by a more sophisticated examination of word order than the strictly linear approaches (basically, 'what comes before and after') both critiqued and offered by Cripe and Wallace, whereby the contours and structure of the writing is viewed as a vehicle of the author's thought expressed in a manner consistent with the desired rhetorical emphasis.[150]

However, even without engaging in such a more nuanced word order analysis, we can already suggest that, for the purposes of emphasis and rhetorical shift, it seems obvious that the greater specificity of the proper name, Titus, trumps a mere pronoun,[151] even if that pronoun finds an antecedent in the preceding context. In the clause under review, the switch of focus is made even more apparent by the new subject being made even more heavily marked with an extra description giving him even greater specificity: τὸν ἀδελφόν μου 'my brother'. This description associates him with the apostle in a relationship described with familial intimacy. Although the resultant IOS word order may be unusual according to Cripe, this is irrelevant—as he also admits—because even if there was a usual word order pattern, it can be varied for desired rhetorical effect. On this reading the subject falls in the final position in the clause, adding further emphasis to that already achieved by the proper name carrying the extra weight of its appended description.

If the results of this review of the infinitival clause are granted, Paul says that in Troas he did not experience relaxation from his troubles, 'while Titus my brother was not finding me', or 'while Titus my brother had not (yet) found me'.

Having discussed the trials and tribulations he was enduring when he arrived in Troas (1:3—2:11), such that, as suggested here, he came to the view that the 'great distress' was commencing before the coming of the End, Paul drew his readers into his resultant state of 'lacking any relaxation', before providing the accompanying circumstances of that

---

150 See, for example, the older and more sophisticated approach of Weil, *Order of Words*, not acknowledged by Cripe-Wallace, who identified five ways words are arranged in order to express ideas (p.70): the descending construction; the ascending construction; the order of enclavement or inlocked construction; the dispersed construction (=hyperbaton); the compound word.
151 See John 1:48, which Wallace, *Greek Grammar*, 196, lists (without comment) as an illustration of S-O and which can therefore be regarded as formally parallel to 2 Cor. 2:13.

moment which entailed a dramatic switch of subject to Titus, and the declaration that Paul's lack of rest was accompanied by 'Titus my brother not having found me'.

Titus, as we will learn, is already well-known to the Corinthians (7:7,13–14; 8:6 [cf. 1 Cor. 16:1–4],16–17,23), but by being marked out here in relation to the affectionate relationship with the apostle, he is drawn towards Paul's troubles, while at the same time being excluded from them, by his absence. The significance of introducing Titus at this point in Paul's autobiographical account—his first appearance in the letter—must await Paul's return to the story when he recounts their happy reunion (7:5–16).

To press this further, contrary to the frequent and prevailing interpretation of this verse, Paul did NOT go to Troas with the expectation of finding Titus because of some supposed prior arrangement between the two men. With the benefit of hindsight, he is simply stating a fact. When he was in Troas he was troubled in spirit. What eventually comforted him only came later, after he had reached Macedonia and Titus had brought him good news. After that, he could look back and say that it was even like he had been raised from the dead (1:8–9). However, while he was so troubled in Troas, Titus had not yet found him.

6. A Happy Reunion in Macedonia

In terms of the flow of the letter, the account that Paul opened in 2:12–13 is closed by 7:5–16, just as the real life situation in Troas in which he finds no relaxation with respect to his spirit came to an end in Macedonia by the comfort brought to him by Titus' arrival with news from Corinth. 'As a result, the Corinthian readers are kept in a certain narrative suspense with the apostle throughout the body of the letter (3:1–7:16). His teaching on the calling of an apostle is set within the context of his experience as their apostle. [...] The breaking off of the narrative serves to drive home the true nature of apostolic ministry as that of suffering and comfort'.[152]

The language forges the connections closely:

---

152 Seifrid, *Second Corinthians*, 79–80.

| 2:12 | Ἐλθὼν δὲ | εἰς τὴν Τρῳάδα [...] | | |
| 7:5 | Καὶ γὰρ ἐλθόντων ἡμῶν | εἰς Μακεδονίαν [...] | | |

| 2:13 | οὐκ | ἔσχηκα | ἄνεσιν | τῷ πνεύματί μου |
| 7:5 | οὐδεμίαν | ἔσχηκεν | ἄνεσιν | ἡ σὰρξ ἡμῶν |

Since it is clear from 7:5 and 8:13 that 'the opposite of external and internal θλῖψις is ἄνεσις',[153] the eschatological understanding of θλῖψις means that its 'relaxation' also becomes an eschatologically loaded term in the Pauline usage. The eschatological overtones are crystal clear in 2 Thessalonians 1:7, where the Thessalonians will find the 'relaxation of their troubles' at the (day of) revelation of the Lord Jesus (alongside the just retribution of trouble for their troublers). In an intriguing suggestion on this same verse, Bultmann compares ἄνεσις with ἀνάψυξις in Acts 3:20,[154] where, for Luke, 'the times of refreshment from the presence of the Lord' (v.20 καιροὶ ἀναψύξεως ἀπὸ προσώπου τοῦ κυρίου) anticipate the restoration of all things (cf. v.21... ἄχρι χρόνων ἀποκαταστάσεως πάντων). Following this lead, ἀνάψυξις may well stand as a one-word alternative for Paul's phrase (... ἄνεσιν τῷ πνεύματί μου) in 2 Corinthians 2:13.[155] What he was unable to enter in Troas, he was able to experience in Macedonia after Titus came to him (7:5–7,13), and in the midst of the eschatological woes, he experienced this refreshment of spirit (and Titus his, 7:13) as a taste of the resurrection to come (1:9), just as he had done before and will do again (1:10–11; 4:7–12). The mutual comfort and joy that once again bound together the apostle, Titus, and the Corinthian church, then issued in a 'haste' (7:11; 8:7–8,16) which overflowed in generosity (8:2), that would then

---

153 Schlier, 'θλῖψις', 3.147, also noting 2 Thess. 1:7; Act. Pl. et Thecl. 37; Act. Pt. 2; Act. Thom. 39. Cf. LSJ I.2 *remission, abatement*, opp. θλῖψις.
154 Bultmann, 'ἀνίημι, ἄνεσις', 365.
155 Weil, *Order of Words*, 70, treats compound words as another form of word order since they encapsulate ideas that could be rendered by another group of words.

be expressed in the collection for the Jerusalem saints[156] as the final act of Paul's mission to the nations—in itself an expression of the last days and so a hastening and harbinger of the End.

The comfort at the start of this chain is clear when Paul appeals to the Corinthians to travel with him in his missionary journey (7:2–3). Paul informs them that he is filled with encouragement and overflowing with joy about everything 'in our suffering' (v.4b, τῇ θλίψει ἡμῶν). As the reason for this encouragement and joy, he reports on his change of state provoked by Titus coming to him in Macedonia (7:5–7). When Paul had arrived in Macedonia, he had been in the same state as he was in Troas (v.5, cf. 2:13), with his flesh having no relaxation, but, instead, 'afflicted in every way, quarrels without, fears within' (ἐν παντὶ θλιβόμενοι· ἔξωθεν μάχαι, ἔσωθεν φόβοι)—further reinforcing his view that if the 'great distress' had begun, the End was nigh. But, while he was in such a state, 'the God who comforts the humiliated comforted us in the coming of Titus' (v.6, ὁ παρακαλῶν τοὺς ταπεινοὺς παρεκάλεσεν ἡμᾶς ὁ θεὸς ἐν τῇ παρουσίᾳ Τίτου). But God was operative, not only in Titus' coming, but also 'in the comfort which he was comforted about you' (ἐν τῇ παρακλήσει ᾗ παρεκλήθη ἐφ' ὑμῖν), with Titus reporting to Paul the Corinthians' longing (ἐπιπόθησις), mourning (ὀδυρμός), and zeal (ζῆλος) on behalf of Paul (v.7, see further, v.11), which had resulted in the apostle greatly rejoicing.

This comfort issued in 'haste', or 'eagerness'. Paul attributes the change in the Corinthians to repentance 'according to God' that was prompted by his painful letter, making him glad that he wrote it, despite the sorrow it caused (7:8–12; cf. 2:3–4). His ultimate aim in writing, as now shown

---

156 Despite the LSJ gloss (I.3) for ἄνεσις as 'relaxation, recreation opp. σπουδή (2 Cor. 7:11,12; 8:7,8,16)', ἄνεσις is actually the experience that issues in σπουδή. Of the twelve occurrences in the NT, five are in 2 Cor. and all related to the passages concerning Titus, whether the Corinthian response to the severe letter he reported (7:11–12); or their subsequent eagerness to be involved in the collection, which Paul now hopes mirrors that of the Macedonians (8:7–8), and of Titus himself (8:16). Gal. 2:10 supplies a further instance involving both the collection and Titus, and, depending upon how they are read (see below), the references in the Pastoral Epistles which indicate the haste with which Paul is regathering representatives of his mission team (Titus 3:12; cf. 2 Tim. 4:9,21; ?cf. 1 Cor. 16:6,10), may find their historical grounding in the haste with which the final collection was gathered and then sent. Thus the word is not simply a 'zealous concern' both similar to and different from that of the Stoics (so Harder, 'σπουδάζω', 566–567), but it is also an eschatologically conditioned attitude (cf. Heb. 6:11) that found concrete expression in the 'moment' represented by the collection.

retrospectively in its result (ἄρα),[157] was ἕνεκεν τοῦ φανερωθῆναι τὴν σπουδὴν ὑμῶν τὴν ὑπὲρ ἡμῶν πρὸς ὑμᾶς ἐνώπιον τοῦ θεοῦ (v.12). Although this is commonly explained in terms of the Corinthians' 'devotion to' the apostle at last being manifest,[158] if this were his meaning, it would seem more natural for Paul to utilise the simple dative, or the prepositions πρός, περί or εἰς rather than ὑπέρ.[159] When the pronouns and prepositions are untangled, Paul's language points in a different direction. Rather than the apostle's 'primary concern [striking] a somewhat egocentric note',[160] it is directly in line with his missionary purposes. This is revealed in the cluster of prepositions governed by the article showing that it is in apposition to the noun. Paul wrote to bring out their 'haste' or 'eagerness' (σπουδή) 'on our behalf towards you in the sight of God'. σπουδή followed by 'on our behalf' (ὑπέρ) should be taken in the sense of acting with diligence 'in discharge of an obligation or experience of a relationship' (BDAG), indicating that the Corinthians have come back in line with Paul's cause (cf. 2:14–17; 3:3; 4:10–12; 5:10,11–15,16–21; 11:6).[161] However, far from this being 'egocentric', since he is the apostle to the Gentiles whose cause is 'for you' (πρὸς ὑμᾶς) and the arena in which it is playing out is 'before God' (ἐνώπιον τοῦ θεοῦ) (cf. 2 Cor. 4:2; cf. 5:16–17 and 12:19). They were previously on a pathway towards 'eschatological death' (7:10) they have once again embraced the apostle's message that brings life to the dead (cf. 4:7–5:10).[162] Even if perhaps self-inflicted, the Corinthians have come through their own affliction (1:4–7; 4:17; cf. 2:2–10 and 7:8–9) and, through its impact upon Paul, they have also become caught up in his afflictions, which as their apostle, he suffers for their sake (cf. 1:6–7). Now their renewed σπουδή for the gospel cause has brought him great joy.

With Christ's sufferings clearly in the background (4:10–12; 5:14–15; 13:4), Paul described his overwhelming experience in Asia as death-like, and his deliverance from it as being raised from the dead (1:8–10). After the Asian experience, viewing it as the 'great distress', he came to

---

157 Thrall, *2 Corinthians*, 495; Harris, *2 Corinthians*, 544.
158 Thrall, *2 Corinthians*, 496; Harris, *2 Corinthians*, 546, both citing BDAG.
159 Harris, *2 Corinthians*, 546, suggests that σπουδή, '[when] followed by ὑπέρ, signifies "devotion"'.
160 Thrall, *2 Corinthians*, 496.
161 Cf. Harder, 'σπουδάζω', 559: σπουδάζω 'means intrans. "to make haste" and is thus closely related to "to be zealous, active, concerned about something"'.
162 Thrall, *2 Corinthians*, 492–493, 496.

Troas for the sake of the gospel of Christ. However, with a door open for further mission, he decided to leave Troas in a state of 'no relaxation' (2:12–13), which even continued when he came into Macedonia (7:5), 'being troubled (θλιβόμενοι) in every way: conflicts on the outside, fears inside'. It was in this very situation that Titus found him, bringing news of Corinth. This was the event that turned Paul around, such that he was not only comforted (7:5–7,13; cf. 1:3–7), but he now also greatly rejoiced because of how much joy had been sparked in Titus, 'because his spirit was refreshed' by the Corinthians (7:13, ἀναπέπαυται τὸ πνεῦμα αὐτοῦ ἀπὸ πάντων ὑμῶν; cf. 1 Cor. 16:18).

Since Paul's 'lack of relaxation' in the midst of his death-like θλῖψις, ceased after Titus brought him resurrection-like comfort, Titus is a key player in the gospel movement from 'death' to 'life' that is embodied in the news that he brought for Paul. The Corinthians, of course, already knew of the encouragement that their renewed enthusiasm for the Pauline mission brought Titus before he went to Macedonia to share the news with Paul. Now the letter informs them of the effect that this mutual comfort had on the apostle Paul, even though it came to him when he was still reeling under the impact of his affliction in Asia and then in Macedonia. Rhetorically speaking, after being drawn into the apostle's experience of distress (2:12–13), the readers are drawn into his experience of him being comforted (7:5–16).

In these final stages of the letter, on the eve of his third visit (12:14; 13:1), Paul continues to make his appeal to the Corinthians to join with him and his gospel cause (10:1–2; cf. 6:1–2, 7:2), with a view to their 'restoration' (13:9,11). Now he wants them to move further into that experience by giving expression to their eagerness on behalf of the mission. Just as it was with the previous letter (7:12), this must also be the ultimate aim of the letter that Titus (presumably) now carries with him as he returns to Corinth.

7. Return to Corinth

The newfound eagerness of the Corinthians will be expressed (cf. 8:7) in their involvement in the collection for the saints. They commenced in the previous year (8:10; 9:1–5; 1 Cor. 16:1–4) at the instigation of

Titus (8:6), and now they are able to complete their contribution also under his leadership (8:6,16–17,23; 12:18). Paul urged Titus to finish the job he had started (8:6), but already displaying the same eagerness (σπουδή) for the Corinthians (8:16; cf. 7:11), as the Macedonians (8:8), the unknown brother (8:22), and now, thankfully, also the Corinthians were displaying for Paul and his mission (7:11–12), Titus welcomed Paul's appeal because he had already decided to do the same thing on his own authority (8:17, ὑπάρχων αὐθαίρετος). His greater eagerness on behalf of the Corinthians was then displayed in his 'rushing off' to return to Corinth (8:17, σπουδαιότερος δὲ [...] ἐξῆλθεν πρὸς ὑμᾶς). After he had arrived back in Corinth and the letter was read out, Paul expected the Corinthians to recognise instantly that Titus was not motivated by greed, and neither was the apostle (12:17–18). There was something larger at stake in this collection.

Although it cannot be explored at length in this essay, both the 'haste' (σπουδή) to be involved in the Pauline mission and the collection for the saints need to be set against the eschatological constraint that Paul considers the world to have fallen under with the coming of the Christ (see above).[163] The Corinthians, however, have been slow to catch onto Paul's vision of the future that is determined by Christ's own resurrection from the dead (cf. 1 Cor. 15), especially how the future resurrection day becomes the key to transformation in this life resulting in abounding in the work of the Lord (1 Cor. 15:58; cf. 2 Cor. 4:7–5:10). This gospel-shaped existence is embodied in the apostles, but now, at last, the Corinthians seem to have caught up as demonstrated by their σπουδή in the midst of afflictions. But if 'urgency' (σπουδή) is an eschatologically-loaded term, the great eagerness with which Titus returned to Corinth to recommence his task shows that he must have shared Paul's view of the times, especially if he accepted Paul's view that the 'last distress' has now commenced with the Asian crisis.

For, of all people, even if recent events pressed the urgency upon him even more, Titus would have already had a sense of Paul's plans in the light of God's eschatological purposes. Soon after he was converted to Christ, Paul took him to Jerusalem, where he witnessed the esteemed leaders of the Jerusalem church making an agreement with Paul that

---

163 This eschatological context is overlooked by Harder, 'σπουδάζω'.

they would go to the Jews and he to the Gentiles. At this point, they also urged that Paul would remember the poor (Gal. 2:10), a self-reference to the Jerusalem church being the 'eschatological poor'—the Zion community redeemed by the Messiah in the last days.

The collection needs to be understood within the same eschatological framework. It is not simply about economics. Paul's use of Isaish 55:10 and Hosea 10:12 (2 Cor. 9:10) alludes to: 'the miracle of Israel's returning home and the eternal covenant between God and Israel. Israel will call all other peoples, and they will come'.[164] In the last days the nations will stream to Zion (Isa. 2:2–4; 66:18–24). Through Paul's gospel both Jew and Greek have come to the Messiah, but it appears that the Gentiles were now preceding the Jews, as an eschatological incentive for Israel to also return to their God through their messiah (cf. Rom. 9–11).[165]

> Read in conjunction with its eschatologically interpreted biblical background, II Corinthians 9:10 means that the Creator is allowing the eschatological miracle of the pilgrimage of the peoples to Jerusalem to coincide with the collection of Pauline congregations (consisting in the majority of Gentiles) taken up for the Jesus-believing congregation at Jerusalem.[166]

However, just as it completely misses the point to see the collection simply in economic terms, so too is it short-selling the collection to see it solely as a symbol of Jew–Gentile unity,[167] if this unity is not set against the eschatological expectations of the Old Testament prophets. The collection symbolises the unity between the Jerusalem church as the fountainhead of the gospel, in their witness to the events of Jesus' death and resurrection, and the recipients of their gospel (via Paul) amongst the nations. Those drawing spiritual benefits now repay materially (cf. Rom. 15:27). However, this unification of Jew and Gentile is itself a feature of eschatological expectation.

---

164 Georgi, *Remembering*, 100.
165 Georgi, *Remembering*, 100.
166 Georgi, *Remembering*, 101.
167 Georgi, *Remembering*, 16–17: 'the Tübingen school, read it as a unifying attempt between Jew and Gentile, to check Judaizing opposition to ensure the continuation of [Paul's] mission'.

> Hence, if Paul saw such a connection between the motif of the eschatological pilgrimage of Jews and Gentiles to Jerusalem and the collection (and its transference to that city), he must have considered the collection itself a signal of the last times.[168]

As Paul lays it out to the Romans in broad sweep, because of the sufferings of Christ, being justified by faith enables both Jew and Gentile (Rom. 1–4) to endure suffering in this fallen world in the hope of the glory to come (Rom. 5:1–5; 8:18–39). Although it may seem that the work of the gospel amongst the Gentiles is more successful than it is amongst the Jews, this is all part of God's plan to bring all people together. As Paul explains, the conversion of the Gentiles is meant to provoke Israel to envy, so that they too might be saved. But this, in turn, will trigger the day of resurrection (Rom. 11:13–15). This is, in fact, the *modus operandi* of the gospel in these last days (11:25–26, οὕτως 'in this manner').[169] Thus, as he perceives the mission to the nations drawing to a close, the collection that is both a symbol and a harbinger of the End, must be taken to Jerusalem (15:17–27).[170]

With such a strategy in view, the significance of the collection for Paul's mission is not surprising. As noted by Georgi:

> As the collection was a constant concern of Paul's from the days of the convention at Jerusalem until his last journey to that city, its story can be viewed truly as a mirror of the apostle's missionary effort as a whole. Hence, depicting the occurrences linked to the collection must inevitably entail a step-by-step study of Paul's mission itself. The difficulties and risks involved in this kind of historical and chronological evaluation are obvious; it must be of a hypothetical nature by necessity. But hypotheses are the daily bread of scholarship; there can be no scientific endeavor without them'.[171]

---

168 Georgi, *Remembering*, 100.
169 See Robinson, 'Salvation of Israel', esp. p.60.
170 Even as he sensed an ending to his mission amongst the nations, Paul held out the possibility of further mission fields opening up in Rome and further west (15:27–29). However, always guided by circumstances changing under the sovereign hand of God, these travel plans, like others before them, also had to be modified as events unfolded.
171 Georgi, *Remembering*, 15.

Because of Titus' close engagement with the collection, the final section of this essay will attempt to draw together his movements in relation to Paul's mission, well aware of the same 'difficulties and risks' required to make the necessary hypotheses.

3. Towards the Missionary Titus Emerging from the Shadows

Having raised questions about the usual picture and with the riddles of the syntax solved differently, what new portrait of Titus emerges? With the attitude of suggesting further hypotheses to be tested, this final section weaves together evidence from the wider New Testament and interpretive hints found already in the scholarship, in order to sketch the contours of Titus, his movements, and his role within the early Gentile mission.

With 2 Corinthians 2:12–13 read differently, there is no reason to suppose that Titus was (like Timothy), a travelling companion of Paul, more 'apostolic' than 'congregational', nor that he had previously been sent to Corinth as the apostle's envoy, whether as letter-carrier or trouble-shooter.[172] Without the need for a pre-arranged rendezvous,[173] the evidence is more than adequately accounted for by Titus coming to Paul as a leading member of the Corinthian congregation, who, like others associated with that congregation, in its later stages of the Gentile mission also took on a wider role.

Although meeting Paul earlier (Gal. 2:1–10), when converts to Christ broke with the synagogue in Corinth to form the city's first Christian congregation, Titus was most likely its host. At Acts 18:7 the manuscript evidence includes early and reliable witnesses that name the man who opened his home next door to the synagogue, not Titius, but *Titus* Justus.[174] In any case, there is no real difference between Titus and

---

172 Barnett, *2 Corinthians*, 136 n.13.
173 Cf. Lightfoot, 'Mission', 284, who for different reasons also saw 'no reason for supposing that they had agreed to meet at Troas'.
174 Manuscripts reading Titus Justus include the 4th c. and well-reputed Sinaiticus (ℵ), and some Syriac and Coptic translations have Titus alone, with syr^p originating in the early fifth century and cop$^{sa,\ bo}$, in the 3rd. Titus Justus was read by 'Chrysostom, Ammonius, etc.', Lake and Cadbury, *Beginnings*, 4.225; see also Robinson, *Redating*, 35. For further discussion, see Bolt, '(Gaius) Tit(i)us Justus'.

Titius, since in the Latin *nomen gentilicium* the -i- is simply the form indicating patrilineal ancestry, 'son of'.[175] Since every descendant bore this family name, the distinguishing of individuals had to come from one of the other names, whether the *praenomen* or, increasingly as time went on, the *cognomen*.[176]

It is therefore interesting that Luke's Tit(i)us Justus fulfills the same role as Paul's host in Corinth when he was writing his letter to the Romans (Rom. 16:23).[177] This in turn becomes a bridge to identifying him with the Gaius who was one of Paul's earliest converts in Corinth and a prominent member of their congregation (1 Cor. 1:14)—thus, especially because accompanied by Crispus, providing a Pauline parallel with the Acts account (cf. Acts 18:7–8).

Thus, it appears that the host of the Corinthian congregation and a foundational member within it, in line with the common Roman practice at the time, bore a threefold name: Gaius Tit(i)us Justus.[178] Because of the flexibility of address afforded by the three names, Gaius would be used amongst those more familiar with him, but Titus, as the *nomen*—his family name—could equally be used in both formal or familial settings.[179]

An argument commonly made against this identification of Titus is that he clearly had dealings with Paul prior to the apostle's arrival in Corinth (Gal. 2:1–10; cf. Acts 15:2) and Tit(i)us was a Corinthian, whereas Titus was more likely an Antiochian.[180] The force of this argument, however, is weak. No claims are made by Luke about the events of Acts 18 being some kind of 'first meeting' between the two men.

---

175 Salway, 'What's in a Name?', 125–126.
176 For discussion see Salway, 'What's in a Name?'.
177 This identification ensures his presence amongst the greeters in 16:21–23, which was missed by Robinson, *Redating*, 81. Once his presence is acknowledged and the 'slender thread of evidence' upon which to hang a theory (Porter, 'Pauline Chronology', 80) removed, the chronology can also be adjusted, as below. I no longer consider this Gaius to be unknown; see Bolt, 'Untangling', 419.
178 See Ramsay, *Pictures*, 205 n.2; Goodspeed, 'Gaius'. Cf. Moo, *Romans*, 951; Fee, *1 Corinthians*, 64.
179 See Salway, 'What's in a Name?', 126, 130, 144. In some contexts he could have also been called Justus. Since the second century bc the use of a cognomen was increasingly common, by the end of the first century bc overtaking the older function of the praenomen as the individual signifier (p.130), and by the end of the first century ad well on its way to its eclipse from the third century and beyond (cf. Salway, 131, 135–136, 144–145). Although arising earlier in the elite families, 'the first examples of cognomina amongst the *plebs ingenua* are not until c. 125 bc and they were not to be common for over a century' (p.127).
180 E.g. Lake and Cadbury, *Beginnings*, 4.225. The fact that Paul might meet Titus in Antioch, or Priscilla and Aquila in Corinth—or they him!—is not an indicator of place of origin, but of mobility.

Similarly, to derive from his one known early visit to Jerusalem a long-term travelling career for Titus at the side of Paul seems an unwarranted generalisation. Another alternative would be that this Corinthian, for whatever reason (and there are many possibilities),[181] was in Antioch when he met Paul and there converted by his ministry (cf. Titus 1:4). He then travelled to Jerusalem to become the parade example of a Gentile converted without being circumcised (a role filled for Peter by Cornelius; Acts 10–11). By being alongside Paul on that occasion, he was associated with the comity arrangements made in relation to the gospel mission to Gentiles and Jews, as well as the call for Paul to remember the Jerusalem saints as the eschatological poor, which will prove foundational for the 'collection for the saints' with which Titus at a later date became so intimately involved. Rather than the two men meeting for the first time when Paul came to Corinth, with this previous relationship in the background, it makes it likely that Paul decided to go to Corinth because he knew Titus was already there, pleasingly making some headway as a godfearer in the synagogue next door to his home.

These identifications made, Titus would have been part of the congregation (note 1 Cor. 1:14) who had requested and subsequently received information about the collection for the saints (1 Cor. 16:1–4) and, in fact, according to Paul's own words in 2 Corinthians, he was the one who initiated it (8:6) in the year previous to their receipt of 2 Corinthians (8:10–12). With insight into the apostle's thinking on this matter from his previous engagement with the Jerusalem congregation (Gal. 2:10), he was already motivated when news came that the Galatians were getting their collection ready. In other words, when Titus commenced the collection in Corinth it was not as an apostolic delegate sent from Paul for this task,[182] but as a congregation member exercising leadership in his local church.

Along with his instructions for the organisation of the collection

---

181 Cf. the argument mounted by Reicke, 'Chronology', in favour of the empire-wide mobility of Onesiphorus, benchmarked against the known mobility of Aquila and Priscilla (and cf. James 4:13); accepted by Robinson, *Redating*, 75.
182 Although he still had Titus sent from Paul, Lightfoot, 'Mission', 281, was sure that he had less influence than others such as Tychicus, Trophimus, Apollos or Timothy. 'The fact that an Epistle of St Paul bears his name leads us almost unconsciously to assign a rank to him which he probably did not hold in the estimation of his contemporaries. Titus then does not appear to have had a church-wide reputation at this time'.

(1 Cor. 16:1–4), Paul's reply also outlined his travel plans. At that stage, after going through Macedonia (v.5), he was planning a lengthy stay with the Corinthians before the gift would be sent to Jerusalem (v.3), perhaps across the three months of the coming winter (v.6–7). He was still uncertain whether he would go to Jerusalem himself or whether he would move on to another destination (vv.4,6). At the time of writing, however, he was in Ephesus and planning to stay there until Pentecost, because of a large and active open door for him (v.9). In the interim, Timothy would pay a passing visit on his way back to Paul (vv.10–11; cf. 4:14–17).

But after this promising beginning, perhaps as an extension of some of the internal problems in the congregation already brewing when Paul sent 1 Corinthians, relationships also soured with their apostle. Although the details are obscure,[183] probably in an attempt to assist with the congregation's problems Paul had visited them briefly. This visit did not go well, with the troubles revolving around a particular individual and the congregational response to him (2 Cor. 2:5–10). Although it appears that Paul told the Corinthians that he intended to visit twice, before and after he went through Macedonia prior to going to Judea with the collection (2 Cor. 1:15–17), he changed plans to spare them 'another painful visit' (2:1). Therefore without knowing the current situation in the congregation or their relationship towards him, when the 'great distress' apparently began in Asia and he experienced his turmoil in Troas, Paul did not return to Corinth, but instead went directly to Macedonia (2 Cor. 2:12–13). Presumably as the Corinthians heard about this change in itinerary, some were upset at his apparent fickleness (2 Cor. 1:17), perhaps using this to further inflame dissension.

Where was his old friend Titus in all this, and why didn't he exercise his long-standing position within the congregation to intervene in the internal leadership struggles that involved the tarnishing of Paul's reputation? Given Titus' role in the congregation, what if the troubles both arose and remained because Titus was absent for this period leaving something of a leadership hiatus? In fact, the hole in congregational leadership had become rather large as several key persons

---

183 'The reason for the clouding of the relationship between Paul and the community is difficult to determine exactly', Kümmel, *Introduction*, 283.

had moved outwards for the sake of the wider mission—perhaps also taking other members of their house-churches with them.[184] In this period, the Corinthian congregation had been potentially 'devastated' from the top, after releasing key people to serve the mission elsewhere. Apparently Titus was also amongst that number.

Although the chronology of the Pastoral Epistles, especially in relation to that of Paul, has been hotly debated for some time,[185] if their incidental personal references are taken seriously, we know that Titus engaged in gospel work in both Crete (Titus 1:5) and Dalmatia (2 Tim. 4:10).

Rather than indicating that Paul himself engaged in mission on the island, ἀπέλιπον indicates that it was at Paul's suggestion and under his authority that Titus was 'appointed to' Crete (Titus 1:5)[186]—perhaps to step into one of the remaining mission fields about which Paul himself was hesitating (1 Cor. 16:4,6) at Easter-time in the year prior. But as he penned the letter to Titus, he was already making adjustments to his travel plans. Now he calls upon Titus to join him urgently in Nicopolis in Epirus where he has decided to spend the winter (Titus 3:12). With the Corinthians' attitude towards him in decline, and the disaster of his brief visit to them (perhaps to fill the breach during Titus' absence), it would no longer be possible to winter in Corinth (cf. 1 Cor. 16:6), but he nevertheless wanted Titus with him, bringing news of his work in the mission.

When Paul wrote his first letter to Timothy, Timothy was appointed to Ephesus as Paul was moving towards Macedonia (1 Tim. 1:3), and Paul was expecting to return soon even though he was aware that he might be delayed (3:14; 4:13). Although Timothy's ministry will not be without its difficulties and there are people for him to guard against (1:19–20; 4:1), in the rather settled feeling of the letter there is no hint of him having to endure suffering and neither do the touches of eschatology bristle with any urgency (4:1,8–10; 5:21; 6:7,12,15,17,19). If this letter was to be placed amongst the events of relevance to this essay,

---

184 Aquila and Priscilla (1 Cor. 16:19); Apollos (16:12); Stephanas, Fortunatus and Achaicus (16:17). For the suggestion that 'house churches' were mobilised as missionary sodalities, see Bolt, 'Untangling', 411–413.
185 Already noted by Lightfoot, 'Date', 399; for updated discussion, see Porter, 'Pauline Chronology', and 'Pauline Authorship'.
186 Robinson, *Redating*, 76; Porter, 'Pauline Chronology', 68.

then it would have been written soon after Paul left Ephesus for his final visit to Macedonia (1 Cor. 16:5-9; 2 Cor. 1:15-16; cf. Acts 20:1), in order to reinforce the tasks he had set for Timothy (1:3), but prior to the crisis that confronted him somewhere in Asia on his 360km journey towards Troas.

Perhaps written even in the midst of this overwhelming experience,[187] and probably already viewing it as the start of the 'great distress' before the End, Paul's second letter to Timothy had a markedly different tone.[188] Urging him to be ashamed neither of himself nor his gospel, Paul warned Timothy to be prepared to suffer along with him (1:8,12; 2:3,9; 3:10-12; 4:5). As regards eschatology, Paul is not only concerned about his own individual departure, but the coming of the kingdom with the appearing of Christ (4:8,18) has also drawn closer on his horizon and 'that day' becomes a motivator for Timothy as well (1:12,18; 4:8). Warning Timothy against the same named opponents as previously (2:17; 4:14-15; cf. 1 Tim. 1:20) and more (1:15; 2:17), Paul is sure that by this time Timothy knows about all of Asia deserting him (1:15) as well as other former companions (4:10). But despite his troubles, Paul is sure that he was and will be delivered so that his mission to the nations can be completed (4:17) before the kingdom arrives for him to enter it (4:17-18).[189] No doubt with this future mission in view, Paul appears to be gathering his forces, wanting Mark to join Luke (4:11) and calling upon Timothy to come to him by winter time (4:21)— which, if taken along with Titus 3:12, would be in Nicopolis with Titus. However, by this time of trouble, Titus has left Crete and is apparently moving in the general direction of Nicopolis, for Paul informs Timothy that he is now in Dalmatia. It remains for both Timothy and Titus to catch up with Paul in Macedonia (2 Cor. 1:1; 7:5-7), and both of them are back in Corinth alongside Paul while he wrote to the Romans on

---

187 Some argue that Paul was arrested in Troas, as noted by Harris, *2 Corinthians*, 240, refering to Hemer, 'Troas', 106; Yamauchi, 'Troas', 666.

188 It is notoriously difficult to date 2 Timothy, or to align it with the information in the other Pauline epistles, see, e.g. Knight, *Pastoral Epistles*, 15-18, 'Incongruences', and it is usually placed in Paul's imprisonment in Rome (e.g. Knight, *Pastoral Epistles*, 9), or Caesarea (Reicke, 'Caesarea', 'Historical Setting', accepted, with modification of details, by Robinson, *Redating*, 73-85).

189 He may well have also written 2 Thessalonians in this period, since he is on his way to Macedonia and the eschatology of the letter also has an imminent feel, even if Paul attempts to stay expectations somewhat.

the eve of departing for Jerusalem (Rom. 16:21,23). If the evidence of Luke is admitted, as originally planned they were able to spend their last winter together in Corinth (Acts 20:3a),[190] due to the fact that relationships had been repaired between Paul and the Corinthians. How did this come about?

Perhaps a final hint towards the backstory of Titus and his movements can be gleaned from Paul's reflections upon coming to the end of his mission to the nations (Rom. 15:14–33). When writing 2 Timothy while undergoing his afflictions, Paul was convinced that he had been delivered so that 'through me the message might be fully proclaimed and all the Gentiles might hear' (δι' ἐμοῦ τὸ κήρυγμα πληροφορηθῇ καὶ ἀκούσωσιν πάντα τὰ ἔθνη, 4:17). When he wrote Romans, he believed that that event was now accomplished (Rom. 15:17–20), for 'I, from Jerusalem and in an arc to Illyricum, have fulfilled the gospel of Christ' (ὥστε με ἀπὸ Ἰερουσαλὴμ καὶ κύκλῳ μέχρι τοῦ Ἰλλυρικοῦ πεπληρωκέναι τὸ εὐαγγέλιον τοῦ Χριστοῦ, v.19). As with Crete, what if this was not Paul's direct work, but Titus who completed it on his behalf in Dalmatia/Illyricum?[191] When he returned home to Corinth, what if the news of the mission's completion played a part in moving the Corinthians back towards the apostle and to regain their eschatological eagerness to get involved? Recognising their change of heart and their longing for the apostle who was now once again 'theirs', Titus rushed off to Macedonia where he found Paul and gave him the news that was so refreshing to his spirit. At the same time he could report his completion of the missions to Crete and Illyricum. When Paul shared his view that the 'great distress' had begun, the next steps would be clear. The gospel that began with the Jerusalem saints, had now also been believed amongst the nations. With that gospel bringing together both Jew and Gentile (Rom. 15:1–13), the eschatological expectations of the Old Testament were being realised (v.16: Isa. 66:20; v.21: Isa. 52:15;

---

[190] Thus, the visit to Nicopolis does not prove problematic for the relationship between the Pastoral and other Pauline Epistles, because absent from Acts (e.g. Lightfoot, 'Date', 405), because it never actually happened. Like other travel plans (cf. 1 Tim. 3:14; 2 Cor. 1:15–23; Rom. 15:28), Paul's wintering arrangements were also modified with his changing circumstances.

[191] This removes the need to squeeze another mission field into the Acts account, raised as a problem by Robinson, *Redating*, 42. Robinson is also correct to note that the Pastoral Epistles need not imply for Timothy and Titus 'extended supervision over designated areas. But in fact the instructions relate to specific short-term tours' (p.83).

v.25: Isa. 2:2–4 and 66:18–24). With the day of resurrection now just around the corner (Rom. 11:15), the final act before the coming of the End is for the Gentiles who have shared in the Jews' spiritual things to now offer a service with their material things (15:27b) to 'the [eschatological] poor saints in Jerusalem' (15:26; cf. Gal. 2:10).

Chronologically speaking, the last we see of Titus is back where he belongs in Corinth (Rom. 16:23), as the final preparations were being with this End in view. He is hosting Paul as the apostle writes his *magnum opus*, with Timothy packing his bags to join the Jerusalem party (cf. Acts 20:4). With his missionary stint over, his local congregation's collection stands ready to be included in the gift, whose beginnings he himself had witnessed (Gal. 2:10). Having fought the good fight and fulfilled his own ministry, Titus can now continue to host the congregation at Corinth, rejoicing that they, too, caught the gospel vision in time to participate in both symbolising and hastening the Day of Resurrection.

Bibliography

Bachmann, P.	*Die zweite Brief des Paulus an die Korinther* (KzNT 8; Leipzig, ⁴1922 [1909]; Reprint: Wentworth, 2018).
Barnett, P. W.	*The Second Epistle to the Corinthians* (NICNT; Grand Rapids: Eerdmans, 1997).
Barrett, C.K.	*The Second Epistle to the Corinthians* (HNTC; New York: Harper and Row, 1973).
Barrett, C. K.	'Titus', in C. K. Barrett, *Essays on Paul* (London: SPCK, 1982), 118-131. Originally published in E. E. Ellis and M. Wilcox (eds.), *Neotestamentica et Semitica, Studies in Honour of Matthew Black* (Edinburgh: T&T Clark, 1969), 1-14.
Bauernfeind, O.	'ἀναπαύω, ἀνάπαυσις, ἐπαναπαύω', *TDNT* 1.350-351.
Beale, G. K.	*The Book of Revelation: A Commentary on the Greek Text* (NIGTC; Grand Rapids: Eerdmans, 1999).
Betz, H. D.	'Corinthians, Second Epistle to the', *ABD* 1.1148-1154.
Bolt, P. G.	'(Gaius) Tit(i)us Justus in the service of the Gentile Mission (Acts 18:7)', in Peter G. Bolt (ed.), *Rebuilding the Fallen Tent* (Norwest, NSW: AUCD Press, forthcoming [2026]).
Bolt, P. G.	'Untangling the Pauline Handshakes: Who is Greeting Whom in Romans 16?', in Peter G. Bolt and James R. Harrison (eds.), *Romans and the Legacy of St Paul. Historical, Theological, and Social Perspectives* (Occasional Series 1; Macquarie Park, NSW: SCD Press, 2019), 391-427.
Bultmann, R.	'ἀνίημι, ἄνεσις', *TDNT* 1.365.
Burdick, D. W.	'With Paul in the Troad', *Near Eastern Archaeological Society Bulletin* n.s. 12 (1978), 31-65.
Burton, E. de W.	*Syntax of the Moods and Tenses in New Testament Greek* (Edinburgh: Clark, ³1898 [1888; revised and enlarged 1893]).
Campbell, C. R., Fanning, B. M. and Porter, S. E.	*The Perfect Storm: Critical Discussion of the Semantics of the Greek Perfect Tense under Aspect Theory* (SBG, 21; New York: Peter Lang, 2021).
Campbell, C. R.	*Advances in the Study of Greek. New Insights for Reading the New Testament* (Grand Rapids: Zondervan, 2015).

Campbell, C. R.   *Verbal Aspect and Non-Indicative Verbs. Further Soundings in the Greek of the New Testament* (SBG, 15; New York: Peter Lang, 2008).

Campbell, C. R.   *Basics of Verbal Aspect in Biblical Greek* (Grand Rapids: Zondervan, 2008).

Campbell, C. R.   *Verbal Aspect, the Indicative Mood, and Narrative. Soundings in the Greek of the New Testament* (SBG, 13; New York: Peter Lang, 2007).

Comrie, B.   *Aspect: An Introduction the Study of Verbal Aspect and Related Problems* (Cambridge Textbooks in Linguistics; Cambridge: Cambridge University Press, 1976).

Crellin, R. S. D.   'The perfect system in Ancient Greek', in R. Crellin and T. Jügel (eds.), *Perfects in Indo-European Languages and Beyond* (Current Issues in Linguistic Theory, 352; Amsterdam: John Benjamins, 2020), 435–482. https://doi.org/10.17863/CAM.57320 [pagination differs from published version]

Crellin, R. S. D.   *The Syntax and Semantics of the Perfect Active in Literary Koine Greek* (Publications of the Philological Society, 47; Malden, MA: Wiley-Blackwell, 2016).

Crellin, R. S. D.   'Abstract: The Greek Perfect Active System 200 bc—ad 150', *TynB* 64.1 (2013), 157–159.

Crellin, R. S. D.   'The Greek Perfect Active System 200 bc —ad 150' (unpublished PhD diss., University of Cambridge, 2012).

Cripe, M. A.   'An Analysis of Infinitive Clauses Containing Both Subject and Object in the Accusative Case in the Greek New Testament' (unpublished ThM thesis; Dallas Theological Seminary, 1992).

Fanning, B.   *Verbal Aspect in New Testament Greek* (Oxford Theological Monographs; Oxford: Clarendon, 1990).

Fellows, R. G.   'Was Titus Timothy?', *JSNT* 81 (2001), 33–58.

Furnish, V. P.   *2 Corinthians* (AB 32A; New Haven: Yale, 1974).

Garland, D. E.   *2 Corinthians* (NAC 29; Nashville: Broadman & Holman, 1999).

Georgi, D.   *Remembering the Poor: The History of Paul's Collection for Jerusalem* (Ingrid Racz, transl.; Nashville: Abingdon, ET 1992 [German: 1965]).

Gillman, J.	'Titus (Person)', *ABD* 6.581–582.
Goetchius, E. V. N.	*The Language of the New Testament* (New York: Scribners, 1965).
Goodspeed, E. J.	'Gaius Titius Justus', *JBL* 69 (1950), 382–383.
Harder, G.	'σπουδάζω, σπουδή, σπουδαῖος', *TDNT* 7.559–568.
Harris, M. J.	*The Second Epistle to the Corinthians* (NIGTC; Grand Rapids: Eerdmans, 2005).
Hemer, C. J.	'Alexandria Troas', *TynB* 26 (1975), 79–112.
Holl, K.	'Der Kirchenbegriff des Paulus in seinem Verhaltnis zu dem Urgemeinde [1921]', in *Gesammelte Aufsätze zur Kirchengeschichte II* (Tubingen: Mohr, 1928), 44–67.
Hughes, P. E.	*Paul's Second Epistle to the Corinthians* (NICNT; Grand Rapids: Eerdmans, 1962).
Jannaris, A. N.	*An Historical Greek Grammar Chiefly of the Attic Dialect* (London: Macmillan, 1897).
Kee, H. C.	'Titus Companion of Paul', *IDB* (Nashville, TN: Abingdon, 1962), 4.656–657.
Kerr, C.M.	'Silas', *ISBE,* s.v.
Knowling, R. J.	'The Acts of the Apostles', *Expositor's Greek Testament* (Reprint: Grand Rapids: Eerdmans, 1961 [1897]), 2.1–554.
Kruse, C. G.	*2 Corinthians* (TNTC, 8; Nottingham: IVP, 1987).
Kümmel, W. G.	*Introduction to the New Testament* (Howard C. Kee, transl.; ET: London: 1975; [6]1987 [German: [17]1972).
Lake, K. and Cadbury, H. J.	*The Beginnings of Christianity. Part 1. The Acts of the Apostles.* Vol. 4: *Translation and Commentary* (London: Macmillan, 1933).
Leaf, W.	*Strabo on the Troad Book XIII, Cap. 1* (Cambridge: Cambridge University Press, 1923).
Lightfoot, J. B.	'The Date of the Pastoral Epistles', *Biblical Essays* (London: Macmillan, [2]1904 [1893]), 399–410.
Lightfoot, J. B.	'The Mission of Titus to the Corinthians [1855]', *Biblical Essays* (London: Macmillan, [2]1904 [1893]), 273–84. Reprinted from the *Journal of Classical and Sacred Philology* 2 (1855), 194–205.

McKay, K. L.	*A New Syntax of the Verb in New Testament Greek. An Aspectual Approach* (SBG, 5; New York: Peter Lang, 1994).
McKay, K. L.	'Syntax in Exegesis', *TynBul* 23.1 (1972), 39–57.
McKay, K. L.	'The Use of the Ancient Greek Perfect Down to the End of the Second Century AD', *Bulletin of the Institute of Classical Studies* 12 (1965), 1–21.
Martin, R. P.	*2 Corinthians* (WBC 40; Grand Rapids: Zondervan, 2014).
Moeller, H. R., and Kramer, A.	'An Overlooked Structural Pattern in New Testament Greek', *NovT* 5 (1962), 25–35.
Moule, C. F. D.	*An Idiom Book of New Testament Greek* (Cambridge: Cambridge University Press, 1953, repr. 1982).
Moulton, J. H.	*A Grammar of New Testament Greek.* Vol. I: *Prolegomena* (Edinburgh: T&T Clark, ²1906).
Murphy-O'Connor, J.	*Paul: A Critical Life* (Oxford: Clarendon, 1996).
Plummer, A.	*The Second Epistle of Paul the Apostle to the Corinthians* (CGT; Cambridge: Cambridge University Press, 1915).
Porter, S. E.	'Pauline Chronology and the Question of Pseudonymity of the Pastoral Epistles', in S. E. Porter and G. P. Fewster (eds.), *Pauline Studies vol. 8: Paul and Pseudepigraphy* (Leiden: Brill, 2013), 65–88.
Porter, S. E.	'Pauline Authorship and the Pastoral Epistles: Implications for Canon', *BBR* 5 (1995), 105–23.
Pratt, R. L.	*I & II Corinthians* (HBC, 7; Nashville: Holman, 2000).
Ramsay, W. M.	*Pictures of the Apostolic Church: Its Life and Thought* (Philadelphia: Sunday School Times, 1910).
Ramsay, W. M.	'Roads and Travel (in the NT)', in *HDB* 5.375–402.
Ramsay, W. M.	*St Paul the Traveller and the Roman Citizen* (London: Hodder & Stoughton, 1897; Reprint: Grand Rapids: Baker, 1962, ⁹1974).
Reed, Jeffrey T.	'The Infinitive with Two Substantival Accusatives: An Ambiguous Construction?', *NovT* 33 (1991), 1–27.
Reicke, B.	Chronology of the Pastoral Epistles [1976]', in D. P. Moessner and I. Reicke (eds.), *Re-Examining Paul's Letters: The History of the Pauline Correspondence* (Harrisburg, PA: Trinity Press International, 2001), 105–120.

Reicke, B.	'The Historical Setting of Colossians [1973]', in D. P. Moessner and I. Reicke (eds.), *Re-Examining Paul's Letters: The History of the Pauline Correspondence* (Harrisburg, PA: Trinity Press International, 2001), 121–130.
Reicke, B.	'Caesarea, Rome, and the Captivity Epistles [1970]', in D. P. Moessner and I. Reicke (eds.), *Re-Examining Paul's Letters: The History of the Pauline Correspondence* (Harrisburg, PA: Trinity Press International, 2001), 131–140.
Robertson, A. T.	*A Grammar of the Greek New Testament in the Light of Historical Research* (Nashville: Broadman, 1934^4 [1914]).
Robertson, A. T.	*Word Pictures in the New Testament.* Vol. IV: *The Epistles of Paul* (6 vols.; Grand Rapids: Baker, 1931 [1930]).
Robinson, D. W.B.	'The Salvation of Israel in Romans 9–11', in P. G. Bolt and M. D. Thompson (eds.), *Donald Robinson Selected Works. Vol 1: Assembling God's People* (Camperdown and Newtown: Australian Church Record and Moore College, 2008), 47–63.
Robinson, J. A. T.	*Redating the New Testament* (Eugene: Wipf and Stock, 2000; orig. London: SCM, 1976).
Schlier, H.	'θλίβω, θλῖψις', *TDNT* 3.139–148.
Schmiedel, P. W.	'Silas, Silvanus', in T. K. Cheyne and J. S. Black (eds.), *Encyclopaedia Biblica* Vol. IV: Q to Z (Toronto: George N. Morang and Co., 1903), 4514–4521.
Seifrid, M. A.	*The Second Letter to the Corinthians* (PNTC; Grand Rapids: Eerdmans, 2014).
Thrall, M. E.	*The Second Epistle to the Corinthians. Vol. I: Introduction and Commentary on II Corinthians I—VII* (ICC; 2 vols.; Edinburgh: T&T Clark, 1994).
Turner, N. and Moulton, J. H.	*A Grammar of New Testament Greek.* Vol. III: *Syntax.* (Edinburgh: T&T Clark, 1963, repr. 1980, 1988).
Votaw, C. W.	*The Use of the Infinitive in Biblical Greek* (Chicago: C. Votaw, 1896).
Wallace, D. B.	*Greek Grammar. Beyond the Basics* (Grand Rapids: Zondervan, 1996).
Wallace, D. B.	'The Semantics and Exegetical Significance of the Object-Complement Construction in the New Testament', *GTJ* 6 (1985), 91–112.

Weil, H.	*The Order of Words in the Ancient Languages Compared with that of the Modern Languages* (Charles W. Super, transl.; Amsterdam Classics in Linguistics, 14; Amsterdam: John Benjamins, 1978, New edition; ET: Boston: Ginn & Company, 1887). French original: *De l'ordre des mots dans les langues anciennes comparées aux langues modernes* (Paris 1844).
Windisch, H.	*Der zweite Korintherbrief* (MeyerK, 6; Göttingen, Vandenhoek & Ruprecht, ⁹1924 [original?] reprinted 1970).
Winer, G. B.	*A Grammar of the Idiom of the New Testament. Seventh Edition, Revised by Gottlieb Lünemann* (Edward Masson, transl.; JosEph. H. Thayer, ed.; Andover/ London: Draper/ Trübner, ET: 1869 [German: 1867]). Original: *Grammatik des Neutestamentlichen Sprachidioms* (Leipzig: Vogel, 1822, ²1825, ³1830, ⁷1867).
Winter, S. F.	'"He Will Rescue Us Again": Affliction and Hope in 2 Corinthians 1:8–11', *Religions* 11.5, 222 (2020), 1–9.
Yamauchi, E. M.	'Troas', *ABD* 6.666–667.
Young, D.	'The Eschatological Significance of Paul's Collection for Jerusalem', (Unpublished STM thesis, Concordia Theological Seminary, 1967). <https://schoar.csl.edu/stm/493>

CHAPTER 12

Of Grief that Turns to Comfort: MT Echoes Resounding in the Background of 2 Corinthians 7:5–16?

Emmanuel Nathan

In his well-known book, *Echoes of Scripture in the Letters of Paul*, Richard Hays mentions the following in his opening chapter on the puzzle of Pauline hermeneutics:

> Quotation, allusion, and echo may be seen as points along a spectrum of intertextual reference, moving from the explicit to the subliminal. As we move farther away from overt citation, the source recedes into the discursive distance, the intertextual relations become less determinate, and the demand placed on the reader's listening powers grows greater. As we near the vanishing point of the echo, it inevitably becomes difficult to decide whether we are really hearing an echo at all, or whether we are only conjuring things out of the murmurings of our imaginations.[1]

My paper will attempt, by means of a short intertextual exercise, to delve further into the question why Paul found it useful to rely upon prophetic traditions of comfort and restoration in order to link his usage of λύπη

---

1   Hays, *Echoes*, 23.

and παράκλησις language in 2 Corinthians 7:5–16. While Paul's deep familiarity with the LXX text is most often presupposed, this paper will argue that perhaps Paul's knowledge of the MT ought not to be precluded. The verse I will be concentrating on for that is 2 Corinthians 7:10, ἡ γὰρ κατὰ θεὸν λύπη μετάνοιαν εἰς σωτηρίαν ἀμεταμέλητον ἐργάζεται· ἡ δὲ τοῦ κόσμου λύπη θάνατον κατεργάζεται. I will ask whether the double meaning of the Hebrew verb נחם as denoting both comfort and regret/grief contributes to our further understanding of 'a godly grief producing a repentance that leads to salvation'. But first I will briefly enumerate the options that commentators have offered on this verse as possible parallels.

Possible parallels?

According to Paul Barnett, 'Paul may have in mind the examples of David's genuine sorrow of heart over his sin in contrast with Esau's shallow remorse'.[2] He goes on to cite Psalm 51:1–11 (David's psalm of repentance after the Bathsheba incident) and Genesis 27:38,41 (Esau's grief at realising his father Isaac had only one blessing) as examples. For the latter case, Barnett makes a comparison to Hebrews 12:16–17:

¹⁶ μή τις πόρνος ἢ βέβηλος ὡς Ἠσαῦ, ὃς ἀντὶ βρώσεως μιᾶς ἀπέδετο τὰ πρωτοτόκια ἑαυτοῦ. ¹⁷ ἴστε γὰρ ὅτι καὶ μετέπειτα θέλων κληρονομῆσαι τὴν εὐλογίαν ἀπεδοκιμάσθη, μετανοίας γὰρ τόπον οὐχ εὗρεν καίπερ μετὰ δακρύων ἐκζητήσας αὐτήν.	¹⁶ See to it that no one becomes like Esau, an immoral and godless person, who sold his birthright for a single meal. ¹⁷ You know that later, when he wanted to inherit the blessing, he was rejected, for he found no chance to repent, even though he sought the blessing with tears.

These examples were already listed by Ralph Martin in his commentary (who in turn cited Windisch and Hughes) but he went on to state that '[t]he contrast between Peter's failure and recovery and Judas' fall (cf. Matt. 27:3: μεταμεληθείς, repented = felt regret; Matt. 21:30,32.

---

2   Barnett, *The Second Epistle*, 377 n.20.

Contrast Luke 22:31–34) is even more obvious'.³ For convenience, they are reproduced below.

Matthew 27:3	Matthew 21:29,32	Luke 22:31–34
³When Judas, his betrayer, saw that Jesus was condemned, he repented and brought back the thirty pieces of silver to the chief priests and the elders.	²⁹He answered, 'I will not'; but later he changed his mind and went. ³²For John came to you in the way of righteousness and you did not believe him, but the tax collectors and the prostitutes believed him; and even after you saw it, you did not change your minds and believe him.	³¹'Simon, Simon, listen! Satan has demanded to sift all of you like wheat, ³²but I have prayed for you that your own faith may not fail; and you, when once you have turned back, strengthen your brothers.' ³³And he said to him, 'Lord, I am ready to go with you to prison and to death!' ³⁴Jesus said, 'I tell you, Peter, the cock will not crow this day, until you have denied three times that you know me.'

Going back even further, Alfred Plummer's commentary⁴ mentions that the examples of Cain, Esau and Judas illustrate the wrong kind of sorrow and that the *Testament of Gad* (5:7) has a phrase reminiscent of this Pauline verse: 'For godly and true repentance destroys ignorance and drives away darkness, and it enlightens the eyes and gives knowledge to the soul, and it leads the disposition to salvation'.⁵

None of these supposed parallels really helps to shed much light on the way Paul uses ἡ κατὰ θεὸν λύπη μετάνοιαν εἰς σωτηρίαν in 2 Corinthians 7:10. Of course, the immediate context is itself instructive on how we should understand this. For instance, Murray Harris states: 'The phrase κατὰ θεόν occurs three times in vv.9–11, in each case qualifying the λυπ- root [...] Although the phrase need not be translated the same way in each verse, it always depicts the λύπη as being in conformity to God's will and purpose [...] It may therefore be rendered 'in accordance with the will of God' (Lang 31; Thrall 486), 'in a godly

---

3 Martin, *2 Corinthians*, 233.
4 Plummer, *A Critical and Exegetical Commentary*, 222.
5 Translation from Hollander and De Jonge, *The Testaments*, 328.

way' (Moule 59; Turner 268), or 'in God's way' (Zerwick and Grosvenor 548)'.[6] Harris follows the classical view that the Corinthian sorrow was intended by God in order to bring on the desired repentance and there is nothing to seriously dispute this reading of the plain sense of the text.

From a structural point of view, it is striking to notice the move from παράκλησις language in 2 Corinthians 7:6–7 (consolation at the arrival of Titus) to the language of λύπη in vv.8–11 (both godly and worldly), and then back to παράκλησις language in v.13. While we are wont to look to Greek literature where Pauline texts are concerned (and with good reason), I would like, in what follows, to take another path for a change. I shall embark on a short intertextual journey into the Hebrew verb נָחַם, which, interestingly, in its *niphal* form can denote both comfort and regret/grief. At the end of this, I will ask whether these findings contribute anything further to our understanding of 'a godly grief producing a repentance that leads to salvation'.

A Short Intertextual Exercise in the MT

Genesis 6:6

וַיִּנָּחֶם יְהוָה כִּי־עָשָׂה אֶת־הָאָדָם בָּאָרֶץ וַיִּתְעַצֵּב אֶל־לִבּוֹ׃

'And the LORD **was sorry** that he had made humankind on the earth, and it grieved him to his heart.'

Genesis 6:6 uses נָחַם, here more specifically in the *niphal* form as a *waw* consecutive imperfect third person masculine singular, to portray God's regret at having created humankind before the onset of the deluge. Holladay's lexicon lists the verb נָחַם in its *niphal* form as having the primary meaning of 'regret' or 'change of heart', followed by a second meaning, in this specific Genesis instance, of 'allowing oneself to be sorry'.[7] So it is that the NRSV translates the verse as 'the Lord was sorry'. The NIV translates as 'the Lord regretted', while the KJV even translates as, 'And it repented the Lord'. While one can entertain here the notion of a divine grief, so to say, there is no actual repentance in

---

6   Harris, *The Second Epistle*, 537.
7   Holladay (ed.), 'נחם', 234.

view, other than the Lord repenting of the idea, that is to say, regretting the fact that he had created humanity. This is reinforced in Genesis 6:7 by the direct speech of God: כִּי נִחַמְתִּי כִּי עֲשִׂיתִם – 'for I am sorry that I have made them'.

What *is* interesting, however, is that God's decision to blot out all of creation is not without an exit strategy. One man finds favour in God's sight – Noah, a righteous man, blameless in his generation. It is through Noah that humanity and all creatures with him gain a second chance. Noah steers this remnant to salvation and, as a result, the earth is repopulated.

Exodus 32:14

וַיִּנָּחֶם יְהוָה עַל־הָרָעָה אֲשֶׁר דִּבֶּר לַעֲשׂוֹת לְעַמּוֹ

'And the Lord **changed his mind** about the disaster that he planned to bring on his people.'

Another setting where the same grammatical instance of נחם appears is Exodus 32:14, when God relents from his plan to destroy the Israelites after their sin with the golden calf. In this particular sentence there is no divine regret, but rather a divine relenting. However, the relenting only occurs as a result of Moses' intercession to spare the people. The divine regret is quite evident in v.7 when God tells Moses to descend Mount Sinai immediately. God distances himself from the people in the process. '*Your* people, whom *you* [that is to say, Moses and no longer God] brought up out of Egypt, have acted perversely.' In v.9 they are no longer God's people or even Moses' but simply, 'I have seen *this* people, how stiff-necked they are'. However, Moses is able to stay the divine wrath by reminding God that the Israelites are in fact *his* people: 'O Lord, why does your wrath burn hot against *your* people, whom *you* brought out of the land of Egypt with great power and with a mighty hand?' (Ex. 32:11). Even though the people have not yet repented of their sin, in succeeding to get God to 'repent' (KJV) of the people's destruction and in this way securing their salvation, Moses is then able to hasten down the mount to confront the Israelites with their sin.

Jonah 3:10

וַיַּרְא הָאֱלֹהִים אֶת־מַעֲשֵׂיהֶם כִּי־שָׁבוּ מִדַּרְכָּם הָרָעָה וַיִּנָּחֶם הָאֱלֹהִים
עַל־הָרָעָה אֲשֶׁר־דִּבֶּר לַעֲשׂוֹת־לָהֶם וְלֹא עָשָׂה

'When God saw what they did, how they turned from their evil ways, **God changed his mind** about the calamity that he had said he would bring upon them; and he did not do it.'

The same use of נָחַם as divine relenting occurs in 2 Samuel 24:16 and 1 Chronicles 21:15, both accounts dealing with the plague ensuing from David's desire to conduct a census of his fighting men and thereby eliciting God's anger. Interestingly, in these two parallel accounts, the divine relenting (God staying the angel's hand from destroying Jerusalem with the plague) occurs as a result of David's confession of guilt and a public display of repentance. A more collective and equally public display of repentance occurs in Jonah 3:10, when the king of Nineveh, along with the city's inhabitants and their animals, don sackcloth and commence a fast in direct response to Jonah's terse (only five Hebrew words, six if one counts the conjunction) announcement of doom awaiting the city. God sees their repentance (the Hebrew verb שׁוב 'turning/returning' used in this instance will in time become the technical term used for repentance, תְּשׁוּבָה) and decides to spare the city. In other words, in the book of Jonah נָחַם does not simply refer to God changing his mind ('repenting' or relenting) with regard to the evil he planned to visit on the city, but is also situated within an actual context of repentance that leads to salvation. This is different than in the case of Moses earlier where Moses' intercession effects the divine change of mind before even the people's repentance has taken place. It is slightly different from the Davidic instances, too, in that it was not just the king who was at fault and hence responsible for making atonement. In the book of Jonah, too, there is nothing to suggest a prior regret or grief on God's part that prompted him into threatening destruction. Nonetheless, there is a sense of aggrievement at injustices done. After all, the Book of Jonah opens with the divine commission to Jonah to go immediately to Nineveh and denounce it because 'its wickedness has come up before me' (Jon. 1:2).

Jeremiah 31:15

> כֹּה ׀ אָמַר יְהוָה קוֹל בְּרָמָה נִשְׁמָע נְהִי בְּכִי תַמְרוּרִים רָחֵל מְבַכָּה
> עַל־בָּנֶיהָ מֵאֲנָה לְהִנָּחֵם עַל־בָּנֶיהָ כִּי אֵינֶנּוּ׃

> 'Thus says the LORD: A voice is heard in Ramah, lamentation and bitter weeping. Rachel is weeping for her children; she refuses **to be comforted** for her children, because they are no more.'

A very different instance of נחם occurs in Jeremiah 31:15. Here, still in the *niphal* form but as an infinitive construct (with preposition), it takes on the third meaning of נחם in the *niphal* form, that of comfort and consolation, specifically in the context of mourning.[8] In this verse it is a question of Rachel's refusal to be comforted because of her inconsolable grief at the loss of her children. Yet her grief is situated within a larger context of restoration for the exiled people of Israel. In the verses immediately preceding v.15 we are told that God 'will turn their mourning into joy, I will comfort them [וְנִחַמְתִּים, *piel* form], and give them gladness for sorrow'. The verses immediately following v.15 (vv.16–20) speak of divine restoration brought on by repentance, a repentance that interestingly relies once again upon נחם in the *niphal* form (v.19):

> [16] Thus says the LORD: Keep your voice from weeping, and your eyes from tears; for there is a reward for your work, says the LORD: they shall come back from the land of the enemy;[17] there is hope for your future, says the LORD: your children shall come back to their own country.[18] Indeed I heard Ephraim pleading: 'You disciplined me, and I took the discipline; I was like a calf untrained. Bring me back, let me come back, for you are the LORD my God. [19] For after I had turned away **I repented** [נִחַמְתִּי, *niphal* form]; and after I was discovered, I struck my thigh; I was ashamed, and I was dismayed because I bore the disgrace of my youth.' [20] Is Ephraim my dear son? Is he the child I delight in? As often as I speak against him, I still remember him. Therefore I am deeply moved for him; I will surely have mercy on him, says the LORD.

---

8 Holladay (ed.), 'נחם', 234.

Rachel's inconsolable grief, brought on by the loss of her children, presumably to exile, will in fact be transformed to comfort at witnessing their return from exile. Ephraim, figuratively representing the people as Israel's firstborn son (v.9, cf. v.20), acknowledges that the hardship of exile was in fact a discipline sent by God that would lead to a change of heart, a turning away from past ways and a return to God and, as reward, a return to the land. Here perhaps, more than in the previous examples, we notice a complex of ideas within a context of comfort and restoration, that most closely resembles a 'grief in accordance with the will of God producing a repentance that leads to salvation'.

Before returning to the Pauline verse in question, let me first summarise what this brief intertextual exercise has yielded. Examining four instances of the verb נָחַם in *niphal* form in the Hebrew Bible (MT), I discovered that it has been used to portray God's regret at having created humankind (in Gen. 6:6). It has also been used to describe a divine change of mind from anger (and intended destruction) to mercy (and a staying from carrying out this destruction). This has been then been variously translated as God relenting or repenting of the judgment he had planned to execute (in Ex. 32:14 and Jon. 3:10). In both these instances there is divine regret or aggrievement to begin with (at acting idolatrously or unjustly), but whereas in Exodus it is Moses' intercession that effects the divine change of mind, in Jonah it is in fact the people's repentance at Jonah's pronouncement of doom which brings about God's sparing of Nineveh. Finally, Rachel's refusal to be comforted in Jeremiah 31:15 is enveloped by a context of comfort and restoration. This comfort and restoration follows upon a period of exile that the people of Israel will acknowledge as having been intended by God as a disciplinary punishment so that they will repent/have a change of heart, return to God, and, as reward, return to their land.

Do We Now Understand 2 Corinthians 7:10 Any Better?

At the end of my brief intertextual interlude, I would now like to ask whether these findings in any way help to further our understanding of 'a godly grief producing a repentance that leads to salvation'. Perhaps I should put this more bluntly by echoing the quotation from Richard

Hays that I started this paper with: are we dealing here with any meaningful echoes from the MT at all, or have I merely been conjuring things out of the murmurings of my own imaginations? I have already admitted to venturing down a road less travelled in Pauline scholarship where, with good reason, one looks to parallels in Greek texts and, therefore, in contrast to the MT, the LXX would normally be the more reliable place to look. That being said, on the basis of my intertextual look at possible MT echoes, I also suggested that the complex of ideas in Jeremiah 31:15 and following, within a context of comfort and restoration, perhaps came closest to the Pauline statement of 2 Corinthians 7:10. This should actually not surprise us since the chapter in question, whether Jeremiah 31 MT or Jeremiah 38 LXX, was probably well known to Paul, given his use of the term 'new covenant' (καινὴ διαθήκη) in 2 Corinthians 3:6, which is generally argued to have had v.31 of this Jeremiah chapter in mind.[9] But it does not get us much closer to answering the question whether Paul relied on MT echoes in addition to the more reliable quotations, allusions, and echoes from the LXX.

Hays has listed seven criteria with which to test whether an echo of a prior text is indeed present and credible.[10] Since these criteria are presented as questions, I shall apply them to the intertextual exercise I made and immediately supply answers to them:

(1) availability: *was the prior text available to the author and readers?* Here the answer of whether the MT wordplay/echo was available would at best be a probable (but not provable) yes for Paul the author and merely a possible (but unlikely) one for Paul's readers;

(2) volume: *how much explicit repetition of words or syntactical patterns are there?* On the one hand, this is a hard one to answer since the exercise was to suggest that the Hebrew verb נחם seems to capture within its ambit the spectrum of emotions from grief/regret through repentance to comfort/consolation. On the other hand, since the question is also how distinctive or prominent the precursor text was within Scripture, I would say that if the Jeremiah text was the precursor text, it would certainly have been well known, but then again, in both LXX and MT versions;

---

9   See, for instance, among others, Scott Hafemann, *Paul, Moses.*
10 Hays, *Echoes,* 29–32.

(3) recurrence: *does Paul cite or allude to the same scriptural passage elsewhere?* As with the foregoing question, I have argued that Paul would have been at least familiar with the Jeremiah text since he seems to have relied on another term from the same chapter elsewhere in his epistle, but it does not prove that Paul was relying on the MT rather than the more plausible LXX;

(4) thematic coherence: *how well does the echo fit within Paul's line of argument?* As with (2), I have tried to suggest that the Hebrew verb נחם, in *niphal* form, seems to capture within its ambit the spectrum of emotions from grief/regret through repentance to comfort/consolation represented by distinct Greek terms in this Pauline verse (and pericope). I would argue that the MT echo is at least as worthy of speculation as the comparisons that commentators have until now been considering (namely, Gen. 27:38, Ps. 51:1–11, Heb. 12:16–17; Matt. 27:3; Matt. 21:30,32; Luke 22:31–34; *Testament of Gad* 5:7);

(5) historical plausibility: *did Paul intend the alleged meaning effect and would his readers have understood it?* If I wanted to make a strong case I would say that Paul fully intended to play upon the different meanings of the verb נחם in *niphal* form, especially since due attention has been given to Paul's use of παράκλησις terminology in 2 Corinthians.[11] However, evidence of παράκλησις terminology in 2 Corinthians hardly proves that Paul also had נחם terminology in mind when writing the letter. And I would have to be extremely honest that his Greek-speaking hearers or readers would have failed to understand it. This latter consideration in itself weakens the case for Paul having relied upon MT echoes (as opposed to LXX echoes), although it need not since it goes to the heart of how reader-sensitive a writer Paul was. In a minimalist sense, though, I feel more comfortable in stating that while Paul himself may not have necessarily intended an explicit meaning effect, the different meanings of the verb נחם in *niphal* form *may* have been playing in the background of Paul's mind as a 'distant' echo;

(6) history of interpretation: *have these echoes been noticed by other readers, ancient and modern?* As already mentioned, due attention has been given to Paul's use of παράκλησις terminology in 2 Corinthians, but I do not think any attention has really been given to whether Paul

---

11 See especially Bieringer, 'The Comforted Comforter'.

also had נָחַם terminology in mind. However it is entirely possible that I have not read extensively enough on the subject, and I would in fact welcome coming across something along these lines since it would go some way to confirming my own position.

(7) **satisfaction:** *does this reading make sense?* I argued earlier that the comparisons given by commentators do not really help to shed much light on the way Paul uses ἡ κατὰ θεὸν λύπη μετάνοιαν εἰς σωτηρίαν in 2 Corinthians 7:10. In fact, I went on to state that the immediate context of the pericope gives us enough information to understand the verse without any further need of parallels or echoes. That being said, unearthing a possible Jeremian echo may serve to complement (and certainly not negate) the more usual look to Paul's use of Deutero- and Trito-Isaiah in this epistle.[12] Reimund Bieringer has noted that, '[u]sing παρακαλέω in the Deutero-Isaian sense, Paul also suggests that the conflict between him and the Corinthian community had a devastating effect on their relationship and required παράκλησις and οἰκοδομή, a sustained effort at reconstruction, encouragement, strengthening and rebuilding'.[13] It is perhaps worth adding to this that Jeremiah 31:38 MT/38:38 LXX both speak here of 'rebuilding' (וְנִבְנְתָה/οἰκοδομηθήσεται), a chapter, even at the risk of repeating myself, laden with the language of comfort and restoration.

Conclusion

My paper has been an attempt, by means of a short intertextual exercise, to delve further into the question why Paul found it useful to rely upon prophetic traditions of comfort and restoration in order to link his usage of λύπη and παράκλησις language in 2 Corinthians 7:5–16. While Paul's deep familiarity with the LXX text is most often presupposed, I tried to show that perhaps Paul's knowledge of the MT ought not to be totally excluded from the picture. As my exercise I picked 2 Corinthians 7:10, ἡ γὰρ κατὰ θεὸν λύπη μετάνοιαν εἰς σωτηρίαν ἀμεταμέλητον ἐργάζεται· ἡ δὲ τοῦ κόσμου λύπη θάνατον κατεργάζεται, and inquired

---

12   See, for instance, Gignilliat, *Paul and Isaiah's Servants*.
13   Bieringer, 'The Comforted Comforter', 7.

whether the double meaning of the Hebrew verb נָחַם, in its *niphal* form, as denoting both comfort and regret/grief, contributes to our further understanding of 'a godly grief producing a repentance that leads to salvation'. I suggested that Jeremiah 31:15 and its immediate context of comfort and restoration offered a complex of ideas that most closely resembled a grief in accordance with the will of God that would bring about a repentance, which in turn would lead to restoration.

Should my intertextual exercise fail to persuade, however, I nonetheless take solace (or should I rather say, comfort?) in the knowledge that perhaps another view on intertextuality (as given in the quote with which I choose to close this paper) might at least be a little more accommodating of the reading I have offered here, and maybe even facilitate a different kind of Pauline 'theology in the making'.

> The Bible is notorious for the paucity of detail of certain sorts within its narrative. Erich Auerbach described this as being 'fraught with background'. The gaps are those silences in the text which call for interpretation if the reader is to make sense of what happened, to fill out the plot and the characters in a meaningful way. [...] There is even a native rabbinic saying for this quality of the text: 'this verse cries out, 'interpret me!''[14]

---

14 Boyarin, *Intertextuality*, 41.

Bibliography

Barnett, P. — *The Second Epistle to the Corinthians* (NICNT; Grand Rapids, MI: Eerdmans, 1997).

Bieringer, R. — 'The Comforted Comforter: The Meaning of παρακαλέω or παράκλησις Terminology in 2 Corinthians', *HTS Teologiese Studies/Theological Studies* 67/1 (2011). doi: 10.4102/hts.v67i1.969.

Boyarin, D. — *Intertextuality and the Reading of Midrash* (Bloomington and Indianapolis: Indiana University Press, 1990).

Gignilliat, M. — *Paul and Isaiah's Servants: Paul's Theological Reading of Isaiah 40–66 in 2 Corinthians 5:14—6:10* (Library of New Testament Studies 330; London: T&T Clark, 2007).

Hafemann, S. J. — *Paul, Moses, and the History of Israel* (WUNT 81. Tübingen: Mohr Siebeck, 1995).

Hays, R. B. — *Echoes of Scripture in the Letters of Paul* (New Haven-London: Yale University Press, 1989).

Holladay, W. L. (ed.) — 'נחם,' in *A Concise Hebrew and Aramaic Lexicon of the Old Testament* (Leiden: Brill, 1998).

Harris, M. J. — *The Second Epistle to the Corinthians: A Commentary on the Greek Text* (NIGTC. Grand Rapids, MI: Eerdmans, 2005).

Hollander, H. W. and De Jonge, M. — *The Testaments of the Twelve Patriarchs: A Commentary* (Leiden: Brill, 1985).

Martin, Ralph P. — *2 Corinthians* (WBC 40; Waco, TX: Word Books, 1986).

Plummer, A. — *A Critical and Exegetical Commentary on the Second Epistle of St Paul to the Corinthians* (ICC; Edinburgh: T&T Clark, 1915 repr. 1970).

CHAPTER 13

Crucifixion, the Spirit, and Christian Identity in Galatians

Grant Buchanan

Introduction

Galatians is vital for understanding Paul's thought, providing important insights into his theology—especially concerning Christ, law, justification, faith and Christian identity. Scholarship, on the whole, tends to focus on Christology in the letter, as this is a central theme throughout Paul's thought. More recently, however, there has been a growing focus on the Spirit in Galatians, and the place and purpose the Spirit has to Paul's argument.[1] Given that Galatians is, in part, Paul's manifesto of the Holy Spirit, this current and dynamic conversation is proving useful to better understand what Paul is attempting to do with his gospel message and his presentation of Christian identity in the letter.

Nevertheless, while this focus on the Spirit is most welcome, in most commentaries and secondary literature the emphasis tends to primarily be on how the Holy Spirit relates to Paul's Christology. In other words, how Paul's Spirit-language serves his Christological argument in Galatians. This is driven by both exegetical and theological concerns that seek to be faithful to Paul's understanding of Christ.[2] A second

---

1   Buchanan, *The Spirit*; Cosgrove, *The Cross*; DeSilva, *The Letter*; Fee, *God's Empowering Presence*; Keener, *Galatians*; Lull, *The Spirit*; Yates, *The Spirit*.
2   Kwon, *Eschatology*; Ferguson, *The Spirit*; Barclay, *Obeying*.

common emphasis focuses on how Paul's Spirit-language serves his ethics, especially in the latter part of Galatians.[3]

In *Eschatology in Galatians,* Yon-Gyong Kwon cogently observes that, while in Galatians 3:1–5, 'Paul begins with the crucified Christ... [he] moves quickly to the Spirit which takes up his main interest here'. Thus, Kwon argues, Paul 'appeals to Christ crucified in order to speak of the Spirit.'[4] The passage reads as follows:[5]

> Ὦ ἀνόητοι Γαλάται, τίς ὑμᾶς ἐβάσκανεν ᵀ, οἷς κατ' ὀφθαλμοὺς Ἰησοῦς Χριστὸς προεγράφη ᶠ ἐσταυρωμένος; τοῦτο μόνον θέλω μαθεῖν ἀφ' ὑμῶν· ἐξ ἔργων νόμου τὸ πνεῦμα ἐλάβετε ἢ ἐξ ἀκοῆς πίστεως;
>
> **3:1** You foolish Galatians! Who has bewitched you—blinded you with the evil eye (τίς ὑμᾶς ἐβάσκανεν)? Before your very eyes Jesus Christ was clearly portrayed (προεγράφη ἐσταυρωμένος) as crucified.
>
> **3:2** I would like to learn just one thing from you: Did you receive the Spirit by the works of the law or by believing what you heard [through seeing my performance message]?

As this passage shows, in Galatians 3:1–5 there is both explicit crucifixion language and explicit Spirit language.[6] In other words, as Kwon notes, rather than Paul's Christology and crucifixion language in 3:1 being the main focus of 3:1–5, his Christology and crucifixion language in 3:1 is in preparation for what he will talk about *the Spirit* in 3:2–5. In my recent study on the Spirit and Christian Identity in Galatians 3:1—6:17, I have noted a similar relationship, where there is a colocation of crucifixion language with Spirit-language at other points throughout the letter.[7]

The aim of this chapter is to consider whether this relationship of crucifixion, the Spirit and Christian identity in Galatians is deliberate on Paul's part, and ultimately, whether the same argument of Kwon's

---

3 Barclay, *Obeying*; Lull, '"The Law"'; Rabens, *The Holy Spirit*.
4 Kwon, *Eschatology*, 178.
5 Unless otherwise stated, the main Greek text is the NA28, and all translations are my own.
6 See Fig. 1 below.
7 Buchanan, *New Creation*, 68–70; 148–149.

could be made further on in Galatians where other explicit language is used, and in an earlier passage in 2:19–21 and later in Gal. 6:14–17, where explicit crucifixion language is used with no explicit mention of the Spirit.

Passage	Crucifixion Language	Person	Spirit Language
Gal. 2:19–3:5	Explicit	Christ and Paul	Explicit
Gal. 3:13–14	Implicit	Christ	Explicit
Gal. 4:4–7	Implicit	Christ	Explicit
Gal. 5:22–25	Explicit	Believers	Explicit
Gal. 2:19–2:1	Explicit	Christ and Paul	Implicit
Gal. 6:14–16	Explicit	Paul	Implicit

Fig. 1. Passages that highlight a correlation of Crucifixion and Spirit Language in Galatians

Setting the Scene

At the beginning of Galatians, Paul establishes the parameters of his gospel. Firstly, he is an ἀπόστολος—an apostle sent not from or on behalf of any human group, nor through any person but *through* Christ (διὰ Ἰησοῦ Χριστοῦ) and God the Father (καὶ θεοῦ πατρός), whom Paul describes as 'the one who raises Jesus from the dead' (τοῦ ἐγείραντος αὐτὸν ἐκ νεκρῶν).[8] Although the genre of this language is clearly apocalyptic,[9] Paul's introduction is not so much a statement of or from theology (whether apocalyptic or Christological), even though it is theologically derived and 'theologically significant'.[10] Neither does it suggest that Galatians should be read entirely through a Jewish apocalyptic lens.[11] Rather, it is language Paul draws on to establish his

---

8   Significantly, this is the only time in Galatians that Paul speaks of the resurrection.
9   Also in 1:4: ἐκ τοῦ αἰῶνος τοῦ ἐνεστῶτος πονηροῦ; 12: δι' ἀποκαλύψεως Ἰησοῦ Χριστοῦ; and 16: ἀποκαλύψαι τὸν υἱὸν αὐτοῦ ἐν ἐμοί; see also 2:2.
10 de Boer, *Galatians*, 24.
11 Keener, *Galatians*, 5. Das, *Galatians*, 86, states that 'Galatians does not conform to the literary genre of an apocalypse', but 'Paul's writings are 'apocalyptic' in worldview'.

cosmically derived authority to speak to the Galatians, and to challenge the authority and gospel of his opponents who are trying to sway the Galatian believers away from his gospel. Nonetheless, it does clearly point to a strongly Christological tone prevalent throughout the letter. All other mentions of Christ in Galatians refer to the place believers have 'in Christ' or Christ has in believers or concern his crucifixion or the effect of what he did through the cross.[12]

While the discussion of Paul's 'in Christ' language is important, it is beyond the scope of this paper. In at least four places, Paul's crucifixion language—whether Christ's, Paul's or the believers' crucifixion—and associated redemption motifs, are closely correlated to explicit Spirit-language.[13] This relationship not only affirms Kwon's argument regarding 3:1–5, it also invites us to consider other passages where this relationship explicitly occurs. If there is sufficient evidence that this pattern is consistent throughout Galatians, then worthy of exploration are other passages where Paul employs crucifixion language and motifs ***without*** any subsequent explicit mention of the Spirit, and whether sufficient evidence exists for an implicit pneumatology. The following discussion explores further passages other than and subsequent to Galatians 3:1–5 that have both explicit and implicit crucifixion and/or Spirit language where such a correlation can be identified. The closest passage that has a similar correlation is Galatians 3:13–14 where an implicit crucifixion reference correlates to an explicit mention of the Spirit.

Galatians 3:13–14: Implicit Crucifixion (Christ) and Explicit Spirit Language

Χριστὸς ἡμᾶς ἐξηγόρασεν ἐκ τῆς κατάρας τοῦ νόμου γενόμενος ὑπὲρ ἡμῶν κατάρα, ὅτι γέγραπται· ἐπικατάρατος πᾶς ὁ κρεμάμενος ἐπὶ ξύλου, ἵνα εἰς τὰ ἔθνη ἡ εὐλογία τοῦ Ἀβραὰμ γένηται ἐν ⌜Χριστῷ Ἰησοῦ⌝, ἵνα τὴν ⌜ἐπαγγελίαν⌝ τοῦ πνεύματος λάβωμεν διὰ τῆς πίστεως.

---

12 Significantly, the mention of Christ in 1:12 is to further reiterate the source of Paul's authority and gospel. I do not suggest that this is not apocalyptic language nor that it has theological weight for Paul. Its use in this part of the argument, however, suggests that Paul is not making a statement so much about Christ, but about his message and authority.

13 See Fig. 1 above.

3:13 Christ redeemed us (ἡμᾶς ἐξηγόρασεν) from the curse of the law by becoming a curse for us (ὑπὲρ ἡμῶν)—for it is written: 'Cursed is everyone who is hung on a tree.'

3:14 in order that (ἵνα) the blessing given to Abraham might come to the Gentiles through Christ Jesus, so that (ἵνα) by faithfulness we might receive the promised Spirit.

Once again, in 3:13-14, there is a definite colocation of crucifixion language—inferred by the imagery of Christ being hung on a tree—and the reception of the Holy Spirit. This explicit colocation echoes what Paul has previously argued in 3:1-2. Firstly, the language of law, crucifixion and Christ, reveals a continuity with what Paul has already argued in 2:19—3:2. Secondly, there is a direct correlation between crucifixion and the reception of the Spirit. As we will see in the next passage in Galatians 4:4-7, the motifs of redemption (ἐξαγοράζω) and the reception of the Spirit are also closely collocated.

Galatians 4:4–7: Implicit Crucifixion (Christ) and Explicit Spirit Language

Ὅτε δὲ ἦλθεν τὸ πλήρωμα τοῦ χρόνου, ἐξαπέστειλεν ὁ θεὸς τὸν υἱὸν αὐτοῦ, γενόμενον ἐκ γυναικός, γενόμενον ὑπὸ νόμον, ἵνα τοὺς ὑπὸ νόμον ἐξαγοράσῃ, ἵνα τὴν υἱοθεσίαν ἀπολάβωμεν. Ὅτι δέ ἐστε υἱοί, ἐξαπέστειλεν ⸂ὁ θεὸς⸃ τὸ πνεῦμα ⸂1τοῦ υἱοῦ⸃ αὐτοῦ εἰς τὰς καρδίας ⸂ἡμῶν κρᾶζον· αββα ὁ πατήρ. ὥστε οὐκέτι οεῖ δοῦλος ἀλλ' υἱός· εἰ δὲ υἱός, καὶ κληρονόμος ⸂διὰ θεοῦ⸃.

4:4 But when the set time had fully come (πλήρωμα τοῦ χρόνου), God sent (ἐξαπέστειλεν) his Son, born of a woman, born under the law,

4:5 to redeem (ἐξαγοράσῃ) those under the law, (ἵνα) that we might receive adoption to sonship (τὴν υἱοθεσίαν ἀπολάβωμεν).

4:6 Because you are his 'sons', God sent (ἐξαπέστειλεν) the Spirit of his Son into our hearts, the Spirit who calls out, 'Abba, Father.'

4:7 So you are no longer a slave, but God's child; and since you are his child, God has made you also an heir.

While there is no explicit mention of crucifixion in this passage, the motif of redemption (ἐξαγοράζω) echoes the language of 3:13 (ἡμᾶς ἐξηγόρασεν), which explicitly and directly relates to Christ being hung on a tree; something we have noted, is a motif for crucifixion. Furthermore, the language of sending (ἐξαποστέλλω) in this passage reveals that God sending his son *is in order that* God will send the Spirit of his son into the hearts of believers. Once again, we see is a clear relationship between crucifixion language, this time implicit, and the Spirit.

Galatians 5:22–25: Explicit Crucifixion (Believers) and Spirit Language

Our third passage, Galatians 5:22–25, mentions both the Spirit and crucifixion. Here the Galatians are the active participants of crucifixion, something that will prove important for the final passage we explore below. The passage reads as follows:

> Ὁ δὲ καρπὸς τοῦ πνεύματός ἐστιν ἀγάπη χαρὰ εἰρήνη, μακροθυμία χρηστότης ἀγαθωσύνη, πίστις πραΰτης ἐγκράτεια^T· κατὰ τῶν τοιούτων οὐκ ἔστιν νόμος. οἱ δὲ τοῦ Χριστοῦ ο[Ἰησοῦ] τὴν σάρκα ἐσταύρωσαν σὺν τοῖς παθήμασιν καὶ ταῖς ἐπιθυμίαις. Εἰ ζῶμεν πνεύματι, ⌜πνεύματι καὶ⌝ στοιχῶμεν. μὴ γινώμεθα κενόδοξοι, ἀλλήλους προκαλούμενοι, ⌜ἀλλήλοις φθονοῦντες.

5:22 But the fruit of the Spirit is love, [consisting of:] joy, peace, patience, kindness, goodness, faithfulness,

5:23 gentleness and self-control. Against such things there is no law.

5:24 Those who belong to Christ Jesus have crucified (ἐσταύρωσαν) the flesh with its passions and desires.

5:25 Since we live by the Spirit (Εἰ ζῶμεν πνεύματι), let us keep in step with the Spirit (πνεύματι καὶ στοιχῶμεν)

Clearly 5:24 does not mention *Christ* 'crucified' per se. Instead, the crucifixion language used here reflects a similar idea to what Paul stated in 2:20. The relationship between crucifixion and life in both passages clearly reflects this.

Because Paul has already mentioned that *his* life is one that is located in the crucified Christ, and is also a life crucified to the law, and that by inference, Paul has the Spirit, it is not unreasonable to suggest that Paul argues here that the Galatian believers have experienced something similar and he appeals to their experience as a result. Furthermore, because they received the Spirit at the point of acknowledging and accepting the gospel of the crucified Christ, similar to Paul, they also are experiencing a co-crucified existence that is enlivened by the Spirit—albeit this time with contrast to flesh (σάρξ) rather than law.[14] Once again Paul's crucifixion language appears to be in service of his Spirit-language, which is also here intimately connected to his life-language.

Each of these three passages discussed so far highlight a close collocation of explicit or implicit crucifixion language and explicit Spirit-language. This, therefore, extends Kwon's assertion beyond 3:1–5 to include these other passages as well. The question remains, however, whether we can say the same of Paul's crucifixion language in a further two passages, Galatians 2:19–21 and 6:14, where there is an *explicit* mention of crucifixion, but *no* explicit mention of the Spirit.[15] This indicates a movement on the movement from 2:20 to Paul's conclusions in Galatians 6.

---

14 I consider the language of 'in Christ' and 'promise' in Gal. 3:28–29 represents another indirect correlation.
15 An earlier passage in Gal. 1:3–4 could also be explored. Here explicit crucifixion and redemption language is collocated with an implied new creation motif. However, because the purpose of this section of Galatians is less parenetic and more introductory, designed to set up Paul's credentials and the foundations on which Paul's gospel has validity, it has less relevance to my argument.

Galatians 2:19—3:5: Explicit Crucifixion and Spirit Language (Christ and Paul)

Returning to the earlier part of the letter, although most agree that 3:1 represents a distinct shift in Paul's argumentation—especially given the vocative nature of his language at the very start of 3:1—and, therefore, begins a new section of his argument, for the sake of this paper, I will begin our exploration of the text at 2:19. This well-studied passage is located in the context of Paul's rebuke of Peter for trying to compel the Galatian believers (τὰ ἔθνη) to live 'Jewishly' (τὰ ἔθνη ἀναγκάζεις ἰουδαΐζειν; 2:14), and Paul's subsequent discussion on how or where a person finds covenant acceptance (justification), i.e. 'by faith' and 'in Christ' (ἐν Χριστῷ; 2:17).

Having established both method (by faith) and location (in Christ), Paul then speaks of his own situation in Christ. The passage reads as follows:

> Ἐγὼ γὰρ διὰ νόμου νόμῳ ἀπέθανον, ἵνα θεῷ ζήσω. Χριστῷ συνεσταύρωμαι· ζῶ δὲ οὐκέτι ἐγώ, ζῇ δὲ ἐν ἐμοὶ Χριστός· ὃ δὲ νῦν ζῶ ἐν σαρκί, ἐν πίστει ζῶ τῇ τοῦ ⸂υἱοῦ τοῦ θεοῦ⸃ τοῦ ἀγαπήσαντός με καὶ παραδόντος ἑαυτὸν ὑπὲρ ἐμοῦ. Οὐκ ἀθετῶ τὴν χάριν τοῦ θεοῦ· εἰ γὰρ διὰ νόμου δικαιοσύνη, ἄρα Χριστὸς δωρεὰν ἀπέθανεν.

> **2:19** For through the law I died to the law so that I might live for God (ἵνα θεῷ ζήσω)

> **2:20** I have been crucified with Christ (Χριστῷ συνεσταύρωμαι – mid?) and I no longer live (ζῶ δὲ οὐκέτι ἐγώ), but Christ lives in me (ζῇ δὲ ἐν ἐμοὶ Χριστός). The life I now live in the body (ὃ δὲ νῦν ζῶ ἐν σαρκί), I live in faithful obedience to the Son of God, who loved me and gave himself for me.

> **2:21** I do not set aside the grace of God, for if righteousness could be gained through the law, Christ died for nothing!'

Here Paul is clearly contrasting himself with Peter (Κηφᾶς), the 'certain men' (τινας) who came from James, other Jews (οἱ λοιποὶ Ἰουδαῖοι) and Barnabas. He is also preparing his readers for what he is about to say about crucifixion and the Spirit in 3:1–2. This makes the connection between 2:21 and 3:1–2 significant.

Rereading Galatians 2:19—3:2 Without Chapter Breaks

To highlight this preparation, reading Galatians 2:19—3:2 without chapter breaks highlights in broader correlation what I am arguing for. This reading requires us to consider Paul's argument again at 2:20 and move straight from this verse into what follows in 3:1–2.

> **2:20** I have been crucified with Christ (Χριστῷ συνεσταύρωμαι·) and I no longer live, but Christ lives in me. The life I now live in the body, I live in faithful obedience to the Son of God, who loved me and gave himself for me...
>
> **3:1** You foolish Galatians! Who has bewitched you—blinded you with the evil eye (τίς ὑμᾶς ἐβάσκανεν)? Before your very eyes Jesus Christ was clearly portrayed (προεγράφη ἐσταυρωμένος) as crucified.
>
> **3:2** I would like to learn just one thing from you: Did you receive the Spirit by the works of the law or by believing what you heard [through seeing my performance message]?

When read this way, two things stand out.

Firstly, in 2:19–20, Paul places *himself* within his crucifixion language. The significance of this is twofold. It first highlights an existential reality that is experienced through the Christ-event. Paul's life has been radically transformed where his value system and understanding of life has been changed in light of Christ crucified. Second, by placing himself squarely in the event of Christ crucified, it is his own life that acts as the model of the faithful believer—in some sense a witness to the crucifixion event, and as an embodied example himself of the crucified Christ that was placarded by Paul before the eyes of the Galatian believers.

Secondly, that, in accordance with Kwon and clearly seen here, Paul's crucifixion language prepares his audience for what he will say about the Holy Spirit in 3:1–5. It is not just 3:1 that does this, but the whole preceding argument from 2:19 on speaks about Christ crucified and the *life* that comes from this event when people actively participate with Christ.

Because in Jewish thought and elsewhere in Paul the Spirit is directly related to life,[16] the language of life (ζάω) in 2:19–20 *may* infer the presence of the Spirit. But it is the explicit mention of the Spirit in 3:2, as the experienced consequence of accepting the crucified Christ, that stands out here. Furthermore, because the Galatian believers have already received the Spirit (3:2), like Paul the Galatian believers are also incorporated into the life of Christ and, by inference, into the crucifixion event that Paul places himself within.

Galatians 6:12–16 Explicit Crucifixion (Paul) and Implicit Spirit-Language

While my main thesis that expands on Kwon's initial statement can be argued effectively from the previous passages, there is one further major passage, Gal. 6: 12–16, which includes important crucifixion language with no explicit mention of the Spirit as in the previous passages discussed above. This begs the question whether my argument falls short at this point, or whether there is something in this closing section of Galatians that still upholds the original thesis. I propose there is. The passage reads as follows.

Ὅσοι θέλουσιν εὐπροσωπῆσαι ἐν σαρκί, οὗτοι ἀναγκάζουσιν ὑμᾶς περιτέμνεσθαι, μόνον ἵνα τῷ σταυρῷ τοῦ Χριστοῦ ᵀ μὴ ⌜διώκωνται. οὐδὲ γὰρ οἱ ⌜περιτεμνόμενοι αὐτοὶ νόμον φυλάσσουσιν ἀλλὰ θέλουσιν ὑμᾶς περιτέμνεσθαι, ἵνα ἐν τῇ ὑμετέρᾳ σαρκὶ καυχήσωνται. Ἐμοὶ δὲ μὴ γένοιτο καυχᾶσθαι εἰ μὴ ἐν τῷ σταυρῷ τοῦ κυρίου ἡμῶν Ἰησοῦ Χριστοῦ, δι' οὗ ἐμοὶ κόσμος ἐσταύρωται κἀγὼ κόσμῳ. ⌜οὔτε γὰρ⌝ περιτομή τί ⌜ἐστιν οὔτε ἀκροβυστία ἀλλὰ καινὴ κτίσις. καὶ ὅσοι τῷ

---

16 See, e.g. Boakye, *Death and Life*; Buchanan, *New Creation*; Burke and Warrington, *A Biblical Theology*; Firth and Wegner, *Presence*; Hildebrandt, *An Old Testament Theology*; Konkel, 'The Vision'; Levison, *The Spirit*; Levison, *The Holy Spirit*; Lowther, *Spirit and Life*; Moltmann, *The Spirit of Life*; Turner, Marshall, Rabens, Bennema, and Cornelis, *The Spirit and Christ*.

κανόνι τούτῳ ⌜στοιχήσουσιν, εἰρήνη ἐπ' αὐτοὺς καὶ ἔλεος καὶ ἐπὶ τὸν Ἰσραὴλ τοῦ θεοῦ.

6:12 Those who want to impress people by means of the flesh (ἐν σαρκί) are trying to compel you to be circumcised. The only reason they do this is to avoid being persecuted for the cross of Christ.

6:13 Not even those who are circumcised keep the law, yet they want you to be circumcised that they may boast in your foreskins.

6:14 May I never boast except in the cross of our Lord Jesus Christ, through which the world has been crucified to me, and I to the world (δι' οὗ ἐμοὶ κόσμος ἐσταύρωται—mid?— κἀγὼ κόσμῳ).

6:15 Neither circumcision nor uncircumcision means anything; what counts is the new creation.

6:16 Peace and mercy to all who keep in step (στοιχήσουσιν) with this rule—and upon the Israel of God.

Galatians 6:12–16 represents the closing argument of Paul's letter. It is more than a mere postscript to what precedes it but represents everything that he has been arguing for and drawing the Galatian believers towards all throughout the letter. This passage presents one of the most direct and concentrated discussions on crucifixion in Galatians. Once again, the language of crucifixion, law and Christ are evident. Once again, Paul places *himself* squarely in the event and the effects of crucifixion. Furthermore, the language of καινὴ κτίσις (new creation) and κόσμος reveal the apocalyptic worldview that Paul operates from within and that was evident in his language at the beginning of the letter. But in the context of Galatians 6:12–17, this language is not future oriented as was common in many Jewish apocalyptic genres but is grounded in Paul's *present* ethic.

Furthermore, what Paul says of the cross here in chapter 6 adds to what he said of crucifixion and himself back in chapter 2. By involving his life in the crucified it means that not only has he 'crucifixionly' died to the cosmos, but the cosmos has 'crucifixionly' died to him as well. While cross and crucifixion language is clearly evident in this passage, the thesis of my paper is not just to affirm the presence of these motifs but to consider whether there is any associated colocation of crucifixion language with Spirit-language. Given the lack of explicit Spirit-language in 6:12–16, some would argue this represents a major challenge to my thesis. There are, however, things that suggest an *implicit* pneumatology.

Hubbard rightly argues that, because the Spirit is central to so much of Galatians, 'it is utterly inconceivable that Paul could summarise this letter's central themes and entirely omit any reference to the Spirit'.[17] So, although there is no explicit mention of the Spirit in this passage, there is a growing consensus that Paul's new creation language in 6:15 is informed by his pneumatology.[18] DeSilva, for example, states that, '"New Creation" is what comes about by the Spirit indwelling each Christian and thus the Christian community'.[19]

Moo takes another trajectory.

> Paul does not use 'new creation' in Gal. 6:15 as a metaphor referring to the renewed person or the renewed community. He uses it to denote a concept: the radically new state of affairs that Christ's death has inaugurated.[20]

The Spirit is the agent and manifestation of this new state of affairs. Whichever position we take, whether new creation or a new state of affairs, or even, as I do, somewhere in between, the Spirit is central to these ideas.

Additionally, the parallel between 6:15 and 5:6 is well noted. In 5:6 Paul also contrasts circumcision and uncircumcision, but this time in relation to faithfulness energised through love (ἀλλὰ πίστις δι' ἀγάπης ἐνεργουμένη). On this point DeSilva notes that

> the parallelism suggests that 'faith working through love' is integral to the emergence of the new creation and thus, by application, is the 'walking in the Spirit' or the 'falling in step

---

17 Hubbard, *New Creation*, 226.
18 Buchanan, *New Creation*, 154–158.
19 DeSilva, *Galatians*, 510.
20 Moo, 'Creation', 99.

with the Spirit' that is of focal concern for Paul as he explicates what it means for faith to become effective through love in 5:13—6:10.[21]

Given that this love encompasses the character of the Spirit in 5:22, this strongly supports an implicit pneumatology in Paul's new creation language in 6:15.

Secondly, the language of στοιχέω in 6:16, where Paul conveys peace and mercy on those who *keep in step* (στοιχήσουσιν) with the ethic and rule of the new creation/state of affairs, echoes the same language of keeping in step with the Spirit in 5:25. As I have argued elsewhere, Paul deliberately uses this term, not only because of the strength of its meaning, but also to remind his readers that keeping in step with the Spirit relates to the transvaluation of reality that has occurred with the New Creation and, along with it, a change of a socio-cosmic ethic—something Paul has clearly located in Christ c rucified and experiences in the Spirit.[22] Thus, Paul's new creation language describes the new order in which the Galatians experience the Spirit as a cruciform community of cruciformly transformed individuals.

Consequently, while there is no explicit mention of the Spirit in 6:12–17, given the emphasis of the Spirit in correlation with the crucifixion, life and Christ language in the other passages explored, and including the fact that both Paul and the Galatian believers have the Spirit as a result of Christ crucified, I suggest that Paul's crucifixion language in 6:14 is also in preparation for what he will say of a radical new existence in the Spirit in 6:15–16—albeit implicitly defined.[23]

Conclusion

Based on my analysis, a case can be made for a direct and ***intentional*** correlation between the mention of crucifixion and the Spirit throughout Galatians. This does not suggest that Christ is in any way subordinate to

---

21 DeSilva, *Galatians*, 511.
22 Buchanan, *New Creation*, 132–133; Buchanan, 'Identity', 62.
23 See also Hubing, *Crucifixion*. Note that Keener, *Galatians*, 572, also views a connection between crucifixion to the Spirit in Gal. 6:14.

the Spirit in Paul's thought here. Instead, this correlation, and a deliberate inclusion and focus on the Spirit at key points throughout the letter, further highlights and elevates the importance of the Spirit for understanding Paul's argument in Galatians.

The Spirit is more than merely experiential proof in service of Paul's Christology. The Holy Spirit is central to Paul's argument and should not be considered as merely one of a number of secondary foci or proofs for Paul's Christological argument. Furthermore, Paul's crucifixion in relationship with his Spirit-language directly informs and shapes the language of Christian identity.[24]

It is because of the Spirit in the life of the believer and believing community that Christians can identify themselves as children of God and call God Father. It is through the Holy Spirit that the Christian community walk in ways that echo and reflect the new creation life of the Spirit—especially in the way they treat others— and that is transformed into the Spirit of God's son (Gal. 4:6). And it is by the Spirit that the Christian community can crucify the flesh just as Paul crucified the world. Consequently, I believe Kwon's assertion regarding crucifixion and the Spirit in 3:1–5 can be extended; that every time Paul employs crucifixion language in Galatians—whether Christ's, Paul's or the believers'—it is in order for (*hina*) Paul to explicitly or implicitly speak of the Spirit as well, in order to (*hina*) establish Christian identity firmly in Christ and of the Spirit.

---

24   See further, Buchanan, *New Creation*; Buchanan, 'Identity'.

Bibliography

Barclay, J. M. G. — *Obeying the Truth: A Study of Paul's Ethics in Galatians* (Vancouver: Regent College, 1988).

Boakye, A. K. — *Death and Life: Resurrection, Restoration, and Rectification in Paul's Letter to the Galatians* (Eugene, OR: Pickwick Publications, 2017).

Buchanan, G. — 'Identity and Human Agency in Galatians 5–6', *ABR* 68 (2020), 50–62.

Buchanan, G. — *The Spirit, New Creation, and Christian Identity in Galatians* (LNTS; London: T&T Clark, 2023).

Burke, T. J. and Warrington, K. — *A Biblical Theology of the Holy Spirit* (Eugene, OR: Cascade Books, 2014).

Cosgrove, C. H. — *The Cross and the Spirit: A Study in the Argument and Theology of Galatians* (Louvain; Macon, GA: Peeters; Mercer, 1988).

Das, A. A. — *Galatians* (Concordia. St. Louis, MO: Concordia Publishing House, 2014).

de Boer, M. C. — *Galatians: A Commentary* (NTL; Louisville, KY: Westminster John Knox Press, 2011).

DeSilva, D. A. — *The Letter to the Galatians* (NICNT. Grand Rapids, MI: Eerdmans, 2018).

Fee, G. D. — *God's Empowering Presence: The Holy Spirit in the Letters of Paul* (Peabody, MA: Hendrickson, 1994).

Ferguson, S. D. — *The Spirit and Relational Anthropology in Paul* (WUNT 2/520; Tübingen: Mohr Siebeck, 2020, doi:9783161590764).

Firth, D. G. and Wegner, P. D. (eds.) — *Presence, Power and Promise: The Role of the Spirit of God in the Old Testament* (Nottingham: Apollos, 2011).

Hildebrandt, W. — *An Old Testament Theology of the Spirit of God* (Peabody, MA: Hendrickson Publishers, 1995).

Hubbard, M. V. — *New Creation in Paul's Letters and Thought* (SNTSN 119; Cambridge: Cambridge University Press, 2002).

Hubing, J. — *Crucifixion and New Creation: The Strategic Purpose of Galatians 6.11–17* (LNTS; London: Bloomsbury, 2015).

Keener, C. S.	*Galatians: A Commentary* (Grand Rapids, MI: Baker Academic, 2018).
Konkel, M.	'The Vision of the Dry Bones (Ezekl 37.1–14), Resurrection, Restoration or What?', in W. A. Tooman and P. Barter (eds.), *Ezekiel: Current Debates and Future Directions* (FAT, 107–119; Tübingen: Mohr Siebeck, 2017).
Kwon, Y-G.	*Eschatology in Galatians: Rethinking Paul's Response to the Crisis in Galatia* (WUNT 2/183; Tübingen: Mohr Siebeck, 2004).
Levison, J. R.	*The Holy Spirit Before Christianity* (Waco, TX: Baylor University Press, 2019).
Levison, J. R.	*The Spirit in First Century Judaism* (Leiden: Brill, 1997).
Lowther, R. J.	*Spirit and Life: The Holy Spirit and the Practice of Christian Living* (Milton Keynes: Paternoster, 2016)
Lull, D. J.	'"The Law Was Our Pedagogue": A Study in Galatians 3:19–25', *JBL* 105, no. 3 (1986), 481–498.
Lull, D. J.	*The Spirit in Galatia: Paul's Interpretation of Pneuma as Divine Power* (Dissertation Series - SBL 49; Eugene, OR: Wipf and Stock, 2006).
Moltmann, J.	*The Spirit of Life: A Universal Affirmation* (Minneapolis, MN: Fortress Press, 1992).
Moo, D. J.	'Creation and New Creation', *BBR* 20, no. 1 (2010), 39–60.
Rabens, V.	*The Holy Spirit and Ethics in Paul: Transformation and Empowering for Religious-Ethical Life* (2nd ed.; Minneapolis, MN: Fortress Press, 2014).
Turner, M., Marshall, I. H., Rabens, V. and Bennema, C.	*The Spirit and Christ in the New Testament and Christian Theology: Essays in Honor of Max Turner* (Grand Rapids, MI: Eerdmans, 2012).
Yates, J.	*The Spirit and Creation in Paul* (WUNT 2/251; Tübingen: Mohr Siebeck, 2008).

CHAPTER 14

The Connection of Σάρξ and Circumcision in Galatians 5:13–26 in Light of Philo's Writings

Sunny Chen

The meaning of Paul's use of σάρξ in Galatians has posed a challenge to Pauline scholars. Not only are there diverse understandings of its connotation, there is also a lack of analysis on how the use of the term in Galatians 5:16—6:10 connects to the rest of the letter; in particular, how σάρξ is used in the σάρξ–πνεῦμα juxtaposition in 5:13–26. Previous scholarly interpretation of σάρξ in this antithesis has varied, from sin, to an evil force, to fallen human nature. Both John Barclay and Charles Cousar have commented on this debate. For Barclay the term 'is an extremely complex and slippery word in Paul's vocabulary';[1] and for Cousar the term 'presents difficulties to translators and interpreters'.[2] Although modern interpreters hold different interpretations of σάρξ in Galatians 5:13–26, it has been suggested that the term has an indirect reference to circumcision in Paul's use of σάρξ.[3] Given the discussion of circumcision is arguably the prime focus in Galatians, this study aims to answer the following question: does σάρξ in Galatians 5:13–26 have any direct or implicit reference to circumcision? To answer this question, I

---

1 Barclay, *Obeying the Truth*, 110.
2 Cousar, *Galatians*, 136.
3 For example, see Cousar, *Galatians*, 138.

first survey the overall usage of σάρξ in Galatians, and then review various interpretations of the term in Galatians 5. Subsequently, I examine the works of Philo, to obtain new insights into the connection between the σάρξ–πνεῦμα antithesis and circumcision. My analysis will demonstrate how the antithesis in Galatians 5 alludes to circumcision.

Σάρξ recurs eighteen times in Galatians, making it the fifth most frequently occurring noun in the letter.[4] The ratio of its occurrences is the highest among all of Paul's authentic letters.[5] The lexical meanings of σάρξ in both Classical Greek and Koiné Greek include, literally, 'flesh', referring to 'the material that covers the bones'[6] or a piece of meat;[7] synecdochically, the whole body; and metaphorically, the seat of affections and lusts.[8] The textual context dictates how σάρξ is interpreted in a text, for example, the term in Galatians denotes the whole body in one sentence,[9] and a piece of meat in another.[10]

1. Σάρξ in Galatians

In Galatians, the word σάρξ is usually repeated in close proximity, which this study calls a cluster.[11] There are four major clusters of σάρξ, appearing in four different discussions throughout the letter. The table below shows where those clusters are located.[12] Intriguingly, apart from σάρξ–

---

4 The occurrences of σάρξ are as follows: 1:16; 2:16,20; 3:3; 4:13,14,23,29; 5:13,16,17(twice), 19,24; 6:8 (twice), 12,13. Its number of occurrence is identical with that of πνεῦμα, only ranking behind Χριστός (38), νόμος (32), θεός (31), and πίστις (22) in the letter.
5 In the seven letters that are commonly considered Paul's authentic works, the ratio of σάρξ's occurrences per 1000 words is as follows: Galatians, 8.06; Romans, 3.66; Philippians, 3.07; Philemon, 2.97; 2 Corinthians, 2.46; 1 Corinthians, 1.61; and 1 Thessalonians, 0.
6 BDAG, s.v. 'σάρξ.'
7 It is conjectured that the word is derived from σύρω (related to σαίρω), signifying *what can be stripped off* from the bones'; Thayer, 'σάρξ', 569.
8 LSJ, s.v. 'σάρξ.'
9 See the analysis of Gal. 4:13 below.
10 See the analysis of Gal. 3:3 below.
11 The single occurrence of σάρξ in 1:16 is an exception. Paul first uses the term to denote human beings. de Boer, *Galatians*, 95, notes that the phrase σαρκὶ καὶ αἵματι 'is an idiom that functions as a metonym for human beings as distinct from God [...] emphasizing in this context their insignificance'.
12 As I hypothesise the connection between σάρξ and circumcision, it is important to note the high occurrence of other words relating to circumcision, including περιτομή, περιτέμνω, and ἀκροβυστία. Περιτομή occurs in 2:7 (three times), 12; 5:6,11; περιτέμνω, 2:3; 5:2 (twice); 6:12 (three times); ἀκροβυστία, 2:7; 5:6; 6:15.

πνεῦμα antithesis in Galatians 5, three of those discussions clearly have direct or indirect reference to circumcision.

Σάρξ and Circumcision in Galatians

Letter Opening 1:1–10	1:11–2:21	3:1–4:31	5:1–12	5:13–26	6:1–10	Letter Closing 6:12–18
	* [**]	* [** **]		[* *** *] *	* [*]	[**]

*: a single occurrence of σάρξ;   ▭ : cluster of σάρξ

The first cluster of σάρξ is located near the end of 1:11—2:21, where the focus is on justification. The phrase πᾶσα σάρξ (2:16) refers to people in general, which Betz suggests is a Jewish phrase.[13] Contextually, the phrase πᾶσα σάρξ is used to articulate people's need for God's justification. It is likely that σάρξ here follows the connotation it had when it appeared previously in 1:16, alluding to human limitations in comparison to divine power and wisdom. Dunn suggests that πᾶσα σάρξ points to the contrast between humanity and God, highlighting the limitations of humanity.[14] Importantly, the discussion of justification is a response to the issue of circumcision (2:1–14).[15] Following that, the apostle makes his own account of justification: ὃ δὲ νῦν ζῶ ἐν σαρκί, ἐν πίστει ζῶ τῇ τοῦ υἱοῦ τοῦ θεοῦ τοῦ ἀγαπήσαντός με (2:20).

The discussion of justification then proceeds to the apostle's rhetorical question in 3:3, within the segment 3:1—4:31: οὕτως ἀνόητοί ἐστε, ἐναρξάμενοι πνεύματι νῦν σαρκὶ ἐπιτελεῖσθε;. It has been argued that

---

13 Betz, *Galatians*, 118.
14 Dunn, *The Epistle*, 146, holds that the term highlights the 'human bodily existence in all its weakness and corruptibility'. Bruce and Longenecker hold a different view, arguing that the term is 'non-theological', simply referring to the 'mortal body'. On the other hand, Betz suggests the polemic usage of the terms here. See Bruce, *The Epistle*, 145; Longenecker, *Galatians*, 93; Betz, *Galatians*, 125.
15 The word περιτομή, together with its cognate περιτέμνω, and its antonym, ἀκροβυστία, appears six times in 2:1–14.

the term here simply refers to the 'fleshy works of the law', underlining the antithesis between the 'two [mutually exclusive] principles, Spirit-faith and flesh-works'.[16] However, Martyn emphasises that the reference, although highlighting this antithesis, is intended by Paul 'in the first instance to refer literally to the foreskin of the penis'.[17] Similarly, Borgen advocates the notion that σάρξ in 3:3 carries the reference of circumcision, as Paul challenges the idea that 'the observance of circumcision should follow and complete the ethical circumcision.'[18] Glick believes that it is Paul's desire to pursue the '[a]dmission of Gentiles into the fellowship' by abandoning 'the insistence on conversion to Judaism'. The traditional Judaism

> was the religion of a single people, set apart by adherence to a Law requiring ethnic separation confirmed by physical practices—'external' signs, 'matters of the flesh': circumcision, dietary taboos, animal sacrifices, regulations and prohibitions of every sort.[19]

Paul's argument leads to a key proclamation in 3:8, which for Martin demonstrates that circumcision is at the heart of the Galatian controversy: προευηγγελίσατο τῷ Ἀβραὰμ ὅτι ἐνευλογηθήσονται ἐν σοὶ πάντα τὰ ἔθνη.[20]

In short, this first clustered use of σάρξ begins with the apostle using the term to refer to humans and concludes with an explicit reference to the cutting of the foreskin. In this cluster, Paul employs σάρξ to highlight the flawed practice of mandatory circumcision, a practice that is as limited and frail as human beings, which is contrary to God and the justification that God offers.

The second cluster of σάρξ appears near the end of 3:1—4:31, in the discussion located in 4:13–20. The term occurs twice to depict Paul's own frail physical body: ἀσθένειαν σαρκὸς (4:13) and τῇ σαρκί μου

---

16 Fung, *The Epistle*, 134.
17 Martyn, *Galatians*, 294.
18 Borgen, *Paul Preaches*, 39.
19 Glick, *Marked*, 36.
20 Martin claims that despite his reconstruction of the letter being different from that of Martyn, they both hold that circumcision is the key issue, and the covenant in Gen. 17:9–14 can explain the three antitheses in Gal. 3:28. Martin, 'The Covenant', 116.

(4:14). The term ἀσθένεια is associated with the term σάρξ. Martin contends that ἀσθένεια 'never means sickness in the extant writings of non-Christian authors before the seventh century CE'.[21] He then concludes that the phrase ἀσθένειαν τῆς σαρκὸς signifies 'the Galatians' condition when Paul initially evangelized them'.[22] Paul is alluding to his own circumcision not being an issue for the Galatians to despise and mock when the apostle first approached them.[23]

The term re-emerges in a new sense, depicting Hagar's son as παιδίσκης κατὰ σάρκα (4:23) and ὁ κατὰ σάρκα (4:29). The introduction of the antithesis between σάρξ and Spirit from 3:3 also re-emerges here in contrast with God and God's promise (4:23), and in contrast with God's Spirit (4:29). The usage of σάρξ illustrates natural human heredity,[24] and also underlines human weakness.[25] The term seemingly has no direct reference to circumcision. Nonetheless, Paul's argument here proceeds directly to his discussion of circumcision in 5:1–12, which is illustrated by the clustered appearance of περιτομή and its cognate.[26] The emphatic expression in 5:2, Ἴδε ἐγὼ Παῦλος λέγω ὑμῖν, is immediately followed by the following clauses: ὅτι ἐὰν περιτέμνησθε, Χριστὸς ὑμᾶς οὐδὲν ὠφελήσει. μαρτύρομαι δὲ πάλιν παντὶ ἀνθρώπῳ περιτεμνομένῳ ὅτι ὀφειλέτης ἐστὶν ὅλον τὸν νόμον ποιῆσαι. The two discussions in 4:13–20 and 5:1–12 are not isolated. Rather, the earlier argument about Hagar's son forms the foundation for Paul to repudiate the practice of circumcision in 5:1–12. In fact, Paul is adding to the earlier association between σάρξ and foreskin (3:3) by developing a fuller argument, with σάρξ referring to the opposite of God and God's promise in 4:13–20. Circumcision is directly denounced in the immediate context, 5:1–12. Paul summarises this argument by making a very strong statement: Ὄφελον καὶ ἀποκόψονται οἱ ἀναστατοῦντες ὑμᾶς;

---

21 Martin, 'What Flesh?', 66.
22 Martin, 'What Flesh?', 78.
23 Martin, 'What Flesh?', 90
24 Das, *Galatians*, 494.
25 Dunn, *Galatians*, 246.
26 Words relating to circumcision appear five times in close proximity within ten verses: περιτομή occurs in 5:6,11; περιτέμνω, 5:2 (twice); and ἀκροβυστία, 5:6.

the verb ἀποκόπτω carries a direct reference to circumcision.[27] In this statement, Paul is bringing together both the association between σάρξ and foreskin, as well as the fuller argument about σάρξ as the opposite of God.

The third cluster of σάρξ is located in 5:13–26, with six occurrences of the term appearing in this passage. The πνεῦμα and σάρξ antithesis is located in Galatians 5, part of the segment 5:13—6:10. As Barclay notes, interpreters hold a 'wide spectrum' of views about what this segment is, including an unrelated section, a paraenesis, and an apologetic appendix.[28] Paul details the juxtaposition of σάρξ and πνεῦμα, elaborating the mutually exclusive nature between the two (5:17), detailing τὰ ἔργα τῆς σαρκός (5:19–21) and ὁ καρπὸς τοῦ πνεύματός (5:22–24). The list of τὰ ἔργα τῆς σαρκός can be categorised as sexual, religious, and communal sins.[29] The list of sins was not 'particularly unique' in that era: both Greeks and the Hellenistic Jews would be familiar with the items in it.[30] The analysis of this 'σάρξ cluster' will be detailed later.

The fourth and final cluster of σάρξ appears in 6:1–10 and the letter's closing (6:11–18). The first occurrence reiterates the antithesis of σάρξ and πνεῦμα, seemingly echoing the argument in 5:13–26. The term recurs in 6:12–13, showing a clear reference to circumcision. First, the term περιτομή, together with its related cognates, appears in a cluster in 6:1–10 where the 'σάρξ cluster' is located. Second, the two concepts relating to flesh and circumcision are intertwined in Paul's discussion, as demonstrated by the explicit reference in 6:12–13,

> Ὅσοι θέλουσιν εὐπροσωπῆσαι ἐν σαρκί, οὗτοι ἀναγκάζουσιν ὑμᾶς περιτέμνεσθαι, μόνον ἵνα τῷ σταυρῷ τοῦ Χριστοῦ μὴ διώκωνται. (13) οὐδὲ γὰρ οἱ περιτεμνόμενοι αὐτοὶ νόμον φυλάσσουσιν ἀλλὰ θέλουσιν ὑμᾶς περιτέμνεσθαι, ἵνα ἐν τῇ ὑμετέρᾳ σαρκὶ καυχήσωνται.

---

27 Edwards, 'Galatians 5:12', observes that all the occurrences of ἀποκόπτω 'indicate the cutting off of a physical member or object', and when considering the reference to circumcision in the preceding verses, it is clear that ἀποκόπτω carries the reference of circumcision. He also maintains that 5:12 simultaneously carries two references: Jewish circumcision and pagan cultic castration.
28 Barclay, *Obeying*, 9–12.
29 For a detailed analysis of those categories, see Das, *Galatians*, 567–75; de Boer, *Galatians*, 357–60.
30 de Boer, *Galatians*, 357.

The σάρξ in 6:13 is best interpreted in a literal sense, referring to the cutting of the foreskin—the act of circumcision.[31]

de Boer observes that 'in 3:3 [σάρξ] stands for circumcision and by extension for the remaining "works of law" (3:2,5)';[32] and in 5:13—6:10 it denotes an evil power that ruins a community; however, in 6:12–13, it is used 'explicitly in connection with circumcision'.[33] Tarazi also suggests that in Galatians the antithesis, σάρξ and πνεῦμα, first develops in 3:3, then in 4:29, 5:13–26, and finally in 6:8.[34]

Having reviewed three of the four clusters in which σάρξ occurs, Paul's usage of the term exerts a degree of negativity. In the first cluster, Paul employs σάρξ to highlight human weakness and limitations in his initial discussion of circumcision. In the second cluster, σάρξ carries a literal sense as Paul uses the term to refer to the foreskin cut off in circumcision. Having articulated the opposition between σάρξ and πνεῦμα in the third cluster, Paul repeats the term in the fourth and final cluster, with an explicit reference of σάρξ to the foreskin in a passage where the concepts of flesh and circumcision 'collide'. In other words, the use of σάρξ across those three clusters appears in the context that has direct or indirect discussion relating to circumcision. In light of this, it would be unlikely that the term recurring in 5:13–26 merely articulates a list of immoral behaviours without any subtle reference to circumcision—the central discussion of the letter.

2. Σάρξ in Galatians 5:16–20

My literature review of modern interpreters reveals that there are three major views on the meaning of σάρξ as it occurs in 5:13–26. First, the term is considered fundamentally sin related, being understood as

---

31 Dunn, *Galatians*, 336, also holds this view, as he argues that the clause εὐπροσωπῆσαι ἐν σαρκί 'clearly refers to circumcision (literally "in the flesh"), which most Greeks would regard as a form of mutilation'. Das, *Galatians*, 634, invokes the image of ancient statues of the naked human body with an ironic twist: focusing on 'a *different* body part' that was 'commonly perceived by the gentiles as a *mutilation* of that flesh'. For Bruce, *Galatians*, 268, 'the literal sense of σάρξ cannot be excluded where circumcision is the subject'.
32 de Boer, *Galatians*, 336.
33 de Boer, *Galatians*, 336–37.
34 Tarazi, *Galatians*, 291.

'the impulse to sin,'[35] 'sinful inclinations,'[36] 'religion by limited human strength [...] with sinful behavior,'[37] or 'the entire potency of sin... [which] is identical with *sin*'.[38]

Second, σάρξ is interpreted as a form of evil force, denoting 'a supra-human power... with the intention of destroying [the Galatians churches] as genuine communities,'[39] 'the force for evil,'[40] or 'an active quasi-personified force that challenges God and his people'.[41]

Third, some argue that the term broadly refers to humans' fallen or weak nature, illustrating 'an essential [but corrupted] aspect of mankind's present human condition,'[42] 'human nature weakened, vitiated, tainted by sin,'[43] 'human fallenness and weakness,'[44] 'the seat of sin,'[45] or 'fallen mankind itself'.[46]

These views are not always as distinct as one would hope. Some interpreters hold a view that cannot neatly fit into one of these three categories. For instance, σάρξ is understood as referring to the whole person,[47] the evil threatening moral life,[48] an expression of ethnic identity and selfish desire,[49] the human tendency of selfishness,[50] or the realm that human operates on in opposing God.[51]

One particular view, which is less common in the scholarship, is shared by some modern interpreters—there is an implicit reference

---

35 Moo, *Galatians*, 354.
36 Witherington, *Grace*, 394.
37 Keener, *Galatians*, 252.
38 Findlay, *The Epistle*, 351.
39 de Boer, *Galatians*, 336.
40 Burton, *A Critical and Exegetical Commentary*, 300.
41 Das, *Galatians*, 558.
42 Longenecker, *Galatians*, 240.
43 Barclay, *Flesh*, 22.
44 Schreiner, *Galatians*, 167, 184.
45 Fung, *Galatians*, 250.
46 Fung, *Galatians*, 253; Morris, *Galatians*, 164.
47 Käsemann, *Perspectives*, 25–26, also argues that Paul's usage of σάρξ here 'derives neither from Greek thought, nor from pre-Qumran and pre-Philonic Judaism' as the concept of flesh in the Old Testament 'is not a hostile active power [opposing] the divine Spirit'.
48 Barclay, *Obeying*, 110.
49 Dunn, *Galatians*, 298. Concerning national identity, Smallwood, *The Jews*, 196, points out that circumcision, along with other religious practices, demonstrated the ability of Hellenistic Jews since the Diaspora 'to preserve [their] national identity even after generations of residence among gentiles'.
50 Matera, *Galatians*.
51 Cousar, *Galatians*, 138.

to circumcision in Paul's use of σάρξ in Galatians 5:13–26. Cousar observes that the term has appeared in 3:1–5, in connection with 'its religious expression', including circumcision, 'correct pedigree, or zealous; piety'; and this religious expression 'may not be far from Paul's mind in [5:16–21]', the works of the flesh.[52] Similarly, Dunn suggests that the term in the letter contains a negative association between circumcision and forbidden desire due to human weakness,[53] although Dunn does not explicitly state that this particular association is deliberate. In his analysis of the σάρξ–πνεῦμα juxtaposition, Betz states, '[u]ltimately, of course, Paul alludes to the rite of circumcision at present by the Galatians',[54] despite his explicit definition of σάρξ in Galatians 5 being 'active, a force which carries our intentions—of course, evil intentions'.[55]

One of the most comprehensive analyses concerning the association between σάρξ in 5:13–26 and circumcision is that of Jewett. He considers σάρξ to be 'Paul's term for everything aside from God in which one places his final trust.'[56] The apostle uses the word to speak against 'the Judaizer threat' that advocates a view in which '[t]rust in the circumcised flesh for the Judaizers had replaced trust in the crucified Lord.' He then asserts that σάρξ 'is not rooted in sensuality but rather in religious rebellion in the form of self-righteousness'.[57] Jewett summarises the meaning of σάρξ in Galatians as follows:

> In summary, σάρξ was first used as a technical term in connection with the circumcision problem raised by the Judaizers; it developed through Paul's typological exegesis into a full dialectical counterpart to the spirit.[58]

As discussed above, the association between circumcision and σάρξ in

---

52 Cousar, *Galatians*, 138.
53 Dunn, *Galatians*, 104, 287, 297.
54 Betz, *Galatians*, 134.
55 Betz, *Galatians*, 278.
56 Jewett, *Anthropological Terms*, 103.
57 Jewett, *Anthropological Terms*, 114. This idea is also advocated by Bruce; see Bruce, *Galatians*, 250.
58 Jewett, *Anthropological Terms*, 114. Jewett's argument is repudiated by Schreiner, who holds that in some occurrences of σάρξ the term 'may be an allusion to circumcision, which involves a cutting of the flesh'. Thus Jewett's suggestion that 'Paul's theology of "flesh" derived from the controversy over circumcision... though stimulating, is impossible to verify'. See Schreiner, *Galatians*, 184.

5:13–26 has been suggested by some modern interpreters. Nonetheless, there is one missing link: the antithesis itself in Galatians 5 displays neither explicit nor implicit connection with circumcision. The focus, as discussed above, is solely on the contrast between σάρξ and the divine Spirit.

Usually, the corpus of Paul's letters provides some helpful clues. However, the σάρξ–πνεῦμα juxtaposition appears nowhere in Paul's authentic letters, except in Romans 8:1–11.[59] Paul urges his audience not to walk κατὰ σάρκα, but κατὰ πνεῦμα, since they are not ἐν σαρκὶ ἀλλ' ἐν πνεύματι (Rom. 8:4–9). The passage concludes the discussion of sin, law and death (Rom. 5–7), and commences the description of the Spirit and its work (Rom. 8). However, the σάρξ–πνεῦμα antithesis there does not shed much light on how Paul is linking σάρξ and circumcision, as it has no reference to circumcision.[60] To address this, we need to examine extra-biblical texts to gain some much-needed insights.

3. Σάρξ in the Works of Philo

Although there are numerous works that mention σάρξ in Koiné Greek literature in the first century, the work of Philo deserves special attention. Philo was a Hellenistic Jew, a contemporary of Paul, who composed an extensive corpus of writings in the first century. Like Paul, many of his works contained his analyses and interpretations of the Scriptures. Philo lived in Alexandria, a city with a large Jewish community where Hellenistic culture flourished. His brother, Alexander, was appointed as the *alabarch*, the leader of the Jews in Alexandria.[61] Alexander was pious and generously donated to the expensive building materials in the Second Temple.[62] Belonging to a wealthy and prominent family, Philo had every opportunity to indulge his love of philosophy, but also to be acquainted with Jewish traditions of study and exegesis. Philo was no outlier as he represented an intellectual strand of Judaism that was most

---

59 Romans, 1 Corinthians, 2 Corinthians, Galatians, Philippians, 1 Thessalonians, and Philemon are widely considered as the authentic works of Paul. See Dunn, *The Theology of Paul*, 13.
60 In fact, the words περιτομή and περιτέμνω never occur once in Rom. 5–14.
61 Josephus, *Ant.* 20.100.
62 Josephus, *B.J.* 5.205.

prominent in Alexandria but not confined to it, namely Greek-speaking Diaspora Judaism. Maren Niehoff argues that Philo should be placed at the 'elitist and philosophical-pious end of the spectrum' of Judaism in the city.[63] Philo's writings were formed and influenced by conversations with many Hellenistic Jews. In fact, he encountered many Jews as well as proselytes who travelled to Pharos, a neighbouring island that was approximately one kilometre opposite Alexandria, to celebrate an annual festival that honoured the Greek translation of the Bible, the Septuagint.[64] Given his brother's prominent role in Alexandria, one can imagine the manifold opportunities that Philo had in interacting and exchanging thoughts with various visitors. In light of this, Philo's work 'percolated through the Greek-speaking Jewish world, migrating from Alexandria to Antioch and other major Jewish centres, whilst stimulating a response within Judaism itself'.[65] Later in life, Philo was selected to be the principal ambassador to defend the Jews in the presence of the Roman emperor Gaius Caligula.[66]

Given the wide connection with various Jewish people across the Empire, it is likely that Philo's writings, or ideas similar to what is found in them, would have had currency among Greek-speaking Jewish communities outside Egypt.[67] These writings would have likely influenced Paul, during the apostle's studies in Jerusalem under Gamaliel,[68] in the Greek-speaking synagogues before his Damascus experience, or in Antioch through Barnabas and other Graeco-Palestinians.[69] Philo was about twenty years senior to Paul. Both men were skilled in rhetoric and regarded their opponents as sophists.[70] The year of Philo's death was not too far off from the time when Paul wrote Galatians, hence Philo's

---

63 Niehoff, 'Ist Philon ein typischer Vertreter?', 145.
64 Philo, *Mos.* 2.41; Josephus, *Ant.* 20.100. The translation of the Torah into Greek, the origin of the Septuagint, took place in Pharos during the time when Ptolemy II was the ruler of Egypt in the third century BCE.
65 Hadas-Lebel, *Philo*, 201.
66 Josephus, *Ant.* 18. 259.
67 Although there is little direct evidence, it is worth noting that it was probable that Josephus knew the work of Philo, given that Philo was 'an important predecessor of Josephus in Rome'. See Niehoff, 'Josephus and Philo', 139.
68 Hadas-Lebel, *Philo*, 202.
69 Holtz, 'Von Alexandrien'.
70 Winter, *Philo and Paul*.

writings could have strong resonance for Paul.⁷¹

There have been attempts to examine Galatians 5 in light of Philo's work. In Brandenburger's work, published more than five decades ago, he asserts that insights from the Philonic materials are helpful in understanding the Pauline usage of the σάρξ–πνεῦμα antithesis.⁷² He proposes that the dualistic type of wisdom in Hellenistic Jewish thought in the σάρξ–πνεῦμα antithesis is the same approach adopted by Paul.⁷³

Following Brandenburger, Borgen argues that Philo's writings in the discussion of circumcision 'reflect the actual debates and conflicts which existed in the Alexandrian Jewish community'.⁷⁴ He compares Paul's discussion with Philo's work, and argues that for Jewish people the meaning of circumcision contained an ethical dimension as it 'portrayed the excision of pleasure and all passions', and consequently, the apostle's discussion in Galatians 5:11—6:10 'deals [...] with the [opponents'] ethical ideas and way of life associated with circumcision'.⁷⁵ In other words, Borgen suggests that Paul preaches ethical circumcision, but this does not mean that bodily circumcision is to follow.

de Boer maintains that Paul employs σάρξ in a polemical context, with the desire of σάρξ in 5:16 denoting the 'evil inclination or impulse'.⁷⁶ He explains this inclination, which is marked by the Hebrew phrase יצר התוב (or simply יצר), by referring to Philo who understands that יצר can be 'metaphorically identified with the foreskin, suggesting that literal circumcision of the fleshy foreskin is a cutting away of the fleshy inclination to do evil'. ⁷⁷

Barclay compares the views of Paul and Philo on circumcision. In a

---

71 Regardless of North Galatia Theory or South Galatia Theory, the date of Galatians is placed within the range of 50 CE to 57 CE. See Brown, *An Introduction*, 476–477. On the other hand, Philo died ca. 50 CE. See Hadas-Lebel, *Philo*, 201.
72 Brandenburger, *Fleisch*, 116–118.
73 Brandenburger, *Fleisch*, 128–129.
74 Borgen, *Philo*, 61.
75 Borgen, *Circumcision*, 16–18. Borgen further explicates this through the idea that 'the foreskin of the heart is to be circumcised in addition to the circumcision of the body', as found in Qumran's writings. See Borgen, *Circumcision*, 20.
76 de Boer, *Galatians*, 337.
77 de Boer, *Galatians*, 337. de Boer is not alone in drawing on Jewish tradition for his interpretation. For example, Martyn refers to the teachings in the Qumran community, and then defines the antithesis in Gal. 5 as two 'supra-human, apocalyptic powers', as Paul 'transform[s] what had traditionally been a form of moral discourse [...] into marks lefts on communities by these two apocalyptic powers'. Martyn, *Galatians*, 484–85.

discussion at the beginning of his treatises on the *Special Laws,* Philo lists six reasons for the custom of circumcision, ending with two allegorical explanations: circumcision is a symbol of cutting away the pleasures (*Spec.* 1:1–11).[78] Despite these allegorical interpretations, Philo does not reject the literal practice. In *Migr.* 91–92, he offers the same allegorical explanations, but he also emphasises that the literal observance should be maintained as he wants to avoid the censure of the masses and their accusations (*Migr.* 93). Having analysed the Philonic texts, Barclay discusses Rom. 2:25–29, where Paul argues that the only circumcision that matters is the circumcision of the heart. In contrast to Philo, Paul is not concerned about the opinion of the masses. Barclay concludes that 'Paul emerges as socially far more controversial than Philo, willing to face Jewish unpopularity where Philo wishes to avoid "censure"'.[79]

The insights gained from the above findings provide some helpful understanding between the word σάρξ and circumcision. Nevertheless, they shed little light on the missing link: the connection between the unique σάρξ-πνεῦμα juxtaposition and bodily circumcision. This study endeavours to identify that link by further examining Philo's writings.

4. Σάρξ-Πνεῦμα & Ἡδονή According to Philo

Σάρξ appears 98 times in the work of Philo. Not only does a σάρξ–πνεῦμα antithesis appear in Philo's work, the antithesis also provides a clue concerning the above-mentioned missing link. As detailed in the following, Philo considers the pleasure of the flesh as antithetical to the divine spirit, and so the ritual of circumcision symbolises the removal of this pleasure. His understanding reflects the reality that circumcision involves cutting off foreskin, a piece of meat—σάρξ in its literal sense. The σάρξ–πνεῦμα juxtaposition, the excision of ἡδονῇ, especially sexual pleasure, and the practice of circumcision, are linked together in his writings.

To provide context, the collection of some of the Philonic texts analysed below had a broader readership than others, illustrating the wide impact of Philo's works on both the Hellenistic Jews and the Gentile

---

78 Barclay, 'Paul and Philo'.
79 Barclay, 'Paul and Philo', 555.

proselytes. For instance, it is agreed in modern scholarship that the Exposition of the Law, of which the treatises on Special Laws forms a part, not only has a Gentile audience in mind but is also directed at Jewish readers.[80] As Philo comments on the Decalogue, he begins his work in discussing circumcision, prioritising this issue 'over other laws, even over the prohibition against idolatry'.[81] Philo understands that the practice of circumcision was 'apparently an object of ridicule among many people', and therefore, attempts to explain this practice by citing 'medical, ritual, and symbolic' reasons.[82] The fact that the treatises on the Special Laws begin with the illustration of circumcision and its symbolism indicates a broad audience for his theme, which includes the excision of passions and so has at least an indirect connection with flesh. Niehoff links these treatises with Philo's stay in Rome in 38 CE, which suggests a broader readership than just Alexandria.[83]

First, an antithesis between σάρξ and πνεῦμα appears in Philo's work *Quis rerum divinarum heres sit*. The occurrence is revealing. In his discussion on the nature of the soul, Philo has the contrast between the two anthropological creation texts in Genesis 1:27 and 2:7 in mind, and thus argues that the race of humankind is twofold, one living by τὸ μὲν θείῳ πνεύματι λογισμῷ, the other, τὸ δὲ αἵματι καὶ σαρκὸς ἡδονῇ (*Her*. 57). The word σάρξ is placed antithetically in relation to the divine spirit (and also allegorically to reason, the part of the soul that has the ability to control the passions). Most importantly σάρξ is directly associated with ἡδονή, pleasure, a term that shows a link with circumcision in Philo's various writings. Although the passage in *Her*. 57 does not concern circumcision, the direct association between ἡδονή and σάρξ, and the link between ἡδονή and circumcision in Philo's works, provide an important clue to the missing link that we have previously discussed. The link between ἡδονή and circumcision is explained below.

As indicated in previous scholarship, including the works of Borgen, de Boer, and Barclay mentioned above, there is a connection between circumcision and pleasure according to Philo. The following briefly surveys this connection in various Philonic materials. Philo defines

---

80 Sterling, 'General Introduction', xiii.
81 Hadas-Lebel, *Philo*, 95.
82 Hadas-Lebel, *Philo*, 95.
83 Niehoff, *Philo*, 2–11.

circumcision as the excision of pleasure in *De migratione Abrahami*: τὸ περιτέμνεσθαι ἡδονῆς (*Migr.* 92). In *Quaestiones in Exod.um II*, Philo allegorically depicts sojourners[84] as those who οὐχ ὁ περιτμηθεὶς τὴν ἀκροβυστίαν ἀλλ' ὁ τὰς ἡδονὰς (*QEx*. 2:2), with the idea of cutting off ἡδονή being mirrored with circumcision. Throughout his writings, Philo consistently interprets ἡδονή as passion, and consequently, a source of evil, with circumcision symbolising the act of cutting off it. For example, wars between the Greeks and the Barbarians are caused by ἐπιθυμίας ἢ χρημάτων ἢ δόξης ἢ ἡδονῆς· περὶ γὰρ ταῦτα κηραίνει τὸ τῶν ἀνθρώπων γένος (*Decal.* 151). What leads to covetousness, the violation of one of the Ten Commandments, is τὸ πάθος αὐτῆς ἡδονή (*Decal.* 143).

Although previous scholarship pointed out the excision of pleasure as a symbol of circumcision, an important nuance is overlooked: the focus of sexual pleasure and circumcision. In *De specialibus legibus* (1:8–9), Philo suggests that circumcision is the symbol of two essential matters. One of them is ἡδονῶν ἐκτομῆς, in particular, the pleasure of ἡ ἀνδρὸς πρὸς γυναῖκα συνουσία, depicting sex between man and woman.[85] Furthermore, in Philo's explication of this symbol, he emphasises mutilation, by stating that the lawgivers think positively about ὄργανον ἀκρωτηριάζειν, the organ that serves sexual intercourse (τὸ ὑπηρετοῦν ταῖς τοιαύταις ὁμιλίαις).

Ἡδονή is also negatively associated with illicit sexual pleasure and fornication. As illustrated in two texts, Philo articulates ἡδονή and πόρνη in the same context. The first text articulates an indirect relationship between the two, as Philo compares people who make ἡδονή as ὁ ψυχῆς τέλος with τῶν ἐκ πόρνης ἀποκυηθέντων (*Conf.* 144). However, in the second occurrence, he discusses people of other nations visiting prostitutes after the age of fourteen, before emphasising the purpose of sex being οὐχ ἡδονὴν ἀλλὰ γνησίων παίδων σποράν (*Ios.* 43).

The pleasure of sex is central to Philo's understanding of circumcision. Paul expresses the same idea embraced by Philo. In Galatians 5:19, the first three words emerging from Paul's discussion about the works of σάρξ are πορνεία, ἀκαθαρσία, and ἀσέλγεια, all portraying immoral

---

84 Perhaps the translation 'proselytes' is more suitable in that context.
85 The second is a symbol of a man knowing himself, casting away a burdensome disease, which allegorically refers to the opinion of the soul. *Spec.* 1:10.

sexual behaviours. Of interest, the trio only appears twice in Paul's authentic letters. Apart from Galatians 5, it also occurs in 2 Corinthians 12:21, with ἀκαθαρσία preceding πορνεία and ἀσέλγεια. In other words, one must not presume that Paul always places πορνεία as the first word in the trio. On the contrary, the placement of πορνεία is a deliberate act. Amongst the immoral sexual behaviours, πορνεία, a word that has direct reference to prostitution, leads the list. Furthermore, Paul's argument concludes that those who belong to Christ have τὴν σάρκα ἐσταύρωσαν σὺν τοῖς παθήμασιν καὶ ταῖς ἐπιθυμίαις (5:24). Σάρξ is portrayed as being crucified together with παθήμασιν and ἐπιθυμίαις. The first word πάθημα primarily means suffering. Nonetheless, this is not the meaning in this context. Rather, the plural form of πάθημα portrays sexual desires, as the word is known to denote strong physical desires, especially of sexual nature.[86] The second word ἐπιθυμία can refer to sexual desire.[87] In this particular context, the pairing of πάθημα and ἐπιθυμία forms a hendiadys, conveying Paul's strong emphasis on sexual desires in his conclusion of the σάρξ-πνεῦμα antithesis. Of interest, the first word on the list of works of σάρξ is πορνεία, but the first word on the list of the fruit of the Spirit is ἀγάπη. Ἀγάπη seems to be deliberately chosen, creating a subtle contrast to another word for love, Ἔρως, which is also the Greek god of sex. In light of all of the above, one can detect a profound sexual undertone in Paul's argument surrounding σάρξ in Galatians 5. Although the word ἡδονή is absent in Galatians 5, the concept behind it, sexual pleasure of the flesh, permeates Paul's discussion. This echoes the Philonic argument, pointing to a shared underlying belief that circumcision symbolises the excision of ἡδονή, first and foremost, sexual pleasure.

Besides sexual pleasure, Paul also echoes Philo's highlight on mutilation in his discussion of law and circumcision. As previously mentioned, Philo states that the lawgivers consider ὄργανον ἀκρωτηριάζειν to be good (*Spec.* 1:9). The verb ἀκρωτηριάζω connotes mutilation. On the other hand, leading into the juxtaposition in 5:13–26, Paul concludes his previous argument by cursing those law-abiders,[88] who propagate

---

86 L&N, s.v. 'πάθημα.'.
87 BDAG, s.v. 'ἐπιθυμία.'
88 Paul describes those agitators as Ὅσοι γὰρ ἐξ ἔργων νόμου εἰσίν (3:10), and accuses them of hypocrisy, as they, who practice circumcision, do not really obey the laws (6:13).

circumcision amongst the Galatians, 'ἀποκόψονται' (5:12). The word ἀποκόπτω signifies castration in this context, which is the extreme form of mutilation—cutting off the foreskin and the male reproductive organ to which it attaches. While Paul and Philo emphasis mutilation in their discussion of law and circumcision, the former opposes while the latter supports the practice.

My analysis is consistent with one of the most recent research concerning some interesting insight into ancient circumcision. Blanton shows the connection between foreskin and lust in the ancient world. He surveys literary and artistic depictions of the prepuce in the Classical world, and suggests the large, exposed glans was negatively associated with lust, while the slender, small prepuce was associated with self-control.[89] Philo leans into the negative connotations, when he emphasises the fertility of the Jewish (and Egyptian) people.[90]

To sum up, the connection between the σάρξ–πνεῦμα antithesis and circumcision would be a known concept understood by at least some of the contemporary Hellenistic Jews and Gentile proselytes, including Paul and likely the Galatians, as reflected in Philo's writings. In placing the word σάρξ antithetically in relation to the divine spirit, Philo directly associates σάρξ with ἡδονή. For the philosopher, circumcision symbolises the excision of ἡδονή, especially sexual pleasure. In Philonic materials, a connection between ἡδονή and immoral sexual pleasure emerges, encapsulated by the term πορνεία. In his discussion of law and circumcision, Philo highlights mutilation. Paul takes up those thoughts. In writing the σάρξ-πνεῦμα antithesis in Galatians 5, he commences his argument by listing the works of σάρξ. Immoral sexual behaviours, which is accentuated by πορνεία, lead the list. He concludes his argument, employing a hendiadys to highlight immoral sexual desires. Despite the absence of the phrase ἡδονή σαρκὸς in Galatians 5, the notion of sexual pleasure dominates Paul's discussion, creating an indirect reference to circumcision. Finally, before introducing the

---

89 On the other hand, Blanton cites medical reasons for circumcision, suggesting the semen flows more easily into the female for reproduction and emphasising the value of circumcision in the prevention of phallic infections, particularly in warmer climates. These environmental and medical explanations stand in addition to his allegorical understanding of circumcision as an excision of passion from the soul. See Blanton, 'The Expressive Prepuce'.
90 Blanton, 'The Expressive Prepuce'.

juxtaposition, Paul concludes his previous discussion of law and circumcision by cursing those law abiders. Echoing Philo's discussion of law and circumcision, Paul also highlights mutilation. All of the above shows that the σάρξ-πνεῦμα antithesis in Galatians 5 carries an indirect reference to circumcision.

Overall speaking, Paul employs the first clustered use of σάρξ in 2:16—3:3 to highlight the flawed practice of mandatory circumcision. He then uses the second cluster of σάρξ in 4:13-29 to emphasis the association between σάρξ and foreskin, and the fuller argument about σάρξ as opposing God. In the third cluster in 5:13-26, Paul's depiction of sexual pleasure underlines the σάρξ-πνεῦμα juxtaposition, indirectly illustrating the antithesis of ἡδονῇ σαρκὸς and πνεῦμα, and referring to circumcision. Paul argues against circumcision in his last cluster of σάρξ in 6:8-13, with the last occurrence of σάρξ in Galatians directly denoting the cutting of the foreskin (6:13).

Conclusion

The juxtaposition of σάρξ and πνεῦμα dominates Paul's discussion in Galatians 5:16—6:10, in particular, 5:13-26. By examining Philo's writings, I attempted to overcome some of the deficiencies in understanding σάρξ in Galatians 5:13-26.

I first reviewed the occurrences of σάρξ in the entire letter, ascertaining that the term appears in the context that has direct or indirect reference to circumcision. Therefore, the reference to circumcision in the context of σάρξ in the σάρξ-πνεῦμα antithesis would possibly exist. Subsequently, I examined the works of Philo, showing ἡδονή (σαρκὸς), in particular, sexual pleasure, as the clue to the missing link between the σάρξ-πνεῦμα antithesis and circumcision.

The reflection on the usage of σάρξ, and its reference to circumcision, reminds us that 'ethnic identity and self-serving desire',[91] signified by circumcision as well as certain religious practices, have no place in the Gospel.

There are some implications of the findings in this study. It has been

---

91 As previously mentioned, Dunn uses those terms. See Dunn, *Galatians*, 298.

argued that Paul transcends his usual 'moral catechesis' into an argument that condemns the practice of circumcision.[92] The practice of circumcision carried a positive connotation amongst the Hellenistic Jews during Paul's time, primarily due to its covenantal connection, as stated in the Torah (Gen. 17:10–12). It was also a common practice that some contemporary Jews and proselytes regarded as a symbol of the excision of sexual pleasure. Yet, in Galatians, Paul argues against the mandate of this practice amongst the Christian community. The reference to circumcision by σάρξ in Galatians 5 is set in opposition to the divine spirit, contradictory to the contemporary common perception. Would it be that Paul argues for an 'ethical circumcision', but against physical circumcision? Would it also be that the apostle counters the positive connotation behind circumcision, by employing the σάρξ–πνεῦμα juxtaposition, to subvert that common understanding? In other words, the term does not merely denote sin, an evil force, or human's sinful nature; nor is the list in 5:19–20 purely a manifesto of the working of σάρξ. Rather, through using the term in a juxtaposition, he creates a negative connotation on circumcision. Consequently, Paul seems to associate his opponents' insistence on circumcision with a force opposing the divine Spirit and a list of immoral behaviours known to be the works of σάρξ. The verification of this conjecture of subversion as well as the notion of 'ethical circumcision' would require further study.

---

92 O'Donovan notes that the common view on 5:16–26 is that the passage concerns a 'sustained moral catechesis', with the antithesis aiming to 'frame the ethical questions', and to 'project across the field of moral life a narrative of liberation'. See O'Donovan, 'Flesh and Spirit', 271, 283.

Bibliography

Primary Sources

Josephus, Flavius   *Flavii Josephi Opera* (ed. Benedictus Niese, 7 vols; Berlin: Weidmann, 1887–1895).

Novum Testamentum Graece   (Nestle-Aland 28th ed.; Stuttgart: Deutche Bibelgesellschaft, 2012).

Philo   *Philonis Alexandrini Opera Quae Supersunt* (ed. L. Cohn, P. Wendland and S. Reiter, 7 vols; Berlin: Georg Reimer, 1896–1930).

Commentaries

Betz, H. D.   *Galatians: A Commentary on Paul's Letter to the Churches in Galatia* (Hermeneia: A Critical and Historical Commentary on the Bible; Philadelphia: Fortress, 1979).

Bruce, F. F.   *The Epistle to the Galatians: A Commentary on the Greek Text*. The New International Greek Testament Commentary. Grand Rapids, Mich.: Eerdmans, 1982.

Burton, Ernest De Witt.   *A Critical and Exegetical Commentary on the Epistle to the Galatians*. International Critical Commentary on the Holy Scriptures of the Old and New Testaments. Edinburgh: T. & T. Clark, 1921.

Cousar, Charles B.   *Galatians*. Interpretation: A Bible Commentary for Teaching and Preaching. Atlanta: John Knox, 1982.

de Boer, M. C.   *Galatians: A Commentary* (The New Testament Library; Louisville, KY: Westminster John Knox, 2011).

Das, A. A.   *Galatians* (Concordia Commentary; Saint Louis: Concordia, 2014).

Dunn, J. D. G.   *The Epistle to the Galatians* (Black's New Testament Commentaries; London: A & C Black, 1993).

Findlay, G. G.   *The Epistle to the Galatians* (The Expositors Bible. London: Hodder and Stoughton, 1908).

Fung, R. Y. K.   *The Epistle to the Galatians* (NICNT; Grand Rapids, Mich.: Eerdmans, 1988).

Keener, C. S.   *Galatians* (New Cambridge Bible Commentary; New York: Cambridge University Press, 2018).

Longenecker, R. N.	*Galatians* (Word Biblical Commentary 41; Waco: Word Books, 1990).
Martyn, J. L.	*Galatians: A New Translation with Introduction and Commentary* (New York: Doubleday, 1997).
Moo, D.	*Galatians* (Baker Exegetical Commentary on the New Testament; Grand Rapids, Mich.: Baker Academic, 2013).
Schreiner, T. R.	*Galatians* (Zondervan Exegetical Commentary on the New Testament; Grand Rapids. Mich.: Zondervan, 2010).
Tarazi, P. N.	*Galatians: A Commentary* (Orthodox Biblical Studies; New York: St Vladimir's Seminary Press, 1994).
Witherington III, B.	*Grace in Galatia, A Commentary on St Paul's Letter to the Galatians.* Grand Rapids, Mich.: Eerdmans, 1998.

Other Works

Barclay, J. M. G.	*Obeying the Truth: A Study of Paul's Ethics in Galatians* (Studies of the New Testament and Its World, ed. J. Riches; Edinburgh: T. & T. Clark, 1988).
Barclay, J. M. G.	'Paul and Philo on Circumcision: Romans 2.25–9 in Social and Cultural Context', *New Testament Studies* 44 (1998), 536–556
Barclay, W.	*Flesh and Spirit: An Examination of Galatians 5.19–23* (London: SCM, 1962).
Bauer, W.	*A Greek–English Lexicon of the New Testament and Other Early Christian Literature* (tr. W. F. Arndt and F. W. Gingrich; Chicago: The University of Chicago Press, 2000).
Blanton IV, T. R.	'The Expressive Prepuce: Philo's Defense of Judaic Circumcision in Greek and Roman Contexts', *The Studia Philonica Annual* 31 (2019), 127–161.
Brandenburger, E.	*Fleisch und Geist Fleisch und Geist: Paulus und die dualistische Weisheit* (Wissenschaftliche Monographien zum Alten und Neuen Testament, Band 29; Neukirchen-Vluyn: Neukirchener Verlag, 1968).
Borgen, P.	*Paul Preaches Circumcision and Pleases Men, and Other Essays on Christian Origins* (Trondheim, Norway: Tapir, 1983).

Borgen, P.	*Philo, John, and Paul: New Perspectives on Judaism and Early Christianity* (Brown Judaic Studies 131; Atlanta, GA: Scholars Press, 1987).
Brown, R. E.	*An Introduction to the New Testament* (The Anchor Bible Reference Library; New York: Doublebay, 1997).
Dunn, J. G.	*The Theology of Paul the Apostle* (Grand Rapids, Mich.: Eerdmans, 2006).
Edwards, J. R.	'Galatians 5:12: Circumcision, the Mother Goddess, and the Scandal of the Cross', *Novum Testamentum* 53 (2011), 319–37.
Glick, L. B.	*Marked in Your Flesh: Circumcision from Ancient Judea to Modern America* (New York: Oxford University Press, 2005).
Hadas-Lebel, M.	*Philo of Alexandria: A Thinker in the Jewish Diaspora* (Studies in Philo of Alexandria 7; Leiden: Brill, 2012).
Holtz, G.	'Von Alexandrien nach Jerusalem. Überlegungen zur Vermittlung philonischalexandrinischer Tradition an Paulus', *Zeitschrift für die neutestamentliche Wissenschaft und die Kunde der älteren Kirche* 105, no. 2 (2014), 256–262.
Jewett, R.	*Paul's Anthropological Terms: A Study of Their Use in Conflict Settings* (Leiden: Brill, 1971).
Käsemann, E.	*Perspectives on Paul* (The New Testament Library, tr. M. Kohl; London: SCM, 1971).
Liddell, H. G., Scott, R. and Jones, H. S.	*A Greek-English Lexicon* (9th ed., with Revised Supplement; Oxford: Oxford University, 1996).
Louw, J. P. & Nida, E.	*A Greek-English Lexicon of the New Testament: Based on Semantic Domains* (New York: United Bible Societies, 1988).
Martin, T. W.	'The Covenant of Circumcision (Genesis 17:9–14) and the Situational Antithesis in Galatians 3:28', *Journal of Biblical Literature* 122, no. 1 (2003), 111–25.
Martin, T. W.	'What Flesh? What Temptation? (Galatians 4.13–14)', *Journal for the Study of the New Testament.* 74 (1999), 65–91.
Niehoff, M. R.	'Josephus and Philo in Rome', in H. Howell Chapman and Z. Rodgers (eds.), *A Companion to Josephu* (Blackwell Companion to the Ancient World 110; Chichester, West Sussex: Wiley Blackwell 2016), 135–146.

Niehoff, M. R.	'Ist Philon ein typischer Vertreter des Diasporajudentums?', in M. R. Niehoff and R. Feldmeier (eds.), *Abrahams Aufbruch. Philon von Alexandria, De migratione Abrahami* (SAPERE 30; Tübingen: Mohr Siebeck, 2017), 139–145.
Niehoff, M. R.	*Philo of Alexandria: An Intellectual Biography* (Anchor Yale Bible Reference Library; London: Yale University Press, 2018).
O'Donovan, O.	'Flesh and Spirit', in M. Elliot et al. (eds.), *Galatians and Christian Theology: Justification, the Gospel, and Ethics in Paul's Letters* (Grand Rapids: Baker Academic, 2014), 271–84.
Smallwood, E. M.	*The Jews Under Roman Rule* (Leiden: Brill, 1976).
Sterling, G.	'General Introduction', in E. Birnbaum and J. Dillon (eds.), *On the Life of Abraham: Introduction, Translation, and Commentary* (Philo of Alexandria Commentary Series 6. Boston: Brill, 2020).
Winter, B. W.	*Philo and Paul among the Sophists* (Society for New Testament Studies Monograph Series 96; Cambridge: Cambridge University Press, 1997).

CHAPTER 15

'An Antiquated Exegetical Convention'?
Ὅτε δὲ and Paul's Chronology of the Incident at Antioch in Galatians

Brent Niedergall

Introduction

Paul narrates two discrete historical episodes in Galatians 2. The first episode occurred in Jerusalem. Paul, in response to divine revelation, returned to Jerusalem with Barnabas and Titus (Gal. 2:1–10). There he met with 'those who seemed influential' (Gal. 2:2,6)—a group that included James, Peter, and John (Gal. 2:9), seeking approval of his gospel message to the Gentiles. Paul reports that he received their approval.[1]

The second episode (Gal. 2:11–14) occurred in Antioch. Paul confronted Peter for his hypocritical behaviour regarding Gentile interaction (Gal. 2:13). At first, Peter ate with Gentiles. But when 'certain men' from James arrived, Peter stopped eating with Gentiles because he feared 'those of the circumcision' (Gal. 2:12).

Given the agreement between Peter and Paul at Jerusalem, the disagreement at Antioch seems perplexing. Did Peter forget or misunderstand the resolution made at Antioch for Paul and Barnabas to take

---

1 For the purposes of this essay, it makes no difference whether Galatians 2:1–10 should be identified with Acts 15 or Acts 11:28–30. On the potential impact this decision makes on an overall chronological reckoning of Paul's ministry, see Reisner, *Paul's Early Period*, 320.

the gospel to the Gentiles? In response to a perceived contradiction, some have suggested Paul does not present these events in chronological order. A trickle of scholars going back to Augustine has suggested that Paul's narrative in Galatians 2 does not follow a chronological arrangement.² Augustine almost offhandedly comments that he was 'more inclined to think' that 'Peter did this [came to Antioch] before the meeting of that council at Jerusalem.'³ Centuries later, others developed this postulation much more. Proponents of the non-chronological reading have suggested multiple lines of argumentation, and there is a larger chronological question on the relationship between Galatians 2:1–10 and Acts.⁴ Other arguments and considerations aside, this essay will focus on only one claim used to advance the non-chronological view—Paul's use of ὅτε δὲ in Galatians 2:11. Potential implications for such a shift include an adjustment to our understanding of Paul's chronology and perhaps even our dating of Galatians.⁵ Ultimately, the claim for a 'chronological rearrangement'⁶ stands or falls on the pragmatics of these two tiny conjunctions.

Non-Chronological Reading Advocates

Most advocates of the non-chronological reading are twentieth-century French and German scholars. Theodor Zahn embraced a non-chronological reading, claiming 'The common opinion that this [the incident at Antioch] followed the visit of Paul and Barnabas in Galatians

---

2   It is outside of the scope of this essay to consider the additional reasons why Zahn, Munck, and Lüdemann argue that the incident at Antioch occurred before the Jerusalem meeting.
3   Augustine, *Letters* 82.2.11.
4   Scholars differ on whether Gal. 2:1–10 refers to Acts 15 or Acts 11:27–30. For a recent bibliography of proponents for each view, see Gibson, *Peter*, 216n.2.
5   The relationship between Galatians 2:1–10 and Acts is the primary consideration every scholar attempting to date Galatians must grapple with. Craig Keener recognizes at least six positions. The two most popular positions are Galatians 2:1–10 is (1) the famine visit referenced in Acts 11:30 and 12:25 or (2) the Jerusalem Council referenced of Acts 15. If 2:1–10 is referencing the Jerusalem Council (ca. AD 48/49), then Paul must have written Galatians after that event. See Keener, *Galatians*, 8. Those preferring the non-chronological view tend to correlate Galatians 2:1–10 with Acts 15. In accord with my own summarising question of 'Given the agreement between Peter and Paul at Jerusalem, why then the disagreement at Antioch?', it is easier to grant the Galatians 2 event the weight of Acts 15 if one allows for chronological rearrangement.
6   Lüdemann, *Paul*, 58.

2:1–10 cannot be justified from the text.'[7] André Mehat, holding to a non-chronological reading, claims regarding the connection between the episodes at Jerusalem and Antioch, 'The link is logical, not chronological'.[8] Gerd Lüdemann, commonly cited as one of the more recent defenders of the non-chronological position, asserts, 'The view that the *hote de* in 2:11 continues the narrative (Oepke, 87–88) is just an antiquated exegetical convention that is unable to explain why *epeita* is not used'.[9] According to these scholars, the incident at Antioch occurred before the meeting in Jerusalem.

Some make the non-chronological claim but omit explanation or support.[10] Others, such as Matthias Schneckenburger, acknowledge the possibility of both the chronological and non-chronological reading, making claims such as this: 'ὅτε δὲ can designate any time'—before or after the council described in Galatians 2:1–10.[11] While each scholar's arguments merit individual attention, we will examine grammatical arguments used to support the non-chronological view.

Grammatical Claims for the Non-Chronological View

Lüdemann offers little grammatical explanation, but he does reference the issue raised by Zahn and Munck.[12] Zahn and Munck both present

---

7   Zahn, *Der Brief des Paulus*, 110
8   Mehat, '"Quand Kèphas vint à Antioch"', 33.
9   Lüdemann, *Paul*, 77. Albrecht Oepke, whom Lüdemann references, states 'δὲ simply continues the narrative. T. [Theodor] Zahn and V. [Valentin] Weber try in vain to deny the following falls temporally behind the Apostolic Council'. Oepke, *Der Brief*, 87–88. John Bligh, who discounts Lüdemann's chronological claim, acknowledges that Paul's language 'does not necessarily imply temporal sequence'. Bligh, *Galatians*, 178.
10 Hans-Joachim Schoeps includes in a footnote, 'The incident at Antioch ... probably occurred before the Apostolic Council' [Gal. 2:1–10]. Schoeps, *Jewish Christianity*, 19. Stählin also submits, 'What we have here is probably one of the not uncommon cases in which Paul does not follow a strict systematic or chronological order.' Yet, unfortunately, Stählin does not reference any other such cases. Stählin, *Die Apostelgeschichte*, 209.
11 Schneckenburger, *Ueber den Zweck*, 109. Johannes Munck and Josef Hainz are also open to both possibilities. According to Munck, 'The text at least leaves open the question whether the clash in Antioch took place before or after the conference in Jerusalem'. Munck, *Paul and the Salvation of Mankind*, 100. Hainz also believes that a non-chronological order is 'thoroughly possible'. Hainz, *Ekklesia*, 121, cited by Lüdemann, *Paul*, 125 n.108.
12 For support, Lüdemann also cites Quintilian's advice on deviating from chronological order when presenting a defence before a judge. In *Institutio Oratoria*, Quintilian acknowledges, 'Neither do I agree with those who assert that the order of our *statement of facts* should always follow the actual order of events, but have a preference for adopting the order which I consider most suitable' (4.2.83). See Lüdemann, *Paul*, 57–8.

the same substance of a grammatical defence. According to Zahn, 'There is no definite or indefinite chronological indication, such as that which linked all previous historical memories.'[13] He notes Paul's prior use of ὅτε δὲ in Galatians 1:15, which is followed by three statements introduced with ἔπειτα ('then'). Because Paul introduces the incident at Antioch not with ἔπειτα, but with ὅτε δὲ, Munck claims 'we have here a fresh beginning.'[14] H.-M. Féret concurs, acknowledging that while ὅτε δὲ can both indicate chronological sequence and an absolute beginning, Paul would have used ἔπειτα to express a chronological sequence, as he did in 1:18, 1:21, and 2:1.[15] According to Zahn, Munck, and Féret, Paul chose this phrase to avoid marking the incident at Antioch as a sequential event to the meeting in Jerusalem.

Mehat differs slightly in his argumentation, but his overall position strongly resembles that of Zahn, Munck, and Féret. Focusing on δὲ rather than ὅτε, he claims the conjunction is neutral when it comes to indicating chronological succession and is most probably adversative.[16] He also reasons that if Paul intended to denote a chronological sequence, he would have indicated so with a Greek word for 'later' or 'afterwards'.[17]

Almost every modern commentary argues for or assumes Antioch chronologically follows Jerusalem. One notable exception is Steven Runge, who acknowledges the possibility of a non-chronological reading. He raises the possibility that this passage compares to other 'sidebar-type comments' that include δέ, such as 1 Corinthians 1:16 and Galatians 1:20.[18] While Runge believes Paul's construction could be a legitimate instance of a non-chronological note, he concludes—based on the protracted length of the episode—that the possibility is unlikely.[19]

---

13 Zahn, *Der Brief*, 110–11.
14 Munck, *Paul and the Salvation of Mankind*, 101.
15 Féret, *Pierre et Paul*, 45. In Dupont's extensive rebuttal to Féret's work, he claims that Paul uses ὅτε δὲ when there is a change in subject and ἔπειτα when the subject remains the same. Dupont, 'Pierre et Paul', 53. Dupont's claim seems to generally hold true, although the sample size is small and 1 Corinthians 15:46 is an exception in which Paul uses ἔπειτα when there is a change in subject.
16 Mehat, '"Quand Kèphas vint à Antioch"', 33.
17 Mehat, '"Quand Kèphas vint à Antioch"', 33. Mehat does not identify any specific Greek words, but perhaps he means μετά with the accusative as a marker of time or the adverbial use of ὕστερος.
18 Runge, *High Definition*, 'Orienting the Events'.
19 Runge, *High Definition*, 'Orienting the Events'.

Semantics and Pragmatics of Δὲ and Ὅτε

Christopher Fresch, in his analysis of papyri from the third to first centuries BC, concludes that the coordinating conjunction δέ functions as a 'segmentation device'.[20] Fresch explains that 'consistently, δέ appears to be used for structural purposes, explicitly marking out distinct segments within the discourse'.[21] Paul's use of δέ in Galatians 2:11 aligns with Fresch's conclusion and also with Steven Runge's claim that δέ signals 'a distinct development in the story'.[22]

The subordinated conjunction ὅτε introduces a temporal clause containing an aorist verb.[23] A temporal clause is subordinate to the main clause and indicates the 'reference time with respect to which the main clause must be interpreted'.[24] The temporal particle ὅτε is a conjunction that normally appears with indicative verbs.[25] And while these verbs can be past, present, or future, the present is rare, and 'the great bulk of the examples [in the NT] are in the past with the aorist indicative'.[26] In a temporal clause, this conjunction indicates simultaneity by either indicating that one point of time coincides with another time (translated 'when' in English) or that a period of time coextends with another period of time (translated 'as long as' or 'while' in English).[27] Heinrich von Siebenthal notes that the temporal clause specifies the time of the '"situation" referred to by the subordinate construction', answering the question 'When?'. He includes Galatians 2:11 as an example in which the 'situation' of the subordinate clause is anterior to the 'situation' of the main clause.[28] The anterior situation found in the subordinate clause is that Cephas came to Antioch. The situation of the main clause is that Paul opposed Cephas to his face.

---

20 For the terminology of 'segmentation device' (or 'chunking device') see Fresch, *Discourse Markers*, 85.
21 Fresch, *Discourse Markers*, 59. Fresch adds that 'δέ functions to close off or begin new sections (relative to its scope), encouraging the reader to process smaller, more manageable pieces of the discourse at a time'. He finds the same to be true in the Twelve of the LXX and cites scholarship making similar claims for Classical and Postclassical Greek. See pp. 60, 79–89.
22 Runge, *Discourse Grammar*, 31.
23 For more on temporal clauses, see van Emde Boas et al., *The Cambridge Grammar*, 536.
24 Luján, 'Temporal Clauses', 3:374.
25 Porter, *Idioms*, 214. The particle ὅταν (ὅτε + ἄν) often occurs with the subjunctive.
26 Robertson, *A Grammar*, 971.
27 BDAG, s. v. 'ὅτε.' See also Luján, 'Temporal Clauses', 374–75.
28 von Siebenthal, *Ancient Greek Grammar*, 511–13. Wallace agrees that ὅτε 'gives the time of the action'. Wallace, *Greek Grammar*, 677. See also Köstenberger, Merkle and Plummer, *Going Deeper*, 414. They classify ὅτέ as a temporal ('telling the time of') subordinating conjunction.

Ancient Greek Evidence

What should we make of Paul's use of ὅτε δέ? And, hypothetically, if Zahn, Munck, Lüdemann, etc. are correct, do we encounter this phenomenon anywhere else? Can we identify other instances in Greek narrative in which ὅτε δέ arguably prefaces the insertion of an earlier event? Ben Witherington's claim sounds reasonable: the Galatians would expect the events 'to be recorded in order unless there were signals in the text and strong reasons behind them for not doing so'.[29] Using a corpus-based analysis, I will examine the evidence from Classical and Post-Classical Greek to determine if the non-chronological claim has any merit and conclude with some observations on the use of ὅτε δέ in narrative material.[30]

The temporal construction ὅτε δέ occurs 17 times in the New Testament, all but one of which prefaces an aorist verb.[31] Douglas Moo is correct when he writes, 'Every other occurrence of the phrase ὅτε δέ in the NT introduces something that follows what comes before it'.[32] The same is true for the Greek Old Testament. In Rahlfs' edition of the Septuagint, ὅτε δέ occurs only eight times, each occurrence prefacing an aorist verb and introducing something that follows in temporal sequence.[33] What then of other evidence? In what follows, I present my analysis of a broad sampling of literary texts, papyri, and inscriptions. A careful study of ὅτε δέ, as it occurs in a temporal clause at the beginning of a sentence, reveals three common uses:

---

29 Witherington, *Grace in Galatia*, 149. Gibson also reasons, 'Absent any textual indication, it is more natural to accept Paul's chronology, especially since Paul appears to be providing a biographical account in chronological order in his first chapter'. Gibson, *Peter Between Jerusalem and Antioch*, 218 n.12.

30 For this essay, I evaluated 290 occurrences of ὅτε δέ as it appears in the LXX, New Testament, classical literature, Jewish and early Christian writings, documentary papyri, and inscriptions. For a complete list of sources considered in this chapter, see Appendix: List of Sources Considered. Although the *Thesaurus Linguae Graecae* currently registers 6,748 hits for 'ὅτε δε', many of these are 'ὁτὲ μέν ... ὁτὲ δέ ...' expressions. For more on this structure, see BDAG, s. v. 'ὁτέ'.

31 The temporal clause in Acts 12:6 contains the imperfect verb ἤμελλεν. Note also that NA28 critical apparatus lists five variant readings in the manuscript tradition that include ὅτε δέ (Matt. 13:48; Mark 8:20; Luke 7:1; Acts 13:34; Jude 9). None of these variants introduce non-chronological material into a narrative. The temporal construction καὶ ὅτε occurs 26 times in the NT, none of which, to my knowledge, has generated arguments in favour of non-chronological readings in narrative.

32 Moo. *Galatians*, 145 n.2.

33 See Ezra 5:12; Esth. 1:5; Jdt. 5:18; Tob. 2:1,13; 8:1,3; Dan. 6:5. Codex Sinaiticus also contains a variant reading in 1 Macc. 12:48 in which a scribe wrote ὅτε δέ instead of ὅτι. This reading would not disrupt the chronology. For textual evidence, see Rahlfs and Hanhart, *Septuaginta*.

1. Mere temporal specification of an action
2. Resumptive repetition
3. Boundary marking (e.g., change of scene, new narrative unit)

My decisions to assign occurrences to each of these three categories involves some measure of subjectivity, but my overall purpose is to categorise a large number of occurrences and determine if any introduce non-chronological material within a narrative. In other words, an incorrect choice between mere temporal specification and resumptive repetition will not skew my overall conclusions. After examining these three categories of ὅτε δέ uses, we can evaluate our exegetical options for interpreting the temporal sequence of Galatians 2:11.

Category 1: Mere Temporal Specification of an Action

By 'mere temporal specification', I mean only that the temporal clause beginning with ὅτε δέ does not correspond with boundary marking (see next section). Albert Rijksbaron observes how a class of ὁτέ-clauses 'provides a temporal specification for isolated statements, that is, statements that do not form part of the surrounding narrative ... the ὁτέ-clauses usually follow the main clause'.[34] There are many examples in which ὅτε δέ provides temporal specification and, also, forms part of the surrounding narrative but does not mark a discourse boundary. I have grouped all such cases together under the category of mere temporal specification.

Mere temporal specification is the most frequent function of ὅτε δέ in the New Testament. Matthew 21:34 serves as a representative example. After Jesus explains in v.33 of his parable of the tenants how the master of the house planted a vineyard and went on a journey, he specifies in v.35 when the master dispatched his servants to collect fruit from the vineyard with the temporal clause ὅτε δὲ ἤγγισεν ὁ καιρὸς τῶν καρπῶν ('And when the time for fruit drew near').[35]

---

34 Rijksbaron, *Temporal and Causal Conjunctions*, 136.
35 Other examples of mere temporal specification in the New Testament can be found in Matt. 13:26; 21:34; Luke 15:30; Acts 8:12,39; 11:2; 12:6; 21:5,35; Gal. 1:15; 2:12; 4:4; Titus 3:4. For the LXX, see Ezra 5:12; Esth. 1:5; Jdt 5:18; Tob. 2:13; 8:3.

We find an abundance of examples outside of the New Testament. Diodorus Siculus, after describing how the once beautiful Queen Lamia transformed into a ferocious beast and murdered children, tells how she was not a threat when inebriated: 'But whenever [ὅτε δὲ] she drank freely, she gave to all the opportunity to do what they pleased unobserved'.[36] Here, δὲ has an adversative function, contrasting the safety that accompanied her drunkenness with the terror that accompanied her sobriety. Again, ὅτε δὲ merely provides temporal specification for an isolated or, in this case, recurring event.[37] The documentary papyri also offer a representative example of this use of ὅτε δὲ. In Dionysia's letter to Theon dated 127 BC, she describes a chain of events in which a man named Neon seized Theon's mattress. Dionysia, after obtaining the right to petition a city official for the mattress, narrates, 'And when [ὅτε δὲ] he went down to confront me, having treated me terribly, it was decreed that it should be secured and stored in the public office until the moment you are present'.[38]

Category 2: Boundary Marking

The use of ὅτε δὲ in Galatians 2:11 goes beyond providing temporal specification by also marking a discourse boundary. In some instances, ὅτε δὲ introduces a new narrative unit consisting of new information. This function corresponds to Runge's observation about temporal frames, which, in narrative texts, 'are associated with discourse boundaries, such as changes of scene or pericope'.[39] Rijksbaron calls this function an absolute temporal adjunct that does 'not contain any elements

---

36 *Diodorus Siculus*, 20.41 (Geer, Loeb Classical Library).
37 For other examples, see also Xenophon, *Anabasis*, 2.6.20; 3.1.33; Clement of Alexandria, *Exhortations* 11; *Epistle of Barnabas* 5.9; *Life of Adam and Eve* 21.2; 33.3; *Acts of Philip* 28.7; 61.1; 126.2. For an example in which a sentence introduced by ὅτε δὲ follows a sentence introduced by ἔπειτα, see Hippocrates of Cos, *Epidemics* 5.20. Although predating Galatians by many centuries, it provides another example of a chronological narrative that uses both words in succession.
38 P.Bad.4.48 (ed. F. Bilabel, 4:107–8). For an epigraphic example from late 2nd–early 3rd century BC, Panamara 226, ll. 11–14 records 'When [ὅτε δὲ] he was priest for the second time, he served as priest also of Hecate at a time of need'. Translation from Oliver, *The Sacred Gerousia*, 154. Also see IKret 3.4.9, l. 131 (and the identical IMagnMai 160, l. 103) for a lacunose example from 112/111 BC that seems to evidence mere temporal specification.
39 Runge, *Discourse Grammar*, 216. See also Bakker, 'Boundaries'.

that refer back to the preceding context'.⁴⁰ Paul's use of ὅτε, much like his use of the conjunction δέ, would signal a new development.

This use does not appear in the LXX and appears in the New Testament only in Galatians 2:11—our passage under consideration. For a representative example outside of the New Testament, we can look to the *Letter of Aristeas*. King Ptolemy welcomes the Septuagint translators and holds seven symposia in their honour. After a prayer before the meal, Aristeas records, 'When, after an interval, an opportunity presented itself, the king asked him who occupied the first place at the table [...] how he should preserve his kingdom unimpaired to the last'.⁴¹ According to Benjamin Wright, this occurrence of ὅτε δέ marks a major break and begins the first of the seven symposia, each comprising a 'self-contained unit'.⁴² This narrative unit follows in chronological order.⁴³ In my research, I discovered that the vast majority of ὅτε δέ clauses occurring at discourse boundaries introduce chronologically arranged material, but there are exceptions. We will consider these after an explanation of the final function of ὅτε δέ.

Category 3: Resumptive Repetition

A third use associated with a preceding ὅτε δέ clause is *resumptive repetition*, which Phil Quick defines as 'a discourse feature used to resume a previous topic, story line or theme line that has been interrupted by a span of information that is related but diverges for a short or long gap before being resumed'.⁴⁴ This corresponds to Rijksbaron's claim that

---

40 Rijksbaron, *Temporal and Causal Conjunctions*, 132.
41 *Letter of Aristeas* 187; Thackeray, *The Letter of Aristeas*, 60.
42 Wright, *The Letter of Aristeas*, 55.
43 Other discourse breaks marked by ὅτε δέ can be found in Aelian, *Historical Miscellany* 12.1; Aristotle, *Rhetoric to Alexander* 1427b.10; Parthenius of Nicaea, *Sufferings in Love* 8; Pausanias, *Descriptions of Greece* 10.32.4; Plato, *Laws* 956b.
44 Phil Quick, "Resumptive Repetition—Introduction to a Universal Discourse Feature," Linguistika 14.26 (2007), 1. Resumptive repetition sometimes takes the form of what Stephen H. Levinsohn calls 'tail-head linkage'. This type of repetition 'in NT Greek involves the repetition, in an adverbial or participial clause at the beginning (the head) of the new sentence, of the main verb and other information that occurred in the previous sentence (the tail). This repetition may be thought of as a rhetorical device that slows the story down prior to the significant event or speech'. Levinsohn, *Discourse Features*, 197. See also Runge, *Discourse Grammar*, 163–177. *Life of Adam and Eve* 40.3 repeats the main verb (κηδεύω) from 40.2 in a participial clause in 40.3.

the second way that a preceding ὅτε-clause can function is to serve as a continuative adjunct that 'presents, on the basis of some earlier information, a new element in the story, which new element, in its turn, serves to locate in the, newly introduced, information of the main clause'.[45] Resumptive repetition with ὅτε δὲ occurs several times in the LXX and New Testament.[46]

Outside of Scripture, we find an example of resumptive repetition in the *Martyrdom of Polycarp* 13.2. After the crowd collects the necessary wood, Polycarp prepares for martyrdom by burning. The introductory phrase, 'But when [ὅτε δὲ] the pile was made ready' is background information prefacing Polycarp's preparatory actions for martyrdom. Another example of resumptive repetition can be found in *Acts of Thomas* 33.8. After a dragon uses its mouth to suck the venom out of a young man, we read 'And when [ὅτε δὲ] the dragon had drawn out all of the poison into himself, the young man, standing up, stood, ran, and fell at the feet of the apostle [Thomas]'.[47] The ὅτε δὲ clause in Galatians 2:11 is not an instance of resumptive repetition, although the one found in Galatians 2:12 could be classed as such.

Examples of Ὅτε δὲ with Implications for Galatians 2:11

My search identified two occurrences of non-chronological material introduced with ὅτε δὲ. The first appears in a speech by Aeschines entitled 'Against Timarchus' (345 BC). In this text, Aeschines reports that Arizelus, the father of Timarchus, dies, manages an estate, and dies again, in that order.

> There were three brothers in this family, Eupolemus, the gymnastic trainer, Arizelus, the father of the defendant, and Arignotus, who is still living, an old man now, and blind. Of these, Eupolemus was the first to die, before the estate had been

---

45 Rijksbaron, *Temporal and Causal Conjunctions*, 131.
46 See Tbt. 2:1; 8:1; Dan. 6:5; Matt. 9:25; Acts 27:39; 28:16.
47 Other examples of resumptive repetition appear in *Acts of Philip* 123.1; Appian, *Civil Wars*, 4.483; Athenaeus, *The Learned Banqueters*, 11.470d; XII.514c; Herodotus, *The Persian Wars*, 9.8; Hippocrates of Cos, *Epidemics* 2.5.85; Thucydides, *History of the Peloponnesians War*, 2.55.3; Xenon, *Hellenica*, 3.25; Xenophon, *Anabasis*, 1.8.8; 2.6.12.

> divided; next, Arizelus, the father of Timarchus. So long as [ὅτε δὲ] Arizelus lived, he managed the whole estate, because of the ill-health of Arignotus and the trouble with his eyes, and because Eupolemus was dead. By agreement with Arignotus he regularly gave him a sum of money for his support. Then Arizelus, the father of the defendant Timarchus, died also.[48]

In this instance of boundary marking, ὅτε δὲ introduces a rather lengthy aside that extends beyond the quotation above, but also appears amid clear contextual signalling that these events occurred while Arizelus was alive. The second case, appearing in the third-century AD work *Lives of Eminent Philosophers* by Diogenes Laertius, is similar:

> The same authority, Apollodorus, states that Eudoxus of Cnidos flourished about the 103rd Olympiad, and that he discovered the properties of curves. He died in his fifty-third year. When [ὅτε δὲ] he was in Egypt with Chonuphis of Heliopolis, the sacred bull Apis licked his cloak. From this the priests foretold that he would be famous but shortlived, so we are informed by Favorinus in his *Memorabilia*.[49]

According to this text, Eudoxus of Cnidos made a geometrical discovery, died, and—while still alive—had his cloak licked by a bull in Egypt. In this second instance of boundary marking, ὅτε δὲ introduces a lengthy narrative unit that extends beyond the quotation above, but an individual's death signals the non-chronological ordering of these events. Neither of these examples fits Runge's classification of 'side-bar-type comments'[50] since both are protracted narrative units. But, significantly, both examples offer clear contextual cues signalling their status as non-chronological material.

---

48 Aeschines, *Speeches*, 'Against Timarchus,' 101.
49 Laertius, *Lives of Eminent Philosophers* 8.90.
50 Runge, *Galatians*, 'Orienting the Events'.

Conclusion

My survey of 282 occurrences of ὅτε δὲ has found that only on rare occasion do these two words introduce a narrative segment in a different order than that in which it occurred. Furthermore, the two instances that I did identify, one predating and one postdating the composition of the New Testament, contain overt signals that the material was non-chronologically arranged. In Galatians 2:11, Paul used ὅτε δὲ to mark a discourse boundary, but he did not overtly signal to his readers that he was presenting chronologically rearranged narrative material. Therefore, we can confidently discount Lüdemann's proposal for explaining Peter's puzzling behavior at Antioch. Peter certainly could have misapplied or misunderstood the resolution made at Jerusalem, or he could have succumbed to peer pressure. Paul's account in Galatians indicates that Peter's conduct in Antioch was wrong. Jews and Gentiles could freely eat together.[51] The true gospel does not require Gentiles to live like Jews (Gal. 2:14).

---

51 For discussion on Jews and Gentiles eating together, see deSilva, *The Letter to the Galatians*, 198–203; Dunn, *The Epistle to the Galatians*, 117–22; Keener, *Galatians*, 152–155; Schreiner, *Galatians*, 141–42.

Bibliography

Augustine	'Letters of St. Augustin', in P. Schaff (ed.), *The Nicene and Post-Nicene Fathers: Series 1, Vol. 1* (14 vols; Peabody, MA: Hendrickson, 1994 [orig. 1886–1889]).
Bakker, E. J.	'Boundaries, Topics, and the Structure of Discourse: An Investigation of the Ancient Greek Particle Dé', *Studies in Language* 17.2 (1993), 275–311.
Betz, H. D.	*Galatians: A Commentary on Paul's Letter to the Churches in Galatia* (Hermeneia: A Critical and Historical Commentary on the Bible; Philadelphia: Fortress Press, 1979).
Bilabel, F.	*Veröffentlichungen aus den badischen Papyrus-Sammlungen* (vol. 4; Heidelberg. Göttingen: Hubert & Co., 1924).
Bird, M. F.	*An Anomalous Jew: Paul Among Jews, Greeks, and Romans* (Grand Rapids: Eerdmans, 2016).
Bligh, J.	*Galatians: A Discussion of St. Paul's Epistle* (Householder Commentaries 1; London: St. Paul Publications, 1970).
Burton, E. De W.	*A Critical and Exegetical Commentary on the Epistle to the Galatians* (International Critical Commentary; New York: C. Scribner's Sons, 1920).
deSilva, D. A.	*Galatians: A Handbook on the Greek Text* (Baylor Handbook on the Greek New Testament; Waco, TX: Baylor University Press, 2014).
Dunn, J. D. G.	*The Epistle to the Galatians* (Black's New Testament Commentary; Peabody, MA: Hendrickson, 1993).
Dupont, J.	'Pierre et Paul à Antioche et à Jérusalem', *Recherches de Science Religieuse* 45 (1957), 42–60.
Emde Boas, E. van, Rijksbaron, L. H. and de Bakker, M.	*The Cambridge Grammar of Classical Greek* (Cambridge: Cambridge University Press, 2019).
Féret, Henricus M.	*Pierre et Paul à Antioche et à Jérusalem: Le 'conflict' de deux apótres* (Paris: Cerf, 1955).
Fresch, C. J.	*Discourse Markers in Early Koine Greek: Cognitive-Functional Analysis and LXX Translation Technique* (Septuagint and Cognate Studies 77; Atlanta: SBL Press, 2023).
Giannakis, G. K. (ed.)	*Encyclopedia of Ancient Greek Language and Linguistics* (3 vols; Leiden: Brill: 2014).

Gibson, J. J.	*Peter Between Jerusalem and Antioch* (WUNT 345; Tübingen: Mohr Siebeck, 2013).
Hainz, J.	*Ekklesia* (Biblische Untersuchungen 9; Regensburg: Friedrich Pustet, 1972).
Keener, C. S.	*Galatians: A Commentary* (Grand Rapids: Baker Academic, 2019).
Köstenberger, A. J., Merkle, B. L. and Plummer, R. L.	*Going Deeper with New Testament Greek: An Intermediate Syntax of the New Testament* (Nashville: B&H Academic, 2016).
Lüdemann, G.	*Paul, Apostle to the Gentiles: Studies in Chronology* (tr. F. S. Jones; Philadelphia: Fortress Press, 1984).
Mehat, A.	"'Quand Kèphas vint à Antioch ...' que s'est-il passé Pierre et Paul?', *Lumière et Vie* 192 (1989), 29–43.
Moo, D. J.	*Galatians* (Baker Exegetical Commentary on the New Testament; Grand Rapids: Baker Academic, 2013).
Munck, J.	*Paul and the Salvation of Mankind* (tr. F. Clarke; Richmond, VA: John Knox, 1959).
Oepke, A.	*Der Brief des Paulus an die Galater* (rev. J. Rohde; Theological Handkommentar zum Nuen Testament 9, 3rd ed; Berlin: Evangelische Verlagsanstalt, 1973).
Oliver, J. H.	*The Sacred Gerousia* (The American Excavations in the Athenian Agora; Baltimore: J. H. Furst, 1941).
Porter, S. E.	*Idioms of the Greek New Testament* (2nd ed; Sheffield: Sheffield Academic, 1994).
Quick, Phil.	"Resumptive Repetition—Introduction to a Universal Discourse Feature." *Linguistika* 14.26 (2007).
Rahlfs, A. and Hanhart, R.	*Septuaginta: Editio Altera* (2nd rev. ed.; Stuttgart: Deutsche Bibelgesellschaft, 2006).
Reisner, R.	*Paul's Early Period: Chronology, Mission Strategy, Theology* (tr. D. Stott; Grand Rapids: Eerdmans, 1998).
Rijksbaron, A.	*Temporal and Causal Conjunctions in Ancient Greek: With Special Reference to the Use of* ἐπεί *and* ὡς *in Herodotus* (Amsterdam: Hakkert, 1976).
Robertson, A. T.	*A Grammar of the Greek New Testament in the Light of Historical Research* (Nashville: Broadman, 1934).

Runge, S. E.	*High Definition Commentary: Galatians* (ed. B. Ellis; High Definition Commentary Series; Bellingham, WA: Logos Bible Software, 2019).
Runge, S. E.	*Discourse Grammar of the Greek New Testament: A Practical Introduction for Teaching and Exegesis* (Peabody, MA: Hendrickson, 2010).
Schneckenburger, M.	*Ueber den Zweck der Apostelgeschichte: Zugleich eine Ergänzung der neureun Commentare* (Bern: Bruck und Verlag von Chr. Fischer, 1841).
Schoeps, H.-J.	*Jewish Christianity: Factional Disputes in the Early Church* (tr. D. R. A. Hare; Philadelphia: Fortress, 1969).
Siebenthal, H. von	*Ancient Greek Grammar for the Study of the New Testament* (Oxford: Peter Lang, 2019).
Silva, M.	'Text and Language in the Pauline Corpus: With Special Reference to the Use of Conjunctions in Galatians', *Neotestamentica* 24.2 (1990), 273–281.
Stählin, G.	*Die Apostelgeschichte* (NTD 5; Göttingen: Vandenhoeck & Ruprecht, 1978).
Wallace, D.	*Greek Grammar Beyond the Basics: An Exegetical Syntax of the New Testament with Scripture, Subject, and Greek Word Indexes* (Grand Rapids: Zondervan, 1997).
Wechsler, A.	*Geschichtsbild und Apostelstreit: Eine forschungsgeschichtliche und exegetische Studie über den antiochenischen Zwischenfall (Gal. 2,11–14)* (Berlin, Boston: De Gruyter, 1991).
Witherington III, B.	*Grace in Galatia: A Commentary on Paul's Letters to the Galatians* (Grand Rapids: Eerdmans, 1998).
Zahn, T.	*Der Brief des Paulus an die Galater* (Leipzig: Deicherische Verlagsbuchhandlung Nachf. Georg Böhme, 1907).

Appendix: List of Ancient Sources Considered

Septuagint
Ezra 5:12
Esther 1:5
Judith 5:18
Tobit 2:1,13; 8:1,3
Daniel 6:5
1 Maccabees 12:48 (*v.l.*)

New Testament
Matthew 9:25; 13:26,48 (*v.l.*), 21:34
Mark 8:20 (*v.l.*)
Luke 7:1 (*v.l.*); 15:30
Acts 8:12,39; 11:2; 12:6; 13:34 (*v.l.*); 21:5,35; 27:39; 28:16
Galatians 1:15; 2:11,12; 4:4
Titus 3:4
Jude 9 (*v.l.*)

Loeb Classical Library
Aelian: *Historical Miscellany*
Aelius Aristides: *Orations, Testimonia*
Aeschines: *Against Timarchus*
Anaxagoras: *Testimonia*
Appian: *Roman History*
Aratus: *Phaenomena*
Archippus: *Testimonia and Fragments*
Aristotle: *Metaphysics, Meteorologica, On Coming-to-Be and Passing-Away, On Plants, On Sophisticated Refutations, On the Soul, Parva Naturalia, Politics, Prior Analytics, Problems, Rhetoric to Alexander*
Athenaeus: *The Learned Banqueters*
Atomists
Basil: *Letters*
Clement of Alexandria: *Exhortation to the Greeks*
Demosthenes: *Orations*
Dinarchus: *Against Aristogiton*
Dio Cassius: *Roman History*
Diodorus Siculus: *The Library of History*
Diogenes Laertius: *Lives of Eminent Philosophers*
Dionysius of Halicarnassus: *Roman Antiquities*

Epictetus: *Discourses, Fragments*
Eusebius: *Ecclesiastical History*
Galen: *On Hygiene, On the Constitution of the Art of Medicine*
Gellius: *Attic Nights*
Herodotus: *The Persian Wars*
Hesiod: *Catalogue of Women*
Hippocrates of Cos: *Diseases, Diseases of Women, Epidemics, Joints, Precepts, The Sacred Disease*
Homer: *Iliad*
Isocrates: *Discourses*
John of Damascene: *Barlaam and Ioasaph*
Josephus: *Jewish Antiquities*
Longinus: *On the Sublime*
Longus: *The Story of Daphnis and Chloe*
Lucian: *Dialogues of the Courtesans, Dialogues of the Gods, The Passing of Peregrinus*
Melissus: *Testimonia*
Parthenius of Nicaea: *Sufferings in Love*
Pausanias: *Descriptions of Greece*
Philo: *Allegorical Interpretation of Genesis 2, 3, On the Decalogue, On the Eternity of the World, Who Is the Heir of Divine Things*
Philostratus of Athens: *The Life of Allonius of Tyana, Lives of the Sophists*
Philostratus the Elder: *Letters*
Philoxenus of Leucas: *Fragments*
Plato: *Critias, Laws, Mathematical Works, Theatetus*
Plotinus: *Enneads, Moralia*
Polybius: *The Histories*
Ptolemy: *Tetrabiblos*
Quintus Smyrnaeus: *Posthomerica*
Select Papyri: *Official Documents, Private Affairs*
Sextus Empiricus: *Against the Ethicists, Against the Physicists*
The Apostolic Fathers: *The Epistle of Barnabas, The Martyrdom of Polycarp*
The Greek Anthology
Theophrastus: De Causis Plantarum, Enquiry into Plants
Thucydides: History of the Peloponnesian War
Xenophon of Athens: Anabasis, Cyropaedia, Hellenica, On Hunting

Papyri and Inscriptions
IKret 3.4.9
IMagnMai 160
P.Bad.4.48

P.Cair.Zen.2.59251
P.Neph.3
Panamara 226

Other Sources
Acts of Philip 28.7; 61:1; 123.1; 126.2
Acts of Thomas 17.1; 20:1; 22:4; 33.8; 41:1
Letter of Aristeas 187
Life of Adam and Eve 21.2; 33.3; 40.3
Testaments of the Twelve Patriarchs 12.10

CHAPTER 16

'As Many as will Conform to this Rule' (Galatians 6:16): Missionary Hospitality, Table Fellowship, and the Occasion of Galatians

Lionel J. Windsor

1. What was going on in Galatia?

The occasion of Galatians is critical for the letter's interpretation, yet it is fiercely debated. Some things are clear. Certain 'agitators' or 'disturbers' (1:7; 5:10,12) are causing the Gentile Galatian believers to follow calendrical observances (4:10) and to want to be 'under the law' (4:21), some even to the point of being circumcised (5:2–3). Paul regards this situation as disastrous because it means the Galatians are turning away from their divine calling, grace, the gospel, Christ, the Spirit, freedom, and truth (1:6–7; 3:3; 5:1,4,7–8) to embrace a rival gospel (1:6–9). The Galatians are also being factious (5:15,26). The key debates surround the precise nature of the agitators' identity and their preaching.

On the question of the agitators' *identity*, there are sound reasons to adopt the majority position that they were Jesus-following Jewish preachers, ostensibly associated with Jerusalem, whom Paul regarded as rival missionaries.[1]

Regarding the agitators' *preaching*, the issues are more debatable. While most investigations focus on the *contents* of the rival gospel the agitators preached,[2] far less attention has been paid to their associated missionary *activity* amongst the Galatians.[3] Nevertheless, missionary activity is a prominent theme in Galatians. Missionary actions involving table fellowship were fundamental to Paul's conflict with Peter and the other Jews in Antioch (2:11–14).[4] Paul's primary accusation was not that they were verbally propagating a rival *message*, but that they were *acting* with 'hypocrisy' (2:13) and 'not walking straight (ὀρθοποδοῦσιν) by the truth of the gospel' (2:14). Furthermore, at several points, Paul presents his own missionary activities and motivations as a contrast to Peter's and the agitators' activities and motivations (compare 1:10 with 2:12; 4:12 with 4:17; 5:11 with 6:12; cf. 2 Cor. 10–12; Phil. 1:15–18).[5] This focus on motivations and actions is particularly prominent in the introduction (1:6–10) and conclusion (6:11–16) of the letter.[6] This suggests missionary activity is more significant for understanding the letter's occasion than is often assumed.

In view of these observations, this essay aims to examine Paul's description of the *concrete social activities* of the agitators as they engaged in their missionary endeavours in Galatia. Two interrelated first-century phenomena are particularly germane to this question: 1) Jewish concerns about accommodation in table fellowship and 2) early Christian concerns about hospitality for travelling missionaries. It will be seen

---

1 Keener, *Galatians*, 13–15; deSilva, *Galatians*, 10; cf. Barclay, 'Mirror-Reading', here 380–81. The terms εὐαγγέλιον and εὐαγγελίζω (1:6–9) imply that the agitators were Jesus-following preachers; see Martyn, 'Law-Observant Mission', here 353; *pace* Nanos, *Irony*, whose understanding of these terms as ironic has not been convincing to the majority of interpreters. The verb εὐαγγελίζω also implies that they were missionaries from outside the Galatian community (cf. 1:11,16,23; 4:13–14; Rom. 10:15; 15:20; 1 Cor. 1:17; 2 Cor. 10:16; Eph. 2:17); see Keener, *Galatians*, 14; *pace* Hardin, *Imperial Cult*, 85–147. The present tense 'those who are circumcised' (οἱ περιτεμνόμενοι) (6:13) is most likely customary, as elsewhere (cf. Josephus, *Ag. Ap.* 1.169–71; 2.141–42; Herodotus, *Hist.* 2.104; Justin, *Dial.* 123.1), which implies that they were Jewish; see Martin, *Regression*, 40–46; *pace* Munck, *Paul*, 87–134. While the agitators were *ostensibly* associated with Jerusalem (4:25), they were not necessarily endorsed by the Jerusalem apostolic community (2:9; cf. Acts 15:1,24); see Keener, *Galatians*, 14–15.
2 For a classic clarification of the methodological issues see Barclay, 'Mirror-Reading.'
3 Hardin, *Imperial Cult*, 100.
4 Keener, *Galatians*, 92.
5 Hardin, 'Without a Mirror', here 296–98; cf. Hardin, *Imperial Cult*, 97–101.
6 Smit, 'Deliberative Speech', 46, 56.

that these two concerns appear explicitly at various places in the letter. It will be argued that they are especially prominent in the conclusion (6:11–16). The essay will, accordingly, include a detailed re-reading of the conclusion, including a re-assessment of the significance of the parallel between 'as many as (ὅσοι) want to make a good showing in the flesh' (6:12) and 'as many as (ὅσοι) will conform to this rule' (6:16).

2. Table Fellowship and Hospitality for Missionaries in the First Century

2.1 Table Fellowship

In the ancient Mediterranean world, table fellowship was an important means of defining group identity by including insiders and excluding outsiders.[7] This was undoubtedly true for Jewish communities.[8] Table fellowship practices varied among Jewish groups, leading to various concerns about accommodation when members of different Jewish groups dined together.[9] These concerns extended to discussions about accommodation when dining with Gentiles.[10] Some Jews forbade eating with Gentiles altogether (e.g., Jub. 22:16; Acts 10:28). Others generally avoided eating with Gentiles, mainly to avoid food contaminated by idolatry or prohibited by biblical dietary laws (e.g., Add. Esth. 14:17c; Tob. 1:10–12). Nevertheless, some Jews were willing to eat with Gentiles under certain circumstances (e.g., Jdt. 12:17–20).

The Letter of Aristeas is especially apposite since it depicts respected Jewish teachers who, while deeply conscious of their distinctiveness (Let. Aris. 139, 142), are nevertheless prepared to become guests of Gentiles at a lavish banquet, prepared in line with Torah regulations, so they can share the riches of the Torah's wisdom with them (Let. Aris. 181–86). While the account is probably fictional, it indicates a broader association between table fellowship and instances of 'Jewish outreach' to Gentiles (cf. 1 Cor. 9:19–23).[11]

---

7 Referring to ancient associations, Kloppenborg refers to this phenomenon as 'segregative commensality'; see Kloppenborg, *Christ's Associations*, 146–51.
8 Magness, *Jewish Daily Life*, 77–84; cf. Dunn, 'Incident', here 207–19.
9 Rudolph, *A Jew to the Jews*, 116–25; cf. Dunn, 'Incident', 209–12.
10 Rudolph, *A Jew to the Jews*, 125–30.
11 Rudolph, 130–42.

2.2 Hospitality for Missionaries

Hospitality for 'travelers on official and private business' was a common means for cementing friendship and inter-group ties in the ancient Roman Empire.[12] In early Christian sources, concerns about hospitality for missionaries appear frequently. Furthermore, these concerns are often associated with a greeting of 'peace'/*shalom*.

In Synoptic accounts of Jesus sending out the Twelve or Seventy-two, Jesus instructs them to rely on the hospitality of those they encounter (Matt. 10:9–15; Luke 10:4–8). These missionaries should give a greeting of 'peace'/*shalom* to households that receive them. However, this *shalom* is conditional upon whether the messenger and message are received worthily:

> Whatever house you enter, first say, 'Peace/shalom to this house (εἰρήνη τῷ οἴκῳ τούτῳ).' And if a person of peace is there, your peace will rest upon them (ἐπαναπαήσεται ἐπ' αὐτὸν ἡ εἰρήνη ὑμῶν). But if not, it will return upon you (ἐφ' ὑμᾶς). (Luke 10:5–6; cf. Matt. 10:12–14)

While 'peace'/*shalom* was a stereotypical Jewish greeting (cf., e.g., Judg. 19:20), it takes on further eschatological overtones in the Synoptic accounts.[13] This is because those who provide hospitality for these missionaries are effectively receiving the Lord Jesus himself, and so will receive an eschatological reward; conversely, those who do not provide hospitality will receive eschatological punishment (Matt. 10:40–42; Luke 10:10–12,16; cf. Mark 9:41). The same principles apply to those from 'all the nations' who receive Jesus' disciples (Matt. 25:31–46, quoting v.32).

Paul is also concerned with hospitality for travelling missionaries. He refers to a key saying from 'the Lord' contained in the aforementioned Synoptic accounts as a warrant for providing materially for travelling missionaries: 'the worker deserves their food/wages' (Matt. 10:10; Luke 10:7; referred to in 1 Cor. 9:14; cf. 1 Tim. 5:18). Paul's reference in Romans to 'hospitality' (φιλοξενίαν) (Rom. 12:13) is also likely to have referred to practices including 'welcoming and economically supporting

---

12 Nicols, '*Hospitium*' quoting 322.
13 Nolland, *Luke 9:21–18:34*, 552.

itinerant missionaries' (cf. Rom. 15:24; Phlm. 22).[14] Paul also uses a formulation involving 'peace' in his instructions for the Corinthians to provide hospitality and support for Timothy: 'send him on his way in peace (ἐν εἰρήνῃ)' (1 Cor. 16:11).

In Acts, Peter's evangelism of the Gentile Cornelius occurs in the context of accepting hospitality amid concerns over table fellowship (Acts 10:17–11:18). Luke also highlights many people who provide lodging for Paul and his associated missionary workers, often naming them individually (Acts 16:14–15,33–34; 17:7; 18:2–3; 21:7–8,16; 27:3; 28:7).[15] When travelling envoys from Jerusalem, including Paul, deliver the apostolic decree that circumcision is not required for Gentile believers, then enjoy warm fellowship in Antioch, several of them are 'sent away with peace/*shalom* (μετ' εἰρήνης) from the brothers/sisters to those who had sent them' (Acts 15:33).

While the Synoptic accounts are primarily concerned with the need for missionaries to exercise discrimination in deciding whom they receive hospitality *from*, other early Christian sources call on believers to exercise discrimination in deciding which missionaries they provide hospitality *for*. The letters of John, for example, commend hospitality and support extended to true missionaries (3 John 5–8) but warn against providing hospitality for false missionaries; such hospitality is signalled by a 'greeting' (χαίρειν) (2 John 10–11)—a Greek equivalent of the Semitic 'peace'/*shalom*.

Didache 11 also provides detailed rules about receiving travelling apostles and prophets, probably stemming from Jewish traditions concerning travelling *sheluhim*.[16] Hospitality for such missionaries is conditional not just on the content of their teaching (Did. 11.1–2) but on their moral conduct when receiving hospitality and other economic benefits (Did. 11.3–12). These regulations for receiving missionaries are designated 'the rule of the gospel' (τὸ δόγμα τοῦ εὐαγγελίου) (Did. 11.3). Missionary conduct in table fellowship as a guest, including the avoidance of hypocrisy, is a particular concern:

---

14 Oakes, 'Economic Approaches', 81–83, quoting 82; Meeks, *Christians*, 109–10; cf. Ricker, *Ancient Letters*, 88.
15 Stanton, 'Accommodation'.
16 van de Sandt and Flusser, *Didache*, 353–55.

And every prophet who sets limits at table (ὁρίζων τράπεζαν)[17] in the Spirit will not eat from it; if it is otherwise, they are a false prophet. So, every prophet who teaches the truth but does not practise what they teach is a false prophet. (Did. 11.9–10)

3. Table Fellowship and Hospitality for Missionaries in the Argument of Galatians

Concerns about accommodation in table fellowship and hospitality for missionaries arise in several prominent places in Galatians.

3.1 Galatians 2:7–16

In 2:7–10, missionary concerns come directly into focus. Paul describes himself as a missionary 'entrusted with the [preaching of the] gospel to the uncircumcision' and Peter as a missionary 'to the circumcision' (2:7).[18] He groups Peter with James and John as authority figures in Jerusalem (2:9; cf. 1:18–19). He notes that these individuals 'gave me the right hand of fellowship', with reference to their respective spheres of missionary activity (2:9); the 'right hand' was a regular token of guest-friendship in the ancient Empire (e.g., Tacitus, *Hist.* 1.54; 2.8).[19]

In 2:11–14, Paul recounts Peter's missionary activities in Antioch. Peter had previously accepted hospitality as a missionary guest of Gentiles and so had engaged in table fellowship (συνεσθίω) with them (2:12a; cf. Acts 11:3). However, he had subsequently withdrawn, 'fearing those from the circumcision' (2:12b), leading other Jews to do the same (2:13). Peter's fear had most likely arisen from the prospect of persecution from zealous Jews. Paul himself had once 'persecuted' (ἐδίωκον) (1:13) the church of God as a 'zealot' (ζηλωτής) for his

---

[17] Commentators regard the Greek phrase as being 'not entirely clear'; see Niederwimmer, *Didache*, 179. However, the idea of expressing scruples over table fellowship or food provides a straightforward reading of the phrase and fits the context well.
[18] Here taking εὐαγγέλιον as a verbal noun and the genitives τῆς ἀκροβυστίας and τῆς περιτομῆς as objective; see Schreiner, *Galatians*, 128.
[19] Nicols, '*Hospitium*', 328–29.

ancestral traditions (1:14; cf. 4:17–18).[20] Following his encounter with Christ, however, Paul's perspective had changed so radically that he felt it necessary to *condemn* Peter for his actions in withdrawing. The problem, as Paul described it, was not simply Peter's cowardly motivations. Peter's actions were 'compel[ling] the Gentiles to Judaise' (τὰ ἔθνη ἀναγκάζεις ἰουδαΐζειν) (2:14).

The word 'compel' (ἀναγκάζω) here most likely refers to the concrete application of social pressure. While the Gentile Jesus-followers in Galatia would formerly have relied on social networks associated with pagan associations, they now would have had a new reliance on this Jewish-centred network, the *ekklēsiai* (cf. 1:2,13,22).[21] Under these circumstances, when a respected Jewish missionary guest such as Peter withdrew from table fellowship on the basis of his hosts' lack of conformity to Jewish customs, the hosts would have felt a strong social compulsion to adopt such customs, i.e., 'to Judaise' (ἰουδαΐζειν).[22]

For Paul, these issues of table fellowship are not merely a matter of social conformity; they have a deep eschatological significance. Paul rebuked Peter for not paying due regard to justification by faith in Christ (2:15–16), which he regards as an eschatological issue (2:17–21; cf. 1:3–4; 5:4–5).[23] This eschatological framing of table fellowship is probably influenced by the apocalyptic motif of the 'Messianic banquet'.[24] Isaiah 25:6–8 (cf. Isa. 55:1–5) describes a great feast 'for all peoples' and 'all nations' on 'this mountain' (the eschatological Zion; cf. Gal. 4:26) associated with the end of death. In the Gospels, expectations of the Messianic banquet also involve the ingathering of the nations to share table fellowship with the patriarchs (Matt. 8:11–12; Luke 13:28–29). While the Messianic banquet was typically regarded as a future event (1 En. 62:12–14; 2 Bar. 29), concrete communal meals could be idealised as Messianic banquets (e.g., 1QSa ii.11–22). This explains why Paul regards table fellowship between Jews and Gentiles as so eschatologically significant. It is not merely a matter of custom but an expression

---

20 This is not necessarily a reference to the Zealot party. Such zeal was likely a general phenomenon patterned on that of Phinehas (Num. 25:11,13) and the Maccabean revolts (1 Macc. 2:24,26,27,50,54); see Dunn, 'Incident', 204–7, 227–29; Gil Arbiol, 'Ioudaismos and Ioudaizō'.
21 cf. Korner, *Ekklēsia*, 213–58.
22 Cf. de Silva, *Galatians*, 199; Dunn, 'Incident', 225–30.
23 Schreiber, 'Politische Sprache', 386–87.
24 Smith, 'Messianic Banquet'.

of the new creation having come in Christ. For Paul, therefore, making distinctions in table fellowship based on circumcised status is not merely socially inappropriate; it effectively denies the gospel itself.

By using the phrase 'compel to Judaise' (ἀναγκάζεις ἰουδαΐζειν) (2:14), Paul stresses a key point of comparison between the situations in Jerusalem, Antioch and Galatia.[25] In Jerusalem, Titus was not 'compelled to be circumcised' (ἠναγκάσθη περιτμηθῆναι) (2:3). In Antioch, Peter was 'compelling' the Gentiles 'to Judaise' (ἀναγκάζεις ἰουδαΐζειν) (2:14). In Galatia, the agitators are 'compelling you to be circumcised' (ἀναγκάζουσιν ὑμᾶς περιτέμνεσθαι) (6:12). Although Judaising and being circumcised are not strictly synonymous, the ideas are closely related.[26] To 'Judaise' means to adopt Jewish customs; to be circumcised represents its most extreme form (Josephus, *J.W.* 2.454; cf. Esth 8:17 LXX). In Paul's mind, therefore, the prior situation in Antioch—involving missionary hospitality and table fellowship—has strong parallels with the present situation in Galatia.

3.2 *Galatians 4:12–20*

In 4:12–20, issues involving table fellowship and hospitality for missionaries return to prominence. Paul here recalls the history of his own missionary activities among the Galatians. His entreaty, 'become as I am, for I also became as you were' (4:12), most likely refers to his willingness as a Jewish missionary to share table fellowship with the Gentile Galatians (cf. 1 Cor. 9:20–22).[27] He reminds them that their hospitality was extraordinary. Despite the difficulty and weakness of his missionary circumstances (4:13), they had 'received' him 'as an angel of God' (4:14; cf. Heb. 13:2). In doing so, they had pronounced a 'blessing' (μακαρισμός) on him (4:15; cf. Josephus, *Life* 273).[28] Indeed, they were willing to go to such extraordinary lengths as gouging out their own eyes and giving them to him—a hyperbolic reference to tokens of hospitality (4:15).[29]

---

25 Gil Arbiol, 'Ioudaismos and Ioudaizō', 232–33.
26 Dunn, 'Incident', 220–21; *pace* Esler, 'Incident at Antioch', here 278.
27 Keener, *Galatians*, 199.
28 Here reading 'your blessing' (ὁ μακαρισμὸς ὑμῶν) as transitive with a subjective genitive; see deSilva, *Galatians*, 381–82.
29 Cf. Nicols, '*Hospitium*', 328.

In describing this positive history of hospitality and fellowship, Paul depicts himself as a direct contrast to the agitators who are deliberately withdrawing fellowship: 'They want to exclude (ἐκκλεῖσαι) you so that you might be devoted to (ζηλοῦτε) them' (4:17). There is a strong parallel between this phrase and Paul's description of the Antioch incident: Peter 'withdrew and separated himself' (ὑπέστελλεν καὶ ἀφώριζεν ἑαυτόν) in table fellowship from Gentiles (2:12) and thereby 'compelled the Gentiles to Judaise' (2:14). This parallel implies that the agitators in Galatia are Jewish missionaries who are exercising scruples about accommodation in table fellowship with uncircumcised Gentiles, thereby applying social pressure for them to adopt stricter Jewish customs.[30]

3.3 Galatians 5:2–12

In 5:2–12, Paul again presents himself as a foil to the agitators. Many of the features previously identified in relation to table fellowship and hospitality reappear at this point. The Gentiles are under pressure to adopt Jewish customs to the point of being circumcised (5:3; cf. 2:3; 2:14). Paul uses eschatological themes—justification, the Spirit, and the hope of righteousness (5:4–5)—to critique attempts to make distinctions on the basis of circumcision (5:6; cf. 2:11–3:14). He cites his own exemplary reversal from preaching circumcision—which is like the agitators—to being willing to face persecution for the sake of the cross of Christ—which is a contrast to the agitators (5:11; cf. 1:10–24).[31]

3.4 Galatians 6:6–10

In the final exhortatory section before his conclusion, Paul returns to the topic of sharing material benefits with teachers. Just as the Galatians had provided hospitality for Paul when he came to them as a missionary (cf. 4:13–15), so now he generalises the principle: 'Let the one who is instructed in the word share with the one who instructs in all good things' (6:6; cf. 1 Cor. 9:14; Matt. 10:10; Luke 10:7).[32] In light of this

---

30 Cf. Keener, *Galatians*, 208.
31 Hardin, 'Circumcision'; cf. Hardin, 'Without a Mirror', 297.
32 Keener, *Galatians*, 274.

parallel, the following description about eschatological punishment and reward based on present activity in relation to the 'flesh' and the 'spirit' (Gal. 6:7–10) may also be particularly applicable to the issue of hospitality for travelling missionaries, as in the Synoptic accounts (cf. Matt. 10:40–42; Luke 10:10–12).

4. Table Fellowship and Hospitality for Missionaries in the Conclusion (Gal. 6:11–16)

4.1 A return to the concerns of the introduction

In 6:11, Paul marks a clear topical shift by stating that he is writing with his own hand. It soon becomes clear that the topical shift involves a return to the focus of the introduction: the contrast between Paul's authenticity and authority as an apostle and that of the rival missionaries (cf. 1:8–9). This suggests that Paul's purpose in his conclusion is not simply to summarise the theology he has outlined in the letter. Instead, his purpose is to *use* this theology for the practical purpose of equipping the Galatians to discriminate among travelling missionaries. In light of the prominence of Paul's concerns for table fellowship and hospitality for missionaries that we have outlined above, it is worth carefully re-reading this concluding section.

4.2 A Direct Contrast between the Agitators and Paul (6:12–14)

Paul's description of the agitators begins with the comparative correlative pronoun 'as many as' (ὅσοι) (6:12). This identifies the agitators as a subset of a larger group of all missionary teachers who have come (or may come) to the Galatians, including Paul (cf. 4:12–20). Thus, ὅσοι deliberately marks out the agitators as *specific missionaries*.

The agitators 'want to make a good showing in the flesh'. The term 'flesh' (σάρξ) has functioned so far in Galatians as a contrast to the eschatological 'spirit' (πνεῦμα) (cf. 3:3; 4:29; 5:16–17,24–25; 6:8). By using this term, Paul deliberately focuses attention on missionaries who do not share his eschatological perspective.

These missionaries 'are compelling you to be circumcised' (ἀναγκάζουσιν ὑμᾶς περιτέμνεσθαι) (6:12). Paul's re-use of this formula (cf. 2:3,14) implies that the agitators, like Peter in Antioch, were exercising scruples about accommodation in table fellowship based on the circumcised status of the Galatian Gentiles (cf. 4:17), resulting in the Galatian Gentiles experiencing intense social pressure to adopt Jewish customs, even to the extent of being circumcised.

Paul believes these scruples were motivated by the Jewish missionaries' fear of being persecuted (6:12). This strengthens the parallel with Peter's withdrawal from table fellowship out of fear of 'those from the circumcision' (2:12).[33] Once again, Paul depicts the agitators' missionary motivations as a foil to his own. The agitators wish to avoid being persecuted for 'the cross of Christ' (6:12), a phrase that represents the eschatological inbreaking of the new order into the old (cf. 2:19).[34] Paul, by contrast, has an entirely new eschatological perspective; he has therefore been transformed from a persecutor (1:13) into a persecuted missionary (1:23; 4:29; 5:11).

In 6:13–14, Paul pushes the contrast between his missionary motives and that of his rivals even further. The agitators' motivation does not stem from a noble ideal of 'guarding the law' (νόμον φυλάσσουσιν) (cf. Acts 21:24).[35] Instead, they want to 'boast in your flesh' (6:13). The terminology of 'boasting' is commonly used by Paul to refer to expressions of pride in missionary endeavours and their results.[36] Paul here contrasts his rival missionaries' 'flesh'-based boast in their missionary endeavours with his own eschatologically-shaped boast 'in the cross of Jesus Christ our Lord, by which the world has been crucified to me, and I to the world' (6:14).

4.3 An Eschatological Principle of Missionary Table Fellowship (6:15)

Since the topic and flow of the discourse up to this point have concerned a strong contrast between the legitimacy of Paul's and the agitators' *missionary activities*, the same topic is a priori likely to lie behind

---

33 Keener, 15–18, 283–84.
34 Schreiber, 'Politische Sprache', 386–87.
35 Du Toit, 'Galatians 6:13'; Hardin, *Imperial Cult*, 89–90.
36 This applies both to Paul's own missionary endeavours (cf. Rom. 15:17; 1 Cor. 9:15–16; 15:31; 2 Cor. 1:12,14; 7:4; 8:24; 9:2–3; 10:8,13,15–17; 11:10; Phil. 2:16; 1 Thess. 2:19) and also to those of his rivals (2 Cor. 5:12; 11:12)

the following statement: 'For neither circumcision nor uncircumcision is anything, but new creation' (6:15). As we have already seen, Paul regards missionary scruples in table fellowship based on circumcised status as a profoundly eschatological issue (2:11–16; 5:2–12). Paul's missionary rivals exercise such scruples; Paul's 'new creation' perspective means that he regards such scruples as illegitimate.

In this understanding, Paul does not primarily intend his formula in 6:15 as a rule to assist the Galatians in testing their *own* theological compliance. While the formula is *based on* and *consistent with* the theology Paul has outlined in Galatians (see esp. 5:5–6), the immediate function of the formula at *this point* in the letter is to inform the Galatians' reception of Jewish missionaries. When any Jewish missionaries come to them, Paul wants the Galatians to observe their practices in table fellowship. Do they (like Paul) practise table fellowship in light of the reality of the new creation in Christ, which means disregarding circumcised status? Or do they (like Peter did) exercise scruples about circumcised status, thus demonstrating they are not taking the gospel seriously in their concrete relationships?

4.4 'As Many As': Delimiting Certain Kinds of Jewish Missionary (6:16)

With this analysis of the discourse topic in mind, we can now examine the details of 6:16:

καὶ ὅσοι τῷ κανόνι τούτῳ στοιχήσουσιν, εἰρήνη ἐπ' αὐτοὺς καὶ ἔλεος καὶ ἐπὶ τὸν Ἰσραὴλ τοῦ θεοῦ. (Gal. 6:16)

The first feature to notice is the return of the comparative correlative pronoun 'as many as' (ὅσοι). A short while earlier, Paul had used this pronoun to identify the agitators among the larger group of Jewish missionaries who come (or may come) to the Galatians (6:12). By re-using the pronoun, Paul is likely again identifying the complementary group: those Jewish missionaries who, unlike the agitators but like himself, *are* driven by an eschatological perspective in their table fellowship practices.

In this understanding, Paul is not using the phrase 'as many as will conform to this rule' (ὅσοι τῷ κανόνι τούτῳ στοιχήσουσιν) to delimit those members of the *Galatian community* who subscribe to Paul's theology. This is a pervasive assumption among interpreters—yet it is an assumption that is almost entirely unexplored.[37] Given the topic and focus of the discourse so far, and the re-use of ὅσοι (cf. 6:12), it is far more likely that Paul intends the phrase to delimit those *Jewish missionaries* who follow his example in practising eschatological table fellowship.[38] As we will now see, this interpretation is borne out by the rest of the verse.

4.5 Conforming to the Rule: A Principle of Missionary Table Fellowship

The term 'rule' or 'norm' (κανών) typically refers to a standard of legitimacy in 'the most varied spheres of life'.[39] Although it *can* be used in a philosophical sense as a standard for truth or doctrine, it can also be used in a more concrete legal sense as a standard for behaviour. Josephus uses it in a discussion of Jewish rules for diet and association, stating that Moses set the Torah as a 'boundary and rule' (ὅρον ... καὶ κανόνα) for Jewish people in relation to their dietary laws, rules of association, and days of rest (*Ag. Ap.* 2.174). At Qumran, regulations for the ordering of Messianic banquets (1QSa ii.11–22) were designated with the term 'rule'/'ruling principle' (סרד) (1QSa i.1).[40] This use of the term κανών and equivalents in relation to meals and rules of association fits with the issues of table fellowship that we have seen are relevant in Galatians. Just as believers' ethical life should conform to the eschatological Spirit (πνεύματι ... στοιχῶμεν) (5:25), so any missionaries who come to the Galatians should conform to Paul's eschatologically-oriented 'rule' of association (6:16; cf. Did. 11.3).[41]

---

37 This is because the famous interpretive crux in the second half of the verse ('the Israel of God') dominates the discussion; see, e.g., Beale, 'Israel of God', 204; Betz, *Galatians*, 321; Dahl, 'Der Name Israel', 168; De Boer, *Galatians*, 403–4; deSilva, *Galatians*, 511–12; Du Toit, *Israel*, 338–39; Eastman, 'Israel', 372; Filtvedt, 'God's Israel', 135; Keener, *Galatians*, 287; Martyn, *Galatians*, 576; Mussner, *Galaterbrief*, 415–16; Schreiner, *Galatians*, 380–81; Schrenk, 'Israel Gottes', 84–85; Williams, *Galatians*, 176.
38 I am aware of only one prior attempt to defend something like the case presented here: Robinson, 'Distinction'; cf. Windsor, *Vocation of Israel*, 55–61, where I briefly raise the idea.
39 Beyer, 'Κανών' quoting 597.
40 Cf. Smith, 'Messianic Banquet', 71.
41 Hence Paul's ethical and missionary concerns are connected but not identical; *pace* Betz, *Galatians*, 321.

4.6 The Greeting of Peace: Hospitality for Missionaries

Paul's phrase 'peace [be] upon them' (εἰρήνη ἐπ' αὐτούς) (6:16) is usually understood as an epistolary blessing given by Paul to those among his recipients who conform to his theology.[42] However, several features of this phrase in its context indicate that it is better understood as Paul's desire for the Galatians to extend a concrete blessing of hospitality to missionaries, similar to the blessing of hospitality they had extended to Paul when he came to them (cf. 4:14–15).

The third person pronoun 'them' (αὐτούς) is correlated with 'as many as' (ὅσοι), which, as we have seen, is not marking out a subset from *among* the Galatians, but a subset of Jewish missionary preachers who have come *to* the Galatians (cf. 6:12). In the rest of the letter, Paul consistently uses the second person 'you' to refer to his recipients (1:3,6–9,11,13,20; 2:5; 3:2–5,7–8,26–29; 4:6–21,28; 5:1–2,4,7,10,12–18,21; 6:12,7,11–13,18), and the third person to refer to the agitators (1:7,9; 3:1; 4:17; 5:7–8,10,12). Therefore, if Paul had wanted to refer to the Galatians unambiguously, he could have said, 'If *you* conform to this rule, peace be upon *you*.' His use of the third person instead implies that he is referring to the agitators rather than the Galatians.[43]

Paul's use of the term 'peace' (εἰρήνη) is consistent with the use of other such 'peace'/*shalom*-greetings in descriptions of providing hospitality for travelling missionaries as we have seen above (Matt. 10:12–13; Luke 10:5–6; Acts 15:33; 1 Cor. 16:11; cf. χαίρειν in 2 John 10–11). Hence Paul's statement, 'As many as will conform to this rule, peace upon them' (6:16a), is best understood as an instruction for the Galatians to extend greetings (with associated hospitality) only to those travelling missionaries who conform to Paul's eschatological principle for table fellowship (6:15). It thereby acts as a counterpoint to the 'curse' (ἀνάθεμα) that Paul has previously pronounced on rival missionaries (1:8–9).[44] Its meaning can be understood thus: 'And as many [of the Jewish missionaries] as will conform to this rule [of table fellowship], [let your greeting of] peace [be] upon them' (καὶ ὅσοι τῷ κανόνι τούτῳ στοιχήσουσιν, εἰρήνη ἐπ' αὐτούς).

---

42 See references in n.37; cf. Doering, *Letters*, 406–15, 422–27, 450–52.
43 *Pace* De Boer, *Galatians*, 403.
44 Cf. Doering, *Letters*, 426.

4.7 Mercy Also upon the Israel of God: Paul's Broader Concerns

This understanding has further implications for debates around the meaning of the phrase 'the Israel of God' (τὸν Ἰσραὴλ τοῦ θεοῦ) (6:16b). The scholarship on this interpretive crux is vast.[45] A key issue is whether 'Israel' is used here in a way that includes Gentile Jesus-followers.[46] Discussions proceed on the almost universal assumption that 'as many as will conform to this rule' refers primarily to Gentile believers in Galatia. However, if the alternative analysis above is correct—i.e., if 'as many as will conform to this rule' is a reference to Jewish missionaries who practice a properly eschatological approach to table fellowship with Gentiles—then a hitherto unexplored possibility arises for understanding Paul's reference to 'the Israel of God'.

After Paul gives his rule for accepting missionaries purportedly from Jerusalem (6:16a), it is natural that his thoughts would progress to the eschatological destiny of the wider group these Jewish missionaries represent: God's Israel. Hence, Paul naturally wishes 'mercy' upon this broader entity (6:16b). An expansive translation would be:

> καὶ ὅσοι τῷ κανόνι τούτῳ στοιχήσουσιν, εἰρήνη ἐπ' αὐτούς καὶ ἔλεος καὶ ἐπὶ τὸν Ἰσραὴλ τοῦ θεοῦ. (Gal. 6:16)
>
> and as many [of the Jewish missionaries] as will conform to this rule [of table fellowship], [let your greeting of] peace [be] upon them, and [may] mercy also [be] upon the Israel of God (Gal. 6:16).

In this interpretation, the Greek text reads smoothly and consistently. Paul first uses the term 'peace' (εἰρήνη) to signal that concrete greetings and hospitality should be extended to travelling Jewish missionaries who come to Galatia and conform to his principle of eschatological table fellowship (6:16a). Then, he uses the term 'mercy' (ἔλεος) to signal a connected ('and', καί) but more expansive ('also', καί) idea: an eschatological wish for God's mercy on the broader group these Jewish

---

45 See references in n.37.
46 Filtvedt, 'God's Israel', 123–24.

missionaries represent, namely, 'the Israel of God'.[47]

In this understanding, Paul's introduction of the term 'Israel' at this point in Galatians is not a confusing development that his readers would have found difficult to grasp. We do not need to account for why Paul suddenly uses 'Israel' in a non-standard way to refer to the church or (alternatively) why he suddenly introduces the concept of a separate entity called 'Israel' into a discussion about Galatian Jesus followers.[48] Instead, in this interpretation, Paul's more expansive concern for the group named 'Israel' arises naturally from his more immediate concerns surrounding table fellowship and hospitality between Gentile Jesus followers in Galatia and Jewish missionaries from Jerusalem. 'Israel' is a term that signals the eschatological hope for the restoration of the whole people of God (cf. Rom. 9–11).[49] Paul first expresses his immediate concerns about the need for the Galatian Gentiles to extend concrete hospitality only to those Jewish missionaries whose table fellowship activities are driven by Paul's eschatological outlook ('peace upon them'). Naturally, he then turns to his broader concerns for divine eschatological mercy to the whole of Israel—mercy which may ultimately even include those Jewish missionaries who are currently his rivals (cf. Rom. 11:30–32).[50]

5. Summary and Implications for the Occasion of Galatians

While the debate over the occasion of Galatians often focuses on the theological *content* of the agitators' teaching, far less consideration has been given to the agitators' concrete social *activities*. This essay has explored this question by bringing to bear first-century concerns about accommodation in table fellowship and hospitality for travelling missionaries.

---

47 There are several ways to read the multiple uses of καί in 6:16b. Grammatically, I follow Eastman, 'Israel'. The second καί in Gal. 6:16 is conjunctive ('and') and the final καί is additive/copulative ('also'). I also follow Eastman in taking the first group ('as many as conform to this rule') as an entity distinct from the second group ('the Israel of God'). However, unlike Eastman, I identify the first group as Jewish missionaries. Therefore, I take the first group as *representative* of the second group.
48 See the summaries of the issues in Filtvedt, 'God's Israel', 133–36; Eastman, 'Israel', 385–90.
49 Staples, *Idea of Israel*, esp. 339–41; Staples, 'All Israel'.
50 Cf. Korner, *Ekklēsia*, 221–29.

In 2:7–16, Paul recounts Peter's missionary activities involving hospitality and table fellowship in Antioch. Paul's explicit problem with Peter was not that Peter's *teaching* explicitly denied the truth of the gospel. Instead, Peter's *actions* in withdrawing table fellowship effectively (if perhaps unintentionally) denied the truth of the gospel. Paul believed Peter was too concerned with avoiding persecution and had not correctly discerned the eschatological implications of his actions. This situation in Antioch is more closely aligned with the situation in Galatia (and Jerusalem) than is often appreciated. In both cases, the phrase 'compel to be circumcised/Judaise' most likely refers to the social pressure for Gentiles to adopt Jewish customs that arises when Jewish missionaries withdraw table fellowship. In 4:12–20, we noted the further prominence of the themes of hospitality for missionaries (both Paul and the agitators) and withdrawal of fellowship. In 5:2–12, we noted the confluence of eschatological themes, distinctions surrounding circumcision, and the fear of persecution. In 6:6–10, we noted the recurrence of concerns for providing materially for teachers alongside the notion of eschatological reward.

This examination prompted a re-reading of the conclusion (6:11–16), where Paul returns to the concerns of the introduction and brings back into focus the direct contrast between himself and the agitators in terms of their respective missionary motivations and activities. Against prevailing yet underexplored assumptions about the meaning of the phrase 'as many as will conform to this rule' (6:16a), we argued that the 'rule' concerning circumcision in 6:15 is a principle Paul gives to his Gentile addressees to enable them to determine whether to greet or reject any present or future Jewish missionaries. It does not function simply as a doctrinal statement; it is, more concretely, a rule of association in table fellowship arising from the eschatological implications of the gospel.

The pronoun 'as many as' (ὅσοι) in 6:16, therefore, does not refer directly to the Galatians. Instead, it acts in direct antithetical parallel to the same pronoun in v.12. It thereby functions to delimit certain kinds of Jewish missionaries. Paul is instructing the Galatians that 'as many' Jewish missionaries (like himself) who conform to this eschatological rule of association should be greeted with 'peace' and thus provided with hospitality, in explicit contrast with 'as many' Jewish missionaries (like the agitators) who do not conform to this rule. Paul then turns from these immediate concerns to express his more expansive eschatological desire for God to extend 'mercy' to the broader group these Jewish missionaries represent: God's Israel.

Bibliography

Barclay, J. M. G.	'Mirror-Reading a Polemical Letter: Galatians as a Test Case', in M. D. Nanos (ed.), *The Galatians Debate: Contemporary Issues in Rhetorical and Historical Interpretation* (Peabody, MA: Hendrickson, 2002), 367–82.
Beale, G. K.	'Peace and Mercy Upon the Israel of God: The Old Testament Background of Galatians 6,16b', *Biblica* 80 (1999), 204–23.
Betz, H. D.	*Galatians* (Hermeneia; Philadelphia, PA: Fortress, 1979).
Beyer, H. W.	'Κανών', in G. Kittel (ed.), *Theological Dictionary of the New Testament* (tr. G. W. Bromiley; 3:596–602; Grand Rapids, MI: Eerdmans, 1965).
Dahl, N. A.	'Der Name Israel: Zur Auslegung von Gal. 6.16', *Judaica* 6 (1950), 161–70.
De Boer, M. C.	*Galatians: A Commentary* (NTL; Louisville, KY: Westminster John Knox, 2011).
deSilva, D. A.	*The Letter to the Galatians* (NICNT; Grand Rapids, MI: Eerdmans, 2018).
Doering, L.	*Ancient Jewish Letters and the Beginnings of Christian Epistolography* (WUNT 298; Tübingen: Mohr Siebeck, 2012).
Du Toit, A.	'Galatians 6:13: A Possible Solution to an Old Exegetical Problem', *Neotestamentica* 28, no. 1 (1994), 157–61.
Du Toit, P. La G.	*God's Saved Israel: Reading Romans 11:26 and Galatians 6:16 in Terms of the New Identity in Christ and the Spirit* (Eugene, OR: Pickwick, 2019).
Dunn, J. D. G.	'The Incident at Antioch (Gal. 2:11–18)', in M. D. Nanos (ed.), *The Galatians Debate: Contemporary Issues in Rhetorical and Historical Interpretation* (Peabody, MA: Hendrickson, 2002), 199–234.
Eastman, S. G.	'Israel and the Mercy of God: A Re-Reading of Galatians 6.16 and Romans 9–11', *New Testament Studies* 56 (2010), 367–95.
Esler, P. F.	'Making and Breaking an Agreement Mediterranean Style: A New Reading of Galatians 2:1–14', in M. D. Nanos (ed.), *The Galatians Debate: Contemporary Issues in Rhetorical and Historical Interpretation* (Peabody, MA: Hendrickson, 2002), 261–81.

Filtvedt, O. J.   '"God's Israel" in Galatians 6.16: An Overview and Assessment of the Key Arguments', *Currents in Biblical Research* 15, no. 1 (2016), 123–40.

Gil Arbiol, C.   '*Ioudaismos* and *Ioudaizō* in Paul and the Galatian Controversy: An Examination of Supposed Positions', *Journal for the Study of the New Testament* 44, no. 2 (2021), 218–39.

Hardin, J. K.   'Galatians 1–2 Without a Mirror: Reflections on Paul's Conflict with the Agitators', *Tyndale Bulletin* 65, no. 2 (2014), 275–303.

Hardin, J. K.   *Galatians and the Imperial Cult: A Critical Analysis of the First-Century Social Context of Paul's Letter* (WUNT 2/237; Tübingen: Mohr Siebeck, 2008).

Hardin, J. K.   '"If I Still Proclaim Circumcision" (Galatians 5:11a): Paul, the Law, and Gentile Circumcision', *Journal for the Study of Paul and His Letters* 3, no. 2 (2013), 145–63.

Keener, C. S.   *Galatians* (NCBC; Cambridge: Cambridge University Press, 2018).

Kloppenborg, J. S.   *Christ's Associations: Connecting and Belonging in the Ancient City* (New Haven, CT: Yale University Press, 2019).

Korner, R. J.   *The Origin and Meaning of Ekklēsia in the Early Jesus Movement* (Ancient Judaism and Early Christianity 98; Leiden: Brill, 2017).

Magness, J.   *Stone and Dung, Oil and Spit: Jewish Daily Life in the Time of Jesus* (Grand Rapids, MI: Eerdmans, 2011).

Martin, N.   *Regression in Galatians: Paul and the Gentile Response to Jewish Law* (WUNT 2/530; Tübingen: Mohr Siebeck, 2020).

Martyn, J. L.   'A Law-Observant Mission to Gentiles', in M. D. Nanos (ed.), *The Galatians Debate: Contemporary Issues in Rhetorical and Historical Interpretation* (Peabody, MA: Hendrickson, 2002), 348–61.

Martyn, J. L.   *Galatians: A New Translation with Introduction and Commentary* (AB 33A; New York: Doubleday, 1997).

Meeks, W. A.   *The First Urban Christians: The Social World of the Apostle Paul* (2nd ed. New Haven, CT and London: Yale University Press, 2003).

Munck, J.	*Paul and the Salvation of Mankind* (tr. F. Clarke; London: SCM, 1959).
Mussner, F.	*Der Galaterbrief* (HThKNT 9; Freiburg: Herder, 1974).
Nanos, M. D.	*The Irony of Galatians: Paul's Letter in First-Century Context* (Minneapolis, MN: Fortress, 2002).
Nicols, J.	'The Practice Of *Hospitium* On The Roman Frontier', in T. Kaizer and O. Hekster (eds.), *Frontiers in the Roman World* (Leiden: Brill, 2011), 321–34.
Niederwimmer, K.	*The Didache* (Hermeneia; Minneapolis, MN: Fortress, 1998).
Nolland, J.	*Luke 9:21–18:34* (Word Biblical Commentary 35B; Dallas, TX: Word, 1993).
Oakes, P. S.	'Economic Approaches: Scarce Resources and Interpretive Opportunities', in J. A. Marchal (ed.), *Studying Paul's Letters: Contemporary Perspectives and Methods* (Minneapolis, MN: Fortress, 2012), 75–91.
Ricker, A.	*Ancient Letters and the Purpose of Romans: The Law of the Membrane* (LNTS 630; London: T&T Clark, 2020).
Robinson, D. W. B.	'The Distinction between Jewish and Gentile Believers in Galatians', *Australian Biblical Review* 13 (1965), 29–48.
Rudolph, D. J.	*A Jew to the Jews: Jewish Contours of Pauline Flexibility in 1 Corinthians 9:19–23* (WUNT 2/304; Tübingen: Mohr Siebeck, 2011).
Sandt, H. van de and D. Flusser	*The Didache: Its Jewish Sources and Its Place in Early Judaism and Christianity* (Minneapolis, MN: Fortress, 2002).
Schreiber, S.	'Politische Sprache, Motive und Kritik im Galaterbrief: Eine Spurensuche', *New Testament Studies* 68, no. 4 (2022), 375–91.
Schreiner, T. R.	*Galatians* (ZECNT; Grand Rapids, MI: Zondervan, 2010).
Schrenk, G.	'Was Bedeutet 'Israel Gottes'?', *Judaica* 5 (1949), 81–94.
Smit, J.	'The Letter to the Galatians: A Deliberative Speech', in M. D. Nanos (ed.), *The Galatians Debate: Contemporary Issues in Rhetorical and Historical Interpretation* (Peabody, MA: Hendrickson, 2002), 39–59.

Smith, D. E.	'The Messianic Banquet Reconsidered', in B. A. Pearson (ed.), *The Future of Early Christianity: Essays in Honor of Helmut Koester* (Minneapolis, MN: Augsburg Fortress, 1991), 64–75.
Stanton, G.	'Accommodation for Paul's Entourage', *Novum Testamentum* 60, no. 3 (2018), 227–46.
Staples, J. A.	*The Idea of Israel in Second Temple Judaism: A New Theory of People, Exile, and Israelite Identity* (Cambridge: Cambridge University Press, 2021).
Staples, J. A.	'What Do the Gentiles Have to Do with 'All Israel'?: A Fresh Look at Romans 11:25–27', *Journal of Biblical Literature* 130, no. 2 (2011), 371–90.
Williams, J. J.	*Galatians* (NCCS. Eugene, OR: Cascade, 2020).
Windsor, L. J.	*Paul and the Vocation of Israel: How Paul's Jewish Identity Informs His Apostolic Ministry, with Special Reference to Romans* (BZNW 205. Berlin: De Gruyter, 2014).

www.ingramcontent.com/pod-product-compliance
Lightning Source LLC
Chambersburg PA
CBHW061228070526
44584CB00030B/4036